STAGE DIRECTION
in Transition

STAGE DIRECTION

DICKENSON PUBLISHING CO., INC.
Encino, Calif. and Belmont, Calif.

Hardie
Albright

IN TRANSITION

Stage Direction in Transition, by Hardie Albright.

Copyright © 1972 by Dickenson Publishing Company, Inc. All rights reserved. No part of this book may be reproduced, stored in a retrieval system, or transcribed, in any form or by any means, electronic, mechanical, photocopying, recording, or otherwise, without the prior written permission of the publisher, 16561 Ventura Boulevard, Encino, California 91316.

Library of Congress Catalog Card Number: 70-163774

ISBN: 0-8221-0013-4

Printed in the United States of America

10 9 8 7 6 5 4 3 2 1

The cover depicts an impressive use of rear projection in a scene from the Company Theatre's production of *Children of the Kingdom.* (Cover sketch by Larry Byrd, adapted from a photo by Ron Batzdorff)

The frontispiece portrays a scene from the award-winning Company Theatre's stirring production of *The Emergence.* (Courtesy of Company Theatre)

Cover designed by Larry Byrd

Book designed by Mary Jones

CONTENTS

v

Contents

PREFACE

Although some older directing books were basically sound when first published, they were written for another time. Some of the best are twenty years old, and in a constantly changing theatre, twenty years—even five years—add newer forms and techniques to the art of directing.

The theatre exists today because it has always been in a state of revolution. Each generation develops its own theatre to meet the demands of its environment. Theatre is distinguished from all other arts in that there is little but the play that remains permanent. But few plays have survived the age for which they were written, and even these, when produced today, are altered so that they are relevant to our times.

The theatre still continues with its revolution, challenging the very foundations of drama as we have known it. Modern dramatists are violating traditional rules of playwriting and directors are doing things which were unheard of as little as five years ago.

This book will present the standards of the traditionally realistic as well as the new theatre, not only to show how modern innovations differ, but because the realistic theatre refuses to die. A full comprehension of today's theatrical innovations requires that we visualize these within the panorama of historical theatre. Each innovation comes into being at its own particular time but with the pressures of the past imprinted upon it. Most of the new theatre concepts are reflections of earlier theatre, such as the improvisational Commedia dell'Arte and the open staging of ceremonials, but our relationship to nineteenth-century realism is ambiguous. For some time we have subconsciously found ourselves in revolt against it, much like a rebellious son set against his father because he wants to be considered as an individual.

If there is to be any choosing up of sides, the reader will need to do so himself. My professional life has been spent in the theatre of realism. This does not mean that I have freely embraced all its ways. I disliked its refusal to recognize that any other theatre form had ever existed and its smugness in believing that realism was the zenith of a long theatrical history. I regretted its faults but loved it still.

I love the new theatre because it returns to theatre's ancient beginnings—to open stages and improvisations, to chants and drums and physical feats, to all the parts that once made drama imaginative and thrilling. Our young strivers and achievers have appropriated *the very idea of theatre*, and bit by bit they are sweeping away the dust of realism.

However, as much as I admire the new theatre, I see faults in it as well. Complete destruction of the old always seems characteristic of revolution in its early stages. Then, little by little, a few of the old ways return to replace the parts of the new which did not work.

There are certain rules of theatre that dare not be violated and still remain theatre. You cannot make a theatre into a lecture hall and still call it theatre. Also, most theatregoers have an ambivalence toward theatrical innovation. To such people, everything on a stage must be "real," because to a great majority of people theatre *is* realism. They expect a protagonist to be someone they can admire, identify with, or at least understand and evaluate. They understand a story told in sequential development with a beginning, a middle, and an end.

And so Ibsen, Chekhov, and Stanislavski live on. The revolution will not be without struggle. We can hope that time will season and mellow the new and that the old will become amenable to change. If only we can have the best of the new and the old—what a theatre we shall have! Until then, a director must feel confident that he can work in either form.

A director places his trademark on each of his productions by his selection of the play, his concept of how the play should be performed, his choice of cast, and his selection of all the visual aspects of his production. There is no way to direct without taking some position on the production—without editorializing. This may also be true in writing a book about directing. I have made a conscious effort to offer pros and cons on all controversial subjects, but I also have my preferences, won in battle with experience. It is certainly the reader's prerogative to disagree, but I hope he will not resent my opinions, for they were not made cavalierly.

What

Most existing texts on directing include such subjects as stage carpentry, makeup, publicity, etc., which leaves limited space for the complicated art of directing as practiced today. While all will agree that a director should know all he can about these tangentially related aspects of production, concern for such details should really be part of his preparation before considering the directing discipline. I prefer to leave such specialized subjects to the wide range of excellent books now available, and to explore, instead, other aspects of directing which are becoming increasingly important.

The role of the director has been amplified and the burden of innovation and creativity has fallen more heavily upon the actor, while the role of the playwright has been attenuated, even threatened. The new theatre places particular accent upon actor-space relationships, multi-electronics, the use of non-proscenium stages, and the values and techniques of training actors in neuromuscular coordination. Although the aim of the theatre has always been to involve an audience in a sensory way, present experiments seek to entice the audience into physical participation in the action. And this is true in the other arts. Museums are displaying "environment forms" which invite spectators to climb into or walk through the creations rather than merely observe.

These are only a few of the subjects that other texts have not adequately covered, and which a young director will be concerned with in the future.

For Whom

This book should be of value to the young student-director who will enter the field at a time when there are fewer limitations than at any other period in theatrical history. One month he may be directing Shakespeare, the next a play for off-off Broadway.

This book might also serve as a handbook for the English teacher who is inexperienced in play-directing but who is suddenly assigned the task of directing the school play.[1]

Because this text concentrates on the practicalities for both the traditional and the new theatre, an experienced director might use it as a guide for defining and solving many problems fostered by change. In any event, it will provide him with an opportunity to test his own methods and techniques against another's. The invitation to experiment and venture into new techniques should be offered to all directors, whether amateur or professional.

Valuable advice and instruction may also be found in this book for that happy innocent who has just been asked to direct a play for his local community theatre. It could be a guide to lead him through the wilderness of controversial theories and methods which exist today about plays, acting, and directing. In fact, this text should interest just about anyone interested in staging new as well as old plays.

Why?

Those teaching drama in education are sometimes put into a position in which they must defend their efforts. One of the most frequently made charges is that drama has little relationship to education and to the preparation of a student for his future in society. While it is true that shoddy commercial plays, produced inexpertly, do not constitute an educational experience, the fact remains that men of the greatest intellects have written for the theatre. Within our heritage of immortal literature there are an impressive number of plays. And yet, in a survey made by an educational testing service, inclusive of 26,000 college-bound students, it was found that among other things, one in five of these students had never read a play by Shakespeare.[2]

If one accepts the viewpoint that the study of drama does not help to

---

[1]In a study on drama instruction in eighty Los Angeles secondary schools, it was found that sixty-three teachers combined drama with English and that twenty combined drama with speech. *Educational Theatre Journal*, Vol. 16 (October 1964), p. 208.

[2]"News & Trends" *NEA Journal*, September 1969, p. 3.

prepare the student to get along in today's world, then he must also agree that creativity, divergent and convergent thinking, training in making value judgments, developing personality, flexibility, planning, and perseverance—in fact, all the elements needed to enrich the individual—are unimportant. But the truth is that all significant advances in the history of civilization have been instigated by creative intellects: those men and women who have been able to extend themselves beyond parroting back information and computerized facts into the realm of imagination and creativity. Certainly a student's cultural tastes will be developed as he becomes associated with worthwhile dramas; but most important, the confidence of the individual is strengthened as he learns to project his ideas to an audience. These are both personal and permanent assets not to be disparaged. Work in dramatic endeavors also develops self discipline and physical control. Students are possessed of great energy and stage work demands a great deal of it. And finally, there is for some that most important reason for studying drama: the training for a future profession.

A Few Facts

A survey made by the American Educational Theatre Association shows that each year fifteen thousand students are enrolled in theatre courses and one hundred thousand undergraduates are involved in play production activities.[3] This seems clear evidence that students do not consider drama in school to be a "frill." Drama attracts more students than do such academic subjects as philosophy and journalism—among many others.[4]

It is gratifying to realize that as Broadway productions steadily decline, universities, colleges, and regional theatres are busily engaged in building large supporting audiences by producing varied repertories of worthwhile plays. University theatre is witnessed each year by almost three times the number of people who attend the Broadway theatre—and this does not include professional regional theatre which frequently presents three hundred plays per season in thirty-six major centers of activity.

In contrast, while eighty New York theatres flourished in 1920, there are less than thirty today, and many of these are threatened with being torn down. Sheer economics is writing them off. The real estate they occupy is too expensive to be supported by two and a half hours of potential money-making eight times a week. That same land might be used to build a high-rise office building which could then be used eight to twelve hours a day for five to six days per week and accommodate hundreds of office personnel. When these theatres are demolished, they will leave behind them many memories and a great deal of sentiment; but the truth is that poor acoustics, crowded backstage space, inadequate seating arrangements, and lack of facilities for the use of modern lighting, projection, and scenery devices make

[3]*Educational Theatre Journal,* November 1966, p. 319.
[4]*United States Office of Education Circular O. E. 54010-62,* Department of Health Education and Welfare (Washington, D.C.).

these old proscenium-type theatres an obstruction to the progress of the theatre. The gilded plaster masks of comedy and tragedy, the crystal chandeliers, and the red velvet curtains will be replaced by newer, more modern interiors now in the planning stage. On the site of Broadway's old Capitol Theatre will be a high-rise office building housing a 1,700-seat musical comedy theatre and below it a 650-seat drama theatre. The high rise at Forty-fourth Street and Broadway (site of the old Astor Hotel) is planned to accommodate both a musical comedy theatre of 1,800 seats and a movie house of 1,500 seats. A small basement theatre of 350 seats is planned for another office tower at Avenue of the Americas and Forty-sixth Street. All of these theatres have already been promised or leased to television, film, or recording interests. Many changes are being activated for the interiors—bars, computer ticket sales, adaptable stages, and complete facilities for multimedia drama.

As if fulfilling a wish, many have predicted the death of the theatre. Its death, like Mark Twain's, seems somewhat exaggerated if the above facts, as reported in *New York* magazine, are to believed. It might be more accurate to say that the theatre is ill, but on its way to the operating room.

THE DIRECTOR 1

Interpreter or Artist?

Some people dream of leading a band; others of directing a play. To sit with a benign possessiveness, shouting orders to a group of actors; to be referred to as director, entrepreneur, maestro, and have friends whisper that you are a temperamental genius, would warm the cockles of anyone's ego.

However, to imply that a considerable amount of work is involved in fulfilling this dream might destroy it. Out of indolence, fear, or just plain ignorance, there are directors who do little or nothing to earn the title. It is a great mistake to suppose that a play will speak for itself. A playwright does not write for readers. As it is written, a play is a beginning. It must be transposed from page to stage. This process is known as stage art and it is a job for an artist. Today we call that artist a director. It is he who creates the living play—visually, aurally, and emotionally.

What's in a Name?

One of the most ridiculous beliefs floating about these days is that the position of director is an innovation of our century. For thousands of years plays have been produced. Who directed these? Someone had to be in charge!

In ancient Rome, the director was called *Archimimus*. Later, the actors of the Commedia dell'Arte referred to him as *Maestro*, and in France, he was known as the *Metteur en Scène*.

No authentic document has yet been found to prove that Shakespeare directed his own plays at the Globe, and yet this is certainly not an unfounded assumption, as he was an actor, as well as author and part owner of the company. During the Elizabethan era and before, it was not unusual for playwrights to direct their own plays. Shakespeare's colleague and close friend, Ben Jonson, directed not only his own plays, but those of other writers as well. Modern-day division of theatrical responsibility simply did not exist in former times. A Greek playwright was also the chief actor in his plays. A play was said to be "done by" him, and in all probability this meant writing, acting, and directing. Certainly Molière directed. We have unimpeachable documentation on this. Not only did he read lines for his actors, but he insisted that they reproduce his every tone, inflection, and gesture. Molière not only directed—*he drilled!* Yes, stage-directing has always existed—even though the Greeks had another name for it.

The Importance of Directing

It should not be difficult to make a list of words which, when considered together, would describe theatre: scenery, lights, stage, music, costumes, props, direction, furniture, dance, tickets, audience, stage crew, programs, and—oh, yes—a play. Suppose we mix all of these ingredients together and distill only the *essence* of theatre. Which elements may we eliminate and *still have theatre?*

Can we eliminate scenery? The great Greek dramas were played in front of a permanent architectural background. Much later the Italians invented scenery as we know it. The Commedia dell'Arte players used none, or at most, a few ragged curtains. Shakespeare was also played against a permanent background patterned after Tudor inn yards. Molière performed his plays against the marble pillars of Louis XIV's Palais Royal. Before World War I, Jacques Copeau was producing plays against a severe permanent structure of various acting levels. And during our own time, Orson Welles' exciting *Julius Caesar* and Wilder's *Our Town* both were acted on a bare stage. Perhaps we can, therefore, eliminate scenery as a *necessity* of theatre.

What about lights? At Shakespeare's Globe, performances were given in broad daylight, as were most plays before that time. The Restoration introduced candles and oil for illumination. Conclusion? Artificial light is expendable.

Is theatre possible without a proscenium stage or even a raised platform? Evidently it is, for both in Europe and America there are many bowl-shaped theatres—both ancient and modern—in which the audience is on a higher level than the actors.

Granted that music is a necessity for musical comedy, it has always been incidental to drama. Costumes, props, dance, furniture, tickets, stage crews, and programs are also pleasant additions to drama, but when narrowing in on the very essence of theatre, we would have to consider these, too, as luxuries.

Can theatre be created without a play? Frequently the Commedia dell'Arte performed without a written play. No rhetoric, not a word is needed for pantomime.

Can theatre exist without an audience? Theatre is not theatre without an audience; it is a rehearsal. An actor must feel he is reaching another human and the response he receives causes him to extend himself. Theatre is an active game between actors and audience, a ball bouncing back and forth, enriching both.

What of the director? Is he indispensable? Shakespeare, Molière, and Sophocles were probably better directors than any we have around today. They were total men of the theatre—actors, playwrights, and directors. Since then, the most significant theatre has been inspired by such directors as Saxe-Meiningen, Antoine, Meierhold, Stanislavski, Reinhardt, Daly, Belasco, Brecht, and Grotowski—to name but a few.

When all our mash has been boiled down, what is distilled? *The essence of the theatre, the indispensable elements are: the art of acting, the support of an audience, and the guiding hand of a director.*

Definition

Way back in 1917, Sheldon Cheney gave a definition for a *director* which remains the best I have been able to find:

> There is in every important drama, a latent art value. . . a synthesis of play, acting, setting and lighting. . . but also a spiritual transformation of the whole through artistic-theatric vision. This implies the existence of a director, who is artist enough to harmonize the provisional or incomplete arts of the playwright, the actor, the scene designer, and at the same time develop by a creative method of production, an inner rhythm, a complete theatre unity.

It seems to be everyone's fate, at one time or another, to suffer through an evening of sheer boredom in the theatre. And so the unlucky spectator sits, thoughts wandering, for nothing seems to hold his attention on stage. He thinks of the bills due tomorrow, of how the brakes on his car need tightening, or he might ask himself, "Why am I so bored? This play is supposed to be good. I had to read it in English Lit. The scenery and lights are beautiful and the actors—well, inexperienced perhaps, but not really bad. Then why is it all so *dull*?"

The play, scenery, and actors constitute the body of theatre. But none of these will come to life on a stage without soul, and the soul of theatre is *vision. The creation of a concept, or vision, is the single most vital function a director can contribute to a production.* Everything is built upon that concept, just as a house is built upon its foundation. The director patterns all

Brilliant young director of the American Conservatory Theatre of San Francisco, William Ball makes final adjustments to makeup of Caliban. (Photo by Hank Kranzler)

of his work with actors, designers—all the components of his production—after this vision which he has conceived. When you are bored in a theatre, you are seeing components, bodies without souls. There is no design, no vision, and nothing lives.

It requires a discerning eye and ear to separate the work of the author, the actor, and the director. An author I know had an idea for writing a play in which the stage was to be divided into two sections. One acting area was to represent an executive office and the other a long diagonal corridor. His idea was that a scene in the office was to be juxtaposed, and yet dramatically contrasted to, one in the hall. As written in manuscript it was so precisely devised and executed that lines, timing, movements—even silences—seemed in counterpoint like an exciting musical score. The play was eventually produced on Broadway. *The critics loved the brilliant direction, but hated the playwriting!*

Qualities Desired in a Director

In the instance related above, you will note that neither the spectators nor the critics knew who was responsible for what they saw. The director is in charge of the entire production. It is he, and he alone, who should know when to slow the tempo, when to make it race, or when the excitement should rise or fall. The greatest value he has is his point of view on the shape, meaning, and rhythm he visualizes for the production. It is his design that places all of the pieces together into an artistic mosaic. He is the master of the production but an apprentice to the play. In the final analysis he must make the final judgments. He will decide what the audience is to see, hear, and feel. Therefore, it is only fair that he has the power to accept or veto all contributions made toward the production. A director should have the ability to make well considered decisions quickly because he knows the play so well, and he must also know how to adjust in order to solve the inevitable problems which arise during rehearsals. As executive director he may be required to attend board and committee meetings, supervise scenery, props, and lighting, hold tryouts, and approve all publicity. He need not be an actor and yet he must understand the actor's ways and means. He must be able to instruct the inexperienced actor who does not know how to get results, and help the experienced actor when his creativity becomes blocked.

All of this should indicate that the director must be able to get along with all sorts of people and possess an aptitude for flexibility in order to see another's point of view as well as his own. Sir Michael Redgrave wrote, "I believe that the first quality of a director (and I am speaking of the qualities which cannot be taught or consciously acquired), is an understanding of human relationships, and the second an understanding of the psychology of his actors, with the power to draw out of them the overtones, the quirks, the individual characteristics most suited to the character."[1]

4

[1]Sir Michael Redgrave, *Mask or Face* (New York: Theatre Arts Books, 1958), p. 158.

In summary, the director should have a love and respect for people and the ability to work with those around him. This is true when working in either educational, avocational, or professional theatre. But a great deal of conscientious effort can be put into a production and yet come to nothing if there is not a firm, sure, and business-like force guiding it. This does not imply that a director should be a despot. But he must command respect of his cast or rehearsals will become a disorderly fiasco. He *will* get respect if he comes to rehearsals with a plan and imparts intelligence, imagination, enthusiasm, good manners, patience, dedication, and honesty and if he displays a sense of fairness along with instinct and emotion. I admit that this is quite an order, and it may not be possible to find such a paragon of virtues. But these qualities are listed here as ideals. If you, as a director, can manage a few, then try to develop others.

A Director's Duties

A director's tasks begin long before his work with the cast during rehearsals. When choosing a play for production, he must first of all find one which excites him. Next he must concern himself with practical considerations. He must ask himself, "Is it a worthwhile play? Does it excite me enough to make the tremendous effort necessary to stage it? Do I have the facilities to produce it? Will my audience like it and pay to see it? Is a theatre available? Will I be able to cast the play? What about scenery, costumes, royalties?" When satisfied that all of his answers are affirmative, he then begins an intensive study of the play. He must imagine it in stage terms—characters, sounds, and movement. He must "see" the play on stage as if in a vision. Eventually, he is going to reproduce that vision so that an audience will also see what he has seen. And this brings us to one of the most important assets a director can possess—imagination. The success of his future work will depend to a great extent upon how well he visualizes the production, although a good deal will also depend upon how well he transmits his concept to his players and his staff. By use of imagination he will actually be constructing his own creation, based upon the play. By placing himself in the center of the play's events as he studies, he will be able to bring that same sense of participation to his audience. In this way he becomes the catalyst between the life of the play and the audience. There are many qualities in a fine production that do not depend upon the written word, and most of these are the responsibility of the director.

A playwright uses life and experience to write a play. A director recreates this on a stage using the tools of the theatre. Although it is his responsibility to transfer the author's printed words into living theatre, there is no reason why the work should be merely interpretive. It is not only the director's right, but also his duty, to add to the playwright's concept however he can. When this is done it becomes the director's individual contribution, frequently surprising and often delighting the author.

Innovations that have been made in the last few years in the director's position have been remarkable. From stage manager of former days, to interpreter of yesterday, the director of today has come to be considered as an individual creative artist. To some degree this change has come about by his success in training and guiding actors, using new techniques in developing characterizations and motivation, and providing spontaneity in their performances. But most of all, he has gained in stature by first conceiving, like any other artist, a vision of the production as the audience will see it.

No longer is he merely a prompter who sees to it that the author's words can be heard and that the actors do not bump into each other. He is now an editor, a teacher, but primarily an artist. It is only natural for the director to meet some opposition on his road up. Critic Walter Kerr, a playwright himself, and husband of another, deplores the shift of the playwright's traditional artistic supremacy to the director. He asks, "Have we so despaired of the writer that we must do his work for him? . . . Whatever may be happening as nontextual elements take over, we had best not go about our practices blindly, supposing we are enriching the theatre's literature by eliminating it."[2]

It is doubtful that Mr. Kerr has the influence to change the new perspective on directing. It may be his impression that the playwright is a manufacturer of a product. A playwright mines the ore, and that raw material is fashioned into a product—which may be good or bad. *Mary, Mary* can be either a delight or an evening of He-She jokes, depending upon the director. The director's newly expanded role has done much toward providing a more fulfilling experience for an audience. This implies that he does his homework properly. During his early study he should come to know the play better than the man who wrote it. Valid decisions as to meaning or business can not be made while actors are standing about at rehearsal. Naturally, he should be receptive to questions or suggestions from the cast—even to those questions which might appear to challenge his knowledge of the play. He should react politely, offering his appreciation for the interest shown. However, when his answers come, they should be so thorough and complete that they build faith in the director and in his concept of the play. And this will happen if he has done his homework. This is not to imply that the director should arrive at the first rehearsal with totally preconceived, inflexible opinions. Much that is effective will occur during rehearsals, either through trial and error, instinct, or even by accident. During rehearsals the director can encourage collaboration and spontaneity by being receptive and showing his own enthusiasm for the work. And now that we are on the subject of the iron fist in a velvet glove, we might consider another facet of a director's disposition. The director must not allow his own tastes or opinions to force a certain play upon his audience. Not every director will be working for a university or for Broadway. Most communities are middle-class American. Polemics, religion, and sex are controversial subjects to unsophisticated audiences.

A few years ago a director of a community theatre or a school could

[2]Walter Kerr, "How Playwrights Lose," *Harper's*, September 1966, pp. 75–80.

choose the plays he wanted to produce from *The Best Plays Of* (*Year*)[3], but as it stands today, this is no longer such a simple matter. In an effort to lure its dwindling clientele back into theatres, New York managers are producing plays on controversial subjects. While such plays may be accepted in metropolitan areas where a relatively sophisticated attitude prevails, the overwhelming majority of theatregoers in urban areas are bewildered by, or openly antagonistic toward, such presentations.

Director John Dexter rehearsing cast for The Kitchen *with author Arnold Wesker seated top right. (Courtesy of The English Stage Company at the Royal Court)*

Some English teachers have argued that whether or not they assign or discuss such books as *Tropic of Cancer, Deer Park, Portnoy's Complaint*, or *Brave New World*, their students are reading and discussing them. They maintain that free and open assignments and discussion of such works in class would provide them the opportunity of weighing the literary quality

---

[3]*The Best Plays of* (*Year*), (New York: Dodd, Mead & Co.). Annually, the ten best plays produced in New York are reviewed in synoptic form with a record of cast, length of run, etc. Published since 1919 and formerly edited by Burns Mantle, the present editor is Otis L. Guernsey, Jr.

of these books against their shock content. Such arguments might very well be made in defense of the present output of New York plays, except that there is a vast difference between reading about an act and seeing it performed on a stage. Sensational sex acts and nihilism are not the elevating verities to which we aspire in theatre.

Any director producing a controversial play must accept the fact that he is playing a kind of Russian roulette. He may win, but the odds are not in his favor, and he must be willing to hazard the consequences. Consider your audience. Choose your play carefully.

Summary

At the risk of oversimplification, let us list some of the director's more important duties:

1. To choose a play not only because he likes it, but because he believes his audience will like it, and to develop and extend a fresh and questioning approach to all areas of his work.

2. To make a thorough study of the play; to find the playwright's intent through research, emotion, and imagination; to record all of his original thoughts and impressions as he studies.

3. To interpret this concept into concrete visual and aural terms, and to decide the emphasis and pace, as he would like to see it staged.

4. To activate and expedite the technical aspects of production, such as music, props, scenery, costumes, etc.

5. To cast actors in parts in which he feels they will give a good account of themselves—and the characters they portray; then to work subjectively with those actors, expanding characterizations, creating solutions for each problem and selecting the most effective—always keeping in mind his original concept.

6. To work always with the audience in mind. The directorial attitude should be: "Do I like it?" and "Will my audience like it?"

7. To use emotional, intellectual, and tasteful values in all judgments.

8. To fuse all contributing parts into a harmonious whole.

9. To display patience with the cast and staff and always retain enthusiasm for the play no matter what disappointments may occur; to be generous in praise and circumspect in criticism.

10. To withdraw from the subjective view during later rehearsals and experience the production from an audience's point of view, because all the work will have been in vain if the audience is not carried back to its own experience.

Further Reading

Archer, William. *About the Theatre*. New York: Benjamin Blom, 1969.

Austell, Jan. *What's in a Play?* New York: Harcourt Brace Jovanovich, 1968.

Bakshy, Alexander. *Theatre Unbound*. New York: Benjamin Blom, 1969.

Beck, Roy A., et al. *Play Production for High Schools*. New York: National Textbooks, 1968.

Braun, Edward, ed. *Meyerhold on Theatre*. New York: Hill & Wang, 1969.

Brustein, Robert. *Revolution as Theatre*. New York: Liveright Publishing Corp., 1971.

Cheney, Sheldon. *New Movement in Theatre.* New York: Benjamin Blom, 1969.

Cohn, Ruby. *Currents in Contemporary Drama.* Bloomington, Ind.: Indiana University Press, 1969.

Cole, Toby, and Chinoy, Helen Krich. *Directors on Directing.* Indianapolis: Bobbs-Merrill Co., 1963.

Esslin, Martin. *Reflections. Essays on Modern Theatre.* Garden City, N.Y.: Doubleday & Co., 1969.

Fuchs, George. *Revolution in the Theatre.* Ithaca, N.Y.: Cornell University Press, 1959.

Gardner, R.H. *The Splintered Stage.* New York: Macmillan Co., 1965.

Gassner, John, and Allen, Ralph. *Theatre and Drama in the Making.* 2 vols. New York: Houghton Mifflin Co., 1967.

Kirby, E. T. *Total Theatre.* New York: E.P. Dutton & Co., 1969.

Kozelka, Paul. *Theatre Student-Directing.* New York: Richards Rosen Press, 1968.

Lahr, John. *Up Against the Wall.* New York: Grove Press, 1970. Essays on modern theatre.

Marowitz, Charles, and Trussler, Simon, eds. *Theatre at Work: Playwrights and Productions in the Modern British Theatre.* London: Methuen & Co., 1967. A collection of interviews and essays.

Marowitz, Charles, et al. *Encore Reader: A Chronicle of the New Drama.* New York: DBX, 1965.

May, R. *Theatremania.* New York: Heinman Imported Books, 1968.

Mitchell, Roy. *Creative Theatre.* New York: Benjamin Blom, 1969.

Rousseau, Jean-Jacques. *Politics and the Arts.* Ithaca, N.Y.: Cornell University Press, 1968.

Seltzer, Daniel, ed. *The Modern Theatre.* Boston: Little, Brown & Co., 1967.

Vaughan, Stuart. *A Possible Theatre.* New York: McGraw-Hill, 1969.

Weissman, Philip. *Creativity in the Theatre.* New York: Dell Books, 1966.

Wight, Edward A. *Primer for Playgoers.* Englewood Cliffs, N.J.: Prentice-Hall, 1969.

Influences Upon Modern Direction

In order to acquire a better understanding of the new directions in the theatre, it may help to consider what has gone before; why changes became necessary and to explore those seminal influences responsible for activating them. New art forms do not burst suddenly into our consciousness. Evolution, in which the old dies gradually while the new is being born, is in both art and life. The cycle of nineteenth-century realism in staging began earlier with the productions of David Garrick, who encased his stage in a proscenium and used painted scenery. Later, realism flourished with productions by Henry Irving, Augustin Daly, Belasco, Antoine, and Stanislavski, culminating finally in the use of that ultimate machine for reproducing life faithfully—the motion picture camera.

In the 1930's the training of actors was confined to some variation of what came to be known as "the method." While always vaguely admitting some association with Stanislavski's theories, each method teacher had his own interpretation of them, usually resulting in an emphasis upon psychological, emotional, and inner-life cant. The new generation of actors and

Italian director Luca Ronconi's brilliant Orlando Furioso *from Rome's Teatro Libero, as staged in a vinyl "bubble" located in New York's Bryant Park. The unseated audience marveled at this production which ionized the jaded atmosphere of New York theatres. (Photo by Martha Swope)*

directors find the style too confining and limited. In *A Possible Theatre*, well-known director Stuart Vaughan expresses some of his difficulties in working with actors trained exclusively in this way: "I had noticed mannerisms which hampered so many Methodists—their inability to speak, their seeming disinterest in anything but contemporary material. I had noticed their insolence toward other theatre practitioners, their assurance that they knew the only way."[4]

But directors, actors, and playwrights are not alone responsible for the present search for new forms of theatre. Now saturated hourly with "real life" from newspapers and TV, audiences seem to be seeking a more imaginative theatre—if we consider the sensations caused by the visits to America by Grotowski's Polish Company, Jean-Louis Barrault's *Rabelais*, and the exciting Roman Teatro Libero production of *Orlando Furioso*, not to mention such American productions as Paul Sill's refreshing *Story Theatre* and *Metamorphoses*, Peter Brook's white-light and aerial *Midsummer Night's Dream*, and some of the more innovative productions of off-off Broadway.[5]

---

[4]Stuart Vaughan, *A Possible Theatre* (New York: McGraw-Hill, 1969), p. 24.

[5]Also to be listed among provocative domestic productions are *The Bacchae, Indians, The Box and Quotations from Chairman Mao-Tse-Tung, The Apple Tree*, and the entire repertory of the Los Angeles based *Company Theatre*.

For this type of production, an actor must have a flexible and expressive body, a voice with range, and an ability to speak the English language well and to speak verse. Also, he must not cringe at the word "technique." He must be proficient in working in many styles of acting, a discipline so evident in the more thoroughly trained and pliable foreign actor.

Actors of this generation have found renewed interest and excitement in their studies through the writings of such men as Antonin Artaud, Bertolt Brecht, Emile Jacques-Dalcroze, and Frederick Matthias Alexander. And young directors are following in the steps of Edward Gordon Craig and Adolphe Appia. Those visits to America by The Polish Lab Theatre, Rome's Teatro Libero, and the Compagnie Renaud-Barrault from Paris have demonstrated how many of their theories can be effectively applied to actual performance.

A rousing "theatrical game," Jean-Louis Barrault's Rabelais *has been a hit in Paris, London, and Rome. Based loosely on the five books by Rabelais, Gargantua, and Pantagruel, this free-form rock-and-strobe extravaganza provided a transfusion to theatergoers in America. (Courtesy of the New York Public Library)*

Revolutions have a way of anticipating themselves. Year after year we have watched the gradual weakening of Broadway's heartbeat. Put simply, some ticket buyers have grown weary of our old banalities: the confining realistic settings, introverted acting, the "boy-gets-loses-gets-girl" plots, and the generation-gap themes. It should not be a shock to anyone that actors, playwrights, and audiences want change—and that the revolution is beginning. But until it is in full flower, there will still be the "real-life" plays, such as *Butterflies Are Free, Child's Play,* and *The Boys in the Band*—which means that actors today must be somewhat ambidextrous.

Those who inspired the present theatrical revolution were mostly prophets, struggling to be heard by their contemporaries; but few would listen. However, their stature seems to grow with time.

Antonin Artaud (1895–1948). Many of the young theatre innovators have recognized their deep indebtedness to this French actor, director, poet, playwright, theorist, and self-styled mad man. Artaud was alienated from his society and remained isolated in his private world of imagination and drugs. But Artaud's writings remain a galvanic force in the new theatre which aspires to be a meeting ground for visceral and spiritual actions and reactions.

His symbolic *Plague* from *The Theatre and Its Double* has been interpreted by the Living Theatre group. They have also done a series of "happenings" called *Mysteries and Smaller Pieces,* based upon his theories. Peter Brook has borrowed Artaud's title The Theatre of Cruelty for his production called *US.* Undoubtedly the inspiration for Brook's production of *Marat/Sade* came from Artaud's notations of projects he planned to stage.

It is almost impossible to give a terse summary of Artaud's sprawling, emotional writings. He rejected all psychological, literary, and didactic concepts, urging a theatre of myths, symbols, and gestures using rhythms, lights, a blending of past and present, conscious and unconscious, the individual and collective-film projections, and sounds emanating from all areas of the theatre in order to rouse the spectators to a peak of excitement and personal experience.

In training actors, Artaud introduced new breathing techniques as the basis for portrayals, with each character a "type," calculated from beginning to end and *with no personal initiative from the actor.* Not only was the proscenium to be abolished, but the platform stage as well, with no barriers between actors and audience. Settings were to be replaced by ten-foot marionettes. Just how much Jean-Claude van Itallie has accepted many of Artaud's ideas may be realized by reading *America Hurrah!*[6]

Bertolt Brecht (1898–1956). Today's theatre has been influenced by Brecht in two ways: (1) As a writer, Brecht believed that the lives of the people on stage could never be separated from social and economic conditions. His brilliant directing style was frankly theatrical—an exciting conglomeration of visible lights, projected slides and films, signs, masks, symbols, songs, and poetry; (2) Actors were to "alienate," that is, stand apart from their characters

---

[6]*A Best Play of 1966–1967* (although it is not one play, but three one-act plays), *America Hurrah!* demonstrates that this long-name playwright, Jean-Claude van Itallie, has been deeply impressed by the writings of both Artaud and McLuhan.

and "demonstrate" them to the audience. In training his actors, Brecht emphasized releasing muscular tensions and developing the actor's physical equipment as an instrument for acting.

Many of the plastic exercises used today in training actors can be directly attributed to three men: Jacques-Dalcroze, Delsarte, and Alexander. The chief goal of these physical exercises is not only to develop the actor's body as an instrument efficient enough to translate emotional stimuli, but to find unstereotyped images and gestures which will create new metaphors for an audience.

Emile Jacques-Dalcroze (1865–1950). Working with his friend and collaborator, Adolphe Appia, Jacques-Dalcroze found certain fundamentals for the individual training of performers. He placed emphasis on the coordination of physical movement with the spiritual and spatial elements. Through exercise, nerves and muscles were trained to react to an emotion automatically, the final purpose being the achievement of a synthesis of body and spirit through plasticity and improvisation. Jacques-Dalcroze repeatedly denied that he was creating a new style of performing, but asserted that he was in search of "a road to art," as investigated by the Greeks. Many of the exercises used by Grotowski are based on Dalcroze eurythmics and then adapted to Grotowski's particular needs.

François Delsarte (1811–1871). Always more popular in Europe than in America, the Delsarte thesis was that reactions in human contact were both introverted and extroverted. The Delsarte charts of bodily attitudes in terms of moods, intuitions, and meanings are now being adapted for training actors in some American educational institutions, if only to form exercises for special requirements.

Traces of François Delsarte's methods may be discovered in the movements and postures as presented by Dalcroze and Alexander. Actors are now placing more emphasis upon the body and voice, which are, and always have been, an actor's most important tools.

The Mark Taper Forum production of The Metamorphoses, *a creation directed by Paul Sills, a Story Theatre transformation of Ovid. (Courtesy of Center Theatre Group, Mark Taper Forum, Los Angeles, Calif.)*

Frederick Matthias Alexander (1869-1955). This Australian-British actor developed what is now known as "The Alexander Technique" of physical reeducation in order to improve himself as an actor. The concept was founded upon the biological principle that each act of the individual involves the entire integrated person. It dealt in part with developing a capacity for neuromuscular coordination and provided escape from clichés. The individual was held to be responsible for, and conscious of, all of his reactions. The discipline begins with learning correct posture and proper use of the breathing apparatus. The body is then trained to respond to outward manifestations of inward tendencies. Pure psychological interpretation often leads to improper physical symptoms. The value in Alexander's exercises is in learning to translate mental, spiritual, and physical aspects into muscular tensions. Alexander considered posture of primary importance and breathing correctly a means of supporting movement.

During his lifetime his students included such eminent men as George Bernard Shaw, Aldous Huxley, and Sir Henry Irving, the foremost English actor of his day. Today the Alexander Technique is included in the actor training programs of the following theatre groups:

> The Tyrone Guthrie Theatre in Minnesota
> The American Festival Theatre in Stratford, Connecticut
> The American Conservatory Theatre (ACT) in San Francisco
> The Juilliard School, Drama Division, Lincoln Center, New York
> The Arena Theatre in Washington, D.C.

In New York, The Center for the Alexander Technique has been established to meet the demands for teachers of this methodology. In Denmark, Israel, France, Italy, and South Africa, instruction in the Alexander Technique has been offered for many years. Even "method" maharishis, who formerly negated the importance of the physical in actor training, are now restructuring classes to include body training. With so many of the "Now Generation" of actors engaged in neuromuscular training, the future seems directed away from a realistically oriented theatre.

Early in this century, Adolphe Appia and Gordon Craig envisioned a new nonrealistic theatre. Ever since, these artists have had a profound influence on scene designers, lighting technicians, and directors.

Edward Gordon Craig (1872-1966). Son of England's luminous actress, Ellen Terry, Craig was himself an actor in Sir Henry Irving's company, but it was as theatre visionary, as well as artist, that he was to make himself immortal. His many handsome books, illustrated by himself, projected his revolutionary theories, founded primarily upon his concept of a single theatre super-artist responsible for sculptural, symbolic settings, contrasting lights, and shadowy illumination with actors who were to be *über-marionettes*. Craig mounted several productions during his lifetime—*Much Ado* in England, and *Hamlet* for Stanislavski in Russia—none of which made a sensation with the people at that time. But, nearly all drama students are thoroughly imbued with the theatre of Gordon Craig through his books, and influenced by him in their own work.

Adolphe Appia (1862-1928). This Swiss musician-architect and prophet of the modern scenic stage, along with Gordon Craig, opened a new vision of theatre. For Appia, the art of stage production involved action of living actors and their reactions to the spaces and masses surrounding them. All inanimate decoration, including the painted scenery and realistic properties, was eliminated, as well as the proscenium frame and the main curtain. Lighting formed a dominating role; indeed, Appia is generally accredited with one of today's standard practices, using light to create mood by casting shadows from light instead of merely lighting the stage for the purpose of illuminating actors' faces.

Both Craig and Appia admitted that their ideas had much in common,[7] and this can be verified by examining their sketches. Both used multiple acting levels and, therefore, the lighting plot was always of primary importance. Appia used little color in his settings and details were architectural rather than painted. His stage was veiled in a mystical penumbra with the emphasis on the cyclorama on which multiple images were projected. During Appia's lifetime there did not exist the necessary equipment to adequately transfer his sketches to the stage. He would approve of our projecting devices today, and of our open space and thrust stages.

The strong resemblance in the work of Craig and Appia can be seen when it is considered that both agreed on space settings, the role lighting must play, the importance of movement, and the concept that the true artist of the theatre should design, write, and direct his own productions. The point of difference is in their attitude toward the actor. In Craig's monumental settings, the actor seems insignificant, but Appia devised all spatial surroundings in scale to the size of the actor.

We cannot properly conclude this section on those men who are influencing the young directors and actors of today without including a writer who is not a theatre man. However, many modern theatre ideas are based upon his revelations.

Marshall McLuhan (1911-   ). The director of the Center for Culture and Technology at the University of Toronto in Canada, Marshall McLuhan is also considered the high priest of pop, and an idol of young theatre workers. In his provocative writings, McLuhan affirms that man has always been influenced by his own means of communication, or "The Medium Is the Massage." Just as Gutenberg created the reader, our electronic age—and especially our TV—has transformed us into creatures of the senses. Translated into theatre terms, this might imply that what we *see* affects our sensibilities more than the meaning of the words we hear; that the tone in which something is said affects our sensibilities as much as the content of a speech.

[7]See Walter Volbach, *Prophet of the Modern Theatre* (Middletown, Conn.: Wesleyan University Press, 1968).

Antonin Artaud

Artaud, Antonin. *The Theatre and Its Double*. Mary C. Richards, ed. New York: Grove Press, 1958.
———. *Anthology*. 2nd rev. ed. Edited by Jack Hirschman. San Francisco: City Lights, 1963.

Bertolt Brecht

Demitz, Peter. *Brecht*. Englewood Cliffs, N.J.: Prentice-Hall, 1962.
Esslin, Martin. *Brecht, The Man and His Work*. New York: Doubleday & Co., 1961.
Gray, Ronald. *Brecht*. London: Oliver & Boyd, 1961.
Munk, Erica, ed. *Stanislavski and America*. New York: Hill & Wang, 1966. See articles: "Exit Thirties, Enter Sixties," by Richard Schechner, pp. 13–23, and "Stanislavski & Brecht," by Eric Bentley, pp. 116–123.
Willet, John. *Brecht*. New York: Hill & Wang, 1959.

Emile Jacques-Dalcroze

Driver, Ethel. *A Pathway to Dalcroze Eurythmics*. New York: Thomas Nelson & Sons, 1957.
Ingham, Percy. *The Jacques-Dalcroze Method*. London: Constable & Co., 1912.
Jacques-Dalcroze, Emile. *Rhythm, Music and Education*. London: Chatto & Windus, 1921.
———. *Rhythmic Movement*. London: Novello & Co., 1921.
Pisk, Paul A. *The Collaboration of Adolph Appia and Emile Jacques-Dalcroze*. Austin, Texas: University of Texas Press, 1966.
Sadler, M. E. Introduction to *The Eurythmics of Jacques-Dalcroze*. London: Constable & Co., 1920.

François Delsarte

Delsarte, François. *A System of Oratory*. Wehman.
Werner, Edgar S. *Delsarte System of Oratory*. 1893.
(Also work by l'Abbe Deleanmosne, translated by Frances A. Shaw).

Matthias Alexander

Alexander's writings include: *Man's Supreme Inheritance* (1910); *Constructive Conscious Control of the Individual* (1923); *The Use of Self* (1932); and *The Universal Constant in Living* (1914). These books are not readily available, and for the director who needs only introductory study, the following is recommended:

Maisel, Edward, ed. *The Resurrection of the Body, Writings of Alexander*. New York: Universal Books, 1969.

Maisel selects from Alexander's writings, correspondence, and transcripts. There is no reliable biography of Alexander, but Maisel includes a brief but lucid word portrait of him.

Edward Gordon Craig

Craig, Edward Anthony. *Gordon Craig, A Biography by His Son*. New York: Alfred A. Knopf, 1968.

――――. *Gordon Craig, The Story of His Life.* New York: Alfred A. Knopf, 1965.

Craig, Edward Gordon. *Books and Theatres.* Facsimile ed. Freeport, N.Y.: Books for Libraries, 1925.

――――. *Ellen Terry and Her Secret Self.* New York: Benjamin Blom, 1932.

――――. *Fourteen Notes.* Seattle: University of Washington Press, 1931.

――――. *Henry Irving.* New York: Benjamin Blom, 1930.

――――. *Mask.* 15 vols., plus index. Edited by L. F. Guidry. Individual volumes available from Benjamin Blom, New York.

――――. *On the Art of the Theatre.* New York: Theatre Arts Books, 1911–1958.

――――. *Radio Talks.* London: Discurion, 1960.

――――. *Scene.* New York: Benjamin Blom, 1968.

――――. *Theatre Advancing.* New York: Benjamin Blom, 1964.

――――. *Towards a New Theatre.* New York: Benjamin Blom.

――――. *Towards a New Theatre, Forty Designs for Stage Scenes.* New York: Benjamin Blom, 1913.

ADOLPHE APPIA

Appia, Adolphe. *Music and the Art of the Theatre.* Coral Gables, Florida: University of Miami Press, 1962.

――――. *The Work of Living Art.* Coral Gables, Florida: University of Miami Press, 1960.

Volbach, Walter R. *Adolphe Appia, Prophet of the Modern Theatre, A Profile.* Middletown, Conn.: Wesleyan University Press, 1968.

Pisk, Paul A. *The Collaboration of Adolphe Appia and Emile Jacques-Dalcroze.* Austin, Texas: University of Texas Press, 1966.

MARSHALL McLUHAN

McLuhan, Marshall. *Understanding Media.* New York: McGraw-Hill, 1964.

――――. *The Medium Is The Massage.* New York: Random House, 1967.

――――. *Verbi-Voci-Visual Explorations.* New York: McGraw-Hill, 1965.

2

THE DIRECTOR AND HIS AUDIENCE

The drama's law the drama's patrons give
And we, who seek to please, must please to live.
                                        —David Garrick

Any work of art presupposes an audience. An aesthetic consideration is that it will enrich the life of the spectator. It matters little that you have chosen to produce a play because you love it, or that you think your production is the best you have ever seen of that play. *If your audience does not like it, you are merely indulging yourself.*

Our American government does not subsidize a professional National Theatre as is done in England and France. An appreciative and enthusiastic audience is our best guarantee of a continuing and vital theatre. Freedom of choice is the opinionated man's means of participation.

No theatre can exist in a vacuum. The continuing goal of a community director is in the creation of a vital and supportive audience. Knowing your audience is more important in regional theatres than on Broadway, where audience preferences are often completely unpredictable.

What sort of monster is an audience? Is it a god sitting in judgment, or is it a demon? It is both! Please it and it is a kind and loving benefactor. Displease it and it will destroy you by ignoring you. If we accept that this god or demon is so vital to our theatre's existence, we might do well to learn more about it.

Primarily, we must accept that no two audiences are ever going to be

Director William Ball (center) directs the American Conservatory's production of Rosencrantz and Guildenstern Are Dead. (*Photo by Hank Kranzler, courtesy of the American Conservatory Theatre of San Francisco*)

the same. Even a Monday audience will differ from one on Tuesday. An audience is not a homogeneous body universally the same, and yet there are some points of similarity—else how would authors, producers, and directors ever reach any standards of acceptance?

We live today engulfed in a menacing atmosphere of realities. These seem so frightening that we are resigned that we are "doomed to living." The theatre also has reality, but its reality is an illusion. Audiences share the hopes, the disappointments, the success, or the death of the characters on stage, and this emotional involvement can be very acute. But members of an audience are also conscious that once outside the theatre they can discard their concern. In real life it is not so easy to dismiss reality. The theatre helps relax the tensions of everyday life and enriches the lives of those who experience it by showing that all mankind share the same fears, hopes, and problems, that all men must live or die with their ideals.

Metamorphosis: People Into Audience

Is an audience singular, a group, or is it a group made up of many different individuals?

> Mr. A is an insurance salesman. He and his wife are giving a dinner for one of his business associates, Mr. B, and his wife. The evening has been planned as an occasion, a celebration, and with this in mind, Mr. A has purchased four tickets for the theatre, which they will attend after dinner.
>
> As they drive to the theatre, the men in front of the car talk of business. Mr. A may offer his opinions of company policies and Mr. B may offer his ideas. Sitting in the back seat, the wives are perhaps talking about

19

clothes or their children. Mrs. A has found a smart little shop where prices are most reasonable. Mrs. B knows the shop but was never able to find anything she liked. All their talk is ego-centered: "What would I do," "If you ask me," "My opinion on that is," "Red is not my color," "My daughter wears it constantly." I—My—Me—Mine!

Now they have arrived at the theatre, and as they enter, one by one, Mr. A follows and hands the tickets to the usher. They find their seats, which are placed in a row among other rows. Unable to continue their private conversations, each of the foursome leafs through his program. Then as the house lights dim, the stage is revealed in a blazing light and the metamorphosis is complete. Our four individuals have now changed into members of a group. Until they leave the theatre, they will respond intellectually and emotionally *as a group*.

Protected by a kind of social anonymity, individual inhibitions will disappear. The tendency will be to react emotionally rather than intellectually, to laugh, cry, or be thrilled along with the group. And as a group they will be more receptive to make-believe and illusion, more inclined to accept lies as truth, than they were as individuals. In such a group the individual gains a kind of security, a safety in numbers.

What makes this metamorphosis possible? When an individual becomes part of a group, either a mob or an audience, there is a strong drive to comply both physically and emotionally with that group. Responses are triggered by stimuli emanating from the stage. These stimuli and the reactions in the audience are absolutely necessary to the theatre experience. Good directors recognize this and approach their work with it in mind. They know that each spectator must be made to feel something of himself on that stage. He must identify with the characters, judge their actions, and take sides. Each has come to the theatre willing to become a part of the play's action, to participate, to fight beside the hero, to punish the villain, to adore the heroine.

This "sharing" of the action, and the constant stress upon the particular in human terms, is the means used in the theatre to reach the universal. Once an audience stops believing in the illusion, you might just as well bring down the curtain. But never blame the audience. The monster is never wrong—you must be! The spectator must remain caught up in the game of make-believe. He must be made to accept that what he hears and sees from the stage is fact, not fiction. This then is the true theatrical experience. The spectator spiritually joins the hero in stabbing the villain, and even though he knows the hero will be punished for it, he also knows that as a member of the audience he will not suffer. When producing a play of realism, a director strives to maintain this invisible division between the stage and the audience.

Aesthetic Distance

We know that in the theatre of Shakespeare's day the acting area thrust out into the audience. Spectators often sat on the stage, and these beribboned

Interior of Ralph Freud Playhouse, U.C.L.A. At right, backstage and elevator forestage. At left, control rooms at rear of auditorium. (Courtesy of Ralph Freud)

dandies frequently interrupted the play with their personal comments or actual participation. Sometime later David Garrick, the leading actor of his day, denied them a place on the stage. This separation of audience and actors, the addition of the proscenium, and other factors opened the way for realism.

During its most popular period, the realistic theatre became so "real" that certain principles had to be established so that spectators would not mistake illusion for fact. Incidents are recorded in which spectators have rushed to the stage to save the heroine from "a fate worse than death." This happened frequently in gold rush theatres. The very human impulse to touch a marble statue, keep time with a rock group, or spar the air while watching a boxing match all stem from our empathetic responses. This becomes even more pronounced when watching real actors on stage involved in real-life situations because this experience is less abstract and more personal. In the theatre, involvement can become so intense that a physical and psychical division between it and actual participation was established. Should the emotional response in the audience become participatory, it could be more uncomfortable than pleasurable. To accept Caesar's blood as real would completely destroy the theatrical illusion. However, it follows that the audience must be aware that what they are experiencing is make-believe. This division between involvement and participation was called *aesthetic distance* by Herbert Langfeld.[1]

The now well-known example used to illustrate this theory involves a man standing on the prow of a boat admiring the rolling of the waves as they lap rhythmically against the side of the ship. His enjoyment of the experience depends upon his artistic detachment. But, if a great mountain of a wave should suddenly engulf the boat threatening his life, this physical involvement would completely destroy that artistic detachment.

The Real and the Imaginary

In spite of the objectives of realism, there are certain theatrical elements which continually deny them. The separation between audience and actor caused by the proscenium, the painted scenery, the artificial light, the makeup, and the projected voices prevents total realism in the theatre. Truth and reality are not the prime objectives of theatre, for it is a place of illusion and magic. This is why it holds its charm for us even in this day when a fantasy like a trip to the moon has become ordinary.

[1]Herbert Langfeld, *The Aesthetic Distance* (New York: Harcourt Brace Jovanovich, 1920).

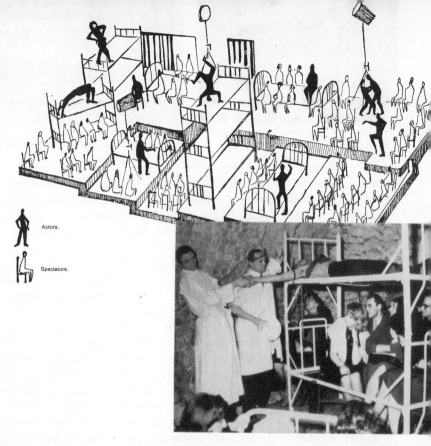

Actors.

Spectators.

Grotowski's Kordian *as shown in both sketch and completed production. Acting space is built to suggest a mental hospital with spectators incorporated into the structure as patients. (Courtesy of Odin Teatret)*

Today there is an active movement to discard the aesthetic distance theory and have the audience participate in the action of the play. We have had the theories of Antonin Artaud and others, and these in turn influenced the current idol of the theatrical intelligentsia, Jerzy Grotowski. The Grotowski company, although working behind the iron curtain, has nevertheless influenced such groups as The Living Theatre, La Mama, The Open Theatre, and the Peter Brook group in England. Grotowski demands direct contact between actors and audience via a series of physical, intellectual, and emotional "shock treatments." The audience, in Grotowski's words, is to be "confronted with a human act and is invited to react totally, even at the moment of performance." This multileveled involvement between the actor and the spectator is believed by some to be a harbinger of future theatre. "Let the most drastic scenes happen face to face with the spectator," Grotowski says, "so that he is within arms reach of the actor, can feel his breathing and smell his perspiration."[2]

When I attended a performance of *Paradise Now*, given by "The Living Theatre," the cast leapt into the auditorium and a girl (or boy, I could not

[2]Jerzy Grotowski, *Towards A Poor Theatre* (Denmark: Odin Teatrets Forlag, 1968), pp. 40–42.

tell which) singled me out to rage against a system that prevented people from walking naked on the street. They followed Grotowski to the letter, even down to the perspiration smell.

Some argue that members of an ensemble company involving audience members directly may violate aesthetic distance for a few but that "artful involvement" for others may be increased through a kind of satanic pleasure at seeing somebody else confronted.

In this day when hardly anyone is building proscenium-type theatres anymore, it is probably safe to say that one of the new directions in stage direction is a complete abandonment of aesthetic distance. My own conviction is that the action of a play may be in and about the spectators and still retain the benefits of aesthetic distance. There is only one requirement and it is that actors do not touch or try to converse with members of the audience, for that personal contact implies a *physical participation by the viewer*, which may be many other things, but never art.

The advantages to be had from the aesthetic distance should not be given up without much thought and certainly not from any desire to be different. Eliminate the proscenium, bring the drama around the audience—but don't touch the spectators. Preserve the illusion.

Some Considerations

Most directors will admit that the choice of plays is a crucial matter to their success. Each play must be matched with an audience. But, too often cliché pieces with clap-trap devices are chosen by a director because they are thought to be the only plays interesting to an audience. Never underestimate the intelligence or taste of an audience!

This is especially true if your production is to be part of the educational system. Some educators have deplored the use of musical comedies instead of worthwhile plays in high schools and colleges. No one will deny that audience acceptance is of great importance, but the education of that audience should also be a continuing goal. It should not be the purpose of drama in schools to cater to the tastes of a mass audience. That is the chief objective of the professional theatre. Educational theatre should elevate and lead the way.

There is no reason to believe that a distinguished play, or even a classic, will be boring to an audience. Everything depends upon what has been contributed by the director, actors, and others responsible for the production. But it is a serious mistake to depend entirely upon the classic, as if all the cast need do is learn the immortal lines and walk about the stage reciting them. Much has been written by indignant scholars about "butchering" great plays. Others are of the opinion that it is a necessity for these plays to be adapted to our time.

The great plays remain great because what they say is universal. They are not for one country or one age, but for all people and all ages. If we neglect them, they will not remain classics much longer. They will then become historical curios. A well balanced season or bill of great plays adds much audience interest in community or educational theatre. Fresh approaches and new life must certainly be contributed to our legacy of great drama, but we must also carefully preserve the timeless values of these plays.

There may be any number of motives involved in the selection of a play. Some plays are predictable successes because of their impact and charm. Occasionally one is selected to encourage new talent. A rugged all-male show will uncover and develop a director's stable of actors, a necessity for casting, as most plays have a predominance of male characters. Also, a director should give high priority to experimental productions which offer the opportunity to attempt innovative and empiric methods.

How much freedom of choice a director will have in the selection of his plays will vary with his particular situation. In the professional theatre a director may refuse a play submitted by a producer. At other times he might, for other reasons, accept a play for which he is less than enthusiastic. Play committees frequently choose plays to be performed by avocational theatres. Throughout this book, it has been necessary to deal separately with variations in professional, university, and community theatres under individual headings.

For the director who is free to choose his own plays, some generalizations can be made. He should choose plays which offer an audience some lasting

The Ghost Sonata *by August Strindberg, as produced at the North Carolina School of the Arts, directed by Ira Zuckerman with sets and costumes by Christina Giannini. (Courtesy of the North Carolina School of the Arts)*

values, a theme of broad universal appeal, skillful writing, rich characterizations, comic or dramatic impact—all adding up to an evening of
full enjoyment for an audience.

Audience Acceptance

Nothing is quite as important to a director as an audience. He may stage
a production which he sincerely believes has great social significance, but
if an audience doesn't care to see it, he is simply indulging himself. In general,
a play should be selected because of its aesthetic validity. Look for *idea
and form.* Does the play have a proportionate assembly of plot, theme, and
interesting characters? Does it have action and that indefinable quality of
uplifting the mind and spirit? If so, and you feel capable of blending these
together into an exciting production, then you should proceed with your
pre-production plans.

This is not meant to imply that there is any infallible formula for pleasing
all audiences. Each audience is individual. They are affected by weather,
holidays, news, strikes, and group psychology. Elizabethan audiences liked
blood. Restoration audiences preferred wit and philandering. And the Victori-
ans bought tickets to see plays of sentiment and morality.

There are also many variables to consider in selecting a play. A play that
is suitable for a state college might not be suitable for a religious college
just a few miles away. A great success in New York is not always a success
elsewhere. Each choice of play must be carefully considered from many
angles before being produced and must be custom-fitted to its audience.
If a director is new to a community, he should learn what sort of play that
particular audience has preferred in the past. If the area has no recent history
of play production, he must then use his reasoning powers to determine
which plays would be appropriate.

In some larger cities and universities, today's focus appears to be on plays
dealing with relevant social issues. Such plays should be considered because
they are the products of our time. *However, the director should feel confident
that the themes and action of such plays will not run counter to the standards
of his particular audience.* The wise director respects his audience—at least
that must always be the professional director's point of view. Disrespect
for an audience is surprisingly confessed by one of the new-wave authors,
Paul Goodman, who states, "The sign of successful new theatre is that the
audience is torn between fascination and the impulse to walk out in disgust."[3]
The present generation of theatre workers may find themselves in the same
predicament as modern painters who have painted themselves into a corner
where no one can follow except a tiny coterie of other far-out painters.
But the most unfortunate aspect is that they do not seem to enjoy what
they are doing. Certainly, perpetual anger will not lift the spirit.

How to choose a play for a particular audience is a lesson I learned the
hard way, and if I may be forgiven for relating a personal experience, my

[3]Alvin Kerman, ed., *Modern American Theatre* (Englewood Cliffs, N.J.: Prentice-Hall, 1967).
p. 120.

Newly constructed 250-seat theatre at Beverly Hills (Calif.) High School. At left, the thrust stage showing the lighting arrangement. (Photo by Ken Gelms) At right, view from the stage showing the light and sound control booth at rear. (Photo by Marc Goldstein)

point might be made better than if I were pedantic.

Several colleagues and I planned a season of professional productions in a quaint old New England town called Guilford. The opening play was *Stage Door*, and the reason the business manager gave for the selection of this play was that there were a few local young ladies who had worked hard to get our season started making speeches to clubs, etc., and as a reward they had been promised parts in *Stage Door*. The opening week's business was far from successful. For our second week we produced a play of social significance, because part of our financial backing had come from a young man who wanted to play the lead. Those two weeks not only depleted our funds but put us in debt. It was obvious that we must close. Both plays had been selected to facilitate "deals," and although I had nothing to do with choosing the plays, I was going back to New York with marks against my career as a director. As I sat in an almost empty theatre, I began studying the few people in the audience. They did not look like Guilford residents. I remembered that the "locals" had not supported our first play in which there were young ladies they had known as children. In the lobby during intermission, I had an opportunity to study individuals. They all dressed and spoke like "summer people," as the natives called them. They were mostly from New Haven, or other metropolitan areas. They had come to Guilford to spend leisurely vacations, to breathe country air, to sun, to swim during the day, and to be entertained at night.

"We're not giving these people what they want," I told the producer. "We should be doing plays about people like themselves, people of intelligence and security, placed in not-too-serious situations, and with some amusing dialogue which they will remember. They don't want problems. They have enough of these in everyday life. These folks are on vacation. They want to be entertained."

As his only other alternative was to close, the producer agreed to try another week. From that time on, we chose plays according to those different standards, and as a result, we became solvent and eventually played twelve weeks, presenting a new play each week to near capacity. Our permanent cast and production staff enjoyed a pleasant summer of gratifying work, and we ended the season with a few dollars for our efforts.

While there is a great deal of satisfaction in working with a play of stature, the plays you will be asked to direct will not always be of literary value. Not one of the plays we did at Guilford would ever be studied in literature classes. Choose, then, plays of *theatrical* significance—those which expose the human condition, using insight and exciting revelation. Such revelation can not "happen" on a printed page, only on a stage. Remember that the great eras of theatre existed when it pleased the greatest number of people.

Pleasing an audience, however, is only one important factor to consider in choosing a play for production. If your theatre is subsidized by one of those Federal Aid to Education grants (National Endowment of the Arts), then you might choose a play simply because you like it and want to direct it. Even so, there could be little satisfaction in sitting alone in a theatre watching a play that you alone enjoy. Certainly actors do not relish playing to empty seats. They have put forth an enormous amount of effort into their work and expect to be seen, and the more who see them the better the actors feel. A director should not make a habit of indulging himself. If he does, the cast may follow his example, and lately, actors seem quite fond of self-indulgence.

Something else to consider when choosing a play is whether or not you will be able to cast it. Suppose your play has eight male characters and two females. Have you the necessary men to produce it? Or, to be more specific, suppose you are considering *Macbeth*. Have you an actor and an actress with enough talent and experience to portray such demanding roles?

Another consideration would be the settings, although this is not the obstacle it was when stage settings had to be realistic. Castle interiors no longer need be authentic reproductions down to the last painted brick. A set piece with some effective lighting will be readily accepted today as Macbeth's great dining hall. Also, most universities of today have at their disposal the very latest and best theatrical equipment—much better than that found in

Director Edward Ragozzino mounts two varied productions for Lane Community College in Eugene, Oregon. At left, The Firebugs *by Frisch. (Photo by Paul Petersen) At right,* The Lark *by Anouilh and Hellman. Both settings by David Sherman. (Photos courtesy of Lane Community College)*

the New York professional theatres. Martin Aronstein, lighting designer of the Broadway hit musical *Promises, Promises*, deplores the lack of front-of-the-house mounting positions for lights in Broadway theatres: "It would be wonderful," writes Mr. Aronstein, "to have theatres on Broadway that are as well equipped as most university auditoriums."[4] It makes one wonder how graduates of such professionally equipped college theatres are ever going to make do with antiquated Broadway equipment.

[4]*Theatre Craft*, May-June, 1969.

THE
DIRECTOR'S
PLAY
SOURCES 3

Classics

In the theatre, a classic is a play worthy of being produced long after the life span of the author who wrote it and the audience for which it was written. Shakespeare did not write for posterity but for a particular audience. That audience is dead and so is Shakespeare, but his plays are experienced today by more people than ever witnessed them at the Globe. Any play which has this sort of immortality is considered to be a classic. Surveys made over a number of years reveal that such classics, especially the plays of Shakespeare, account for the largest single group of plays being produced today outside the commercial theatre.

But there are also plays written a comparatively short time ago which, by theatrical standards, are considered classics. I suggest that any play which moves an audience today, whether written four or four hundred years ago, is contemporary.

However, to the scholar, a classic remains literature; that is, it can be recognized by its distinguished writing, fine characterizations, and universality of theme. There have been a great many literary figures who have attempted the play form with indifferent success, such as Robert Browning with *Strafford*, Shelley with *The Cenci*, and Henry James with *The American*. While these are worthy of study in literature classes because of the author's fame or for the prose or poetry found in them, they are rarely produced on the stage. The true classic should be stage-worthy in any age.

Twelfth Night *in the repertory of the American Shakespeare Festival Theatre, Stratford, Conn. Left to right: James Valentine as Andrew Aguecheek, Patric Hines as Sir Toby Belch, Joan Darling as Viola, and Julian Miller as Fabian. Directed by Frank Hauser. (Courtesy of the American Shakespeare Festival Theatre)*

Coriolanus, *as staged by the American Shakespeare Festival Theatre at Stratford, Conn. Philip Bosco appears at center as Coriolanus, Patrick Hines as Menenius. (Courtesy of the American Shakespeare Festival Theatre)*

Approaching the Classics

In staging classics, most directors follow one of two approaches. Either they are guided by the ritualistic qualities of great masterpieces, or they hope to express some totally original concept in their production.

Each generation should revivify the great dramas of the past. Should no one read, study, or produce the works of Shakespeare, Sophocles, or Molière, then as time passed, young people would become computerized non-humans. But our desire to produce these plays should not be based upon historical factors but upon how they relate to our contemporary experience. There is no law which says we must stage a Shakespearian play inside a reproduction of the Globe Theatre. There is no right way to produce Euripides.

But the production of a classic must never distort the shape of the original. We must respect its form and symmetry, its soaring language, the blinding accuracy of its timeless characters; and above all, we must preserve its trenchant exploration of the human predicament. From the first reading, we must accept the fact that the great masters of drama were not concerned with portraying a realistic representation of life, but rather with expressing some universal meaning in one taut, forceful, and logical event. They did not only write drama, but the *inner meaning of that drama.*

There is some danger in becoming too familiar with the masters. A director should be comfortable in their presence, but he should not allow memories of other productions he has seen to block his own creativity. Conversely, while tradition may be by-passed a little if doing so will lead to fresh ideas and new life, no good will come of throwing out the baby with the bath water.

Try reading the classics as if they were recently completed manuscripts. Obsolete words and phrases may be understood by consulting the many glossaries, concordances, and variorums available to you. Use your research to fortify your instinctive feelings and imagination.

Undoubtedly, some cutting will be necessary—but, do not be in a hurry to do this. Lines which are redundant, puns, and remote Elizabethan humor may be considered at once, but wait until you hear the actors read before you decide on more serious cuts.

The ritualistic quality with which the classics have been endowed is capable of moving and exciting a traditionally oriented audience—if a director does not clutter the play with anachronistic gimmicks. The progressive, accumulative flow of the play must remain inviolate. Scene must follow scene without interruption; in fact, the divisions of scenes found in present printed versions of Shakespeare are thought not to be his but those added after his death by early printers or editors. If we are to take at face value the words of the Prologue in *Romeo and Juliet*, the spectators at the Globe stood in the open air for ". . . Two hours traffic of our stage . . ." Modern audiences do not have such patience. We must, as undoubtedly Shakespeare did, rely upon zest, speed, and fluency in production. There should be no waits between scenes, even if this means that the actors themselves arrange necessary furniture. Try to eliminate as many act divisions as possible, and the curtain. Remember that the Elizabethan and Greek actors had no curtain to separate them from the audience.

Some Differences Between
Staging Classics and Modern Plays

Modern plays are not necessarily easier to stage than classics, but the classics do require better-trained actors. These actors must have a fine coordination between the intellectual, emotional, and physical aspects of acting. Many classics are written in verse or arranged prose. This means that actors should learn about the interplay between long and short accents, as well as learn about the lilting music of the speech and the studied use of consonants and vowels. Obviously, an actor cannot approach a classic using the patterns of colloquial speech. It simply will not fit the luscious rhetoric and lofty metaphors. The language of Euripides or Shakespeare can be perfectly clear

The great classic Antigone, *as presented by the Tufts Arena Theatre, Tufts University, Dr. Marston Balch, Director.* (*Courtesy of the Tufts Arena Theatre*)

today if spoken properly. The inexperienced actor will need to maintain a sustained tone and have great reserves of breath for the towering emotional passages. Development of his breathing muscles will be a necessity until the actor is able to speak six or eight lines of verse with one sustained breath. He must have good enunciation and a sense of phrasing or musical value, and this must never descend into doggerel. All this is required, along with a well trained body, because the characters in the classics are larger-than-life. They can never be reduced to naturalistic portraits. The trick is to capture the human values along with the poetry and style. It is difficult for the inexperienced to comprehend the sheer physical strength required to act *Oedipus* or *Hamlet*. Sir Laurence Olivier has said that the great plays "devour" an actor.

> *You are playing* Othello, *you give it all you've got. The author says to you, "You've given it all you've got? Good! You've done that? Fine. Now, more! More! M-O-R-E!" And your heart and your guts and your brain are pulp, and the part feeds on them. Acting great parts devour you. Great parts are cannibals.*[1]

In the production of a classic, the director should always remember that these plays hold no surprises for an audience. Most people know what happens to Romeo and Juliet. Indeed, it is not unusual to find someone in the front row, book in hand, thumbing along each line as it is spoken. Realizing that the surprise element is denied them, some directors make the mistake of substituting gimmicks and tricks.

Some Mistakes in Directing Classics

A common fault in directing classics is to fill the stage with excessive effects and "busy" movement. One of the differences between the classics and realistic plays is the language. Never apologize for the poetry by distracting an audience.

Allow the immortal lines to carry their own interest, *and* they will! In those lines, Shakespeare illustrates. Don't illustrate the illustrations. The less spectacle an audience sees, the more they will imagine.

Another serious fault is to force the classics, and especially Shakespeare, into our modern speech idiom. Attempts to sound "natural" by breaking the formal style only muddles its clarity. One does not think of a speech such as "The ages of man . . ." on the spur of the moment. Respect the conventions of syllables, accents, and caesuras.

Also, it is not necessary to be freakish to be relevant. Among the abortive attempts to make Shakespeare relevant was one seen recently in New York. The play was *Henry V*, and this particular production erected considerable obstacles between the play and the audience. The stage was a jungle-gym, cluttered with jump ropes, pipes, and swings. The players were literally players, clapping, shouting, and chasing each other through the pipes. Canter-

---

[1]Interview with Sir Laurence Olivier by Kenneth Harris, *Los Angeles Times Calendar*, March 2, 1969. Reprinted by permission of *The London Observer*.

bury and Ely were rag-doll clowns. Perhaps this eccentricity was meant to open up the play to the audience. Instead, the lines were muffled between shenanigans. Concepts such as this seem such a flat denial of the original intent that they appear to be an apology for attempting the play at all. When the antics of the actors or directorial gimmicks detract from the value of the play, the whole system of "modernizing" breaks down. All changes are not improvements.

What Principles Should Guide The Director in Producing a Classic?

A play is an imitation of life, created in the minds of an audience by the use of symbols, moods, and an overall pattern of events. We should never ask, "What does this play mean?" but "How does it have meaning?" A director must clarify that first in his own mind. He must then work from a sense of the whole—the core, the commanding statement, the spine, the

Ellis Rabb directed this modern-dress Shylock for the American Conservatory Theatre production of Shakespeare's The Merchant of Venice *with Peter Donat. (Photo by Hank Kranzler, courtesy of the American Conservatory Theatre of San Francisco)*

dynamic spirit of the play. This is where the meaning will be found. He must then think of ways to clarify it. Such elements as the play's place in theatrical history, the customs of the people of the time, the costumes they wore, and the decor of the production should all be adjusted to and made harmonious with the director's sense of the whole. Elements must never interfere with or dominate over the director's concept of the production. And in acting, it is more important to illuminate the play than to encourage virtuosity in performances. As we cannot fathom the minds of those audiences which first experienced the plays of Euripides or Shakespeare, we must adjust to the minds of the audiences we know. But never neglect the poetry. Conduct some rehearsals in which the actors are instructed to speak their lines as quickly as possible, emphasizing the key words and the music. In this way, the verse will usually impose itself on the actors. Modern plays do not have the selectivity and precision of language used in the classics.

As an example of how to give a classic greater appeal to a modern audience while preserving the sense of the whole play, I reprint the following letter from an imaginative young English director to his cast of *Everyman*. Perhaps it will illustrate points I have been trying to make.

My dear cast,

Here, put down as they occur to me, are some of the ideas that I have for our production of "Everyman" which I think may prove very exciting and which should certainly be stimulating for you to work on.

You know that I have set the play in the present day and I want us to find for the play and for each of the characters a modern counterpart. I do not want it to be pious or beautifully elocuted. The play itself has too much vitality, urgency, austerity, crudity, and innate humour—qualities that are to be found in almost all the medieval morality plays. It is a latter day fallacy that religious plays must be performed piously.

Everyman himself is to be seen as a successful young man—we have no indication as to his age but with a young cast it seemed more interesting to interpret the play from your viewpoint. He might have been a boxer, a film star, but I have asked Bryan Stanyon to present him as a pop singer; Adam Faith is his model. Goods is seen as his manager-cum-agent, Beauty is his girl friend, Strength a weight-lifting chum, Discretion his secretary, Five Wits his legal advisor (a seedy, down-at-heel, whisky-fumed Irish lawyer who perhaps tried for the Church originally and got thrown out of the seminary—this would help to explain his smattering of theology). Build up a sense of community. Five Wits, Discretion, etc. are on one level allegorical figures, but in that we judge a man by his friends and associates, I want them to emerge as actual people, not merely types, the friends and associates of Everyman.

Knowledge is being depicted as an Irish St. Vincent de Paul nun, a bustling, practical and maternal figure, who probably taught Everyman his catechism. Confession is a Dominican friar and Everyman's parish priest. We have to remember that this is a Catholic play, and that Catholic dogma and practice are woven into the play's fabric. In the background of the production, at Chelmsford Cathedral, we shall see in the chancel the figure of Confession, saying mass, hearing confessions, as well as administering extreme unction to Everyman when the time comes. The purpose of all this is to enable the audience to see Everyman as one of the Faithful, even though lapsed. He is not A Man, but Every Man.

*Death—I have had many ideas about this, some influenced by Cocteau—
Death on a motor cycle and so forth, but each time I have come back
to a quiet, sympathetic yet austere figure in a white raincoat, very still
and watchful, rather like M. Henri in Anouilh's* Point of Departure.

*Because of the short rehearsal time available I would like you all to
learn your lines as quickly as possible and then to forget them for the
first week. In this week I want us to improvise around the characters and
situations. Fellowship is Everyman's buddy, his china, and they meet in
a bar and talk over drinks. What is their relationship? Is he a singer also?
Are they boyhood friends? Then let Bryan, as Everyman, imagine that he
has to break the news to him that he has cancer.*

*Get at the emotions behind each situation. Similarly, when Everyman
rings up his manager, Goods, find a comparable situation in which a top
artist might suddenly cease to be of use to his manager, who realizes that
this boy is about to become a has-been, is fast becoming an embarrassment,
a liability.*

*Get your imaginations working. Accumulate a mass of detail. Talk with
each other, have ideas, reject them, try others, until you have a foundation
of creative material from which fruitful improvisations can grow. The attempt, each time, is to try to understand the thought and belief of this
play as it affects people at all times.*

*Finally, this is a piece of theatre. It is also a ritual that I want you
to make your own. I want to see what you have to offer me and out of
all this material we will select, assemble, shape and concentrate the final
result. . . .*[2]

Further Reading: Classics

Boas, Guy. *Shakespeare and the Young Actor, A Guide to Production.* London: Rock-
liffe, Salisbury Square, 1955. By a headmaster of an English boy's school producing
Shakespeare with boys playing Shakespearian heroines as in Elizabethan theatre.
Lists number of lines in famous roles, has photos, etc.

Charney, Maurice. *Style in Hamlet.* Princeton: Princeton University Press, 1969.

Cunningham, J.V., ed. *In Shakespeare's Day.* Greenwich, Conn.: Fawcett Publications, 1970.

deBanke, Cecile. *Shakespearean Stage Production, Then and Now.* New York: Mc-
Graw-Hill, 1954. A compilation of work by eminent authorities on various aspects
of Shakespeare's theatre, including staging, books and references, actors and personnel of the Globe Company, costumes, music, dances, and recordings, with
extensive bibliography and illustrations.

Fergusson, Francis. *Shakespeare, the Pattern in His Carpet.* New York: Dell, 1970.

Guthrie, Tyrone. *In Various Directions.* New York: Macmillan Co., 1965.

Hunt, Hugh. *The Director in the Theatre.* London: Routledge & Kegan Paul, 1954.

———. *Old Vic Prefaces, Shakespeare and the Producer.* London: Routledge & Kegan
Paul, 1954.

Joseph, Bertram L. *Acting Shakespeare.* London: Routledge & Kegan Paul, 1960.

Kernodle, Goerge R. *Invitation to Theatre.* New York: Harcourt Brace Jovanovich,
1967.

Knight, G. Wilson. *Principles of Shakespearian Production.* London: Farber & Farber,

[2]From *Directing a Play,* by James Roose-Evans. Copyright © 1968 by James Roose-Evans.
Reprinted with the permission of the publisher, Theatre Arts Books, New York.

1934; New York: Macmillan Co., 1936., pps. 49–217. With a concept of *Macbeth* by Shakesperian authority.

Spaeight, Robert. *William Poel and the Elizabethan Revival*. London: William Heine-mann, 1954.

Sprague, Arthur Colby. *Shakespeare and the Actors, The Stage Business in his Plays. (1660–1905)*. Cambridge: Harvard University Press, 1944; London: Russell & Russell, 1963.

Traveisi, D. A. *An Approach to Shakespeare*, 3rd ed. New York: Doubleday & Co., 1969. Scholarly tome identifying the discontinuity in Shakespeare's work. Part I, Chronicles; Part II, The Problem Plays & Tragedies.

Watkins, Ronald. *On Producing Shakespeare*. London: Michael Joseph, 1955.

Webster, Margaret. *Shakespeare Without Tears*. Greenwich, Conn.: Fawcett, 1955 (paperback).

American Classics

There is another source of plays which has been a recent happy "discovery" of Broadway. So many of the plays being written today lack craftsmanship and entertainment value. As a result, producers have been obliged to reexamine hit plays of the recent past. Ironically, *The Front Page* was produced by Richard Barr, Edward Albee, and Charles Woodward as a kind of fund raiser for, of all things, developing new playwrighting talent.

The list of successful revivals in recent years is impressive. *You Can't Take It With You, The Show Off, Our Town, The Little Foxes, Beggar on Horseback, Room Service*, and *Harvey* have been revived, not only because they were great successes in their day, but because they have a timeless appeal and are respected examples of the playwrighting art. If we ever have

At left, Director Edward Hastings brought William Saroyan's The Time of Your Life *to the American Conservatory Theatre stage with Ken Ruta (front) and Joy Carlin and Scott Thomas at rear. (Photo by Hank Kranzler, courtesy of the American Conservatory Theatre of San Francisco) Below, Tufts University Arena Theatre stages the American classic* Our Town. *(Courtesy of the Tufts Arena Theatre)*

a national repertory theatre in this country, as they have in England, let us hope that American playwrights such as Wilder, Kelly, Kaufman & Hart, Saroyan, and others will be adequately represented in the repertory of plays.

Contemporary Sources

Broadway Plays: The Hits and Misses

Recently only nineteen new American plays were produced on Broadway proper compared to twenty-five during the previous season, although financially it was the richest season in Broadway history, estimated by *Variety* at fifty-five million dollars. No doubt this was due in part to higher ticket costs.

The term *Broadway* is in itself a misnomer. There are only two theatres on the main stem, while thirty-four theatres are located on side streets both East and West of Broadway. Theatrical unions consider Broadway "an area"—from Thirty-fourth Street to Fifty-seventh Street, and between Fifth and Ninth Avenues. In Broadway terminology, a "hit" is a production which has returned its costs. Recently, out of seventy-eight productions, only two were hits. In the following season the score was thirteen out of eighty-four. These genuine Broadway successes are always in tremendous demand, and rights are not released until years later—and then at premium royalty costs.

Another group of plays usually advertised by play publishers as "Broadway

The Forum of the Vivian Beaumont Theatre produces young playwright James Hanley's The Inner Journey, with Michael Dunn as Antaeus and Robert Symonds as Christian. (Photo by Martha Swope)

Long running on Broadway are these Bremen town animal musicians, (from left) Paul Sand, Richard Libertini, Richard Schaal, and Peter Bonerz in Story Theatre by Paul Sills. (Courtesy of the Center Theatre Group, Mark Taper Forum, Los Angeles, Calif.)

37

successes"[3] are actually Broadway failures, victims of audience apathy or critical assassination.[4] Rarely does one find a play from Broadway with distinction enough to relate to education. Broadway has other standards. One of its main interests is the box office, and a good box office usually means a good sale to films. More and more, lately, the Broadway successes have been plays of shock impact, dealing in "new morality," four-letter words, deviational sex, and nudity. Before selecting a Broadway hit—or miss—I suggest that you do the following:

1. Consider the play from the viewpoint of your audience and community
2. Check the availability of the play
3. Determine royalty costs
4. Obtain clearance from your superiors

Catalog Plays

Business firms who exclusively publish "acting versions" of plays and offer yearly catalogs of them are today caught in a vise. On one side are the customers interested in buying a particular type of play. On the other side is the publishers' traditional source, Broadway, producing a product which is not acceptable to their customers. If we contrast the nay-saying kind of play (which often "nay-says" itself out of communicability and artistic coherence) with those plays which once were staged in a thousand high school auditoriums and Elk's halls throughout America, it is easy to understand why a great majority of towns dare not look to Broadway for plays. But if you believe these smaller towns are square and that it's about time they "get with it"—then that brings up the matter of reform, and that is another subject altogether.

Each Broadway season brings out only a few plays which are commerical successes, and there is frantic competition among publishers for such plays. In order to compensate for the dearth and continue in business, the publishers have plays written under their supervision by experienced playwrights using pseudonyms. These hungry playwrights are instructed in particular formats and in writing down to the tastes of the amateur market located in rural communities. The results are usually better in playwriting technique than in subject matter, which for the most part deals in clichés and pap which these publishers underestimate to be the tastes of the amateur market. Some such plays are even offered royalty free.

Unproduced Plays

This group includes not only plays written by novice writers, but those written by more experienced playwrights who have been unable to have

[3]You may check the validity of these by determining which year they were produced and then looking them up in *The Best Plays of (Year)*. This will inform you of how long they ran on Broadway, and why they were or were not successful.

[4]Each year a Pulitzer Prize Play is, hopefully, chosen by a panel of critics. In the five-year period between 1962 and 1967, only two plays were thought to deserve that award.

their plays produced on Broadway. This does not necessarily mean that because they are unproduced they are bad plays. There is a long history of plays "making the rounds" and being rejected before being produced with outstanding success. Naturally there will be good and bad plays among this group.

In most cases it might be unwise for secondary schools to attempt untried manuscripts, especially those written by students. But among members of a local community may be found a budding author with an interesting unproduced play. If a director has a venturesome spirit (and what director has not?), he should read such plays and seriously consider staging them. There would be local interest, and should the play go on to other successful productions, the director and the group would enjoy the credit of first discovery.

The late Margo Jones, founder of the Alley Theatre in Houston, once said:

> Too many people are saying, "I'll do a new play if I can find a good one." Certainly you must find a good one, but this attitude is not good enough. The plays can be found if you look hard enough. And if you take the violent stand I have spoken about, you will feel obligated to search and search and search until the scripts are discovered. I have a belief that there is great writing in America today and that much of it has not yet been unearthed. . . .
>
> The production of classics is healthy, but it is not a step in the flowering we want to see in the American theatre. We need progress, and the seed of progress in the theatre lies in the new plays."[5]

With such determination Margo Jones discovered playwrights Tennessee Williams and William Inge.

Production costs in New York today have become so monumental that producers can hardly afford to gamble on a new play written by a novice. They do watch the London theatres, and if a new play is a success there, a New York producer might import it. But this procedure does not help the young American playwright to develop by seeing his play before an audience. Our most prominent and prolific Broadway producer has finally staged his *first* new play by an American playwright.[6]

Colleges and universities should certainly include at least one new play per season. Few do. Sensing this need for new plays, several organizations have been instituted. Two of these are The American National Theatre and Academy (Manuscript Service, 139 West 44th St., New York, N.Y., 10036) and The American Educational Theatre Association (1701 Pennsylvania Ave., N.W., Washington, D.C. 20006). Another play agency is the American Playwrights Theatre, located at Ohio State University in Columbus, Ohio. These organizations rent new plays to members, some written by Broadway senior citizens, such as George Sklar, Lawrence & Lee, and others.[7]

---

[5]Margo Jones, *Theatre-In-The-Round* (New York: Holt, Rinehart & Winston, 1951), p. 25. Reprinted by permission of the publisher.

[6]David Merrick's production of *Child's Play*, by Robert Marasco. A mystery melodrama.

[7]See Gerald Weales, *The Jumping-Off Place* (New York: Macmillan Co., 1969), p. 228.

Several years ago, the Rockefeller Foundation provided a grant to Arthur H. Ballet of the University of Minnesota, for the purpose of giving young American playwrights an opportunity to see their work performed before audiences, to experiment, and to learn as much as possible about their craft without the scarifying hazards existing in the hit-flop atmosphere of Broadway. Under the ponderous title of "The Office for Advanced Drama Research," the original intent has been nationalized and now offers $4,500 for each production of fifteen plays chosen by Ballet to whichever American theatre Ballet feels will best serve the playwright.

Reading approximately a thousand playscripts each year, only thirty indicate to Ballet that their authors have "interesting talent or attitude, or something."[8]

Ballet finds that most playwrights are imitating Sam Shepard, or Megan Terry, former finds of the O.A.D.R., along with Terrence McNally and Jean-Claude van Itallie. Although Ballet has the counsel of a committee, the final decision on which plays are selected is his own, as he learned early that committee selections "invariably resulted in compromise and mediocrity." As a result, Ballet finds himself enthroned as a patron saint of undiscovered American playwrights, along with Ellen Stewart of La Mama in New York and Ed Parone of The Center Theatre in Los Angeles.

Some of Ballet's selections may be read in the following four volumes of *Playwrights for Tomorrow:*[9]

> Volume 1: *American Power* (2 Acts) by James Schevill; *Ex-Copper Queen On A Set Of Pills*, by Megan Terry; *A Bad Play for an Old Lady*, by Elizabeth Johnson; *And Things That Go Bump in the Night*, by Terrence McNally.
>
> Volume 2: *Tango Palace* (1 Act) and *The Successful Life of Three* (a skit), both by Maria Irene Fornes; *Shelter Area*, by Nick Boretz; *The Boy Who Came To Leave*, by Lee H. Kalcheim.
>
> Volume 3: *Easy Payments*, by John Lewin; *Where is De Queen?* by Jean-Claude van Itallie; *The Great Git-Away*, by Romeo Muller; *With Malice Aforethought*, by John Stranack; *I, Elizabeth Otis, Being of Sound Mind*, by Phillip Barber.
>
> Volume 4: *The World Tipped Over and Laying on its Side*, by Mary Feldhaus-Weber; *Visions of Sugar Plums*, by Barry Pritchard; *The Strangler*, by Arnold Powell; *The Long War*, by Kevin O'Morrison.

It is only fair to admit that some regional theatre directors who have tried producing new plays would be apprehensive about repeating the procedure. They point out that they lose the ticket-selling potential which comes with a nationally publicized play and that their audiences do not care to pioneer when attending theatre. Such short-sided views might be one of

---

[8]From an interview with Arthur H. Ballet by Dan Sullivan, *Los Angeles Times Calendar*, December 21, 1969.

[9]Arthur H. Ballet, *Playwrights for Tomorrow* (Minneapolis: University of Minnesota Press, 1967).

*Two productions from Northwestern University Theatre, both directed by Robert Scheideman,
with settings by Sam Ball. At left,* The Marriage of Mr. Mississippi *by Friedrich Durrenmatt.
At right,* Finnegan's Wake *by James Joyce. (Courtesy of Northwestern University Theatre)*

the reasons why America has produced only a few great playwrights.

I know one director who has at least solved the publicity problem. He
bolsters the unknown playwright by getting a well-known name in the leading
role. Usually when a playwright is working, he visualizes some particular
actor as his protagonist. This resourceful director asks the author if this is
true in his case. If so, he writes a very business-like letter to the actor,
in care of either Actor's Equity in New York or the Screen Actor's Guild
in Hollywood, and tells the actor that he has an excellent new play he intends
to produce which is ideally suited to the star—in fact, was written with
him in mind. He offers to send the play to the actor so that he may read
it. This either opens negotiations or the inquiry never receives a reply, in
which case, the effort has cost only the price of a postage stamp. It is not
surprising, considering the scarcity of acting opportunities today, that this
director has several times been able to have a well-known actor appear in
a "Pre-Broadway Opening" in his theatre.

Hollywood and New York have many actors anxious to keep active in
a slow market. While granting that the brilliance of some of these stars
may be a bit dimmed, they are still "names" and remembered fondly in
smaller communities.

Modern Foreign Plays

Many more new plays are produced abroad than in America because production costs are much lower there. To produce a typical one-set, six-character
play on Broadway today could involve a minimum investment of $100,000,
while in England the play might be done for one-tenth that cost.

A majority of new plays do not survive beyond their first production.
This does not always mean that they are bad plays, but merely that they
are not considered commercial enough for their particular market. If modern
foreign plays are of interest to you, you might subscribe to some English

theatrical magazines (such as *Plays and Players*)[10] or refer to the seasonal European reports in *The Best Plays* series. Only you will be able to judge if the subject matter of such plays would interest Americans and be acceptable to your particular audiences.

Director John Hirsh used masks to advantage in his production of Bertolt Brecht's Galileo *for the Repertory Theatre of Lincoln Center (New York). (Photo by Martha Swope)*

The Chinese Wall by Max Frisch, as produced by Northwestern University Theatre. Note use of hand masks. (Courtesy of Northwestern University Theatre)

[10]*Plays and Players* is an English monthly theatrical magazine, Artillery Mansion, 75 Victoria Street, London, S. W. 1, England.

Experimental Plays: Off-Broadway

When costs made it impossible to experiment with untried plays on Broadway, smaller theatres in lower-rent districts were engaged, mostly in Greenwich Village, where new plays and revivals might be produced with some hope of meeting expenses. There were also other considerations which made this a logical course of action: the difficulty in booking Broadway theatres, and the reluctance of backers to make any sizable investments in untried and unconventional plays.

Some now well-known plays were first introduced Off-Broadway, such as *Oh Dad, Poor Dad*, by Arthur Kopit, *The Prodigal*, by Jack Richardson, *The Connection*, by Jack Gelber, *The Brig*, by Kenneth H. Brown, and *The Typist and the Tiger*, by Murray Schisgal, who later moved to Broadway with his play *Luv*. Earlier the public had been conscious of Edward Albee because of his Off-Broadway productions of *The Zoo Story*, *The Death of Bessie Smith*, and *The American Dream*.

Today, Off-Broadway continues to sponsor first productions of experimental drama. *America Hurrah* was first performed by experimental groups and then moved to Off-Broadway. The most successful of the Off-Broadway plays have now been published—and even some which had no success at all.

America Hurrah! *as presented by the Long Wharf Theatre of New Haven used sixty black and white slides which were projected on a screen upstage of the action, providing striking juxtapositions of human action against the photographed projections.* (Photo by Maurice Breslow)

43

Groups operating Off-Broadway employ professional Equity actors, sell tickets, invite criticism from newspapers and magazines, and give regularly scheduled performances in small but licensed theatres. The impetus for the entire movement, you will remember, was to save the costs of producing uptown. In the beginning, this was possible. A new play could be successfully mounted and produced with professionals for under a thousand dollars. But, after the movement became established, rents were raised, the unions were more demanding and ticket prices soared as a result. This created a need for another movement.

Off-Off Broadway

In order to escape higher costs which had now become part of the Off-Broadway professional theatres, those still hoping to experiment with new play forms moved to small hidden cafes and coffee houses. With tongue-in-cheek, a newspaper writer dubbed the movement "off-off Broadway." The title is unfortunate in that it suggests an effort which is two steps below the norm. The truth is that these noncommercial groups are displaying more excitement and fresher theatrical concepts than has been generated on the "Great White Way" in some time. It might very well be the answer to the old question, "Where are the new plays and playwrights coming from?" The playwrights themselves instigated off-off Broadway when they became frustrated at finding no doors open to them. And so they made a place for themselves in little Greenwich Village coffee houses until City officials reminded them that cafes were not licensed to stage plays.

Then, beginning around 1960, most of these groups moved into lofts, churches, or libraries. Indeed critic John Chapman is supposed to have once jumped into a New York cab and said, "Take me to an off-off Broadway theatre" and the cabbie replied, "You're in one." Usually the actors in these groups are either students or novices who have other work to support themselves and their groups, which have no other resources than "club dues," collected from spectators. Audiences consist mainly of Village intellectuals and some "with-its" from uptown. The usual run of these plays is three weekends (nine performances), while a "hit" will play to an estimated 1,500 spectators, turning away an additional 2,000.[11]

It is not surprising that these groups have such small audiences, as most of them use theatre to exploit distinctly specialized interests. Traditionally, thesis or political plays have proven very transitory. Working for love and little else, these groups nevertheless have been able to produce many new plays by novice playwrights—more than ever before in American theatrical history. In its first six years, the La Mama group alone has staged two hundred plays, according to the *New York Times Magazine* of July 9, 1967.

Unfortunately, there has been more quantity than quality. Some of these productions were not even plays, if we regard conventional dramatic struc-

[11]Tom Sankey, Introduction to *The Golden Screw*, in Robert Schroeder, ed., *New Underground Theatre* (New York: Bantam Books, 1968).

ture. It may be that these young writers *choose* to ignore form. Or it may be that quite a few of their efforts began as workshop improvisations and then later were "written for an audience," as admitted to be the case in the Obie prizewinner *Viet Rock.*[12] As a result, their next job may be to train an audience to appreciate their unorthodox methods of playwriting.

Harold Pinter has effectively demonstrated that it is possible to combine fresh techniques with traditional play structure.[13] He has won audiences, simply by being more of an observer than an iconoclast. His plays have unity of character and development, with "a beginning, a middle, and an end." One of his greatest assets is his carefully recorded speech. It is language that is amazingly accurate and yet so arranged that it has a musical quality which fascinates, lifting his dialogue into the realm of art. This is the opposite of the case for most off-off Broadway plays, in which the language lacks arrangement, artistic design, literacy, and selectivity, probably because it stems from improvisations. Language used in improvisations is seldom better than banal street talk. Indeed, that is one of the good points in improvisational training. It brings distinguished literature to a level where most actors can understand.

Earlier we considered the difficulty in separating the work of the author, the actors, and the director. This is especially true in the work of off-off Broadway, where the three elements form an almost symbiotic unity. In his book *The Third Theatre,*[14] Robert Brustein affirms that "Among its strengths are the large number of interesting writers it has produced," then quickly adds, "Although none can yet be called a major talent." Well then, if it is not the playwrights who are responsible for the vision and creativity seen in this new theatre, is it the acting personnel? A majority of the actors have little training or experience, and much of their acting is often irrational and over-indulged. The balance between the contributions of the playwright and the producing unit has changed drastically, as we know. I seem to detect the fine hand of the director igniting the spark, guiding the energy, and molding the materials into an exciting and original production.

There is nothing new about using the theatre as a valid social instrument, even if it does muddle politics with art. However, it is most effective when used as Aristophanes used it—to lampoon the Athenian establishment. Note that the key word here is "lampoon"—not "preach" or "lecture." "The artist is not there to indict, nor to lecture, nor to harangue, and least of all to teach," advises Peter Brook,[15] who does not necessarily follow his own advice.

Kenneth Tynan, English critic of *The Observer*, laments "the prime Orwellian sourness of much left-wing drama." It might be that they are trying to persuade us that every time we enjoy ourselves in the theatre we are

[12]Obie is a prize awarded by the *Village Voice*, a "liberal" New York newspaper.
[13]Harold Pinter is today one of the world's leading playwrights of the absurdist or any other school. author of many successful plays, including *The Homecoming*, 1966–67's Best Play, Tony, and Critic's Award winner. Pinter is also resident contemporary playwright for the Royal Shakespeare Company of England.
[14]Robert Brustein, *The Third Theatre* (New York: Alfred A. Knopf, 1969).
[15]Peter Brook, *The Empty Space* (New York: Atheneum Publishers, 1968), p. 134.

either old-hat or dumb. After ten years of productions, no comedy playwright of major importance has emerged from off-off Broadway, and a director would have little success in finding a new comedy to equal a Tory comedy of manners. This may be one reason for the many revivals of comedies by Kaufman, Hart, Cohan, Hecht, MacArthur, Goerge Kelly, and Coward. It does seem odd that today's new playwrights have not realized that laughter can be a more searing weapon than Napalm. But the British know. At age twenty-four, Christopher Hampton has written *The Philanthropist*, a bitter comedy of Wildean wit produced at the Royal Court Theatre. And another Englishman, Henry Livings, has had his farce, *Eh?*,[16] produced at the Circle-in-the-Square Theatre in New York, and directed by Alan Arkin, and after receiving generally excellent reviews, it ran an entire season.

We can wish that the off-off Broadway groups would improve on some levels, but it will in no way detract from what they have already accomplished. Thanks to them, an aspiring playwright now has some chance of seeing a play he wrote produced upon a stage. Also, these groups have mounted the first full-scale assault upon the fly-speck realism which has been holding back creativity in the theatre for much too long. These fervid professional-amateurs are attempting to say things in a different way, choosing metaphors which are not only authentic to interior and exterior patterns, but which are also theatrically true. These metaphors are left for the audience to identify and translate.

As a result of their fresh viewpoints in directing and the visual images which they create, the kind of theatre produced by these groups is for the most part antirealistic, and this, in the opinion of many, has contributed greatly to making their work highly imaginative, exciting, and wholly fascinating to watch. In many productions, startling theatrical effects have been

"This old-hat direction is killing showbiz!"

[16]Henry Livings, *Eh?* (New York: Hill & Wang, 1966). Other plays by Livings are *Kelly's Eye* (a melodrama), *Honour and Offer* (a farce), *Stop it, Whoever You Are!*, and *Variable Lengths and Longer* (3 sketches).

achieved—cadences of movement, brilliant stage business, synchronization of sounds and music.

Concepts such as these are possible only when a director is allowed great freedom of expression. There is no attempt to represent any outside reality. Actors may speak directly to the audience. Such self-conscious theatricalism is characteristic of the entire modern movement in all of the arts. It presumes that a spectator will use his imagination and contribute—which he is apparently most happy to do.

Now what does all this mean to the director looking for a play he can produce?

We must understand that most of these plays were written because their authors were disenchanted with conventional definitions of commercial success. It was more important for them to have freedom of expression—to say what they wanted to say—than to adapt to the market place. They deliberately turned their backs on any audience but their own parochial "in-group." This may be sincere dedication. It may also be self-indulgence or lack of discipline. But the end result is that many off-off Broadway plays would be considered unacceptable in a majority of communities. Even though not all of these experimental plays deal in anger and aggression against America and its institutions, a director would need to use great selectivity in choosing one to produce in other than a university or a large city.

Some such conclusion has been reached by New York producer Joseph Papp and his New York Shakespeare Festival Public Theatre group. Mr. Papp makes the following confession:

> *Most of our initial 10,000 subscribers committed themselves to our first four plays with expectations that the work would in some way reflect the "high moral tone" and visual splendor of the Bard's plays. There was never a performance during the run of our first three plays at which anywhere from five to fifty people didn't storm out of their seats in protest.*
>
> *Obviously, many members of our audience do not share our opinions; they oppose them, in fact, and for a variety of reasons: anti-American, anti-religious, obscene, not to say dull. However we analyze it, it becomes increasingly clear that the audience is leaving us because we are leaving them. There is a coterie that is interested in the kind of plays we are doing, but it is not large enough to support us or to justify the kind of money we must spend. One thing, however, has become very clear: The plays we have produced do appeal to the young. But the young, unfortunately, are not the theatregoers of our time. With few exceptions the large theatres in New York attract theatregoers who both have money and are settled in their attitudes. These people, after reaching an exalted state, have no desire to spend money to hear their ideals assaulted. They cannot tolerate doubts and if they have any they certainly do not want them exposed. That is not unreasonable. It is perfectly human to cultivate, and cater to, the status quo. It is certainly more reasonable to mount a production for an audience that already exists than to do shows that must find their audience.[17]*

[17]Joseph Papp, *New York* magazine, April 21, 1969. Reprinted by permission of Joseph Papp and *New York* magazine.

Pioneers have a way of moving into new territory to blaze trails and cut the vines; and then, when weary from hunger and exhaustion, they fall, others less dedicated but more practical reap the rewards. The commercial theatre may very likely take up the fresh, marketable ideas from off-off Broadway, discard what is not, and use these ideas in new high-rise theatre productions.

Aesthetics and the Market

This section on the experimental theatre should not be taken to imply that the living theatre must be commercially viable above artistic and idealistic considerations. Directing is not an exact science; tastes differ. One student might set his sights on the professional theatre; another's aim might be more aesthetically oriented. Those who seek both commercial and artistic success may find themselves leaning one way or the other now and then. Broadway, educational, community, and regional professional theatres understandably do not share exact goals or interpretation of success. A student interested in becoming a success must choose his own definition of success. This book cannot make that choice, but it *can* explore various theatre forms for the individual.

Further Reading

PLAYS IN COLLECTIONS (LISTED BY AUTHORS)

Benedikt, Michael, ed. *Theatre Experiment.* Garden City, New York: Doubleday & Co., 1967. Contains *Benito Cereno,* by Robert Lowell, *Gallows Humor,* by Jack Richardson, *Santa Claus,* by E. E. Cummings, *What Happened,* by Gertrude Stein, and others.

Dukore, Bernard F. *Off-Broadway And The New Realism.* DeLand, Florida: Everett-Edwards, 1969.

Gassner, John, ed. *Three Plays From the Yale School of Drama.* New York: E. P. Dutton Co., 1964. Contains *Man Better Man,* by Errol Hill, *Here Comes Santa Claus,* by Joel Oliansky, *Hey You Light Man,* by Oliver Hailey.

Hanley, William. *Whisper In God's Ear.* New York: Dial Press, 1963. Contains also *Mrs. Dally Has a Lover, Slow Dance On The Killing Ground.*

Hoffman, William, ed. *New American Plays.* New York: Hill & Wang, 1969. Contains *Futz, Until The Monkey Comes, A Message from Cougar, French Grey, The Abstract Wife,* and others.

Horovitz, Israel, *First Season.* New York: Random House, 1968. Contains *Line, They Called It Sugar Plum, The Indian Wants The Bronx,* and *Rats,* with introduction by the author.

————. *Morning, Noon, and Night.* New York: Random House, 1969. Three one-acts produced on Broadway by Horovitz, McNally, and Melfi.

van Itallie, Jean-Claude. *The Serpent.* New York: Atheneum Publishers, 1969.

————. *America Hurrah!* New York: Coward-McCann, 1967.

Lewis, Allan, ed. *American Playwrights of the Contemporary Theatre.* New York: Crown Publishers, 1965. Contains essays on "contemporary" playwrights O'Neill, Hellman, Miller, Williams, Behrman, and others. Also such "upstarts" as Chayefsky, Schisgal, Kopit, and Alexrod.

McNally, Terrence. *Sweet Eros, Next, and Other Plays.* New York: Random House, 1969. Contains the following short plays: *Botticelli* (Two American G.I.'s setting an ambush for enemy while playing word game; *Sweet Eros* (Kidnapper having an affair with victim); *Cuba Si* (Cuban woman sets up beachhead in Central Park. Effective but controversial—has four-letter words); *Next* (Over-forty man being examined by woman for draft (Solid farce premise.); *Witness* (Window washer tells what he has seen. Immature little one-act which never reaches its potential.)

Parone, Edward, ed. *New Theatre in America.* New York: Delta Books, 1969. Includes *Mrs. Dally Has A Lover,* by William Hanley, *Upstairs Sleeping,* by Harvey Pere, *In A Cold Hotel,* by Ben Maddow, *Match Play,* by Lee Kalcheim, *The 9:00 Mail,* by Howard Sackler, *The Rook,* by Lawrence Osgood, and others. *Playbook,* An Anthology of Plays. New York: New Directions, 1956. Includes *The Long Night of Medea,* by Corrado Alvaro, *Methusalem,* by Yvan Goff, *The Wax Museum,* by John Hawks, *The Assault Upon Charles Summer,* by Robert Hivnor, *Knackery: For All,* by Boris Viam, and others.

Richards, Stanley. *The Best Short Plays, 1970.* Philadelphia: Chilton Books, 1970. Includes one-acts by Bullins, Horovitz, Rattigan, Orton, and others.

Schroeder, Robert, ed. *New Underground Theatre.* New York: Bantam Books, 1968. Contains *Sand,* by M. Medrick, *Fruit Salad,* by Grant Duay, *The Golden Screw,* by Tom Sankey, *Life of Lady Godiva,* by Ronald Tavel, *Red Cross,* by Sam Shepard, and others.

Shepard, Samuel. *Five Plays.* Indianapolis: Bobbs-Merrill Co., 1966. Contains *Chicago, Icarus's Mother, Fourteen Hundred Thousand,* and *Melodrama Play.*

Smith, Michael, ed. *The Best of Off-Off Broadway.* New York: E. P. Dutton & Co., 1969 (paperback). Contains *Forensic and The Navigators,* by Sam Shepard, *Moon,* by Robert Heidi, *Dr. Kheal,* by Maria Irene Fornes, *The Next Thing,* by Michael Smith, *Charles Dickens' Christmas Carol,* by Soren Agenoux, *Mushrooms,* by Donald Kvares, and *Gorilla Queen,* by Ronald Tavel.

———. *Eight Plays From Off-Off Broadway.* Indianapolis: Bobbs-Merrill Co., 1966. Contains *The General Returns From One Place to Another,* by Frank O'Hara, *The Madness of Lady Bright,* by Lanford Wilson, *Chicago,* by Sam Shepard, *The Great American Desert,* by Joel Oppenheimer, *Balls,* by Paul Foster, *America Hurrah!* by Jean-Claude van Itallie, *The Successful Life of Three,* by Maria Irene Fornes, and *Calm Down Mother,* by Megan Terry.

Terry, Megan. *Viet-Rock.* New York: Simon & Schuster, 1966. Also contains other plays by this author.

Whiting, John, *The Devils.* New York: Hill & Wang, Inc., 1961.

Wilson, Lanford. *Balm in Gilead.* New York: Hill & Wang, 1967. Also contains *Home Free, The Rimers of Eldrich, Ludlow Fair,* and other plays by this author.

ESSAYS AND REVIEWS

Brustein, Robert. *The Third Theatre.* New York: Alfred Knopf, 1969.

Cantor, Arthur, and Little, Stuart W. *The Playmakers.* New York: Norton, 1970.

Goldman, William. *The Season, a Candid Look at Broadway.* New York: Harcourt Brace Jovanovich, 1969.

Jacobsen, Josephine, and Mueller, William R., *Ionesco and Genet.* New York: Hill & Wang, Inc., 1969. Critical essays of two avant garde playwrights.

Kostelanetz, Richard, ed., *The Theatre of Mixed Means.* New York: Dial Press, 1968.   **49**

Essays on staging techniques, "happenings," etc.

Lewis, Emory. *Stages.* Englewood Cliffs, N.J.: Prentice-Hall, 1969. The fifty-year childhood of the American theatre.

Pasolli, Robert. *A Book on Open Theatre.* Indianapolis: Bobbs-Merrill Co., 1970.

Rostagno, Aldo; Beck, Julian; Malina, Judith. *We, The Living Theatre.* New York: Ballantine Books, 1970.

Schechner, Richard. *Public Domain.* Indianapolis: Bobbs-Merrill Co., 1969. Mostly articles reprinted from this author's contributions to TDR.

REGIONAL THEATRES (PROFESSIONAL)

Novic, Julius. *The Quest for Permanent Theatres.* New York: Hill & Wang, 1968. Report on regional theatres.

OLDER PLAYS

We have not the space to list plays written before 1960. For this purpose, refer to the following play indexes.

Fidell, Estelle, ed. *Play Index 1961–1967.* Boston: H. W. Wilson Co., 1968. Lists by author and title, and gives cast analysis.

Ireland, Norma. *Index to Full Length Plays 1944–1965.* Boston: F. W. Faxton, 1965. Selective coverage of plays in English indexed according to subject matter, such as "Politics," "Loneliness," "Freud," "Absurd," "Vacations," etc.

Ottemiller, John H. *Index to Plays in Collections 1900–1962.* New York: Scarecrow Press, 1964.

Stratman, C. J. *Dramatic Play Lists 1591–1963.* New York: New York Public Library, 1964.

———. *Index to Plays in Collections 1900–1942.* New York: Scarecrow Press, 1945.

And of course, there are the catalogs by various play publishers.

If your organization can afford a subscription, I recommend:

The Theatre Critic's Reviews. Plays are reviewed by leading critics as they open. These include newspaper, TV, and other reviews in photostat, covering dramas and musicals. Gives award citations. Write to 150 East 35th St., N.Y., N.Y. 10016, or to Four Park Ave., Suite 21D, N.Y., N.Y. 10014.

Theatre Information Bulletin, by the same publisher. Weekly news of Broadway, Off-Broadway, and off-off Broadway, including news of casting, schedules, and plots of up-coming plays.

Drama Review. Formerly *Tulane Drama Review* or TDR, 32 Washington Place, N.Y., N.Y. 10003.

Stage. The London theatrical newspaper. 19 Tavistock St., London WC-2, England.

GLOSSARY

Granville, Wilfred. *Theatre Dictionary.* New York: Philosophical Library, 1952.

OFF-OFF BROADWAY GROUPS:

Ellen Stewart's La Mama.

Kalfin's Chelsea Theatre Center

Richard Schechner's Performance Group
Stephen Aaron's New Theatre Workshop
Herbert Berghoff's Bank Street Studio
Tony Lo Bianco and Burt Brinkerhoff's New York Theatre Ensemble
Ken Eulo's Courtyard Playhouse, producing in a West 45 Street backyard

Black Theatre

A common error is to associate off-off Broadway with the Black Theatre. The only thing they have in common is protest.

An overwhelming number of off-off Broadway plays are antirealistic and lack any resemblance to traditional play form. Characters, for the most part, are simple, cardboard cut-outs—"types." The "common man" is portrayed as a mindless machine moving about with others in drill formation, speaking clichés. Representatives of "the establishment" usually are obese, cigar-chewing martinets. A few lights on a bare stage encourage the spectator to design his own set in his mind's eye. The most successful of these plays, that is, those gaining the most notice from the press, are free-wheeling and indomitably theatrical.

In contrast, the Black Theatre plays are rooted in realism. These authors have chosen, and rightly so, to use locales such as subways, pool halls, barber shops, bars, toilets, and ghetto pads as backgrounds for their plays. The characters, their speech and habits, are so realistic that one of them would not seem strange walking on any Harlem street. Black authors use living people and ghetto locales, and they follow traditional dramatic form to the letter.

Black Audiences

A knowledgeable director always matches a play with an audience. When a playwright begins to write a play, he must ask himself certain questions. One of the first would be, "What audience do I hope to reach with this play?" A black author needs to answer another question: "*Which* audience am I writing for—white or black?"

Scene from the Minnesota Theatre Company production at the Tyrone Guthrie Theatre of Ceremonies In Dark Old Men, *with Maxwell Glanville as Parker and Ron Glass as Theopolis, his son. (Courtesy of the Tyrone Guthrie Theatre)*

Playwrights Langston Hughes and Lorraine Hansberry chose to appeal to both white and black audiences. Hughes's *Mulatto* played to mixed audiences for over a year on Broadway. Miss Hansberry's success *A Raisin in the Sun* was the Best Play of 1959 and was acted professionally and by amateurs all over the country. It eventually sold to films for $300,000. In his review of the play, the New York Times critic, Brooks Atkinson, wrote, "When the mother buys a house in a white neighborhood, *Raisin in the Sun* touches on the inflammatory topic of race relations. Miss Hansberry faces the issue frankly. But she argues no cause." Harlem's *New York Age* said, "Don't go see this play only because a Negro wrote it, a Negro directed it, it's about Negroes and Negroes act in it. Go see it because it is one of the most moving experiences you'll ever have in a theatre." Black audiences appreciated that both Hughes and Hansberry knew what they were writing about, being Negroes themselves. White audiences were moved because the authors adhered to interests which were *universal*—the hopes, joys, sorrows, life, and death of all human kind, white or black.

In the thirties, we had a period of socially conscious plays: *Waiting For Lefty, They Shall Not Die, Bury The Dead, Processional*, and many others. In the sixties, indictments against social injustices were taken up by the Black Theatre, a part of a larger concept, the "Black Art Revolutionary Movement." It proposes a separate symbolism and mythology and a radical reorder of the white cultural aesthetic in the arts of the Negro. The movement centers upon separatism, the belief that there are two Americas—one black and one white, and that the black artist must direct his work not to the whites "with their decadent set of experiences and mercenary goals," but to a black audience. The primal urge of this movement is to incite black audiences to action in their own interests. Newspapers and magazine writers have been impressed by how this goal has succeeded in the plays of the Black Theatre which they have reviewed. Jack Kroll of *Newsweek* (June 2, 1969), reviewing Lonne Elder's *Ceremonies in Dark Old Men*, reports that "the fresh responsiveness of that audience is almost the most interesting thing in the whole

Ceremonies In Dark Old Men, *prize-winning play by Lonne Elder III, as produced by the Minnesota Theatre Company, Tyrone Guthrie Theatre, with Ron Glass, Maxwell Glanville, and Bette Howard. (Courtesy of the Tyrone Guthrie Theatre)*

Black Theatre movement." Reviewing *A Black Quartet,* produced at the Chelsea Theatre Center, Harold Clurman wrote in *The Nation* (May 12, 1969), "the audience with its deeply felt—though intellectually indiscriminate—cries of sympathy are for me the most memorable aspect of the evening." And then further along in his review, "I pray that these representative writers do not fall into the error that vitiated the work of many left-wing dramatists of the thirties, that of following a path that too narrowly interprets their mission, and thus seeking to move their audiences by slogans of which derision, hate, and self-consuming rebelliousness constitute the main characteristics."[18]

When one remembers that Clurman himself was one of those "left-wingers" of the thirties, his advice gains a respectful authority.

While black audiences are always wildly appreciative of these plays, the truth is that they have little money to spend on theatre. White audiences might pay to see these plays, but these plays have not been written for whites. The searing, anti-white dynamism of these plays is not proper collateral to use in exchange for white dollars—dollars which might pay the author's royalties, the rent, the actors' salaries, and a few dollars in reserve for producing the next play. And this is a pity, because these plays, as *plays,* are very, very good! Not only are the characters displayed in rich, full terms, the writing sincere, honest, and passionate, but the plays are mounted in a solid and traditional dramatic form. The acting, especially by the Negro Ensemble Theatre, is laudable. Unlike the expressionistic *Emperor Jones,* these plays have a dead center realism which gives them a factual immediacy. The bleak and sordid settings of actuality enhance their messages of frustration.

Plays of the Black Theatre might very well be considered as possibilities for productions in larger cities where there is a large Negro population to draw upon, or in some universities. There is no doubt that the Black Theatre has contributed to American theatre, when we consider that the Pulitzer Prize Play for 1970 was awarded to Charles Gordone's *No Place to Be Somebody.* Whether or not such plays are suitable for production in a given community is a decision that each director must make for himself.

Further Reading: Black Theatre

Couch, William T. *New Black Playwrights.* Baton Rouge: Louisiana State University Press, 1969. Contains *Ceremonies in Dark Old Men, Day of Absence,* and other plays by black playwrights.

Cruse, Harold. *The Crisis of the Negro Intellectual.* New York: William Morrow & Co., 1967.

Hughes, Langston, and Meltzer, Milton. *Black Mask, A History of the Negro in American Entertainment.* Englewood Cliffs, N.J.: Prentice-Hall, 1967.

Lewis, Emory. *Stages.* Englewood Cliffs, N.J.: Prentice-Hall, 1969. (See Chapter 10, "Blackface, Whiteface")

Litto, Frederic, ed., *Plays from Black America.* New York: Hill & Wang, 1968.

[18]Reprinted by permission of *The Nation.*

Mitchell, Loften. *Black Drama.* New York: Hawthorn Books, 1967. The story of the American Negro in the theatre, and his opportunities today.

TDR, Black Theatre Issue. Vol. 12, No. 4, Summer 1968. New York: New York University Press, 32 Washington Place, N.Y., N.Y. 10003.

An Addendum to Experimental Plays

It should be stated that there are many who believe that what is being accomplished at the experimental level, not only represents the *zeitgeist* of today, but is also a forecast of what is to come in dramatic shapes and styles in the future. They consider the experimental groups of today as a source for future plays and playwrights. Contemplating a more politically and socially oriented commercial theatre, they offer *Hair, The Boys in the Band*, and *No Place to Be Somebody* as evidence of this. These plays moved up from experimental stages to commercial success.

Still others are of the opinion that protest plays have run their course, that they represent merely a phase similar to the left-wing dramas of the thirties. These people expect a pendulum swing to a more humanistic theatre in the future. In his book, *Revolution as Theatre*, Robert Brustein is dubious about the effectiveness of such activity either as politics or theatre. However, few theatre lovers would deny that experimental plays are having a formidable impact upon our theatre.

Royalties

> *Every financial question in the theatre is an artistic one
> and every artistic question is a financial one.*
> —Roger Stevens
> Chairman, National Endowment for the Arts

No matter which play you decide to produce, it is practical to determine early how much the play is going to cost.

Before final selection of a play, write the publisher or copyright proprietors and ascertain if the play is available to your group and at what royalty fee. These costs vary from five to one hundred dollars per performance, with reductions allowed for subsequent performances. This applies to amateur or stock productions only.

Everyone is aware that there is such a thing as a copyright on a play, but few are acquainted with the exact facts of this law.

Copyright. Examination of a published play will disclose if the play has been properly copyrighted. Notice of copyright must be placed either on the title page or on the page immediately following. Such notice must consist of the word "Copyright" or "Copr." with the name of the proprietor and the date on which it was awarded. An unpublished play existing only in manuscript (or typescript) form may be copyrighted under proper entry being made and notice, as above, placed on the title page or the page following.

Infringements, penalties. Any group performing a copyrighted play without having obtained consent in writing of the copyright proprietor before performance is collectively liable to damages of at least one hundred dollars under whatever conditions the performance is given. If performed willfully and for profit, *members of the group are each individually liable to fine and imprisonment under the criminal provision of the act.*

In a professional production, the author's royalties are determined by a Dramatists League standard contract, which provides for an option fee, a date of production, and a percentage of the weekly gross.

Some Considerations on the Choice of the Play

Determine budget. This item usually means, "How many corners can I cut?" Therefore, consider cost of sets, author royalties, costumes, and advertising, just to mention a few items. If stage hands are not salaried, you have already omitted a big cost.

Once a play has been chosen, the first practical step is to determine what expenditures must be made in order to produce that play. It may be that the play you would like to produce will be too expensive. In that case you must either cut corners or choose another. Usually a total sum is allocated and then a budget must be made listing the detailed expenditures. Proportional costs for items of production will vary. New substitutions for old materials appear regularly, and each production has its own variables. Certain effects are critical enough to a particular production that one must either pay the price regardless of cost, and then hope to compensate by reducing expenses on another item, or else elect not to do that particular play.

I cannot agree with those who feel that the play budget has to be outside the directorial field and therefore should be of no concern to him. Sooner or later, even a divinely inspired director must come face to face with inevitable practicalities.

"With the resources I have, what sort of production may I plan?" Answer this from an artistic, as well as a practical, standpoint.

Director of the Living Stage 70, Robert Alexander. (Courtesy of the Living Stage, a project of the Arena Stage, Washington, D.C.)

Rehearsal time. *"How much time do I have to prepare?"* Professional rehearsal time is usually four weeks (or six, with special permission from Equity).

Most community and educational theatres schedule rehearsals anywhere from four to eight weeks. The necessary factor is that the opening date be settled far in advance and the time carefully organized with a detailed schedule made up far in advance.

Problems in choosing a play. What if a community theatre director is not allowed to choose his play? Even if play selection is the responsibility of a committee, the director's opinion should certainly influence their choice to a great extent. Ideally, before a director accepts an assignment, it is agreed that he is to have the right to refuse any play being considered. But if this has not been agreed, then the director should try gracious and convincing arguments. Should this fail and his wishes are circumvented by the committee, he still has a choice. He can simply refuse to stage a play in which he does not believe. If this means his dismissal, then he is better off not to work under such impossible conditions. Should he be financially unable to have freedom of choice, then he has no alternative but to adjust. Perhaps he can find some element in the committee's play which does interest him. Then, in the future he should try to remedy such an artistically inequitable working arrangement. Time may solve the problem. It might be that the committee's play will fail. If so, when considering the next play, they will certainly be more receptive to the director's opinions.

ANATOMY
OF
THE
STRUCTURED
PLAY 4

Reader Vs. Spectator

To sit alone reading a play is an entirely different experience from sitting in a theatre watching a play *happen*. Some believe it is better to read a play rather than see it performed. Rubbish! Plays are not written to be read, but to be acted. A radical difference exists between the purpose, planning, and writing of a play and that of other forms of literature.

Distinguished novelists such as Henry James and Graham Green found it difficult to shrink themselves into the confines of playwrighting conventions. A storyteller projects events in retrospect. Drama consists of events as they happen. A play needs a visible and audible presentation before an audience. It deals with living action or a series of actions. Narrative and descriptions, as used by the novelist, are denied the playwright. He is bound in time and space. Everything he wishes to convey must be accomplished through dialogue, and he cannot *tell* what a character is thinking, he must *invent action* to reveal it. His story must be clear, strong, and highly concentrated. He cannot indulge himself by wandering into flights of fancy, reminiscences, authorial intrusions, or historical comparisons. He has but one device he can use to tell his story—*live action*.

An interesting illustration of the radical differences between the methods of a novelist and those of a playwright would be evident from first reading Melville's *Moby Dick* and then reading Orson Welles' dramatization of that novel. The novelist communicates directly to the individual reader, but the playwright must reach his audience of many individuals through a director and actors.

It is for that reason some find it difficult to read plays. The plays seem sparse to a reader unfamiliar with the techniques of the theatre unless he is able to approximate what he reads to what he should be seeing and hearing on a stage. A reader may think directly to life, from page to reality, but this is an involved way to appreciate a play, which is, in itself, a re-creation of life.

If the theatre is an art, then the art of it can only be tested at the point when all the parts come into contact with the audience. All the private work of preparation, the technical skills employed by the playwright, craftsmen, and actors come to nothing unless they are fused together by a director and presented to a participating audience.

A director should never read a play as he would read a novel. He must contribute the psychology of a group. He must visualize so clearly that he actually sees the play being performed in his mind's eye. He must also remember that theatre is possible only when the audience is accepted as a motivating part of the performance.

But just what is a play? Is there any definition which might encompass *Oedipus, Lysistrata, Macbeth, Love for Love, Tartuffe, Wozzeck, Phaedra, Uncle Vanya, Fashion, Galileo, The Bald Soprano,* and *Marigolds*? Obviously, any description of a play will need to be generic. Here is John Gassner's definition:

> *A sequence of events in which characters express themselves through what happens to them, what they do or fail to do.*

An old English character I once worked with had another definition:

> *You finds an interesting bloke—Act I; you gets him up a tree, end of Act II; you throw rocks at 'im and then get 'im down—end of Act III.*

Whenever rules have been laid down, for crossing an ocean or writing a play, some maverick is sure to come along, break all those rules, and still produce something outstanding. But not all of us are pioneers or geniuses. Just as a bridge-builder understands what stresses each span will bear, so a director must understand the construction he is using. If not, his entire production might collapse because he has failed to understand the function and limits of each part of his play.

Play Form

Let us now examine the elements of a traditional play. At the risk of boring those who have studied play construction (they can skip this section if they wish), a thorough knowledge of such elements is still a requirement for anyone hoping to direct, for it is on this basic construction he will create a production. It seems only reasonable that any director begin his work by a study of his play's structure, genre, language, and techniques of characterization. In this way he is equipped with attitudinal aspects and serviceable tools for projecting the playwright's intentions to actors and technicians, and through them, to an audience.

It is the fashion today to deny that a play needs any structure whatsoever; but without plot, continuity, dramatic situations, and authentic characters, will a play still remain a play? And so, in order to understand the modern non-structured innovations in playwrighting, a director should know exactly what is meant by a structured play.

When a playwright has his first impetus to write a play, he may be inspired by some incident, an interesting character, a theme, a situation, a point of view, or a conviction. Suppose it was an incident; he will need to invent others, as he has only one link in a chain of events. If he begins with a character, he has saved himself some time. He has the *protagonist*, the "one we care about," and now his task will be to supply other elements. He might proceed by asking himself, "What does this protagonist want or care about?" But, suppose he begins with a conviction? He may have a theme, but it will need to be stated in human terms. Characters will have to be supplied and a story constructed to illustrate those social, ethical, or philosophical convictions.

In each of the above suppositions, we have only one link. Others will be needed if we are to have a proper chain of events.

When taken together, these links are meant to represent a *plot*. A study of characters in a play will lead us to the play itself. Let us test this. What do we want to know? Suppose we ask the old standard question, "What does this play mean?" At this time we have a protagonist. Who is he? What is his drive? What does he want? Why does he need it? Now, if the answers to these questions will be in harmony with audience ethics, we have gained an important point. The audience empathizes with the hero's drive. They have sympathy. *They care.*

Who stands in our hero's way, or what obstacle blocks him from his drive? If our plot has no conflict, it has no drama, and no one will be interested in it because nothing happens. If the audience likes our hero and therefore dislikes the antagonist, they will try to anticipate the story. "Oh, yes, I know what's going to happen." When this occurs we have suspense and participation. After several accumulating situations, we come to the showdown, or *crisis*, when the opposing forces meet. Does the protagonist achieve his goal, or is he defeated? This final action will lead us to the *theme*. The play in its entirety will reveal the character of the protagonist and the special world of the play. The overall progression and tone of the plot will give us an impression of the background, or *atmosphere*, of the play we expect to produce.

The World of the Character

Action is the very heart of drama. All other elements revolve around it, unifying the whole. Some believe that emotion is the nucleus of drama, but that is a tribute to the great dramatists who have so skillfully motivated their characters' emotional drives that these seem to motivate the plot. When this happens, we readily accept that the characters are doing only what is right for them to do. Tell the story of a play and you are telling about the characters in that play. Plot is what is done. Characters are the "whodun-its." It should be obvious that we are dismantling the working parts of a play so that the director may examine each part and understand its function. None of this should concern an audience. Moreover, the mechanics should never appear obvious to them.

Characters Plus Action Equals Plot

There are many ways for an audience to understand character. Richard III boasts of his ambitions and his villainy. He speaks directly to the audience, and that is *narrative*. He then proceeds *to do* everything he has talked about. Lady Anne's attitude toward him shows us that *others* consider him a villain. Later, *by her actions, and although he is physically repulsive to her*, she shows us another side of Richard—his evil, but irresistible, magnetism. Here, then, are a few ways in which the director and the actors might demonstrate character to an audience: by the character's appearance and actions, by what he says, and by what others say about him and his actions.

Whenever we have a scene between two characters, we learn a great deal about each of them. In some plays there is often a contradiction between what the character says and what he does. This adds another dimension; but one of the most important considerations for the director is that he must always relate the characters to the plot. A playwright creates characters to further his plot, or the plot is invented to explore the characters. How they affect each other in this relationship and how the director can benefit the production by this consideration is something only the director can decide.

Playwright's Description of His Characters

In published plays there is usually a page of "Dramatis Personæ." Opposite the name of each character is a brief description of the character. Here are some examples:

Behan's *The Hostage*

> TERESA: *A Country Girl.*

Pinter's *The Caretaker*

> DAVIES: *An Old Man.*

Ionesco's *Amédée*

> AMÉDÉE BUCCINIONI: *Aged Forty-five.*

These may be of some value to a reader, but not to a director or an actor. Also, there is little of value in those descriptions of a character making a first appearance in a play. In his prefaces, George Bernard Shaw wrote voluminously of his characters, and these may be found useful. Shakespeare, however, described his characters through lines in the plays.

As has been already said, a playwright formulates specific characters to communicate the meaning of his play to the audience. This meaning may be some truth about life, nature, or experience. Characters are the agents of his theme and they can only fulfill that destiny *in action*. This furnishes the playwright with conflict—the stuff of drama. His invention of subsequent characters must further explore his theme.

Or perhaps an author will begin with an interesting character and then build theme and plot around him. But characters in any structured play are organically interconnected and intended to lead inexorably to the crisis. The director, and only the director, should decide what the audience's reaction will be to a character, if the meaning of the author's play is not to be distorted. A shift in the director's loyalties from author to actor can only end in disaster. To illustrate, let us suppose that in his interpretative studies of the play, the director becomes convinced that the author's intent was that a certain character appear unsympathetic to the audience. Then in rehearsal, he finds the actor, willfully or accidentally, portraying the character sympathetically. Unless the director corrects the error, the play is sure to suffer.

Plot and Protagonist

Plot

What is plot? The usual answer is: "It's the story." British novelist Edward Morgan Forster had a different answer. "When the King dies," he said, "and then the Queen dies,—that is a story. But when the King dies and the Queen dies of grief,—that is a plot." When a plot is really good, it is invisible and therefore unappreciated. Currently, plot is a dirty word. But we should never forget that theatre is a storytelling art. Shakespeare borrowed stories and then turned these into his own masterful plots. Shaw deprecated plot, then proceeded to create very serviceable ones. Chekhov's approach was tangential to plot, but his plays are structured like battleships.

In studying the plot of a play, the director should concentrate upon the *incidents which actively relate to the main drive of the play*. Subsidiary incidents such as background, moral issues, history, narrative, and theme are contributory and should be subordinated in our consideration at this particular time. Strip the tree of all its branches and leave only the trunk. No definition of plot will apply equally to all plays, but a majority of plots will have a sequential and accumulative organization of actions or situations which provide involvement and conflict in the lives of the characters.

The Protagonist

There can be no plot without characters and situations. Usually the dramatic pressure centers upon a protagonist. He is the one who wants something so badly that he is willing to fight, or even sacrifice his life, for it. The motivating force may be love, power, duty, money, politics, freedom, country, morality, honesty, ethics, revenge, or life itself. Hopefully, the audience will see something in this human which relates to them, and *the particular will become the universal.* If the playwright is skillful, we will sympathize with his desires, his hopes, and his needs. Or in another kind of play, we may understand a protagonist's greed, lust, jealousy, or opportunism. No one is perfect; if the protagonist were, he would not be a leading character on a stage, because he would not be human. And so, we accept the protagonist for what he is: a human being like us, faults and all.

As we watch his struggles against overwhelming odds, we may admire his courage, his strength of will, even if he goes down to defeat, as he does in tragedy. In comedy, we are happy when he achieves his goal. In most plays the protagonist will make his objectives plain to us, and hopefully the playwright will, by his skill, obtain our approval. Later in the play the protagonist will be challenged, and he must then reach a decision. This will reveal to us his inner conflicts and the very fiber of the man. Once he makes his decision, there will be no turning back. In his soul-searching we will recognize the dilemma of all mankind. There are times when each of us must reach moral decisions in a universe not receptive to the will of the individual.

Along with the central character (or activist) there will usually be a secondary character or characters almost as important to the plot as the protagonist. He, she, or they may be allies or antagonists. We would be unable to tell the story of *Romeo and Juliet* without mentioning their parents. Hamlet has the King to oppose, Macbeth has Macduff and Lady Macbeth. The only reason these are secondary characters is that it is not their story.

If we were to consider these same secondary characters from a different angle, they might become leading characters. But the plays as written make these contributing characters part of the protagonist's struggles, either aiding or opposing him.

As a director writes his brief of the plot, he will, of course, be required to mention secondary characters; but the protagonist should always be the subject of a sentence. Instead of writing, "The Queen orders Hamlet to her chamber," he should write, "Hamlet goes to his mother's chamber in answer to her order." In this way he will constantly keep in mind the protagonist as the activist. The character of Horatio in *Hamlet* is revealed to the audience as a warm and devoted friend, but he is not a motivating force in the plot. On the other hand, one cannot write a plot-brief without mentioning Claudius, because he stands between Hamlet and his goal, which is to avenge his father's murder. Horatio is one of the branches of the tree, but Claudius is part of the trunk. When a director sits at his desk studying his play, ideas on staging, characterizations, scenery, or even props may occur to him. Such ideas should be noted down for future reference. These early reactions to the play may not happen again when he is deeply involved in the many details of rehearsals. Notes regarding his emotional reactions are probably the most important of all. In looking over some of my old director's books, I find such notations as "Try for gay mood in this scene"; "She should not appear to recognize him"; "This act needs an eerie mood—use lighting effects, tempo, and breathy speech from actors."

We will be discussing such notes later on, but for now, let us get back to our study of the play.

The Plot Brief

In writing a plot brief, the director might begin his thinking by considering the high point of the play, such as the play scene in *Hamlet*. The high point will deal with the protagonist's point of decision, from which there is no return. You will remember that at the conclusion of the play scene, Hamlet chooses the path he will follow. Convinced now that Claudius is guilty, he decides that he must kill him. By finding the high point of a play, the director might then work back toward the beginning and then to the end. This will assure a progressive build in his direction of the play. He will begin as if it were the top of a triangle, think how the play begins, build to the climax and then to the end. If this method is used, he will be literally completing the Aristotelean cycle of "A beginning, a middle, and an end."

When composing a plot-brief, the following might be useful as a guide. Supply characters' names and give details only as needed to tell the story.

BEGINNING

What has happened in the past to influence the present? Opening: (Use the Who-What-Where formula.) What is the world of the characters? Which character should we care most about? What does he want or need? Do other characters care? Is there resistance to him? Will the audience care? Why?

MIDDLE

What is the protagonist doing to reach his goal? Are there complications? What is the tension here? Has resistance now become active? At what cost to the protagonist? What are the complications leading to a definite confrontation? What is the protagonist's emotional attitude toward the confrontation? What might be the audience's feelings of suspense and tension toward his attitude? What is the moment of decision, the point of no return, in this play?

END

What are the reactions to his decision and action? What further actions are shown because of his decision? Has the theme been stated or indicated thus far? If so, write it in one sentence. What constitutes the final actions? Will the ending secure the empathy of the audience? Does the plot illustrate some universal truth? Describe the line of action.

Remember that your plot-brief not only tells the story of the play, *it describes action*. The story will help you know where you are going, and by describing the action, you will be telling yourself how to get there. In writing this brief, you will be forced to neglect certain characters and scenes. This is unavoidable. You are writing a *brief*. You should concern yourself only with *the main line of action*, the protagonist's struggle to reach his goal. You are describing the trunk of the tree, without branches. As an example, here is a plot-brief on *Hamlet*.

EXAMPLE: PLOT-BRIEF

During a ghostly visitation of his father, Hamlet, Prince of Denmark, becomes suspicious that his uncle, the King, has murdered his father. He becomes absorbed with learning the truth, and when a troupe of strolling players visits him, he decides to test the King's conscience by enacting a play in which a player king is poisoned by his brother, who then marries the Queen. When Hamlet sees the reaction of his uncle to the play, he is convinced that they are caused by his guilty conscience, and decides to avenge his father's death. Hamlet visits his mother in answer to her command, and on his way, sees the King at prayers, is tempted to finish him there but decides to wait a more propitious time. Hamlet is reproached by his mother for his behavior, and he accuses her of complicity in the crime, which she denies. Ever suspicious, Hamlet thinks the King is hiding behind a curtain, but stabs the old family counselor instead. This results in the suicide of the old man's daughter, who is also Hamlet's sweetheart.

Hamlet's presence at court is now a danger, and the King sends him to England but makes plans to have him killed en route. The plan backfires. The potential murderers are murdered.

Hamlet returns to Denmark to complete his task. The King arranges a fencing match between Hamlet and Laertes, the son of the murdered counselor, who has agreed that his foil be tipped with poison, hoping to avenge the deaths of his father and sister. And should this fail, the King has provided a cup of poisoned wine for Hamlet. Instead, the Queen drinks it; Hamlet is scratched with the poisoned foil before Laertes is slain. When the King attempts to escape, Hamlet kills him, but the poison is now in his blood and he dies.

The Objective Approach

Another way to write a plot-brief is simply to describe what happens between the time the play begins and ends by pretending that you are seeing the production from an audience point of view. This objective approach is one the director must take later during final rehearsals.

When working with the actors and technical crew, the director will be subjectively engulfed in the production. Later he will sit in the audience section and attempt to view the work objectively, as if seeing it all for the first time. That is the way the audience will judge the production. They will not be aware of all the problems encountered and all the work put into achieving the production.

Now let us return to our earlier definition of plot as "a sequential and accumulative organization of actions or situations which provide involvement and conflict in the lives of the characters."

Without characters and action there can be no plot.

1. Mrs. B gets up each morning at six-thirty, fixes breakfast, and gets the children off to school.
2. She wakes her husband, feeds him, and helps him get off to work.
3. She bathes, dresses, cleans up the breakfast things, and sits down to coffee.
4. Her neighbor, Mrs. C, drops in and joins her.
5. They decide to go shopping. Mrs. C helps her slick up the house and they leave.
6. After a day of shopping, Mrs. B returns home and starts dinner.
7. The children arrive home from school.
8. One of the children cuts his finger and she treats it.
9. Her husband returns home and the family has dinner.
10. She cleans up the kitchen and puts the children to bed.
11. She joins her husband watching TV.
12. At ten-thirty Mrs. B goes to bed.

This list reproduces the everyday surface of *life*—we have *characters* and there is plenty of *action*. But where is the *drama*? A situation may have movement, action, characters, be "real"—*and yet have no drama!* A dramatic incident is a situation made dramatic. Plot is a playwright's means of organizing incidents into chronological order. It not only describes the action of the characters, but builds these actions into a meaningful overall statement. As drama is an art form, plot serves as a catalyst, forming smaller components into an overall design.

The Dramatic Incident

Our next concern is that smallest unit, the atom of a play, called the *incident*, which together with other incidents make up the plot. An incident involves something happening, either intellectually, physically, or emotionally. The episodes in Mrs. B's day are a fair reproduction of life, but taken together the episodes are dull. No theatregoer will make the effort to get to a theatre and pay to see what he sees at home. What, then, must be done to transform *life* into *drama*? A dramatic incident should include:

An Objective

This should relate to the play's overall objective. Any action in a dramatic incident must be motivated by the characters.

Sequential Development

The action must have consequences. In classic plays, for instance, there

65

are extensions; each sequence is anticipatory. Action grows out of previous scenes and suggests other action to come, causing the audience to speculate. Each incident fits into its proper place which, if removed or replaced, causes the structured plot to disintegrate, as will the characters and theme. (Flashbacks, as in *Death of a Salesman*, are accepted deviations.)

CHARACTER EXPLORATION

Each action taken by a character in an incident tells us something about that character. As Oedipus drives on to find the truth, even though he realizes the truth might ruin him, we become conscious of his great courage, and we admire him.

CONFLICT

It may not be possible to have conflict in every scene, but it is certainly desirable. Even in a scene of pure exposition or narration, it will help if there is some disagreement among the characters. It encourages audience participation when they take sides. Conflict does not necessarily denote a physical encounter, but a clash of wills. Conflict allows a director to use color and contrast in his work in the same way an artist uses them in painting a picture.

SUSPENSE

Material should be presented in such a way that the audience has a desire to know what will happen next. This implies that from the start the audience must be made to care. This is usually provided by some stimuli presented when the protagonist (or others) have made their goals clear.

If a number of the above ingredients are not included in the dramatic incidents, then we have only talk, talk, talk. There must be a focal point which unites all the parts or there will be no motivation for the characters. When a director can define the objectives *in each scene* and is able to utilize this knowledge in his staging, he is in a better position to help actors with their characterizations and to understand the total thrust of the play. I add this just in case you are thinking that we are stepping into the domain of the playwright and that it would be better if we stayed on the director's side of the fence. *Any* knowledge of the play is going to make a better-equipped director. He need not be a playwright, but he must be familiar with the playwright's methods.

In order to decide what is wrong with a scene, you must know what is right. If a scene is "not playing," you can locate the trouble—if you know the way it should be. If a playwright has not provided, let us say, suspense in a scene, there are directing methods to provide it.

The following development of a play is not to be considered as a *sine qua non*. There are plays which have no resolutions, others lacking in "rising action." But upon careful examination, you will find that most fine plays do follow this general outline.

The Substance of Plot

In analyzing a plot, there are several parts which may be identified by a director.

OPENING

Usually narrative. Establishment of atmosphere and characters: where they are, who they are, what they want. Disclosures of past as it will affect the play-present. Ideal opening contains dramatic incident. Example: *Romeo and Juliet.*

COMPLICATION

Usually referred to as the "rising action." Series of events building interest toward major climax. Resistance to protagonist's drive. Opposing forces face each other. Changing fortunes.

CLIMAX

Should be preceded by the crisis or turning point, the time of the protagonist's decision to follow one direction from now on. This is the most intense section of the struggle. It creates a new balance of forces. High point of interest, the turning point from which there is no return. The deed begins to yield answers and the deed is always performed by the protagonist.

RESOLUTION OR DÉNOUEMENT

French for "unraveling." In this section, those conflicts which were intensified earlier are finally resolved. The central action is finalized and all subplots are disposed of.

This list was shown to three capable directors, and then the following questions were put to them: "When directing a play, which of the above sections do you consider most important? To which do you devote most time and attention?" No two directors agreed.

The first director unhesitatingly answered, "*The climax!* If that does not satisfy an audience, they feel cheated." The danger here is that there might be a tendency on the director's part to spend too much rehearsal time on the climax at the expense of the play as a whole.

The second director thought all parts of the play were of equal importance. He did not give extra care or rehearsal time to any particular part.

The third director was convinced that the opening scene of exposition, or the preliminary situation, was by far the most important section of any play in performance, and because it is usually narrative, it was particularly challenging to his resources as a director.

Director number two disagreed, and stated that an audience is especially attentive and receptive during the beginning of a play, and saw the opening as no challenge to him at all. In his opinion, the really critical period was immediately *after* the opening.

Director number three thought that number two had made a point, but he still maintained his original position, because, as he put it, "If you haven't caught their interest in the first ten minutes, you can forget about the rest of the evening."

I merely report these opinions and ask that the reader think about the question, then arrive at his own conclusions.

The Proposition

For some reason, this term is seldom heard in professional theatre, although it is a good one. *A proposition describes the main action of a play, without subsidiary plots.* In this book we have referred to it as the *trunk*. It can usually be stated in one sentence if no mention is made of background or motives.

EXAMPLES

TARTUFFE: *A good man is fooled into believing that a confidence man is a saint, and takes him into his house.*

ROMEO AND JULIET: *A son and a daughter of opposing houses fall in love, but cannot achieve happiness because of old hates.*

OEDIPUS: *In order to save his people, a king appeals to the oracle for answers, and learns more than he cares to hear.*

In stating the *proposition* of your play, limit it to a brief generalization of the trunk. Do not complicate it.

Theme

For the proposition of *Romeo and Juliet* we suggested: "A son and a daughter of opposing houses fall in love, but cannot achieve happiness because of old hates." This statement is so general that other plays might be written using the same proposition.[1] "Opposing houses" could be interpreted as family feuds, and in this case we might have a play about mountain people. The advantage in generalizing in this way is to separate the *basic action* from all other elements. But what happens in a play is not necessarily what the play is about.

Now let us consider another element, *theme*. A theme describes the *meaning* of the play. In the best plays it reveals some universal truth with which all can identify. Action and meaning are both intrinsic components of a play, and yet each has its own special function. *Theme is the idea, the meaning, which has guided the author in creating the conflicts of characters or forces in the play, the moral peg on which the author hangs all other elements.*

A clear statement of this theme may often by found in the dialogue or in a speech spoken by a character; on the other hand, it may be expressed

[1]See Peter Ustinov's *Romanoff and Juliet.*

in the unfolding of the plot. This would mean that it may be suggested in the way the plot is structured or in the action of the characters.

Theme directs the action, but neither one can function separately. Action indicates movement, conflict, gestures, feelings, everything physical or emotional.

Theme is more hidden and demands a more intellectual inquiry. It represents the thought, the idea, the philosophy behind all the action in a play. It may have a moral significance, presenting the audience with an opportunity to judge what is right or what is wrong. Or, the viewpoint may be ethical, dealing with duty to ideals, family, country, or another human.

Usually the theme is revealed in terms of action, particularly during the play's climax. Indeed, the climax is the concrete realization of theme.

Unity of Theme-Action-Climax

An affinity exists between theme, action, and climax, and this may be demonstrated by analyzing these three words, starting from either the right or the left. If we begin with theme, we assume that the author has begun with an idea, some universal truth. But this is abstract, nontheatrical. That idea as theme can only be expressed through live events, or action. The most fundamental action of a play is found in the climax. During this principal conflict there is a change in the balance of forces. The winning force should indicate the theme.

Or, by reversing this procedure and reading from right to left, we will begin with the climax, then study the action leading up to it. We will eventually reach the idea which started it all—the theme.

But what if the playwright begins with only an idea of a character? Or what if he has only a situation in mind? The character will eventually come to represent some aspect of theme, and the situation will become an action. Whichever single component is the impetus for the creation of a play, the other missing elements will eventually need to be added, because drama considers theme-action-climax as a unity. Ibsen's notebooks indicate that his creative method was to begin with a theme, supplying action by bringing every dramatic incident into adjustment with the climactic event. The really great plays all have this unity.

Examples of Stating Theme

The key to stating the theme is brevity. The director should not get confused by verbiage concerning plot, but should stay strictly with the theme. He should be able to state a theme in very few words. No one could state the theme of *Romeo and Juliet* more clearly, concisely, or beautifully than Shakespeare himself. In the final scene, the Prince admonishes Montague and Capulet with the following:

> *See what a scourge is laid upon your hate,*
> *That Heaven finds means to kill your joys with love!*

Even in the beginning of the play, the Prologue speaks the author's meaning:

> *A pair of star-cross'd lovers take their life;*
> *Whose misadventured piteous overthrows*
> *Do, with their death, bury their parents' strife.*

We have in the above lines the universality and the philosophic characteristics of a theme.

The theme of *Death of a Salesman*, according to Elia Kazan, director of the original New York production, is competition and love. Protagonist Willy Loman is pulled to pieces by these opposing forces. He wants love and respect from others, and yet he wants to be better than they are. His tragic suicide concludes his inner struggle. Although the dialogue is realistic, the style of the play is unrealistic. The play unfolds as Willy experiences the events *as seen through his mind*.

Thesis

Early in this century, "message" plays were in vogue. Playwrights Pinero and Galsworthy in England, Ibsen in Norway, Brieux in France, and Clyde Fitch in America used the stage to promote reforms in social, ethical, and moral customs.

Later, in America, the *pièces à thèse* was revived during the 1930's with social-revolutionary plays by Rice, Lawson, Odets, and others. Some of these plays timidly moved away from realism, such as Rice's *The Adding Machine*, Lawson's *Processional*, and Odets' *Waiting for Lefty*.

The thesis play survives today. Playwrights have always written thesis drama, but the really lasting plays have found deeper and more lasting goals.

Non-Sequential Development

Someone once asked French director Jean-Luc Godard if he thought a story should have a beginning, a middle, and an end. He replied, "Yes,—but not necessarily in that order."

There are many fine plays which are structured around image clusters, not primarily arranged in chronological or logical sequence. In such plays, present action may be interrupted at various times to present, retrospectively, vital knowledge, characters, or incidents, in order to fill out essential elements in plot development. Or many questions may be left completely unanswered for the audience. As an example, in Harold Pinter's *Dumbwaiter*, there is a succession of events not following any cause-and-effect sequence, reason, or logic, except for the non-logic of everyday life. But there is an overall design or pattern which forms a certain structure in such a play, and this is the rising accumulation of emotional tension.

Breaking traditional rules of structure is but one of the innovations of today. It appears that there is no longer any need to write plays; they can merely be improvised by actors. However, this does jeopardize the high position of the playwright in the theatrical chain-of-command. Instead of

"Yes, I know you have a new play at the Imperial
Theatre—We saw the first act last night"[3]

being a creator, the playwright is little more than a recording secretary; or, as Joseph Chaikin, founder of Open Theatre, has described the role of playwright: "They suggest forms to us; later these are often written out."[2]

U.C.L.A. *Theatre Arts production of* Lazarus Laughed *by Eugene O'Neill, one of the few productions of this play ever attempted. (Courtesy of Ralph Freud)*

[2]Preface to *Viet Rock and Other Plays* (New York: Simon & Schuster, 1966), p. 9.
[3]From the book *Modern Times* by Charles Preston. Copyright © 1968 by Charles Preston. Published by E. P. Dutton & Co., Inc., and used with their permission. This cartoon originally appeared in *The Wall Street Journal*.

Exercise

Study the play *Becket, or The Honor of God*,[4] by Jean Anouilh, and then test your understanding of play structure by answering the following questions:

1. Who is the protagonist of this play?
2. What force or forces oppose him?
3. What is the goal of the protagonist?
4. What is the goal of the antagonist?
5. State the plot of this play in a few sentences.
6. Describe the principal characters.
7. State Anouilh's theme.
8. Would you classify this as a thesis play?
9. In reading this play, did you "feel" a definite atmosphere? Describe it.
10. State: the challenge; the complication; the crisis; the climax, or the resolution of this play.

Atmosphere

Writers of science fiction seem to have a common method of creating an atmosphere of suspense. In a very commonplace locale, they inject furtive hints that in spite of the apparent normalcy, horrendous shadows lurk, great fearful things too awesome to describe. This ambient and threatening atmosphere we have mentioned before as being charactersitic of Harold Pinter's plays. As an example, in *The Dumbwaiter*, two hardened gunmen have taken over a basement room and seem to be waiting to make a kill. Gradually, Pinter exposes their inner strains and fears, alternating hilarity and terror to create an atmosphere of almost unbearable tension.

Among all the contributions a director can make to a production, creation of an atmosphere can be most easily recognized by the audience as being exclusively the director's. He can make actual what the playwright can only suggest. Words can only go so far. They must be translated into atmosphere by the use of actors and the mechanics of the stage. The director must create a *climate* for the play, and this must be expressed to the audience.

A really skilled playwright will first "feel" a scene, then set down the words which he hopes will convey his feelings to others. But a director works in reverse. He must read the words written by the playwright and try to re-create the playwright's "feeling." He is then able to help the actors enter into the situation physically, mentally, and emotionally. The final goal of all this effort is to transmit emotion to the audience, to cause them to "feel" that original emotional atmosphere created by the playwright. In a very few moments this cyclic transference can set the mood for a scene or for an entire play. It is this atmosphere which will arouse an audience's interest in what is to come.

[4]Jean Anouilh, *Becket, or The Honor of God*, trans. by Lucienne Hill (New York: Coward-McCann,
1960).

Let us imagine that we are sitting in an audience waiting for a performance of *Hamlet* to begin. The house lights dim slowly. There is a distant roll of kettle drums. A glow of light appears on the stage, and we can trace outlines of a lone soldier standing high on the ramparts, his form silhouetted by the soft glow of moonlight. Now the drums are more definite, more portentous, and then they begin to fade away. The soldier's cape moves with the wind, but he is static, frozen with fear and cold. There is a pause of expectancy. Then in the blackness we think we see a movement. The soldier springs to life as he wheels about, threatening the shadows with his halberd. His voice is firm and challenging: "Who's there?" Silence again. Now his voice is bolder: "Nay, answer me." Again there is movement in the shadows: "Stand, and unfold yourself." Suddenly from the blackness a shadowy figure steps forth, and we can barely see that it is another soldier. His arm raises sharply, level with his shoulder in a salute. He shouts in a military manner, "God save the King." And our eyes travel back to the soldier high on the ramparts. He brings down the challenging halberd to his side; his taut body relaxes.

The director has created this atmosphere, using four lines from the playwright, but it promises the audience that in the next two hours they are going to be moved "almost to jelly with the act of fear." After such an opening, we are ready for that most profound and elevating probe into the human condition—Shakespeare's *Hamlet*.

The above description is what the audience will see, hear, and feel. It describes their point of view. Now let us consider the same scene from the director's point of view. When he conceived this effect, the director also had to "feel" the scene. Then he put on another hat and began to work with the many tools and techniques which the stage provides him. He and an electrician had to work out the exact timing he wanted for the house lights to dim, the curtain to be parted noiselessly during a second of blackness. He had to find a recording of kettle drums and make a tape. If he could not find a recording which provided the exact effect, then he had to find actual drums and work with a musician to give him what he wanted. The cape on the lonely guard had to be made of some cloth light enough so that the wind machine would whip it about the soldier's body. He had to arrange lights which when reflected on the "cyc" would simulate a cold moonlight. When he had that set and marked, he had to arrange the dim-up position. Light on the soldier had to be balanced with the darkness of the group in the shadows. He had to work with the actors until they achieved the inner feeling he had when he conceived the effect. I have been talking quite a bit about "feeling," and that is a necessity when creating the idea, but the time comes when the director must accept that this is a *theatrical effect, calculated and wrought*. It is the work of an artificer dealing with many nonverbal, nonemotional tools, to produce emotion in the audience. This is the duality in direction. The director must be able to "feel"—but it will help a great deal if he is also a practical technician.

Any director who can impress his audience by the use of atmosphere, not only during an opening, but all through the play, will find it a distinct advantage and well worth any effort made to achieve it.

Suggestion

In contrast to the somber atmosphere created for *Hamlet*, conceive an opening for one of the Restoration comedies, or for one of Oscar Wilde's plays. Write a page description of the opening. What sort of music will you use? Which colors in the setting and costumes? Furniture? Grouping? Lights? *Describe the scene from the audience's point of view.* Then write another page explaining the mechanics, or the specifications (spec-sheet), indicating just how you hope to accomplish the tone or mood you have described on the first page.

Further Reading

Altenbernd, Lynn, and Lewis, Leslie L. *A Handbook for the Study of Drama.* New York: Macmillan Co., 1966.

Austell, Jan. *What's in a Play.* New York: Harcourt Brace Jovanovich, 1968.

Barry, Jackson G. *Dramatic Structure.* Berkeley: University of California Press, 1970.

Clay, James H., and Krempel, D. *Theatrical Image.* New York: McGraw-Hill, 1967.

Grenbanier, Bernard. *Playwrighting.* New York: Crowell-Collier Publishing Co., 1961.

Rossi, Alfred. *Minneapolis Rehearsals, Tyrone Guthrie Directs Hamlet.* Berkeley: University of California Press, 1970.

Rowe, Kenneth Thorpe. *A Theatre in Your Head: Analyzing the Play and Visualizing Its Production.* New York: Funk & Wagnalls, 1960.

Shank, Theodore. *The Art of Dramatic Art.* Belmont, Calif.: Dickenson Publishing Co., 1969.

Taylor, John Russell. *The Rise and Fall of the Well-Made Play.* New York: Hill & Wang, 1968.

Wager, Walter, ed. *The Playwrights Speak.* New York: Delacorte Press, 1969.

Weales, Gerald. *The Play and Its Parts.* New York: Basic Books, 1964.

Whittle, Stuart, and Cantor, Arthur. *The Playmakers.* New York: W.W. Norton Co., 1970.

PLAY
GENRES
AND
PRODUCTION
STYLES 5

If a director is to fully understand a play in order to stage it, he must first decide upon the meaning the author hoped to transmit to the audience. The meaning of a play is usually found in its interior, what one feels, as well as in its exterior, or what one sees. The interior, or emotional, reaction which is incited by a play determines its type, or genre. A drama which appeals, then brings forth compassion, suggests tragedy; one that makes us laugh at ourselves is comedy; actions which are ridiculous, but could happen, might describe farce; while melodrama excites, thrills, and threatens.

A modern drama might embrace two or more genres. Play types should not be accepted as fixed boundaries, but rather as an aid to the director to inspire him with an idea or an approach to the play he will direct.

Subdivisions might include realistic, nonrealistic, absurd, epic, and expressionistic, and in this book such terms are used to express the exterior, or *styles* of, presentation. In other words, we may have a play which is a realistic tragedy, such as Eugene O'Neill's *Beyond the Horizon*, or a nonrealistic tragedy, as in Arthur Miller's *Death of a Salesman*.

Play Genres

Drama runs a gamut from profound grief to outrageous ribaldry. Labels may be put on plays, but they are not always absolute. Boundary lines between some types of plays are almost indefinable. Playwrights today usually avoid labeling their efforts as "tragedy" or "comedy," fearing that this will leave them vulnerable. As a result, most title pages carry the unpretentious but vague description, "A Play." Of course, such ambiguity is useless to a director trying to get at the heart of its meaning.

Unlike the author, a director cannot hide behind vague labels. He must be prepared to answer all sorts of questions about the play, which will surely be put to him by his staff and the cast.

Style, tempo, and mood depend upon whether the play is a comedy, a farce-comedy, a comedy-mystery, etc. Shakespeare satirized the use of play labels when he had Polonius report to Hamlet that the Players had arrived and that they were "the best actors in the world, either for tragedy, comedy, history, pastoral, pastoral-comical, historical-pastoral, tragic-historical, tragic-comical, historical-pastoral . . ."

It is during his early study of the play that the director should decide upon the genre of his play. This may sound fairly obvious, but we often see a play produced as a comedy when it really is a farce.

In the following sections are listed titles of representative plays for each classification. These are given with a warning that few plays are absolute examples of their genre. In *Three Sisters*, Chekhov thought he had written a comedy. Scholars consider it a tragi-comedy. It is usually produced as a tragedy.

When there is any uncertainty in a director's mind regarding just what form his production will take, there is a rule of thumb he might find of some value: *The way the author treats his characters will have a great deal to do with the play's genre.*

Tragedy

No scholar today can tell us with certainty what a tragedy looked like when first produced in 431 B.C. However, there are many suppositions. I suggest that we might experience some of the look and "feel" of these productions by attending a Catholic High Mass. Both began in religious festivals, both remain solemn rituals encompassing processionals and a chorus, and both deal with symbolic articles and movements. In all there is a basic sense of form, although the mood, tone, atmosphere, and organic life might differ. Neither the Athenian stage nor the Greek dramatists were concerned with realism, but rather with an imitation of life, or *mimesis*. The language was different from everyday speech, and actors spoke it with precise diction.

In Greek and Elizabethan tragedy, we are dealing with poetry, cascading metaphors, images made real. Even in some later tragedies, such as the plays of Maxwell Anderson, there is metre.

An important duty for the director in staging tragedy is to create a mood or atmosphere—even before an actor speaks a line. When the curtain goes up, the lights and setting should convey a mood. Consider the lone sentinel in the beginning of *Hamlet* as he stands his watch on the icy ramparts of Elsinore. He transmits to the audience a state of mind, even the emotion for what follows.

In more modern tragedies the protagonist has not the nobility of the poetic heroes of Sophocles or Shakespeare. He is not in conflict with the gods, the powers of nature, fate, or some tragic flaw of character, but struck like Oswald Alving by syphilis, or a victim of his own faulty goals, as in *Death of a Salesman.*

Whatever the conflict, it arouses in us, the audience, either pity for unmerited misfortune, or sympathy because we recognize in him certain frailties which we too possess. The modern protagonist of tragedy is not so much tragic as he is pathetic. His struggle is more likely to be in trying to retain his individuality in an integrated society. But his physical destruction and the tragic atmosphere of doom can still be associated with the classical tragedies. However, tragedy is not all gloom. Usually there is some hint of better things to come; for without hope, life would be meaningless.

Representative Examples of Tragedy

Antigone	*The Dance of Death*
Agamemnon	*Blood Wedding*
Medea	*House of Bernarda Alba*
Oedipus Rex	*Henry IV* (Pirandello)
Faustus	*Ghosts* (Ibsen)
Macbeth	*Justice*
Richard III	*Beyond the Horizon*
Hamlet	*Mourning Becomes Electra*
Othello	*Long Day's Journey Into Night*
King Lear	*The Last Mile*
Don Carlos	*Winterset*
L'Aiglon	*Man for all Seasons*
The Wild Duck	*Murder in the Cathedral*
John Gabriel Borkman	*Death of a Salesman*
	Hogan's Goat

Further Reading: Tragedy

Aristotle, *Poetics*. Edited by A. Gudeman. Translated by Lane Cooper. Ithaca, N.Y.: Cornell University Press.

Bacon, Helen H. *Barbarians in Greek Tragedy*. New Haven, Conn.: Yale University Press, 1961.

Bates, William N. *Euripides: A Student of Human Nature*. Cranbury, N.J.: A. S. Barnes & Co., 1961.

Bieber, Margarete. *The History of the Greek and Roman Theatre*. Princeton, N.J.: Princeton University Press, 1938.

Bowra, C. M. *Sophoclean Tragedy*. New York: Oxford University Press, 1944.

Butcher, S. H. *Aristotle's Theory of Poetry and Fine Art*, with essay by John Gassner. New York: Dover Publications, 1951.

Fergusson, Francis. *The Idea of Theatre*. Princeton, N.J.: Princeton University Press, 1949.

Flickinger, R. C. *The Greek Theatre and Its Drama*. Chicago: University of Chicago Press, 1936.

———. *The Greek Theatre and Its Drama*. Chicago: University of Chicago Press, 1960. Studies the conventions of Greek drama in terms of culture environment.

Gardner, R.H. *The Splintered Stage*. New York: Macmillan Co., 1965.

Gassner, John. *Masters of the Drama*. New York: Random House, 1940, and Dover Publications, 1945.

Grube, G.M.A. *The Drama of Euripides*. New York: Barnes and Noble, 1961. Discussion of his plays.

Harsh, P. W. *Handbook of Classical Drama*. Stanford, Calif.: Stanford University Press, 1944. (Excellent)

Kitto, H. D. F. *Greek Tragedy: A Literature Study*. Garden City, N.Y.: Doubleday & Co., 1960. The form and language of Greek Tragedy.

Lattimore, Richmond. *The Poetry of Greek Tragedy*. Johns Hopkins Press, 1958. Study of the verse.

Lind, L. R. *Ten Greek Plays in Contemporary Translations*. Boston: Houghton Mifflin Co., 1957.

Mantzius, Karl. *History of Theatrical Art in Ancient and Modern Times*. 6 Vols. London: Duckworth, 1903–1921. (The old standard)

Roodman, R. *Drama on Stage*. New York: Holt, Rinehart & Winston, 1961.

Rys, Ernest, ed. *Poetics of Aristotle on Style*. New York: Everyman's Library, E. P. Dutton & Co., 1947. (Recommended)

Sinclair, F. A. *A History of Classical Literature from Homer to Aristotle*. New York: Macmillan Co., 1935.

Steiner, George. *The Death of Tragedy*. New York: Hill & Wang, 1961.

Comedy

When working with a tragedy, a director knows that the hero's fortunes usually go from good to bad, while in comedy, from bad to good. Events are not so real as they are contrived. Usually a comedy begins with some complications, which increase, not only in number, but also in speed. Although characters are socially recognizable, they do not develop to any great extent as they do in tragedy.

In less complicated times, the ending of a play determined whether it was a comedy or a tragedy. If it ended with the defeat or death of the protagonist, it was a tragedy. When all ended happily, it was comedy. Then it was discovered that plays were written in which serious themes were treated in an amusing manner, and in others, amusing characters were heartbreaking to an audience. *A practical consideration for a director would be to determine if the conglomerate of characters, meaning, and developments in the play is basically tragic or comic.* This standard is especially sound when considering the plays of the last few years. Boundary lines between comedy and tragedy are becoming increasingly blurred. Few unadulterated tragedies are being written today and there is much which is deadly serious in present ironic comedies. The joke is on the human race in such plays as *The Homecoming* and *The Boys in the Band*. Ionesco has said, "Comic and tragic are

Comedy version of the Pygmalion legend with Avery Schreiber as the sculptor and Lesley Warren as his ideal woman, in Paul Sills's The Metamorphoses. (Courtesy of the Center Theatre Group, Mark Taper Forum, Los Angeles, Calif.)

merely two aspects of the same situation, and I have reached the stage when I find it hard to distinguish one from another."

The word *comedy* is a generic term embracing many forms—light comedy, which may be almost drama; comedy of manners, in which the follies and vices of the time are mocked; drawing-room or "cup and saucer" comedy; romantic, satiric, and farcical comedy; and bitter comedy, or as it is called today, black comedy.

Obviously, no technique of directing or playing could possibly serve all these different genres equally well. To add further complications, scenes of comedy are frequently interspersed in serious plays in order to provide interest and variety.

Typical comedies are rooted in their characters. The mixture of comedy and seriousness found in O'Neill's *Ah! Wilderness* is in his handling of his characters. One of Guernsey's *Best Plays of 1967–68* deals with the marriage of an English couple and how this marriage is being destroyed because of their ten-year-old spastic child. The dialogue is not particularly witty, and physical handicaps have long been considered taboo as a comedy premise, and so it is remarkable that with such material the play evolves as a warm and tender comedy. The characters make it so by their revelation of a warm and common humanity. As produced in New York with Albert Finney playing the husband, the audience was never allowed to be too close to the horror of a young couple burdened with a child who is no more than a vegetable. *Joe Egg* is an excellent example of the dark or black comedies of interest today.[1]

[1]Peter Nichols, *A Day in the Death of Joe Egg* (New York: Grove Press, 1968).

Another distinctive comedy genre is found in the relationship between humans and animals. A monkey seems amusing only when related to human-like traits. Disney's animals all have human attributes.

When humans are related to machines or machines to humans, we have another source of comedy. Move three or four people in unison about a stage and an audience will be amused. The characters in the *Motel* scene from *America Hurrah!* are really machines. Harold Pinter uses this device in a one-act skit called *The Applicant*.[2] In it we have a machine-like human placed in conflict with an ordinary human; the juxtaposition produces both laughter and social comment.

Closely related and yet different, satire is mocking irony, a caricature of reality. It is aggressive, fast, exposing stuffed shirts and hypocrisy, for its basis is morality disguised as science.

Slapstick begins with sanity, a credible situation which turns into incredibility and finally into complete insanity. On stage, its movement must be free, the pace increasingly quick. Kant refers to laughter as "sustained expectations being suddenly reduced to nothing," and this might explain the oft quoted farcical example of the pompous man striding along proudly—until he slips on a banana peel.

Many comedies are constructed upon a single comic proposition, such as in Peter Shaffer's *Black Comedy*, in which the fuses have blown out so that the action appears blacked-out to the characters but lighted to the audience. Another, and more accumulative, comic method begins with one lie or mistake being accepted which leads to others, until the complications become hilarious, such as in *She Stoops to Conquer*. In a more contemporary play, *Cactus Flower*, a dentist hoping to avoid matrimony tells his mistress he has a wife and three children. When she attempts suicide, he realizes how much she means to him and proposes marriage. But the mistress insists on meeting the nonexistent wife first, and that done, the dentist must then find a man to pretend to be his wife's lover, and then the children must be produced, etc., ending in a mountain of mistakes and farcical situations.

But what do all these disparate forms of comedy have in common? Incongruity.

An Approach to Comedy

When producing a comedy, the director should instruct his actors in the use of a touch which is light and deft, not heavy-handed as in slapstick farce. Satirical humor is wry. Plots are probable, not outlandish and improbable as in farce. Good comedies often have a literary quality. If the director expects his audience to have a good time, he must convince his actors to have a good time playing the comedy. This spirit of gaiety and enjoyment will then be projected into the audience.

Inexperienced actors usually find that comedy technique is difficult to

---

[2]Harold Pinter, *The Applicant*, in *The Dwarfs and Eight Review Sketches* (Dramatists Play Service, 1965), pp. 39–41.

master. In their desire to seem sophisticated or worldly, they only succeed in seeming bored. The light touch, the glancing verbal blow, and the water-fly darts of satire are attributes of comedy. It should never take on the "sock-it-to-'em" methods of farce.

It has been said that comedy should be played "loud and fast." While there is some truth in this, it is also an oversimplification. Directing and acting comedies by Sheridan and Wilde depend largely upon an intellectual approach, an urbanity, precise articulation, and deft movement. The spirit should be bright and vivacious.

In comedy, the director must rehearse his actors over and over so that their movements and speech are as measured as the timing of a watch. One of the classical comedy methods is repetition, either in word or action. Actors must also speak their lines as if they had just thought of them. During rehearsal, particular facets of a character, those which are most typical of the character, should be selected and enlarged. Good traits should be magnified, bad traits justified, for the actor must be in sympathy with each comedy character he plays. He must believe in his character, be he fop or fool.

Representative Examples of Comedy

The Frogs
The Birds
Lysistrata
Taming of the Shrew
Twelfth Night
Midsummer Night's Dream
Volpone
The Would-Be Gentleman
The Imaginary Invalid
Love for Love
She Stoops to Conquer
The Rivals
The School for Scandal
The Guardsman
The Swan
Candida
Pygmalion
Androcles and the Lion
The Devil's Disciple
The Admirable Crichton
Butterflies Are Free

What Every Woman Knows
Our Betters
Playboy of the Western World
The Far-off Hills
The Show-off
Ah Wilderness!
Beggar on Horseback
Once in a Lifetime
Green Grow the Lilacs
Arsenic and Old Lace
Blythe Spirit
Teahouse of the August Moon
Born Yesterday
Mr. Roberts
Bell, Book and Candle
Barefoot in the Park
Enter Laughing
A Thousand Clowns
Madwoman of Chaillot
Mary, Mary
What the Butler Saw

Further Reading: Comedy

Casson, Lionel, ed. and trans. *Masters of Ancient Comedy*. New York: Macmillan Co., 1960. Contains *The Haunted House* and *The Rope*, by Plautus, *The Brothers* and *Phormio*, by Terence; all in anachronistic, modernized versions.

Chapter 5

Champion, Larry S. *The Evolution of Shakespeare's Comedy.* Cambridge, Mass.: Harvard University Press, 1970.

Freud, Sigmund. *Wit and Its Relation to the Unconscious,* in *Basic Writings of Sigmund Freud.* New York: Modern Library, 1938.

Hogan, Robert Goode. *Drama, The Major Genres.* New York: Dodd, Mead & Co., 1962.

Krutch, Joseph Wood. *Comedy and Conscience after the Renaissance.* New York: Russell & Russell Publishers, 1949.

Lahue, Kalton C. *World of Laughter.* Norman, Okla.: University of Oklahoma Press, 1966.

Meredith, George. "An Essay on Comedy." In *Comedy.* Edited by Wylie Sypher. Garden City, N.Y.: Doubleday & Co., 1956.

Muir, Kenneth. *The Comedy of Manners.* London: Hutchinson University Library, 1970. Lively, fresh discussions of Etherege, Dryden, Wycherley, Congreve, Van Brugh, Farquhar, Sheridan, and Wilde.

Olson, Elder. *The Theory of Comedy.* Bloomington, Ind.: Indiana University Press, 1970.

Seyler, Athene, and Harrard, Stephan. *The Craft of Comedy.* New York: Hill & Wang, 1946.

Shaw, George Bernard. *Shaw on Theatre.* Edited by E.J. West. New York: Theatre Arts Books, 1946. See "Rules for Directors."

Treadmill, William. *Fifty Years of American Comedy.* New York: Exposition Press, 1951.

ARTICLES

Brooks, Albert. "School for Comedians." *Esquire,* February 1971, pp. 89–94. (A rib on comics and their methods.)

Rivers, Joan, and Thompson, Thomas. *What Makes Us Laugh. Life,* January 8, 1971, Vol. 70, No. 1, pp. 69–75.

Farce

This ancient and popular type is the mother of comedy. In its earliest form it consisted of low, risqué humor, exaggerated pantomimes, and absurd situations. The physical aspects of farce should always be remembered. Originally, farce performers were superb athletes, expert at juggling, wire-walking, and tumbling. Perhaps the very essence of farce staging is in timing. At its best it has speed, wit, crackling dialogue, and a brilliant use of mechanics: entrances, exits, surprises, climaxes, denouements.

Farce must be played for an audience and to an audience, and is most effective when played with the assistance of an audience. An expert farceur does not concentrate upon any deep inner meaning of lines or characters but upon the technicalities of communication: his timing, action, and gesture. This requires keeping an eye and ear on the audience and their reactions to what is happening.

Just as in some comedies, farce characters are chiefly types. We have the braggart, the innocent but luscious farm girl, the jealous husband, the scamp, the roué, the pedant, and the charlatan. If the farce you have chosen

Stephen Keep as Commedia dell'Arte Arlecchino in Goldoni's The Venetian Twins, *translated and directed by Robert David Macdonald for the Tyrone Guthrie Theatre. (Courtesy of the Tyrone Guthrie Theatre)*

warrants it, settings, costumes, and makeup may be exaggerated and stylized. Music should be used whenever there is an opportunity.

We need not attempt to have an audience identify with farcical characters, nor would we expect any "message" to be conveyed by them. Emotion or "feeling" is the arch enemy of farce. The aim of farce is simple: to entertain, to create laughter. Comedy is cerebral, while farce is visceral.

An Approach to Farce

Many plays which are technically comedies have certain scenes which are pure farce. This is especially true in plays of the absurd and the new theatre. In fact, it is not unusual to find comedy, farce, and tragedy all in one play.

It has long been considered true that a comic is only as funny as his straight man makes him. Several questions the comedy or farce director must always answer for himself are: Should I tell this actor his line is the biggest laugh in the piece or should I run the risk of having him kill the laugh during performance by stepping on it because he doesn't realize it's there? Will the knowledge cause him to overcompensate and punch the line out of existence?

There are also times when even a director is wrong. Suppose there is no laugh there? This would leave the actors standing open-mouthed, holding for a laugh which is not forthcoming. It is much better if the director instructs his actors to sense if a laugh is coming, to hold for an instant until the laugh crests, but if not, to go on. All audiences differ. On Monday a line might cause an audience to roar and on Tuesday that line might be met with a chilling silence. The ability to use instinct and intellect in feeling out an audience is a gift which turns an actor into an artist.

83

If a comedy or farce is to give an audience more than just laughs, it must begin with *theatrically* true characters in a credible situation. These characters and situations need not be "real," that is, the sort encountered in everyday experience, but both must be plausible. It is also desirable if there is a suggestion of some instability in the situation. This allows the audience the enjoyment of contemplating what is going to happen. If the playwright and director are able to surprise them with a more amusing solution than they have contemplated, that is ideal.

But always the opening situation must alter if the plot is to advance. Such changes usually develop out of transformations in the characters themselves. To illustrate these changes is the responsibility of the director and actors.

The approach to farce must be broader than the approach to comedy. Farce is analogous to caricature and the tall tale. Madness is an integral part of it, and this to some extent depends upon the audience's instant recognition of the disparity between what is happening on stage and what happens in everyday life.

Comedy might use a sensible phrase to express an absurd idea, but farce will express an absurd idea by absurd speech, gestures, and movement. A farcical incident always elaborates the physical, while comedy is more intellectual. Characters which develop during the playing of a comedy must be portrayed as having sufficient resemblance to humanity, without encouraging a comparison with actual people. But in farce the characters are acted as types, with the accent placed more upon their physical actions rather than their psychological reasoning. Farce depends more upon imagination than upon logic. What is farcical about the strutting gentleman slipping upon a banana peel, or, for that matter, the pedantic professor who must scratch himself in the middle of a lecture on the Peloponnesian War? Perhaps we are laughing at our humanity. We all share the same fate, the struggle to be better than our animal inheritance. It is absurd, even farcical, that creatures clever enough to fly to the moon must first solve the problems of eating and eliminating food. But it is both amusing and pathetic that man, who can accomplish such a miracle, is, in the final analysis, tethered to his animal heritage. This may be one reason why farce is considered nearer to tragedy than to comedy.

Although the director may accomplish a certain amount of pre-rehearsal blocking for farce, the most effective comic business will be discovered when working with the actors, either through improvisation or through direct contact with the farcical situations in the play.

Representative Examples of Farce

The Comedy of Errors
The Importance of Being Earnest
The Man Who Married a Dumb Wife
Scapin (Molière)
Keep an Eye on Amelie (Feydeau)

The Proposal
Harvest
The Inspector General
Hotel Paradiso
Room Service

Flea in Her Ear (Feydeau)
Charley's Aunt
The Boor
The Magistrate (Pinero)
Waltz of the Toreadors

The Man Who Came to Dinner
You Can't Take It With You
The House of Blue Leaves (John Guare)

Play Genres and Production Styles

Further Reading: Farce

Bergson, Henri. *Laughter in Comedy*. Garden City, N.Y.: Anchor Books, 1956.

Clinton-Baddeley, V.C. *Burlesque Tradition in the English Theatre*. New York: Benjamin Blom.

Esslin, Martin. *The Theatre of the Absurd*. Garden City, N.Y.: Doubleday & Co., 1961.

Feibleman, James K. *In Praise of Comedy*. New York: Horizon Press, 1970.

Lea, K.M. *Italian Popular Comedy, A Study of the Commedia dell'Arte*. 2 Vols. New York: Russell & Russell Publishers, 1962.

Oreglia, Giacomo. *The Commedia dell'Arte*. London: Methuen & Co., 1968.

Moineaux, G., et al. *Farceurs*. New York: Bond pap.

Nicoll, Allardyce. *The World of the Harlequin*. Boston: Cambridge University Press, 1963.

Welsford, Enid. *The Fool: His Social and Literary History*. Garden City, N.Y.: Doubleday & Co., 1961.

COMMEDIA DELL'ARTE

Ducharte, Pierre Louis. *The Italian Comedy*. New York: Dover Publications, 1965. Scenarios, improvisations of the Commedia.

Gassner, John, and Allen, Ralph G. *Theatre and Drama in the Making*. Boston: Houghton Mifflin Co., 1964. Contains a complete scenario, "The Portrait," pp. 222–230.

Herrich, Marvin T. *Italian Comedy in the Renaissance*. Chicago: University of Illinois Press, 1960.

Lea, Kathleen M. *Italian Popular Comedy*. 2 Vols. New York: Russell & Russell Publishers, 1962.

Newton, Douglas. *Clowns*. New York: Franklin Watts, 1957.

Nicholl, Allardyce. *Masks, Mimes, and Miracles*. New York: Harcourt Brace Jovanovich, 1932.

———. *The World of the Harlequin*. New York: Cambridge University Press, 1963.

Smith, Winifred. *The Commedia dell'Arte*. New York: Benjamin Blom, 1964.

Melodrama

This term is frequently used with some contempt. But melodrama is not only the most theatrical of all play forms, it is also the most popular. Except for farce and Shakespeare, it has monopolized the popular stage for the last two centuries. When done expertly, melodramas such as *A Shot in the Dark*, *Inherit the Wind*, and *Child's Play* still please modern audiences.

Unlike comedy and tragedy, this form is so diffuse that it is difficult to define in a few words. Melodrama encompasses tragedy, comedy, pantomine,

George M. Cohan's The Tavern *was one of the American Conservatory Theatre's most successful productions. Directed by Ellis Rabb, the melodrama featured Miss Michael Leanred. (Photo by Hank Kranzler, courtesy of the American Conservatory Theatre of San Francisco)*

and spectacle. In the 1900's it used more or less stock characters, usually a high-minded hero or heroine, a devoted comical friend, and a formidable opponent, developing in situations and plot with conventionally moral, humanitarian, and sentimental standards. The audience focus was upon events rather than the meaning of those events, which were not necessarily revealing of life. The main accent was upon tension and suspense.

Television would not be such an obsession with viewers were it deprived of its daily "soap-operas," "Westerns" (from "Hopalong Cassidy" to "Bonanza"), and crime-detective series. We may reproach a friend for being "melodramatic," but we still like our melodramas.

Representative Examples of Melodrama

Lady of Lyons	*The Demon Barber of Fleet Street*
Richelieu	*The Bells*
The Silver King	*Angel Street*
After Dark	*Night Must Fall*
Under the Gaslight	*The Desperate Hours*
The Ticket-of-Leave Man	*The Birthday Party*
Black-Eyed Susan	*Child's Play*
London Assurance	*Conduct Unbecoming*
The Colleen Bawn	*The Great White Hope*

NOTE: If you plan to stage an old melodrama, investigate the plays by the most popular playwrights of the 1880's and before, such as Dion Boucicault, Tom Taylor, Augustin Daly, Henry Arthur Jones, Wilkie Collins, Pinero, and Scribe.

Further Reading: Melodrama

Baur-Heinhold, Margarete. *Baroque Theatre.* New York: McGraw-Hill, 1967.

Cartmell, Van H., and Cerf, Bennett, eds. *Thirteen Famous Plays of Crime and Detection.* Philadelphia: Blakistan, 1946.

Clark, Barrett, ed. *America's Lost Plays.* 20 Vols. Princeton, N.J.: Princeton University Press, 1940. Includes *Billy the Kid, The Great Diamond Robbery,* and others.

Cerf, Bennett, and Cartmell, Van, eds. *The Most Successful Plays of the American Stage.* New York: Random House, 1944.

Engle, Johann. *Practical Illustrations of Rhetorical Gesture and Action.* Adapted to English Drama by Henry Siddons, 1912. Reprint. New York: Benjamin Blom, 1968.

Foote, Samuel. *Treatise on the Passions.* 2 Vols., 1747. Reprint. New York: Benjamin Blom, 1969.

Gassner, John, ed. *Best Plays of the Early American Stage.* New York: Crown Publishers, 1967.

Goldberg, Isaac, ed. *Davy Crockett and Other Plays* (1887–1938). New York: Frederick Ungar Publishing, 1956. America's Lost Plays.

Lawrence, W. J. *Old Theatre Days and Ways.* New York: Benjamin Blom, 1935.

Nicholl, Allardyce. *A History of Late Nineteenth Century Drama* (1850–1900). 2 Vols. New York: Cambridge University Press, 1949.

Quinn, Arthur, ed. *A History of American Drama From the Beginning to the Civil War.* 2d ed. New York: Appleton-Century-Crofts, 1943.

———. *Representative American Drama* (1767 to present). New York: Appleton-Century-Crofts, 1943.

Rawill, Frank. *The World of Melodrama.* University Park, Pa.: Pennsylvania State University Press, 1967. Contains ten-page bibliography. Sets down guidelines on subject of play texts, and provides information where rare ones may be found.

Rowell, George. *The Victorian Theatre.* New York: Oxford University Press, 1956.

Styles of Production

From past eras the theatre has inherited many forms or styles of production. In this context, style, or form, refers to the particular spirit of a production. Each style was born of its own time, the mother being invention, the father, necessity. Humanity has always had a need for theatre, and when a new era evolved with its own particular needs, older ways were discarded or altered and a new style of theatre was made popular.

Some texts deal with the technicalities of play direction, but few explain how to visualize a play on a stage. Let us assume that a director has read a play he has chosen to produce and has reached a decision as to its content. He must now visualize that content; how it will look, sound, and feel to an audience. This visualization or concept must be clear, and must come to him *before he begins the machinery of production.* And he must never lose sight of it. He must know what it is he intends to do before he does it. For instance, will his play be more effective if done as a "slice of life"? If so, he would have to make his audience forget they were in a theatre, getting them completely engrossed in the life, the people, and the problems of the play. Or does the essence of the play indicate that the audience would enjoy it most if it were stylized? In this instance the director would be admitting frankly to the audience that they were, in fact, in a theatre.

The manner in which the director envisions the play now will show him the proper road and guide him on the journey ahead. A knowledge of different styles of staging will put the director in a better position to decide how to choose actors, what props and costumes will be most suitable, and what he hopes eventually to offer an audience.

The Nonrealistic Style

As this is the oldest style, we should consider it first. This style makes no pretense that the audience is watching real people, real settings, or real events. Events are not accidental, but selected, refined, with the lines written for and then memorized by the actors. The dying man on stage is an actor and not dying at all. Later, we may see him in the restaurant next door having dinner. But as all these things happen on the stage, they must be accepted as real.

Between the audience and the actors there is a convention, an ancient one, which accepts that there will be a *willing suspension of disbelief* between all parties concerned. There are other conventions, too. A person appears before the play begins and tells the audience what they should know. He is usually called "Prologue." Soliloquies and asides are conventions. An audience accepts that when an actor speaks a soliloquy, they are hearing the character's inner thoughts. They accept that the aside they hear from the stage cannot be heard by other actors on stage. When intermission is over, the audience is called back to their seats by a buzzer, and long ago the convention was simply to pound a hammer on the wooden stage. Masks, symbolic props, costumes, even figures of speech, are all theatrical conventions. We have accepted them for so long that we do not think about them any more than we think about breathing. The director will find audiences willing, even eager, to accept that for the period they sit before a play, they enjoy a game of pretending that the unreal is real—that two or three soldiers carrying banners are really an army of ten thousand.

The nonrealistic style was used by the Greeks and is still being used today in its pure form in Oriental theatre. The prop man is visible on stage. He may place a chair at center for the leading character, but the audience accepts that the prop man is invisible. The hero places a foot upon the chair and speaks of his long tiring journey up this mountain. (Incidentally, who placed the thrones on stage for Shakespeare's kings? It may have been some young apprentice so invisible that no Elizabethan writer remembers seeing him.) When the theatre was young, all plays were produced nonrealistically.

All theatrical styles require that the audience accept some conventions. Often these conventions are used to augment other styles. We may have a realistic scene, as in *The Death of a Salesman*, and into it walks the ghost of Uncle Ben. The author sought to step outside the confinements of reality into the realm of memory and imagination, and the audience followed at once. Although this play is basically realistic, it follows the style of the classical tragedy to that extent.

The Realistic Style

Realism is Exposure, whereas Art is Revelation.

—Gordon Craig

As the twentieth century approached, realism had become firmly entrenched in the theatre. Revolving, sinking, and sliding stages made it possible to change solidly built settings in a fraction of the time needed before. Street scenes could now be reproduced complete with architecturally detailed house fronts, and it was possible to dress an interior setting with involved details, interesting but quite irrelevant to the essence of a play.

Stage art was now able to reproduce reality almost as well as the camera. No longer was it necessary for an audience to use its imagination; "real life" was right there on the stage. Of course, it followed that the actor must also be "real"—to feel real emotion and behave on stage as his counterpart would on the street.

Belasco once tore down an actual room and had it rebuilt on stage. Stanislavski tried using real beggars to play beggars in *The Lower Depths*. The idea was that a play was to be viewed as if through a keyhole, or as if one wall of a room was removed so that the audience could eavesdrop on what was happening in the private moments of the characters. Realism is still called the *keyhole* or *fourth-wall* theatre.

Arch-realism as seen in Stanislavski's production of The Lower Depths. *Moscow Art Theatre, 1902. (Reprinted from Norman Marshall,* The Producer and the Play)

When such experts as Stanislavski, Antoine, or our own David Belasco used it, realism was particularly effective. For the greater part of this century, it has dominated the theatre, and hundreds of plays have been written for that style. Even today, Neil Simon's plays are staged in box settings reproducing actual apartments or hotel rooms. To most people realism *is* theatre.

A realistic setting by David Belasco was typically crowded with accuracy. Note the labeled jars on the shelf, the thermometer, dictionary, and other details of real life in the early 1900's. (From the Katherine Grey Collection)

But all during its reign, realism has had its detractors who have pointed out that a play is not, and never can be, "real." It is an artifact having its own milieu, laws, conventions, and limitations. It must not be considered as the only form of theatre. There were other vital theatres before it which may have more affinity with our times. Director Peter Brook is an outspoken critic: "Naturalistic representations of life no longer seem to Americans adequate to express the forces that drive them."[3] The terms *naturalism* and *realism* have muddled the waters for some time. They sound alike, but are they? John Gassner clarified this matter when he wrote: "Naturalism is merely an extreme form of realism."

Our present revolutionary trend in theatre technique may at last indicate that the saturation point of realism has been reached. Many are convinced that the picture-frame theatre is on its way to the boneyard. This may be only wishful thinking, but it is a fact that the objective in all contemporary art is to remove the picture from the frame.

Each play must be the arbiter of the style the director will use to stage it. Should he concentrate upon the characters and their actions, consider their environment, and find the forces affecting them, he will discover the style most effective for staging his play. Another important consideration will be the audience for which the play was originally written.

Many forms of staging are in evidence on the modern stage. Plays are being produced which are a kind of bouillabaisse of comedy, tragedy, fantasy, and realism. Others are pure in their particular style.

[3]Peter Brook, *The Empty Space* (New York: Atheneum Publishers, 1968), p. 27.

Constructivism

We might consider different staging techniques which have distinctive characteristics and are sometimes useful in staging special types of drama. One of these is *constructivism*, the "new thing" of the thirties in New York. It was abandoned until recently and is now once again being used modestly.

Constructivism used an architectural or skeletal background made of lumber or pipe. Its effect is similar to modern sculpture in that open space is employed as part of the design. Usually permanent, various locales can be suggested by the addition of set pieces. Its great advantage is in providing great movement, speed, and action on a variety of acting levels including ramps, ladders, and steps. While constructivism is not much help to dramas in which language is of primary importance, it does enhance plays of the expressionistic or avant-garde schools.

One of the first constructivist settings used in the Meierhold Theatre in Moscow. (Courtesy of the Library and Museum of the Performing Arts, New York Public Library)

A disadvantage is that the set must be constructed and used for all rehearsals so that actors might become accustomed to it. This is a problem if the stage is used for other purposes.

A director should be positive that this form will add to his production. Recently there was a production of *Tartuffe* using a constructivistic setting. The play was "adapted" to an early Monterey period, but neither the setting nor the period change contributed to Molière's satire on hypocrisy. Extra added scenes and the running, shouting, and galumphing smothered poor Monsieur Molière.

Expressionism

One of the earliest attempts at *expressionism* is an old silent film, *The Cabinet of Dr. Caligari*. Even in black and white, the backgrounds were startling in their distortions and dream-like quality. Costumes were "futuristic" and makeup sought to depersonalize the actors. Along with these elements and the story itself, an extraordinary mood of hallucination was achieved. The style was perfectly suited to the story, which centered around the imaginings of a madman. The mask-like faces of the actors, their catatonic

The Cabinet of Dr. Caligari (*1919*).
(*Courtesy of the Museum of Modern Art Stills Archive*)

movements, and the opportunity to use machine-like distortions in the settings makes this style suitable to such plays as *Man and the Masses, The Dance of Death, The Trial,* and *The Adding Machine.*

The Epic Style

The word *epic* recalls to mind those long narrative poems, *The Iliad* and *The Odyssey,* which recount the deeds of legendary or historical heroes. Bertolt Brecht used the term to describe his plays, although in a strict sense his heroes were anti-heroes. But his plays did resemble the epic style in that they were lyrical, vast in scope and range. Brecht remains difficult to stage expertly. When his plays are done well and follow his directing style, they can be exciting, but they have had a monotonous record of failure in New York. When they are done poorly and without proper facilities, they seem crude and didactic. The one exception was his *Threepenny Opera* produced inexpensively in the Village.

The epic style has always been a commodity in the film industry. In fact, the great classical motion pictures, *Birth of a Nation, Ben-Hur, Gone with the Wind, Quo Vadis,* and *Intolerance,* are excellent illustrations of the type.

But no typical example of the true epic stageplay has been evident in years until the Arena Stage in Washington, D.C., produced a new play by Howard Sackler called *The Great White Hope.* Its protagonist, a Negro heavyweight champion, transcends both history and myth. The story is told with the sweep and scope of a novel, using a cast of over thirty, but the author has not forgotten that he is writing for the theatre. As subsequently staged in New York, the play had speed and excitement, and was awarded "The Best Play" of the season. Nothing had been seen in that city to equal its theatricalism since Reinhardt's *Miracle.* The nineteen scenes included two championship fights, a raid, a funeral, and a July Fourth celebration. And so, at last we have a typical epic play winning the Pulitzer, Drama Critics, and Tony awards.

Alienation Theory

Alienation theory is a phrase used by Brecht to describe a technique to be used by actors in his plays. Perhaps the essence of alienation is to make the audience think—not feel. Brecht always thought of his plays as "learning plays." Actors were not to identify with characters. They were "demonstrators," and characters were to be studied in a critical way, not sympathetically. He cautioned actors not to be motivated by any inner-emotion or "hypnotic tension." Brecht often contrasted a scene of lyric beauty with scenes of the grotesque. In his direction he used visible spotlights, placards, film, music, masks, and in fact any device that was theatrical.

The Style of the Absurd

The term *avant-garde*, as used in the modern theatre, is generally applied to almost any play that makes a decided break with realism. *Absurd*, on the other hand, means "out of harmony," or, as Ionesco has expressed it, ". . . cut off from his religious, metaphysical, and transcendental roots, man is lost; all his actions become senseless, absurd. . . ." Plays of the Absurd

Gower Champion directed this Feydeau farce, A Flea in Her Ear, *for the American Conservatory Theatre, featuring Michael O'Sullivan (left) and Herman Poppe. (Photo by Hank Kranzler, courtesy of the American Conservatory Theatre of San Francisco)*

parallel similar trends found in the writing of Joyce and Kafka, in the so-called Cubism and Abstract styles of painting, and in the outlook of the Dadaists of the 1920's.

If there is any directing style already noted which would be suitable to the plays of the Absurd, it is expressionism—but with quite a dash of farce. Absurd plays are certainly not of the "slice-of-life" category, and yet there are realistic scenes in many of them. In fact, an Absurd style would be a conglomerate of expressionism, comedy, tragedy, melodrama—and especially farce. Shock value as displayed in farce is one of the Absurd's chief characteristics. We may have two men seated at a table drinking wine and behaving in a very natural way when suddenly one turns into a rhinoceros. Or, in a farcical situation, the mood could suddenly plunge into tragedy, as in *The Chairs*. Tenderness might be juxtaposed with cruelty or horror, and then burst into a farcical ending. Any combination is possible in plays of the avant-garde. One of the aims of Absurd theatre is to mock our everyday speech—to demonstrate our use of clichés and repetitions, our hypocrisy in saying one thing and thinking another. These plays dissect our ethos as a biology student dissects a frog. In writing of the avant-garde, Robert Corrigan maintains that:

> None of the theatre's revolutionaries . . . have ever resolved so systematically to undermine and destroy not only the superstructure of naturalism, the elaborate setting, the contrived plot, the socially recognizable characters with

Comic absurdity as shown by Robin Gammel (left) and Rene Auberjonois in The American Conservatory Theatre's production of Endgame *by Samuel Beckett. (Photo by Hank Kranzler, courtesy of the American Conservatory Theatre of San Francisco)*

*their all-too-familiar problems but the very foundations of the naturalistic
vision; the laws of logic.*[4]

Summary

The style of a production will depend upon the play and its characters.
All artists avail themselves of styles. A painter may use bright, gay colors
and hard lines when painting clowns; intricate lines and meticulous detail
when painting domestic scenes. The artists of the Renaissance used soft muted
tones when painting religious subjects.

When you have reached a definite decision regarding the style in which
you visualize your production, this will guide you in choosing the type of
background you should use in the settings, costumes, acting method, and
the overall climate of the production. If you remember to relate your play
to its predominate theatrical style, you should have no difficulty deciding
the most effective way to produce the play. If it is a conglomerate of several
styles, as in the absurd, each style will be found useful.

Labels, Labels

This century has been afflicted with the disease of jargonism, especially
in the arts, where a hip vocabulary is bantered about by those who consider
themselves to be "in-the-know"; but few really understand.

The young director should be wary of the plethora of labels used in shobiz.
Some of these are attempts to suggest gradations in staging between the
two basic forms—realism and nonrealism. Others are the inventions of highly
imaginative authors. Let us have a look at some of these.

REALISM

Audience pretends they are watching
real life. Actors pretend that the
audience is not there.
Example: *Lower Depths*

NATURALISM

Extreme realism.
Example: *Dead End*

SELECTIVE REALISM

Only selected realistic pieces used,
such as set pieces, props, etc.
Example: *Mother Courage* as
produced by Brecht.

SUGGESTED REALISM

Indications only. An arch for a
cathedral.
Example: *The Lark*

SYMBOLISM

Use of symbols in scenery, lights, etc.
Example: *He Who Gets Slapped*

NEO-ROMANTICISM

Return to the poetic form.
Example: *Cyrano*

[4]Robert W. Corrigan, *The Theatre in the Twentieth Century* (New York: Grove Press, 1963),
p. 12.

EXPRESSIONISM

Distortion of proportions to express play or moods.
Example: *The Adding Machine*

CONSTRUCTIVISM

Skeletal construction of settings.
Example: *Processional*

SURREALISM OR SUBJECTIVE REALISM

Dream symbols. Free association of ideas.
Example: *Death of a Salesman*

STYLIZATION

"The manner" in acting and production.
Example: National Theatre Company of Great Britain's production of *The Beaux' Stratagem*

THEATRICALISM

Frankly theatre.
Example: *Our Town*

FORMALISM

Classic, permanent set or background.
Example: Greek Tragedy

ENVIRONMENTAL OR PERFORMANCE THEATRE

Communal creation performance by totalitarian togetherness of actors and audience.

EPIC THEATRE

Heroic deeds set within mythical or historical backgrounds of great scope.
Examples: *Abe Lincoln In Illinois*, *The Great White Hope*, and with some variations, the works of Brecht

BLACK COMEDY

Tragedy so contrived and pretentious that it is comic. Also "camp."
Example: Peter Shaffer's *Black Comedy*

ABSURDISM

Sense hidden by nonsense.
Example: *Bald Soprano*

AGIT-PROP

Agitation-propaganda.
Example: *Waiting for Lefty*

THEATRE-OF-FACT

Journalistic drama.
Example: *The Living Newspaper*

THEATRE-OF-CRUELTY

Artaud inspired.
Example: Peter Brooks' *US*

TOTAL THEATRE

Among the first to use the term was Laszlo Moholy-Nagy, who in 1925 drew plans for an actorless theatre based on light, motion, and sound effects alone.

THEATRE-OF-CHANCE

Dialogue spoken is subject to actor's whim.
Example: Judith Malina's *Living Theatre*

THEATRE-OF-THE-RIDICULOUS

Ronald Tavel's definition: "We have passed beyond the absurd; our position is absolutely Ridiculous."

LIQUID THEATRE

Improvisational "events."
Example: Steven Kent's *Company Theatre*, Beverly Hills Productions. "James Joyce Memorial."

NOTE: I believe the above labels are mostly ego-fulfilling on the part of their originators. But students often ask, "Just what is theatre-of-chance, agit-prop, absurd theatre," etc. Even if I think such labels are confining, some people do take them seriously, and that is why I include them here.

Language

Just as no two thumb prints are identical, so each play creates its own identity by means of its own special grammar and syntax. This language helps us understand the play's milieu, characters, and what the playwright had in mind when he wrote the play. Language will also indicate or suggest a form which the play will take in a production.

A playwright's ideas are expressed in words but are communicated to an audience by means of speech. This may vary from the exalted poetic similes of Shakespeare to the gutter talk of LeRoi Jones. In each play, whether the language be colloquial, profane, or scholarly, the author's ideas and feelings will need to be expressed in a special language that is terse, individual, and dramatic. Of necessity, a playwright must speak through his characters. However, this must never become obvious to an audience.

Language also contributes much to the actor's work on characterization, for it is the most effective means of expressing the character's beliefs, background, emotions, and present condition.

This special language which is in a play is always selected and condensed. It differs from other writing in that it is *written to be spoken, not read*. Little relationship exists between everyday speech and the dialogue found in plays. Ordinary conversation abounds in repetitions, hesitancies, and clichés. If such speech were used by a playwright, his audience would soon be fast asleep. The director will find that the language of a play functions to reveal character, further plot, and stimulate the audience either through thought, imagination, or emotion. This should certainly be explained to the cast. There are certain speeches in every play which are most important to the audience's understanding of the play. These may be only a few lines in a scene or a speech, but they become vital when we consider that they are plot lines, that is, they carry information needed by the audience in order to follow the play's progression.

But I want to get back to that point regarding the vast difference between everyday speech and the language of a play. A great many people, and especially actors, have a mistaken idea that the highest ideal of acting is "just being natural." However, it should only *appear* natural. The actor's skill is in making language which is written, contrived, and designed for a purpose sound as if it were extemporaneous. But in so doing, the actor should not be allowed to substitute his own for the author's words. "Oh's," "Ah's," "I mean's" and all other everyday speech habits should be discouraged, and discouraged before they become a stage habit. A playwright may work hours selecting and refining a phrase so that it says precisely what he wants it to say in the fewest possible words.

Another difference between ordinary speech and dialogue is that the language of a play is active. It is not just idle conversation; *it leads somewhere.* **97**

Movement by characters on a stage is often thought to be action. But dialogue can also be active, expressing the theme and characterizations by expressions of vivid and colorful words. In Shaw's *Don Juan in Hell* interlude, language embodies the action almost exclusively. Another example of action in language is found in *The Time of Your Life*, when Kit Carson describes how he drove a swarm of bees across a desert. Even such phrases as "It comes with the territory" in *Death of a Salesman* are not only pungent revelations of character, but they also further the action of the play.

In order to help actors reach their greatest potential, a director should be knowledgeable of the various forms of language used in plays. Such information will also help the actor to reach a sympathetic understanding of his character. Granted that an actor must always possess a flexible body and face to express a wide range of ideas and emotions, he must also understand the importance of language, because in drama, thought and emotions are communicated largely by the human voice. We are going to consider four types of language at this time, although there are others. Each form has its own technique of expression.

Realistic Language

The term *realistic language* comes from an attempt to echo the cadences and rhythms of the current vernacular. It is favored by contemporary playwrights more than any other form. But speaking it on the stage presents some difficulties for the actor and director. A common fault is in neglecting stress or emphasis. Not all words in a sentence are of equal importance. We give emphasis to selected key words even in everyday speech, but often when we read realistic lines on stage they sound either monotonous, slovenly, or drawled. This results in a failure to communicate proper meaning to the audience.

Should this fault become obvious in any of your productions, you should work with the actor by first clarifying the moment; if this fails, then ask him to stress certain words which will carry the meaning. He should then be instructed to speak only those selected words until he becomes convinced that they alone can carry the author's thought. Stress may also be used to project an emotional content in a speech.

An outstanding use of realistic language may be found in the works of English playwright Harold Pinter, author of *The Birthday Party, The Dumbwaiter, The Caretaker*, and *The Homecoming*. Not only does Mr. Pinter have an uncanny ear for common speech, but he adds his own comment to it by making it sound absurd. There is also something sardonic about it, as if the air were filled with some vague lurking menace.

Another English playwright, Arnold Wesker (*Chips With Everything*), perhaps comes closest to accurately reproducing realistic language, but some critics believe he negates his plays by a reforming zeal.

Among current successful Broadway playwrights using realistic language are Neil Simon, Rene Taylor, and Woody Allen, who add the ethnic strains of New York-Jewish cadence and quaint sentence constructions to some characters, somewhat like the language once used by Odets and Arthur Miller. But most other American playwrights are content to write the speech of a less colorful citizenry.

Poetic or Romantic Language

This language can be identified by its use of a kind of lyrical quality. Usually spoken with more speed than everyday speech, it must roll along, articulating over the tongue and lips, stimulating emotional sympathy and excitement. Its greatest individualism might be found in its appeal to the senses rather than the intellect. A sustained tone should be used throughout romantic passages, as in verse plays. This is the language form of Shakespeare. Romantic language is so clearly identified with earlier dramatists that it seems somewhat surprising when a modern playwright uses the form. T. S. Eliot superimposes poetic language upon common idiom in his *Murder in the Cathedral*. Christopher Fry makes no such compromises in *The Lady's Not for Burning* and in his *Venus Observed*; neither did Peter Shaffer in *The Royal Hunt of the Sun*. Another English Playwright, John Arden (*Sergeant Musgrove's Dance*), states that he is "—more concerned with the 'poetic' than with the 'journalistic.'" No American dramatist since the late Maxwell Anderson seems willing to accept the disciplines of this form, although devotees of Tennessee Williams feel that his language frequently rises to the heights of dramatic poetry.

In summary, we may accept that the two language forms discussed so far, the realistic and the poetic, are frequently combined, but for the director and actor they are individual enough to note differences. There are other language styles, perhaps less popular than the two we have discussed, which should be noted at this time.

Symbolic Language

Tennessee Williams once said, "I can't deny that I use a lot of those things called symbols—symbols are the natural speech of drama." Other playwrights such as Andreyev and Maeterlinck are best known for their use of symbolism to suggest an atmosphere engulfing their characters; but Andreyev, Maeterlinck, Pinter, and Williams, all have different methods of achieving their purpose. Maeterlinck may turn a character into a symbol, but Pinter's symbolism is more in the language, in the attitude of his characters toward something outside themselves. In Pinter's *A Slight Ache*, the Matchseller is both a character and a symbol, and as a result the lines he speaks may be more than they seem. While Maeterlinck uses no comedy, Pinter achieves it through irony. Maeterlinck is stylized, lyrical in his language, his people floating upon a blue light; but Pinter's people are very much alive, concerning themselves with acquiring food, money, and love.

There was a Broadway success of some years ago, *On Borrowed Time*, in which one of its leading characters, Mr. Brink, was a symbol of Death. In another play, *Death Takes a Holiday*, Death was an Italian Count who took respite from his grim occupation until a young girl agreed to join him. The symbols used by John Whiting in his *Penny for a Song* and *Saint's Day* puzzled audiences although the plays were otherwise admired.

Rhetorical Language

As we know, *Look Back in Anger* was written in a realistic style. And yet, some of Jimmy Porter's crusading tirades match any by a nineteenth-century melodrama hero denouncing the dastardly deeds of the villain. Dramatists adapt language to suit different characters, but each playwright also has an individual style which can be identified. Read aloud a few speeches from Shakespeare and you know they were not written by Jonson, Congreve, Shaw, or Pinter.

THE
DIRECTOR'S
VISION 6

*Man's desires are limited by his perceptions: none can
desire what he has not perceived.*

—William Blake

Experiencing the Play

One of the most important duties of the director is to form a communicating
bridge between what he reads on a printed page and the actions, characters,
and emotions which are to be felt by the audience. All the play's sights,
sounds, tastes, and feelings have been condensed by the author into those
small lines of print we read upon a page. The director must unscramble
these sensory elements and cause them to live again.

To do this, he will need a period of withdrawal and self-containment in
order to achieve a form or vision of his production. Some may not admit
it, but most successful directors do begin their work with a period of gestation
in which they saturate themselves in all aspects of the play they intend
to produce. All artists need time for contemplation. Creativity happens when
the spirit is ready, usually in solitude, free from distractions. This absorption
is both intellectual and emotional. It is not any logical attitude the director
seeks, but a coherent emotional summary of all the play represents to him.
Drama is narration, but it is also visual and spatial. We understand more
readily what we see than what we hear. Therefore, the director is not so
concerned with surface considerations or intellectual questions as he is with
the moods and atmosphere of the play. After much research into all material
relating to the play, and many, many private readings of it, the director
should gradually develop an image, or vision, of the play as it will look
when performed upon a stage. No two directors will come out of this study
with the same concept of an identical play. Lines should be read for the
action and emotional drives they represent. Try to picture a stage alive with
sights, sounds, color, and movement which your play suggests.

In order to better realize the full spirit and excitement of the play, it

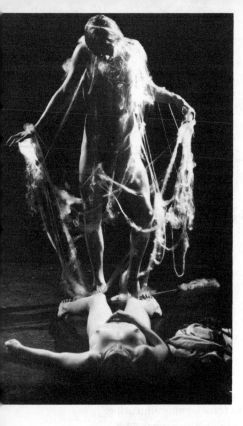

Interesting concept of Satan as presented in this scene from The Emergence *by Ama Giesta Fleming, part of the repertory of the Los Angeles based Company Theatre. (Courtesy of Company Theatre)*

is often helpful to stand, read aloud, and move with the action of the play. This is especially recommended when studying Shakespeare. Hearing the lines spoken often reveals meanings which might otherwise be hidden in the Elizabethan language form.

Moving and speaking seems to turn a printed play into a living experience. Strive to feel the play's inner significance, the thought behind it all, and then the emotional reaction to that thought. When this is achieved, it will be subjective, the result of some personal feeling.

The lighting, scenery, costumes, space, sound, and color, as well as all sensory preferences, to be used will depend upon your concept of the production. And that experience you have had is the same one you will use to transmit your concept to the audience.

Of course, not any of this is going to happen if a director does not study, but merely reads the play casually at odd moments during an ordinary work day. The play must be allowed to grow from the inner convictions of the director. This will give him a clearer understanding of the style and meaning of the play, and more study and readings will deepen his concept. But his very early readings will be the only time when he will be permitted to "feel" the impact of the play as a whole. Only at this time will he be allowed the excitement of a new, fresh experience in which there will be the proper mixture of emotion, imagination, and discovery.

Later, certain obscure impressions will begin to take more concrete forms. A feeling for the mood and style of the play will evoke impressions. These may be gentle, reminiscent of personal experiences, past moods, and actions only half remembered and brought back to reality by the play. These are the visual, aural, and emotional impressions which must be revived, recorded, and used later to create atmosphere, movement, and dramatic impact. At this time, facts, reason, and logic will only block the intuitive grasp.

Intuition and the Director

There is an ever present danger of directing by the head and not the heart. The more experience, background, and imagination a director can bring to his study, the richer will be his contribution to his production. All of the work to follow—the casting, blocking, creation of characters, the tempo and rhythm of the production—will depend upon this first study of the play as noted in his director's book. But he may follow his own blueprint meticulously and yet end with a cold, uninspired production which fails to move an audience *unless he uses his intuition during rehearsals*. Creativity, in our context, is simply a fresh way of organizing. An original musical score is really a rearrangement of traditional notes. A best-selling novel is a reorganization of tried and true dramatic incidents. The ability to benefit from past experience is not only possible in all living creatures, but by being alive we are indeed *forced* to create. As an example of the benefits which might come from a director's intuition, Peter Brook tells of an incident which occurred during a rehearsal of *Measure for Measure*. Just before Isabella was about to kneel and plead for Angelo's life, Brook asked the actress to pause "until she felt the audience could stand it no longer." The silence, in which the invisible elements of the play crystallized a moment of mercy, came out of a purely intuitive inspiration during the rehearsal.

Once satisfied that his concept of the play has been fairly recorded in his director's book, the director next approaches the problem of making a carefully planned rehearsal schedule. Later, as the work matures in rehearsal, he will once again return to a more intuitive approach. After the actors learn the lines and the movement has become more or less automatic, the play will begin to take shape and actually come to life. It is then that the director will begin to feel the dramatic impact of a scene—or the lack of it.

The Director's Point of View

What we see when we look at an object depends upon our point of view. The enjoyment we derive from looking at Cezanne's "Cherries and Peaches" is not from the fruit but from the way Cezanne painted the fruit—his viewpoint. The moment we pick up a play and start reading, interpretation begins, evolving in a point of view. The names of the characters soon become more than names. Printed words become something said by particular persons. A director needs a point of view. You cannot decide upon the height of a platform, the position of a light, or the force of an emotion until you have decided upon the essence and function of your play.

"Your" play, because once you have chosen a play to produce, you break the author's seal. From that time on, it is not Shaw's *Caesar and Cleopatra*, it is yours. However, this proprietary interest carries with it a respect for the author's text. Directing is a process of making value judgments, discovering the angle from which the actions and characters will appear most plausible and most effective to an audience. This concept or point of view (P.O.V.) is exactly what the director hopes to achieve by studying the play. He reads slowly, absorbing everything the play offers.

Reading the playwright's description of the setting, the director tries to visualize the opening, seeing the lights, feeling the atmosphere. Then as various characters enter, his imagination may create a sense of tempo for a speech. Then there is a moment of action, and in his mind's eye he sees the movement of the people on stage. Next, he feels those seconds of hesitancy—the silence of a pause. He may ask, "What is the essence of this scene?" and "What is the relationship of this scene to the play as a whole?" He must try to get variety in the performance, and for this he will need to decide which are the scenes of tension and which are the scenes of ease. As he works at his desk making notes, visual concepts may occur. He may see the kinetics of the story progression and the effect he hopes to give an audience. As he nears the end of his study, he should be able to formulate words to describe the theme to his satisfaction. In so doing, he may realize that certain key words or important phrases or speeches are the building blocks of the play. Characters are certainly important in finding the essence of a play; or he might find the key to the play in the climax. Such introspection can lead to an understanding of the reasons why this particular author wrote this particular play. What is performed on a stage is a concept of a play, not the play itself. No two productions of *Oedipus* are identical. Concepts do not come to a director entirely by conscious effort. Concept in art involves the conscious, unconscious, subconscious, memory, emotion—the sum total of many factors. Except for a thorough investigation of the play, a director would be unable to achieve a concept.

For the most part a concept is made of spontaneous impressions—or so the director might believe, but the process is not as spontaneous as it first appears. There should be no mystery about creative thinking. We use it every day. Each of our efforts begins with a goal, something we hope to achieve. Imagination provides a plan for achieving that goal. While reading a play, the director will recall bits and pieces of his experience which relate to the incidents in the play. Such experiences are rooted in all the perceptions and awareness he feels as an artist. These will be stimulated by his own P.O.V. of the central idea of the play. But these thoughts, or visions, are only the beginning of the creative process. His next task will be to turn his vision into theatrical reality, those sights and sounds, groupings and movement, rhythms, images, and excitement which will best express the play. In short, he will be transferring the abstract into the concrete.

But before these first impressions are lost, they must be recorded. He may even leave the means to express them until later, *but at the moment, he must write them down!* This is an essential and vital part of the director's work. His first impression, his vision of a production, must be described in words. It would be a mistake for him to trust these to his memory. Later, during rehearsals, his mind will become absorbed in the many details of the production. Now, as he studies, every feeling, reaction, even questions, should be written down and preserved. These notes will serve somewhat as a musical score serves a conductor. They will be invaluable not only as a record of first reactions, but as a guide for all the subsequent work ahead.

Such notes should state the background leading to the director's individual P.O.V. Any research materials used in formulating his concept or any particular design approaches that might provide future guidance into production creativity should be noted. An excellent example of a director's P.O.V. is stated in the following letter by Director Earle Ernst to designer Richard Mason for a production of Shakespeare's *King Lear* at the University of Hawaii.

> Lear *will happen two or three centuries after the great atomic holocaust, when the few survivors have worked themselves up to a feudal scheme of things. Not much is left of the earth where anything will grow; that's the reason both for the violent storms and for the greediness. The heath is one of the direct-hit, infertile areas. There are only two classes of people: those at the "courts" and those who live like animals on the heath. The latter are "mutants"; Kent and Edgar in disguise look like them. The "human" survivors occupied the remaining parts of buildings and subsequently built onto them with whatever they could find. This means a disquieting juxtaposition of styles. They used stone, mostly, because there wasn't much wood. Their clothes—they'd have wool, but not silk; I can't think they'd have many dyes. Clothes distinguish the haves from the have-nots, but they're stiff and hard, giving a sense of not belonging on the body, but worn to disguise it and to state rank. Their style is a combination of archaic and spaceship.*
>
> *The general scenic effect is of coldness, hardness, the earth returning to barren rock, man having destroyed it and himself. "This great world shall so wear out to naught." There is no comfort anywhere; the characters are constantly wrenched and tortured by surprise, fearful discoveries, pain; a recurring pattern is their seeing each other in a new, stunning light. The only anodynes in this shattered world are power and sex.*
>
> *The music is electronic (the storm too), except for the Fool's songs. He sings them to the traditional, "remembered" airs:* Tea for Two, Alexander's Ragtime Band, Moritat, *etc.*[1]

[1]Reprinted by kind permission of Prof. Earle Ernst, University of Hawaii.

Shakespeare's King Lear, *as produced by the University of Hawaii. (Photo by Richard Mason)*

Adapting Plays

*Style in dramatic production, as in any work of art, con-
sists in a unity of key that is in harmony with the subject
presented.*

—Gilmor Brown,
Founder-director,
The Pasadena Playhouse

It might be logically assumed that the style of a production would be governed by the play—its type, period, and the manner in which it was originally performed. Meticulously researched productions often seem as interesting to an audience as some carefully preserved historical artifact in a museum. "As originally presented " is one of the revered phrases of theatrical ballyhoo. After Shakespeare's death his plays were produced in almost every conceivable way, culminating in the elaborate scenic productions of Sir Henry Irving. Then William Poel cut through the affectations and presented Shakespeare before a simple, permanent, and formalized background. He also did scholarly research into Elizabethan dress and acting techniques. During the last two decades, "Globe" playhouses have been built all over America notwithstanding the fact that no one knows for sure what the original "Globe" looked like. There were two playhouses by that name and both burned to the ground along with any records which might have provided posterity with accurate information.

David Garrick played Romeo in a periwig. Basil Sydney played Hamlet in a dinner jacket, Richard Burton played the part in rehearsal clothes. While there is nothing wrong in adapting a classic to our own time, the Central Park *Hamlet* in hippy clothes did not please the few who saw it.

Exactly how far a director may supplant the style and values of a classic with his own concept is a matter of taste and judgment.

As a creative artist, a director has every right to produce a play in a style which is not in accordance with previous productions, providing he feels that the inherent values in the play will not be sacrificed. Plays are considered classics when they incorporate timeless and universal appeal which permits adaptation without the loss of their fundamental values. The style of a production should always depend upon the play. When a friend accused Lon Chaney of overacting in the film *The Hunchback of Notre Dame*, his reply was, "Read the book." The style of a production may be influenced by:

EDUCATIONAL INTERESTS

Plays of other lands; such as Spanish, French, or Japanese Nō plays; Agitprop; Black Theatre, and plays of the right or left.

Minor plays of other times written by writers known for other works, such as Byron, Balzac, Pablo Picasso, Gertrude Stein, Victor Hugo, etc. Also, Multimedia, Happenings, etc.

Style must be in harmony with elements of the individual play, its mores, theme, or language: poetic plays or fantasies, such as those by Maeterlinck, Racine, or a play like *Beggar on Horseback*.

PERIOD PLAYS

Styles depend upon a study of periods, the mores and acting techniques popular at the time, such as Commedia scenarios, melodramas, Restoration comedies, Molière, Shakespeare, and Ibsen.

Importance of Concept

The chief influence on the style of a production may be the director's concept. A relevant and inspired example is the University of Hawaii production of *Lear*. The factors listed above are considered *in addition* to the obvious styles of plays, such as realistic, nonrealistic, expressionistic, absurd, etc. A production will also depend upon whether the play is a comedy, farce, melodrama, etc., and such factors are considered by the director when studying the play. Often different scenes or different acts *within the same play* will suggest different styles in treatment.

Once the director has reached his decision about the general style in which he will present his production, it then becomes a matter of *emphasis*. Some plays will depend greatly upon color, sweep, and action, such as the plays of Molière or Goldoni; others will rely upon grandeur, formal speech, and bodily grace, such as the Greek tragedies, Racine, or Shakespeare. All the great acting styles have been individually treated in *Acting: The Creative Process*,[2] and because so many consider style to be the weakest aspect of directing and acting in this country, I recommend either this book or *A Re-Discovery of Style*.[3]

Cutting

Plays are sometimes improved by judicious cutting. During his study of a play, a director may find some passages which seem dull or uninteresting. The fault may be with the author, who has not stayed strictly with his subject matter. Or, he may have put too much emphasis on certain points when these are perfectly clear to an audience. Audiences have an annoying way of being ahead of an author. If so, the director may help a play by careful cutting.

Plays written for another era, such as those from Ancient Greece, the Renaissance, or Restoration period, contain outdated topical references and analogies as well as archaic words, phrases, and puns. They may also contain comedy which was effective only during the time these plays were first

[2]Hardie Albright, *Acting: The Creative Process* (Belmont, Calif.: Dickenson Publishing Co., 1967).

[3]Michel Saint-Denis, *Theatre, a Rediscovery of Style* (New York: Theatre Arts Books, 1960).

presented. Also, some of the early plays are too lengthy to sustain the attention span of today's audiences.

When cutting, a good rule to follow is to respect the play's line of action, its characters, plot, and atmosphere, and to cut only those words or lines which seem superfluous to those elements. Generally, some cuts should be made before rehearsals begin. If these are left until late or middle rehearsals and you deprive an actor of some lines, they are sure to be his favorites. He may even think that they were cut because he was not reading them to suit you, and develop a guilt complex.

Cutting Period Plays

While plays of other eras especially seem to benefit by respectful cutting, this should be done prudently, and only after careful deliberation and research. Of all playwrights the greatest has suffered most from butchery of his plays. Shakespeare was not long in his grave before open season was declared on his works. Many well known theatrical figures set about to "improve" his plays. At least David Garrick, Davenant, and Tate had a modicum of honesty when they called their efforts "adaptations." The hacking, patching, and outright vandalism continues to this day with *Hamlet* the prime target. We have had *Hamlet* with all soliloquies cut and with subplots omitted, and the day may come when we have *Hamlet* without Hamlet. It is ironic that not one word may be cut from a play by a modern playwright without his permission, and yet Shakespeare's plays are mangled by anyone presuming to know more about playwrighting than the world's greatest.

If you contemplate directing a Shakespearean play, you will benefit by consulting the variorums, especially the republished Furness editions and Granville-Barker's *Prefaces to Shakespeare*. It is also important which version of a play you use. Some "Acting Editions" are copies from old promptbooks which were originally butchered to provide a "vehicle" for a former star. There is also the choice to be made between folio and quarto editions. It will save much time and a great deal of wasted effort if you begin with the edition most suited to your needs.

When considering a Greek play for production, a director should first examine the different English translations. For instance, the *Medea* used by Dame Judith Anderson and played so successfully by her was a modern adaptation by the poet, Robinson Jeffers, based upon the Euripides original. Other modern writers such as Giraudoux and Anouilh have made versions of Greek classics. If faithful translations are chosen, special attention should be given to archaic language and to playing time required, and when necessary, cuts should be made, such as those from Molière's original French, and other-language playwrights.

Restoration comedies are frequently pruned. There may be some outspoken language regarding the rake's sexual prowess, or some modification needed of the libertarianism of the philandering ladies of London society, but this can only be judged by the individual director in his special circumstances. However, in pruning the plays of the Restoration, the director should take care to preserve the gaiety and the manner in which they convey the unrestrained modes of that day.

In general, if cutting is done with respect for the playwright and a great deal of intelligence, a director should not consider it sacrilegious. A director is not a translator but a creative artist. He has his cast and his stage to consider, and most important—his audience. When to draw the line between cutting, adapting, and writing his own play is a matter to be decided by the director and his conscience.

Cutting Modern Plays

New York theatregoers have always been considered more sophisticated than those in other parts of the country. Language containing vulgarity and profanity has always been accepted as part of the Broadway norm. Formerly a director could eliminate a few words and produce a play even for the Ladies Aid Society. But now that is impossible. Abnormality, nudity, and physical sex acts have been commodities on Broadway during the last few seasons. Cutting a few four letter words from *The Boys in the Band, Futz,* or *The Killing of Sister George* would be useless. It is the *basic idea* of such plays which unsophisticated audiences would find objectionable. There are some Broadway plays which might be produced other than in New York, or some other such metropolitan area, by doing some cutting, but even these must be selected by the individual director for his particular situation, as he will be held responsible for his selection.

Motivation

In working out the movements for a scene, the director should begin by considering the emotional drives of the characters and the relationship of the scene to the play as a whole. Another scene may be unemotional, such as one of pure narration, but in each case the director should begin by analyzing the characters of the particular scene and play. This will guide him into the movements. Let us take the example of a man and woman seated on a sofa. She is upset by something he has said, and rather than allow him to see her tears, she turns, rises, and moves to DL, not facing him. He rises to above sofa, still taunting her. This upsets her all the more, and covering her face, she crosses angrily in front of him to DR. Realizing he has made matters worse, he decides to lighten her mood by apologizing. He moves to DC, on a line with her. The sheer mechanics might be recorded in the book as follows:

> She rises and moves DL. He balances by rising and walking back of sofa (UR). She crosses to DR, again he balances by moving DC in front of sofa facing her.

We know that movement alone is able to convey a story. There was an English director who always tested movement he had given to a cast by making them run through the play *silently*. When pleased with a particular scene, he would call from the house, "Good, that tells the story." Audiences accept that movement is to direct their attention, or focus, on something important to their understanding of the play. But never mistake activity for action. Many productions of late have a great deal of activity but no real action.

Movement can also be an important means of developing character. When we look at a sketch of weak and strong stage positions, we see at once that characters can be moved not only east, south, north, and west but also parallel to the footlights across the stage, and upstage or downstage in straight lines. The acting space can encapsulate a great deal of movement in what at first appears to be a confining little area. The director's problem in this case would be to prevent confusion and collisions. Solutions will be found in carefully designed and properly motivated blocking. Precision in the timing of moves will be a consideration for later rehearsals and need not be noted in the director's book.

Movement is also valuable in relieving tensions. When two characters are facing each other in a strong stage position, even a slight movement by one or the other will break the tension. An audience can also be distracted from an important scene by movement somewhere else on stage. Movement is often used purposely to provide contrasts, to vary voice sounds, to change pace, or to elicit emotion.

Action and Characters

It is an old American custom to sit on the front porch and watch people walk by. A popular television show adopted this device by placing a silent camera in the street to photograph pedestrians as they walked by the studio. During the TV showing, the master of ceremonies would make a running commentary.

One of the reasons this is entertaining is that there is, in all of us, a deep-seated interest in others. People like to watch people. We study these pedestrians as they walk along, note how they dress, how they walk, what they carry. We speculate as to where they have been, where they are going, where and how they live, and what they do for a living. These simple films are deceptive. They have in them three necessary ingredients of theatre: characters, action, and spectators.

In a theatre, our interest usually begins with characters—how they behave, how they sound, and how they are dressed. But our interest would soon lag if they did not move. Humans are always more interested in objects that move rather than those that remain static. The movements of characters on a stage tell us as much about them as the words they speak. The great pantomimists have proven that by postures, gestures, movements, and attitudes they can tell a complete story.

One of the director's important duties, as he studies and plans his production, is to conceive effective movement for the characters. This movement must not only tell us who and what the characters are, but must also tell their story. On a stage, actions follow certain principles which have proven effective ever since "Roscius was an actor in Rome." These principles were originated to give a better understanding to an audience and are accepted, even expected, by an audience as part of the rules of the game of theatre.

Actions

A character does not generally move about during another character's speech. This is not done out of politeness, but because a character in motion will distract from a speaker. A moving character is dominant and should not be hidden when passing upstage from another character. A move is best made on a character's own line or during the interval between lines. Some directors consider such rules to be old-fashioned; however it seems only common sense to preserve a point of focus for an audience. When one of the characters makes an entrance or exit, some adjustment should be made by the characters remaining on stage. This often introduces a new subject or a change of mood for the audience.

Audience Focus

Principal characters in a play have a great deal more to say than others because *they are the chief means of communicating the story and action to the audience.*

As we see in the figure below, there are weak and strong stage positions. In proscenium staging, characters may be positioned so that an actor with important lines can be assured of the full attention of the audience. Such arrangements are not made primarily for aesthetic reasons, but because they are functional and necessary if the audience is to have a full enjoyment of the play.

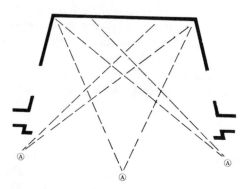

Obviously, such characters with important scenes must be placed in the stronger positions so that they dominate others. We can admit frankly (among ourselves) that these movements are calculated and planned. *But they must never appear so to the audience.* There should always appear to be some reason for a move, as if done in response to a stimulus. In real life we move because of some intellectual or emotional impetus. The very next time you move, determine why you did so. As in real life, a character on stage must seem to move for a reason, too, and when the audience speculates on or understands the reason, it helps to elucidate both character and play.

Justifications for a character's movements are, for the most part, the responsibility of the actor. If the actors do not understand this or have never had the experience of thinking about it, they must be carefully schooled in the process by the director.

Inactive or subordinate characters must not be allowed strong stage positions in which they might become the center of an audience's interest. If so, they can detract from the focus upon the important people and action in the play. When a move is made by a character on stage, others should "balance" his move, or "dress the stage."

Note how the audience's attention is divided between Ramon Bieri and Peter Donat (left) in this scene from the American Conservatory Theatre production of Staircase. *(Photo by Hank Kranzler, courtesy of the American Conservatory Theatre of San Francisco)*

Tension

By moving and thereby relaxing tensions, it is possible for a scene to be made to "build" again. This prevents a long, unrelieved scene of shouting and gives variety to the tonal qualities. However, in building to a climax, movement is generally kept to a minimum, unless a great deal of confusion or excitement is required by the play. Moves should be short in time. Two short moves are more acceptable to an audience than one long one. Ideally, the line spoken and the move made should coincide. In a comedy or farce, moves are made at a much faster pace than in real life, while in tragedy, movement is slower, more deliberate, with attention given to the grace of the movement.

Stress

Moves are often used to give emphasis to a line or a situation. In Act III, Scene v of *Romeo and Juliet,* Juliet considers all alternatives for not marrying Paris. But even her beloved Nurse advises this marriage. After dismissing the Nurse, Juliet throws her cape around her shoulders, then almost in panic, starts out for Friar Laurence's cell. Traditionally, she stops, moves slowly to the table, picks up a small dagger, holds it in both hands against her heart, and speaks quietly—

"If all else fail, myself have power to die."

The movement made with the cape and the move to the door are actions of determination, but this is halted by a more profound and deeper consideration. The slower movement with the dagger and her statement that she will have Romeo or death are actions which help elucidate the significance of the entire play.

Pre-Blocking

If you are so far along that you have narrowed in on direction as a discipline, you probably know, among other things, upstage from downstage, center (C) from left center (LC), and you know that "X" means cross.

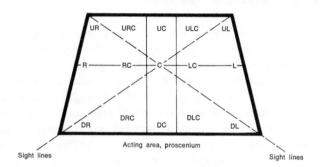

Acting area, proscenium

Sight lines   Sight lines

Usually the various locations are identified as:

Strong	RC, LC	Weak	URC, ULC
Stronger	DRC, DLC	Weaker	DC, UC, L, R
Strongest	C	Weakest	DR, DL, UL, UR

The truth is that these "strong and weak" positions are highly controversial. It is possible for an actor standing at a supposedly weak position (DL) to "steal a scene" from another at the strongest position (C). So many conditions might affect stage positions that a director dare not rely on such generalized pedagogics.

The above positions obviously apply only to realistic box settings on proscenium stages. On an open stage, spotlights and other elements will alter positions, but the greatest contrast is in the position of the audience seated on many sides instead of one. Ramps, platforms, and steps also affect the values. Strong and weak positions for thrust or arena staging will be explored later.

Any blocking which is planned before actual rehearsals begin should not be too involved or detailed. At this time it is quite enough to consider groupings, balance, movement, and the use of space. Later, when working with the actors, the director will adjust this temporary blocking. During rehearsals he will be better able to *sense* where Macbeth should be when he sees the dagger before him. He will sense when a passage should be slow and deliberate in movement or when the action should skip along. There is no adequate way to explain such feelings, as they are rooted in the director's reaction to the individual play and the actors. The nuances of such sensations will not occur during early readings but will be inspired by characterization and the basic gestalt of the production.

Director Jules Irving placed his characters in direct relationship with the audience in this production at Lincoln Center (New York) for James Hanley's The Inner Journey. *(Photo by Martha Swope)*

It is interesting that the term *blocking* is used in other art forms. A sculptor fashions his clay into areas and planes. A head begins with an egg shape set upon a column. Indentations are made as eye sockets, and planes are leveled for cheek areas. At this point the sculptor works *tentatively*, carefully avoiding any detail. He is dealing only with a "rough" (another art term), realizing that these indications must be correct before any detail or refinement is possible. The director of a play must also work tentatively in the beginning. It would be impractical for him to consider much detailed movement before selecting a cast. Individual styles and the personalities of his actors and what they are able to contribute will affect the final movements.

Pre-blocking should be considered only as a blueprint—a "rough"—a means of getting started on the actual construction. Practical necessities and unforeseen elements will no doubt alter some of the early blocking. All during the period of creating the production, the director will rely greatly upon his intuitive reactions. These will influence his approval of the sets and of the colors selected for the costumes and lights—in exactly the same way an artist is guided by his intuition as he sits before a canvas or works in clay.

Later, when we deal with actors, we will develop more on this subject of blocking, but at this point it should be considered as the *general movement of characters on a stage* by means of organic motivations. This in turn will clarify the action for an audience.

The question might very well be asked, If pre-blocking is so tentative and general, why not accomplish all the blocking during the rehearsals? And it must be admitted that many professional directors do wait until they have the actors on stage before they do any blocking. Those using this method

Pleasing arrangement of cast in The Robber Bridegroom, *a stage treatment of a Brothers Grimm tale, directed by Paul Sills. (Courtesy of the Center Theatre Group, Mark Taper Forum, Los Angeles, Calif.)*

believe that pre-blocking places undue emphasis upon the purely mechanical aspects of movement. I have used both methods, but for working with inexperienced actors, I unhesitatingly recommend some tentative pre-blocking. It gives a sense of security to the amateur actor when he needs it. If the blocking is presented as being tentative and adjustable, it will not discourage collaboration by the actors during future rehearsals. When working with inexperienced actors, it is unwise to come to a blocking rehearsal with only a vague idea for moving them about the stage. Just try it once. Tell your amateurs to move about as they see fit and you will soon be convinced how necessary it is that they have some point of reference. Actors often say that they like to be free and move about as they "feel" the character and the scene; but this freedom, if permitted, should always be controlled by the director. If not, rehearsals are sure to become an intolerable muddle of people bumping into each other, all fighting for stage center. Actors expect and respect authority. They are unsure without it. Leniency should never become indulgence. The director will not only save valuable time but will also gain the immediate respect of his cast if he comes to blocking rehearsals with at least a general plan for movement. Later, when the actors are free of scripts and are under the skin of their characters, these moves can be tested. If the pre-blocked moves do not seem right at that time, *then* they can be altered. Naturally an actor should be comfortable in anything he is asked to do, but he is not in a position to see the play from any total perspective. Only a director is able to see the production as a whole. Moreover, another value in having notes on blocking is that it is good psychology. It demonstrates to an inexperienced cast that their director has direction himself.

A director is often able to delineate characters and convey moods by his placement of those characters. The Fool above has discovered that nobility rests in him, while the King realizes that a crown does not automatically make a wise man, in this scene from The Company Theatre's repertory. (Courtesy of Company Theatre)

Stage Composition

Other directing books have devoted many pages to composition, stage pictures, symmetrics, etc. (One of these even has twelve pages of old masters.) We can go to an art gallery to see still life. We go to a theatre to see action. Even the word *drama* is derived from the Greek *dran*—"to do." In the presence of space technology, discotheques, and Picasso, stage tableaus seem pretty square.

While books on theatre have been using Medieval paintings as illustrations of how to arrange actors on stage, all the other arts have been moving into the next century, away from old concepts of space as solid mass. Since the 1950's, the art world has been in an expanding, dynamic period. Exciting work has been done in environment, motion, kinetics, and creations which move and "live." And during this time, theatre, which is supposed to be the liveliest art, has atrophied behind its picture-frame stage.

Thirteen years ago, Gyorgy Kepes was saying that motion was ". . . the simultaneous representation of the numerous visible aspects composing an event." I take this to mean that motion or an action is not truly represented by one phase of the action but by many, as proven in stop-action photos. Kepes was not a theatre man, but he certainly indicated a path we could follow when he said, ". . . motion picture, television, and related techniques have now given us the flexibility we need to mark the time flow of images, the growth, succession, rhythm, and orderly continuity of vision."[4]

Also, in more modern concepts, light has become more than utilitarian. It has developed as a medium for creating art. Moholy-Nagy worked for years creating light sculpture, but most theatre people saw nothing in his accomplishments which they might apply to theatre production. Working with Walter Gropius at the Bauhaus in Germany and later in this country, he sought out the possibilities of an art of real forces, producing an endless transformation of expression in which the spectator could be immersed. The use of light as a dramatic medium is only now being explored. In *Prune Flat* (1965), Robert Whitman presented a provocative use of filmed images in conjunction with live actors. Film is used to enhance or contrast the stage action. In one sequence which articulates the scale of possibilities, a filmed nude was projected upon the white costume of a living actress to make a statement. Materials and revised precepts of space and time relationships could extend our methodology if we are receptive to a redefinement and readjustment of our technologies and materials.

But most especially, a readjustment must be made in our antiquated precept that people on a stage should be considered as solid mass. If we do not make this readjustment, and quickly, then the oft repeated brickbat that theatre always trails behind the other arts will seem true. Adventurous forces in the new theatre no longer consider actors as mass in a fixed space, of classic poses, of geometric compositions, and balance. Actors must be considered *unfettered action forces*. In short, stasis must become kinesis. There

[4]Gyorgy Kepes, *The New Landscape in Art and Science* (Chicago: Paul Theobald & Co., 1956), p. 371.

are many hopeful indications that at last theatre is moving out of its picture frame and antiquated precepts of poses into the free space of open theatre and unbounded imagination.

When you shake your fist at someone, the object is to threaten and not to impress them with your lovely pose. Action through movement can tell a story or convey a mood as well as the words of the text. Some of the new playwrights accept this. Arnold Wesker has stated: "I am working very much towards a reduction not only of scenery, but of dialogue as well, and I bet the rest of my plays are no bloody good. The less I say, the better I like it. This, I think, is the result not so much of my interest in cinematic forms, as of working in the theatre, talking to other playwrights, and becoming aware, more and more aware, that the theatre is a place where one wants to see things happening."[5]

"Seeing things happen" has nothing to do with beautiful groupings. If one gets enamoured with them they can slow down action to the point of boredom for an audience. Once they recognize a stage picture as such, drama will creep out the stage door. In my opinion, this dedication to graceful poses on stage is more harmful to today's nonprofessional productions than any other factor. Don't spend your valuable time carefully arranging posed still life when you should be rehearsing your actors. When they understand their character motivation and emotion, you may then be able to arrange them aesthetically—if that "turns you on." In this way it will not seem as if it has been done out of any desire to make pretty pictures. Unlike static art, a play develops kinetically. The inciting forces are organic. A performance should be an ever-changing, ever-moving picture.

Summary

The director will need a complete knowledge of the play he has chosen before putting it into rehearsals. A period of solitary study will allow for rational analysis and the development of inspirational concepts. The best of this study period should be recorded in a personal book. Later, these fresh impressions and concepts will be developed with the actors, set designer, lighting staff, etc. An important phase of the work is in maintaining an enthusiasm, an emotional delight in the work. If a director retains that, he will inspire others.

Further Reading

Battcock, Gregory, ed. *The New Art.* New York: E. P. Dutton & Co., 1966.
Esslin, Martin. *The Theatre of the Absurd.* Garden City, N.Y.: Anchor Books, 1961.
———. *The Peopled Wound, The Work of Harold Pinter.* Garden City, N.Y.: Doubleday & Co., 1969.
Gropius, Walter. *The New Architecture and the Bauhaus.* Cambridge, Mass.: Massachusetts Institute of Technology, 1965.
Kenny, Sean. *The Shape of the Theatre, Actor and Architect.* Edited by Steven Joseph. Manchester, England: Manchester University Press, 1964.

[5]Arnold Wesker, in *Twentieth Century*, February, 1961.

Kepes, Gyorgy. *The Language of Vision*. New York: Paul Thomas, 1944.
Kostelanetz, Richard, ed. *The New American Arts*. New York: Horizon Press, 1965.
———. *The Theatre of Mixed Means*. New York: Dial Press, 1968.
Moholy-Nagy, Laszlo. *The New Vision*. New York: Wittenborn, 1947.
———. *Vision in Motion*. Chicago: Paul Theobald, 1947.
Motherwell, Robert, ed. *The Dada Painters and Poets*. New York: Wittenborn, 1951.
Nadeau, Maurice. *The Art of Surrealism*. New York: Macmillan Co., 1965.
Naylor, Gillian. *The Bauhaus*. New York: E. P. Dutton & Co., 1968. (Paperback).
Read, Sir Herbert. *The Grass Roots of Art*. New York: Meridian, 1961.
Rosenberg, Harold. *The Tradition of the New*. New York: Horizon Press, 1959.

What is a Director's Book?

A director's book is not to be confused with a stage manager's prompt book, which contains finalized technical instructions pertaining solely to the management of the stage during production and performances. The director's book is his alone, for his own private use, and should not be seen by others. It will note the director's spiritual and theatric vision of the production, along with his early intentions for communicating these to an audience. It will include private notations concerning casting which should never be available to actors.

When beginning his study, the director might ask himself, What is the meaning of this play; what is its central theme? His answer should include the plot-brief and how he intends to convey these matters to the audience. He should write a description of the play *as he would like to see it performed on the stage*. He should detail impressions of the leading characters which justify each action they take in the play. If the play is well known, the book should include notes on anything which has previously been written about the play—its historical and sociological background, etc.—and the director should continue his study until he knows how each scene contributes to the mounting tension, for this will signify the motives he is to reveal, first to the actors, and finally to the audience. During this study he should decide upon the moment of crisis when opposing forces meet, and note where he has found his own interest lagging and indicate what he intends to do about it. In fact, the director's book should contain anything that has helped crystallize his concept.

This may seem like a lot of unrewarding work. But it is not. An example of failure in a director's original concept was apparent in a production of Truman Capote's *The Grass Harp*. The play itself is "talky" and this was certainly obvious to the director during his study of the play, and he probably planned to compensate for its inactivity. But during the rehearsals, he was probably distracted by many other aspects and lost sight of his original concept. He confined his characters into a limited acting space, and as a result the audience had an interminable evening of atrophy and talk. Much sincere effort can come to nothing if the director's original concept is not based upon consideration of the audience and constantly kept in mind during the rehearsal period. The director's book helps to maintain a steady course, if the director will refer to it constantly.

Work on a Director's Book

When you are satisfied that you understand the play thoroughly, measure the stage on which you will produce the play. Next, scale down these measurements on paper to the size of a ground plot with which you can work. This is usually ¼ or ½ inch to a foot.

Now mark in your acting space, and if it is a realistic play and you are using a box set, indicate the limitations of your setting, leaving open spaces for entrances, windows, etc. If the play has more than one setting, have a duplicate made of the stage plot and use a different plot for each setting. Also, when planning more than one set, remember to keep them simple, so that you save time on scene changes. You need not follow the staging plan in acting versions.

A realistic play is usually most effective when the setting contains three separate groups of furniture. This makes it possible for the director to use a variety of acting areas. Each group of furniture should be placed so that there is ample room for actors to move freely around them. And now I am going to make a suggestion which is not always possible to follow, but when circumstances allow, it is certainly ideal. Scene plots should be given to the designer by the director, not the other way around. After you have worked with the actors and the blocking is finalized, then give your ground plot to the scene designer. I realize that if you have six weeks to do a show and you take a full week to block, this means that the technicians must design, construct, and paint your sets in five weeks, and many colleges and universities do not have the technical staff to work that rapidly. A solution might be that the designer and the director confer early and work out compromises. This will prevent the difficult task of adjusting your movements to a strange set. It is the director who should decide the boundary lines of his acting space, where he wants doors and windows, as well as the placement of furniture. These are all related to the director's interpretation of the play.

If the play you have selected to produce is printed, provide yourself with a notebook which is larger than the printed playscript and which has at least double the number of pages. There are several ways of mounting, and one is to simply paste pages into the center of the notebook, using the margins for notes. This will require the purchase of two playscripts, and when complete it is often bulky. Another method is to cut out the centers of the notebook pages, one-quarter inch smaller than the playscript, and paste the script pages into the panel so that each side can be read. Still another, and the most satisfactory method I have found, is to cut away every second page of the notebook, leaving a stub about 1½ inches from the binding,

and then pasting a playscript page to each stub. This allows for marginal notes to be written on the full blank page, indicating moves, line-by-line directions, or overall notes on the scenes. These notes might include comments on the purpose of the scene, the values sought, or the atmosphere to be created. Ink should not be used until rehearsals have finalized the movements. Mark these in soft pencil by numbering the line (or even the word), then using a corresponding number in the margin for the note.

It is also handy to have each scene indexed by the use of tabs for quick location. Using colored pencils, a system may be worked out to differentiate between notes, such as blue for actors' movements, red for moods, tempo, or atmosphere, green for sounds, etc.

Don't be in a hurry to mark furniture, prop trees, rocks, platforms, or ramps on your ground plan just yet. First get some index cards, scale down the pieces in proportion to the plot, then cut out and label each. You might begin by placing the furniture according to the author's description and then experiment by moving the pieces into other positions until you feel you have them in the best locations for your action. When you are satisfied, *then* trace these on the ground plot.

Classics are usually performed in some sort of permanent structure which is adaptable to different scenes by lighting or a few changes of set pieces. Naturally you will hope for the best arrangement which will express your interpretation of the play. But in every type of modern or classic play, you will need to adjust to the resources at hand. A good general rule is to place furniture, props, windows, and doors in accordance with *what is going to happen in each scene.*

Remember that you are a director, not an interior decorator. Keep your settings practical and not cluttered with superfluous gimcracks. A stage setting can become a great overpowering "thing" which devours actors and play. The old professional productions of Irving and Belasco were smothering in detail. But today, simplicity is the goal. Make sure your settings are unobtrusive and can be changed quickly; that they actually function for play and actors, create atmosphere, and serve the action. But if the curtain rises and the setting gets a hand, then you, as director, will be forced to overcome the distraction, to get the audience interested in the play. In early discussions with the scene designer, make it very clear that both you and he are servants of the play.

Index cards may also be used to indicate characters. Trace the outlines of the figures below on cards and cut them with nail scissors. Label each one with the character's name and stand each one upright in a place card holder.

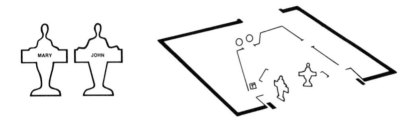

You are now ready to read the play and move your characters about the plot-sheet to suit the action. As you finalize a move, mark it in your director's book. Use the wide margin to indicate the exact line or word on which the move is to be made. When making these notes, always keep in mind that movement can tell a story as well as words. Test all movement by

1. Situation
2. Characters
3. Atmosphere

Place actors according to story progression and the relationships between characters. Use as many contrasting moves as possible in order to insure variety. Do not play too many scenes in the same position, such as on a sofa just off center. Move the characters on their own lines and use their own psychology to justify those moves. This will be easiest for the actor to understand rather than ordering him to do so. All moves should be justified and never made mechanically. Play no movement on plot or comedy lines and avoid two or more movements on any one line, except for comedy effect. If you know that a character will exit soon, get him near his exit and note the preparatory crosses in your book. This will avoid long walks which are not desirable except if done for some specific dramatic purpose.

The work described above should be part of the study made by the director before rehearsals begin. Later, as the actors begin to acquire confidence, the director may then encourage their collaboration. Amazing things can happen when actors and director contribute to the play's action. This may happen intellectually or quite accidentally. Often the most effective moves, from the viewpoint of an audience, have been those which an actor has stumbled upon during rehearsals and then have been developed by the director.

Symbols Used in a Director's Book

Diagrams and/or symbols are neater and take less space than written notes when marking indications in your director's book. As indicated earlier, these should first be made in pencil until after rehearsals are under way and you have decided that they can be made permanent.

CODE

CS	Center Stage		USL	Upstage left
DS	Downstage (toward audience)		USR	Upstage right
			DSL	Downstage left
US	Upstage (away from audience)		DSR	Downstage right

ACTOR'S DIRECTIONS

S, or ↓	Sit	ⓟ	Pause
R, or ↑	Rise		Rise left
K.	Kneel		Circle
Ex.	Exit		Turn right
Ent.	Entrance		Turn left
X.	Cross	⇌	Pace R and L
X3	Cross three steps		Upstage turn
XRT	Cross right of table		Downstage turn
XDL	Cross down left of chair		Pauses before or after crosses

FURNITURE

Chair		Sit in chair		Platform	
Sofa		Sit left of sofa		Steps L	
Table		Fireplace		Steps R	

SHORTHAND FOR SPEECHES AND READINGS:

Delete		Beat or slight pause	|
Insert	∧	Longer pause	‖
Transpose	"or tr"	Topping	T
Up inflection		Broken speech	-------
Down inflection		Change in tone	
Rising pitch		Breath	ℬ
Falling inflection		Fast tempo	///////
Crescendo	<	Audience	ΩΩΩΩΩ
Diminuendo	>	Actor	
Underline for stress	———	Actress	
Greater stress	═══		

Playscripts Vs. Sides

As quickly as the play selection has been finalized and the budget made, manuscripts must be ordered for cast and staff. If the play is published, enough copies must be on hand before the first rehearsals. Until a short time ago, typed "sides" were frequently used. These were half-pages of 8½-by-11 inch sheets, bound by paper and clasps. One or two words as direct cues were given and then the full speeches for the individual part or character. Stage directions for the character were also given. These sides were laconic but also practical, in that an actor could roll them up and put them in his pocket. But they were far from satisfactory to any but a slapdash actor. A "side" might look like this:

. . . . . . going to.

(sinks in chair, winks invitingly to Marvin)

Why don't you say what you mean? You only came here
to ruin me, didn't you?

. . . . . . not a boy!

(You turn sharply UR and exit in a fury)

Obviously, no actor could possibly understand much about a scene or characters from this. It has been said that sides prevented actors from "mouthing" another's lines and that the small paperbound books left the actor's right hand free for business when rehearsing. But sides encourage the "You speak, I speak" habit and never allow the actor to follow the logical sequence of a scene or to know the sense of the speech preceding his. Neither will he know what is said about his character when not on stage. Any study of the play and the relationships of the characters must be done by studying the complete manuscript. But purchasing complete texts for a large cast is expensive. When a director must confine costs within a modest budget, sides may be made for small parts by using copying machines for selected pages. In any case, playscripts or xeroxed sides must be ordered or provided for as soon as there is a firm selection of the play.

Check List for Study of the Play

How many times should a director read a play during his study? If you are able to answer the questions in the check list which follow, you have probably made an adequate study of your play.

1. What is this play about? What is its theme, its plot?
2. Type: comedy, tragedy, farce, melodrama, etc.? Staging: realistic, classic, symbolic, etc.?
3. Time: year, season, day; weather.
4. Place: where does the action occur, geographically and locally?
5. Requirements: cast, settings, lighting, etc.
6. Characters: what person or persons should the audience care about? What is the progatonist's goal?
7. Do I have a complete understanding of all characters?

8. What is the mood or atmosphere of this play?

9. What happens in this play? What is its line of action? How does it begin and end?

10. Which are the key scenes? What impressions do I want to make on the audience? What would I like them to remember about my production? (Director's concept)

Write answers to the above questions at the beginning of your director's book.

If you believe that all this preliminary work is a foolish waste of time and that you should be getting on with rehearsals, perhaps Harold Clurman can convince you of its importance:

> . . . notes set down for my own use when I have read a play at least a half dozen times are never communicated to the actors in the forms which they take in my "little book." They would be unintelligible to actors in this form as well as practically useless. They serve to make the thoughts and sentiments I experience in reading the script somewhat more specific than they might be if I allowed them to remain inchoate within myself. They are springboards and tracers for my own feelings. They lead me on and point to the objectives I hope to attain.[6]

[6]Harold Clurman, *Directing the Play*, ed. by Cole and Chinoy (New York: Bobbs-Merrill Co., 1953), p. 319.

THE
DIRECTOR
AND
THE
STAGE 7

. . . the best thing that could happen to our theatre at this moment would be for playwrights and actors and directors to be handed a bare stage on which no scenery could be placed, and then told that they must write, and act, and direct for this stage. In no time we should have the most exciting theatre in the world.

—Robert Edmond Jones,
The Dramatic Imagination

Different Stages: The Evolution of the Playing Space

Before any further planning can be done on your production, you must decide what sort of stage you will be using. Almost eighty percent of college and high school productions are mounted upon proscenium stages, and in all probability it will be the stage you will use. All of our discussions so far have been based upon that assumption.

For nearly two hundred years, plays have been written for this stage and have been most effectively mounted upon it. These are the plays of realism. It is curious that to most people, even the word *theatre* has come to mean a platform framed by an arch, with the spectators placed on one side directly before the actors. This was not always so. Our little picture-frame stage, which we accept as a venerable tradition, is really a Johnny-come-lately in a long theatrical history.

The Anti-Illusionists

Some very distinguished men of the theatre are of the opinion that we have outgrown the proscenium stage, that we have done all that can be done with it, that it no longer challenges them as artists, that it is indeed stale, rigid, and confining. They predict that if we continue using it exclusively, more and more of our audiences will desert us, wearied by the old peep-hole box with its little marionettes jiggling inside. They feel that this type of theatre, which was once fresh and exciting, has now grown old and tiresome by repetition. It cannot be denied that only in the most expensive seats can a playgoer see and hear a play properly. Others must be content to strain eyes and ears watching something which appears smaller than their TV screens at home. Films and TV are also victims of the proscenium-arch syndrome. Film makers are making every effort to break out of the peep-hole box and frame and increase the viewer's experience of being in or surrounded by the action. Already they have devised three or more screens to function as the eyes do—to rove up, around, down, and capture the whole surrounding environment for the viewer.

Eames, Information Machine. (*Photo by Charles Eames*)

But the chief argument against the proscenium stage is that it sharply divides the players and audience. This hardly encourages an audience to assume its rightful place as a full partner in the theatre experience. The anti-proscenium people propose that the actor-audience relationship be restored by abandonment of the picture frame, the curtains, and the platform. If this were done, they feel, then a maximum number of spectators would be drawn into a total empathetic experience with the actors and the action. It is interesting that this actor-audience relationship is the precise point upon which both sides of the controversy base their arguments.

The Illusionists

Those defending the proscenium argue that when an actor intrudes into the audience section, "he becomes a performer instead of an illusion in the phenomenal world of the stage." They believe that audiences do not pay to participate. When a spectator is forced to collaborate physically, as they are when actors mingle among them and address them directly, then all illusion is shattered. This sudden jolt back into real life, they maintain, destroys any further concentration on the pretend-life on stage. After all, they say, the actors have been rehearsed and know what is expected of them. But when an actor singles out a spectator, for instance, and asks him what he would do in such a situation, as proposed in the play, the spectator is at a disadvantage and bound to be embarrassed. He will take it as a breach of the contract made when he purchased his ticket. Not even the fine print said anything about doing the actor's work for him!

Does the Audience Want Illusion or Participation?

This seems to be the heart of the controversy. At this time you need not decide which is right or wrong, but each time you plan directing a play you must answer this question: "If I had both types of stages available to me, on which would this play be most effectively presented—the open stage or the enclosed stage?"

"Why even consider it," you might be thinking, "I have only one stage." But are you quite sure of that? With a little effort you might convert any room, lodge hall, gymnasium, or warehouse into an intimate little circle theatre. Further along we will consider just how little is needed for center staging. Try not to decide against it until you have finished this chapter, as you may be denying yourself the opportunity of a new experience.

If you are concerned about budgets, and what director is not, then consider the economy of reducing scenery costs and other trappings of the proscenium stage. On open or circle stages, sets are either deleted or kept to a minimum by using only a few set pieces. Gone are wall flats, returns, backings, ceilings, tormentors, border, footlights, and cycloramas, which will result in the elimination of large lumber bills, labor costs, and rental of storage space for inactive settings.

But economy is not the only advantage. No longer need you become frustrated by those long scene changes between acts which ruin the flow of the play. You need not rack your brain about some means to mask necessary lighting equipment. In the space theatre the mechanics are all exposed frankly as theatrical devices. The very key to this type of staging is simplicity. And how many times has it happened that you found the auditorium unavailable for those final, critical rehearsals? But best of all, space staging affords you variety and restoration of adventure in your work. The theatre of today might be characterized by its search for new forms of expression. It matters little if a theatre has no red carpet and plaster cupids if the show is vital and reflects our time. While few proscenium stages are built today, all over America the most modern and impressive theatre work is being accomplished sans proscenium, such as in the New Alley Theatre in Houston, Texas, the Festival Theatre in Stratford, Ontario, The Vivian Beaumont Theatre in Lincoln Center, New York City, The MacGowan Theatre on the UCLA campus in Los Angeles, and The John F. Kennedy Center in Washington, D.C., to mention only a few. The fact that these are not localized in a particular section of the country is indicative of the scope of the movement. New scenic ideas, such as rear projection, and modern sound equipment are already in use. An ambitious director, joined by a forward-looking group, deserves to experiment with forms other than the proscenium stage.

The thrust stage of the Tyrone Guthrie Theatre is used effectively in this scene from The Tempest, *produced by the Minnesota Theatre Company. (Courtesy of the Tyrone Guthrie Theatre)*

Various Stages

In order to clarify different types of stages other than proscenium, let us get back to the actor-audience relationship:

1. When the audience is seated on *one* side of the acting area and the actors are set in a frame, that is *proscenium* staging.

2. Eliminate the picture frame, the curtain, the borders, and the wings, and that is *open*, or *end*, staging.

3. Seat the audience on *three* sides of the acting area and that is *thrust*, or *horseshoe*, staging.

4. Seat the audience on *four* sides of the acting area and that is *circle*, or *center*, staging.

5. Which brings us to early primitive stage.

Now let us read a few details on each, beginning with the most prominent theatre—the proscenium stage. It is not the oldest form of staging when compared with the "new"—which is incredibly old. Previously we have concluded that theatre consists of an audience, some actors, and a story. These are the exact elements, *and the only ones,* that primitive man used to make drama.

Some years ago, playwright Lynn Riggs took me to see a corn festival performed by the Santa Fe Indians. Set in an open space before their tribal hogans, an "audience" of nearly a thousand Indians stood in a great circle around the "actors," who wore masks and enacted a story to the accompaniment of drums and chants, as was done by primitive man thousands of years ago. *Here was a dance-drama being enacted in a central staging area with the audience on all sides of the actors.*

It was also primitive man who contributed the Maypole or some symbol around which festivals were performed. To all intents and purposes, such symbols might be considered as man's first attempt at scenery—for what is a setting but a symbol of a place?

Central Staging Today

Also known as arena, center, environmental, theatre-in-the-round, island, and circus staging, an example of central staging today is The Arena Stage in Washington, D.C.

In primitive staging, actors were on a level with the audience; but in today's center or arena theatres, the actors may be raised above, or placed below, the level of the audience. This variation may be provided for permanently in the architecture or so adapted by using platforms. The Arena Stage in Washington, D.C., has steeply banked rows of 750 seats.

The "circle" of circle theatre may be a square, an oval, a rectangle, or *any acting area which is surrounded on four sides by an audience.*

For those who would like to experiment in center staging but do not have such a facility, the only unconditional requirement is a room large enough to accommodate both an acting and a seating area. Even this might be scaled to how many spectators you will care to seat. Lodge rooms, gyms, classrooms, storerooms, and even garages have been used. Chairs or benches may be placed on floor level, but sight lines will be improved if the audience is seated higher or lower than the actors. In space staging, everyone has the best seat in the house. In either case, differences in height are accomplished by the use of platforms. The circular or four-sided arrangement must provide at least two aisles, but four would be better. These are not only for use by the audience, but they will also serve as entrances and exits for the actors. Place the seats away from the walls of the

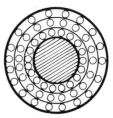

Primitive

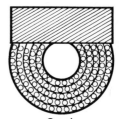

Greek

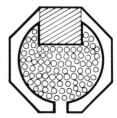

Elizabethan (Thrust)

Proscenium

Circle or Arena

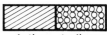

Acting   Audience
Space

At left, the original Arena Stage in Washington, D.C., with properties set for Mother Courage. (*Photo by R. Norman Matheny, Staff Photographer, The Christian Science Monitor*) Above, Tufts University production of Under Milkwood *in an arena theatre.* (*Courtesy of Tufts Arena Theatre*)

room if possible, as this space will be found invaluable for actors to get from one entrance to another. Lights and support stands need not be concealed or masked in any way. Audiences accept the mechanics of space staging, and in fact, enjoy them. They are considered part of the non-illusionary theatre.

Space Settings

As mentioned earlier, one of the advantages of center, thrust, and open (or end) staging is that by returning to the simpler procedures of early stage-craft, the almost prohibitive costs of present production can be greatly minimized.

In proscenium staging, settings usually extend the entire width of the stage; but in space staging, the sets are confined to a smaller area with less material and labor involved. Settings for open or end productions consist of self-supporting units or screens which are hinged or clamped together in desired forms. There are several techniques which might be used for construction of various types of screens. In Richard Southern's *Stage Setting* (London: Faber & Faber, 1967), there is an entire section on this, giving detailed instructions for building different constructions. Hub Electric of Chicago publishes bulletins by James Hull Miller with information adapted exclusively to open or end scenic devices. In any space theatre the director cannot be expected to duplicate the scenic requests indicated by the author at the beginning of the playscript. Settings will need to be adapted to the environment of the stage. The director should be free to use his imagination to provide what is best for the play and his production; however—*anything used must be functional and not illusionistic!*

If a door, a fireplace, or a window is absolutely necessary, these may be constructed as outlines and set into the aisle openings after the audience has been seated. Bamboo strips make excellent material for arches and windows. If the room has sufficient height, set pieces may be suspended above until needed. An outdoor setting may be simulated by using low hedges, benches, and mounds. Bed and living room sets should *only be suggested* by using a few pieces which are low and centrally located.

Floor coverings assume more importance than in proscenium staging, especially if the audience is seated above the acting level. A floor cloth might be painted to represent tiles, bricks, or planking, or it might be decorated in angular color patterns for surrealistic or more imaginative drama. Grass mats or leaves could be used to suggest a forest or garden. At any rate, the flooring or ground cloth can indicate "a place" and not interfere with the view of the audience, but flats, windows, practical doors, high-backed chairs, cupboards, and mirrors are not suitable for space staging.

Set Changing on Space Stages

There are several ways in which this may be done quickly, although it will be found that changing sets is not the complicated task it is in the realistic theatre. If set pieces are used, they should be assembled on smaller units and made portable by using rubber casters. In this way a large structure can be assembled from the smaller units, each unit to be handled by one person. As in the Oriental theatre, stage hands may be visible and work in view of the audience if they are dressed in inconspicuous uniforms. Changes may also be made during intermissions, or in the dark if exits are marked with luminous paint.

At the beginning of the play, the audience must be oriented as to the direction of important areas. Once an aisle is indicated as the passage to the garden, this must be maintained throughout the play. Because of the importance of entrances and exits during rehearsals, each aisle should be given a symbol, such as A, B, C, D or N, E, S, W or the numbers on a clock. In the absence of realistic scenery, and because the actors face more than one direction of audience, some point of reference should be established. This cannot be done by locating other actors, as on the proscenium or end stages. Identification with the aisles seems the most effective method of directing the actors' positions, and should be so indicated in blocking and in the director's book. The terms right, left, upstage, dress, counter, etc., have little meaning in space staging. Also, actors can never be "discovered at rise," as in proscenium staging, but must make entrances or find places in the dark which are then suddenly illuminated.

Lighting in the New Staging

What differentiates the center, open, or thrust forms from the proscenium are: an economy of means and a radical difference in the actor-audience relationship. The boxed-in conventional theatre is confining, closing off space. In contrast, the space stages are free, always in flux, and much more dynamic. In such nonrealistic theatres, lighting has assumed more importance than merely illuminating the set and faces of the actors. In the recent developments, lighting has become part of the drama itself. Donald Oenslager has written: ". . . light became far more than a naturalistic medium toward a realistic end. The audience could see far more than eye to eye with the actor, for it was discovered that light was an emotional and dramatic medium, capable of infinite expression, as subtle as a whispered phrase or as obvious as a comic strip.[1]

What follows is not intended to be technical or specific, or to recommend any light plan or equipment. The objective is only to inform those unfamiliar with the newer lighting concepts as applied to space staging. We must accept at once that the basic philosophy in this case begins with simplicity.

A director need not be a master of every technical craft of the stage. If he were, he would only jeopardize his own specialty. Selling tickets, building sets, and estimating electric power requirements, or knowing how to get the distortions out of a Linnebach,[2] are elements that should be in the hands of capable, responsible people. This sort of advice often instigates the standard reaction, "That's all very well for some, but we're small. If I don't do everything myself, it simply isn't done!" A director needs to value his own time better than that and to depend upon organizing help. Many people will be only too happy to assist if properly approached. Theatre is a social, cooperative venture.

However, a director should have enough knowledge of each craft of the stage so that he understands the particular problems and is familiar with the tools used in each craft. Should he want to change the position of a light during a "tech rehearsal," he should be able to identify the light by name and know what it can and cannot do.

Modern theatrical lighting for thrust or central staging is achieved chiefly by lighting *zones*. Older lighting logistics for the proscenium stage had to deal primarily with illuminating the realistic sets which spanned the stage from side to side. Space staging with its structures arranged in free-form designs do not fill the entire stage, but have space all around them to accommodate exciting new effects in light.

These are the stimulating possibilities of space staging, and there is much more to be gained. And think what we lose—the old front act curtain, the cyclorama cloth, backdrops, ceiling, overhead rigging, and all the dusty passementerie of the proscenium theatre.

Zone lighting can provide effects similar to the long shot, pan, or close-up of films. This is important if we are to catch the interest of a generation accustomed to film and TV.

It is impossible to deal here in specific plans for lighting or to suggest what light units would be needed for particular stages. Texts which are more technically oriented will be listed under Further Reading, but final decisions will need to be made on an individual basis.

[1]Donald Oenslager, *Scenery Then and Now* (New York: Russell & Russell, 1966).
[2]*Linnebach*: The simplest type of direct beam projector with a frame holding cut-outs, painted glass, or anything which will project a soft-edged image.

The Importance of Light for Space Stages

In circle staging we know that particular areas of the acting space will be more important than others. We also know that the distribution of light is more effectively divided into small zones of different intensities. This will allow for flexibility of movement and will affect the way the director plans the movements of his actors. In lighting this type of stage, a very general concept would be to think of light as serving three functions.

1. BACKLIGHTING

To separate forward areas from the background, to add depth to the stage picture, and to outline the actors. (In open or proscenium staging, backlighting is also used to illuminate scenery, cycs, or drops.)

2. SUBJECTIVE LIGHTING

This means lighting the subjects of most interest to the audience.

3. FRONTAL (OR FILL) LIGHTING

This source highlights the actors' faces as well as raising the general illumination for better vision for the audience. It will be noted that this concept of separating the subject from the background and adding highlights from the front is the exact method used in portrait photography.

The director will find that properly placed and controlled light and well chosen colors will contribute much toward creating a mood or an atmosphere. In central staging it is important that the light does not spill into the faces of spectators in the first rows of seats. The type of room and the equipment available make it almost impossible to give any arbitrary rules regarding lighting. In open, end, or proscenium stages, backlighting assumes more importance than it does in center or thrust staging. However, in all cases, for more modern staging, it is important to provide the means to dim or black out acting areas. This control should be independent of the house lights, as in central staging, the blackout or dim-out replaces the old act curtain. Any licensed electrician can devise a system which will comply with local safety codes. Manufacturers of lighting equipment may also be consulted, but in this instance one must be careful not to be sold more equipment than is needed. In center staging it is not necessary to conceal or mask lighting equipment. Not every organization can afford expensive equipment. Many beginning center theatre groups have even improvised temporarily by installing sockets and bulbs into gallon or half-gallon cans.

The Control Board

The most difficult single item to obtain and, therefore, the most costly, is likely to be the control board. This presents a problem to a group just beginning with only modest funds. But studio photographers and display and exhibition organizations use similar control boards, and it might be possible to rent or purchase one no longer used from such an organization, at least until your group is in better financial position. Removing the control board from behind the proscenium to the rear of the "house" is another innovation of the newer theatres.

The importance of lighting in space staging cannot be overestimated, especially for those who have been accustomed to the comparatively simple task of lighting sets on the proscenium stage where illumination is more or less stable. Lighting, of course, will not insure a fine production and neither will possession of a control board. It is the imagination of the director, the spirit of the group that works miracles. I know of one group who learned of an old piano crate type dimmer which was stored in a manufacturer's warehouse. Upon inquiring, they found the owner willing to present them with the control box, and all it cost was the cartage and two season tickets. Nothing seems impossible to a group determined to have their own theatre.

Blocking for Space Staging

Most directors find that blocking movement for end stages is not too different from blocking on a proscenium stage. Ground plans are similar; it is only that the picture frame is removed. But in thrust staging, visual dynamics are altered. The line parallel to the footlights is discarded and characters quite literally step out of the picture frame.

For center staging the directorial perspective must again be altered. He must now be conscious that his action will be completely surrounded. He must think in terms of the circle. Rather than move about the house at rehearsals surveying the action from the audience's view, as he must in a conventional theatre, the director might consider sight lines from the positions of the actors. If an actor can see the audience during an important scene, the audience can certainly see him, but if he is blocked by furniture or other actors, the director should restage that particular scene. Perhaps the essence of central staging is that the focus of interest must influence all movement around it, and when the attention of the audience is sought elsewhere, then the movement must be made to indicate the new focus.

In thrust staging, the director should visualize that the audience is now surrounding the actor on three sides. The exact degree of this arc will depend upon the relationship of the seating arrangement to the playing space. Obviously, spectators seated in different positions in the house are going to see different action and have different impressions. Therefore, the director should consider positions which will be viewed from half a circle instead of the proscenium triangle.

As in all else with the space stage, simplicity and practicality will be the keynotes in placing furniture. Only pieces which are a necessity should be used. They should be placed so that there is no chance that they will block entrances or exits and there should be ample passage room around each piece of furniture. Groupings of furniture for important scenes should be placed a little off-center with smaller pieces at the edges of the playing space. Characters not predominate in a scene should be placed around the periphery and remain motionless while facing the more active characters. The director should move the action and movement outward, toward the audience, instead of toward the center of the stage as in the proscenium theatre.

Exits and entrances are problems in timing for the director. Center theatre is an action theatre. More motivated movement and a faster tempo is required than on the enclosed stage. Moves by individuals should be curved, not direct, and the placement of characters should be rotated frequently so that different actors are visible to the spectators at different times.

Acting on Center Stages

On the conventional proscenium stages, actors are required to "open up" and be conscious of sight lines even in scenes of direct confrontation. But more normal, face-to-face positions are possible in center staging. Makeup and costumes must be faultless and characterizations must be constantly maintained. On a conventional stage an actor may be placed in an inconspicuous position, but in central staging, the director cannot count on much aesthetic distance between players and spectators. As a result, actors must acquire a subtlety and reserve in emotion. But actors will find that enthusiasm and warmth are less difficult to project than on the proscenium stage.

The advantages gained in space staging cannot be taken without some problems. One of these, especially for a director, is learning how to use the aisles effectively. The natural tendency is to consider aisles as a part of "the house." This is untrue in central staging. They are part of the acting area and actors must be in character the instant they are visible to the audience. Aisles are also used to position subordinate or inactive characters who must remain on stage and yet not block the view of the audience. Such actors should be placed with their backs to the aisle and remain motionless with their attention focused upon the important action.

Those working in space staging for the first time find it difficult to adjust quickly to the new and different sight lines. In more conventional staging the actor has learned to concentrate his efforts toward the front. This technique must be unlearned as spectators on one side should not be favored while others are deprived of seeing anything but the back of the actor's head. Unfortunately, this cannot always be prevented, and it will happen now and then during a performance, but it should not be so for the duration of any long scene. The solution to this problem is action. However, activity should not be mistaken for action. Action must be the result of some motivation—attitudes, moods, or reactions of a character to what is happening. Motivations can often be found in the author's lines; if not, they must be supplied by the director or actor.

The intimacy of the actor-audience relationship in space staging, whether center, end, or thrust, does not mean that the actors need not project their voices. True, less volume is required, but the actors must always make sure that their voices reach the spectators on three or four sides instead of just one. Various levels of projection should be tried, as each theatre will be individual and again different when spectators are present.

It is important that scenes vital to the action of the play are seen and heard by as many of the spectators as possible. Such scenes should be played so that inactive characters have their backs against dead spaces, such as set pieces or an aisle.

Actors should consider their positions in center staging as part of a constantly changing series of movements, in which one character moves into the central focus of the audience, then gives way to another, returning to the periphery of the circle, until he again has the dominant lines, and only then, when needed, will he weave back into the central area.

The intensity of concentration possible for the spectators by their proximity to the action might be compared to the effect of looking through a microscope. Every detail is enlarged. Costumes, makeup, and characterizations all must pass the most minute scrutiny. Fakery, acting clichés, and mannered speech, which might pass unnoticed on a proscenium stage, will be observed on a center stage. Here there is no aesthetic distance. The spectators are within arm's distance.

New ventures are constantly plagued by insufficient funds. Of all forms of staging, a circle theatre remains the simplest, and therefore the least expensive to set up. The cost of renting a hall or a tent is far less than the cost of renting a theatre. That is only one consideration. Another is that most established theatre plants with prosceniums have union commitments.

A great deal of work will be required to change a hall into the simplest center theatre, but all things considered, it will provide the advantage of having your own showplace, and at minimal expense. If the venture is successful in finding its own audience, then that support will provide the means for better facilities. All directors should avail themselves of the many possibilities of nonrealistic staging. Even those loyal to the proscenium arch might do well to adapt some of the more exciting space stage techniques to use within their picture frames.

Plays for Space Stages

Formerly, space staging was believed suitable only to the classics. The plays of Shakespeare, Molière, and Greek poets were never written for, nor intended to be produced on, the proscenium stage. They have an affinity to almost any form *except* the Italian picture frame.

All sorts of plays are produced today on center or thrust stages. When a director uses a little ingenuity and imagination, he need not hesitate to consider almost any play, and especially those which one would not ordinarily think possible to produce. Plays of intimacy or pageantry, or those depending greatly upon mood or atmosphere, are effective because of the proximity of the audience. All that is needed is that the director be resourceful.

An individual might live a lifetime without ever attending the theatre.

Tyrone Guthrie produces on an Edinburgh open stage. (Reprinted from Norman Marshall, The Producer and the Play)

He has entertainment in movies and that comfortable commodity, TV. But by denying himself theatre, he would also be depriving himself of something much needed by humans, that sharing of experience with others of their kind; and the feeling that one can reach out and touch the actors provides an almost personal, physical experience with the situation and events of the play.

Central staging in a small theatre, Croyden, England. (Reprinted from Norman Marshall, The Producer and the Play)

The Eclectic Modern Stage

In many ways the new theatres being built and in use today are full of contradictions, conversions, and composites. An example is the Vivian Beaumont Theatre in Lincoln Center for the Performing Arts in New York City. This theatre is electronically controlled to change platforms and seating, converting it into either a thrust or proscenium stage. And the Ahmanson

137

Above, elevation of the thrust stage, Mark Taper Forum in Los Angeles. At left, the stage as transformed in an artist's sketch for the production of The Metamorphoses. *(Photos courtesy of the Center Theatre Group, Mark Taper Forum, Los Angeles, Calif.)*

Theatre in Los Angeles, when used as a thrust stage, also uses the house aisles as entrances, exits, or acting areas for the actors, which was not possible in the first proscenium theatres.

There are many other instances of blending between the old and the new. But our immediate concern is not with theatrical history. We can only pay our respects to old forms and then concentrate upon what is happening today—to the points of similarities and differences. Let us try to chart some of these.

TABLE OF CONTRASTS
FOR CENTER AND THRUST STAGES

Contrasting	Center	Thrust
Facility	Minimum seating. No curtain (lighting only). May or may not have raised stage.	1,000 or more seats. No curtain in front, but may have some at rear. Typical raised stage.
Settings, Costumes	Carefully detailed costumes, props. Functional, low furniture. Settings: limited to screens, "constructive" windows and doors.	Elaborate costumes. Functional furniture and props. Settings: architectural background. Back wall for cyc, projections, or painted drop.
Blocking	Directed toward 360° angle.	Directed toward 180° angle.
Acting	Actors surrounded by spectators. Acting style dependent upon play.	Audience on three sides of actors. Acting style dependent upon play.
Direction	Freedom of movement. Advance to center, strong position. Peripheral movement. Use of aisles for exits and entrances.	Strong position CS. Other positions similar to proscenium stage, *Tyring*° room at rear, side entrances and exits depending on facility.°°

°*Tyring* room is Elizabethan playhouse term for "attiring" or dressing room.
°°Many new thrust facilities have revived the *vomitoria* or entrance/exits passages, cut through and/or under the seating areas.

The Proscenium Stage

We come now to the latest theatre form, which seems so old to us because it is theatre as most of us have known it.

Shortly after the death of Shakespeare, the Puritans gained power in England and were able to have all theatrical performances prohibited. All existing thrust stages were torn down. Much later, when the ban was removed and new theatres were built, many innovations were introduced, all based upon the rococo Italian theatres, including the proscenium arch and painted, realistic scenery. This has dominated plays and players to this day.

We must understand that the picture frame with its elaborately painted perspectives, its wood wings and footlights, was to the Restoration playgoer a novel and refreshing form of theatre. But, we have had the proscenium for so long that our attitude toward it has grown jaded.

Although we have briefly covered the proscenium stage throughout this book, let us now review its outstanding characteristics and contrast it in outline form with other historically popular forms. In the proscenium theatre:

1. There is always a raised platform or stage with space between it and the spectators. (Footlights, orchestra pit, etc.)

2. The stage is always framed by either a square, a rectangle, or an arch. In older theatres there were doors on each side of the opening permitting passage from house to backstage. Two-tier boxes on each side are also typical.

3. Curtains and asbestos drops are required.

4. There is limited audience view except for selected seats near center and in front.

5. The picture frame is meant to provide greater illusion so that the audience feels it is visiting real people and seeing them in real life situations.

6. Wings, drops, borders, flats, and ceilings are typical of realistic decor, and for outdoor scenes scenery is painted to imitate brickwork, street scenes, trees, rocks, and buildings.

7. It is proper that actors be "discovered" at rise of curtain, or make entrances through painted canvas or wooden doors or when "outdoors" through wood wings.

8. To retain the illusion of reality, all mechanics of the stage, anything that might interfere with the picture of reality, are hidden or "masked."

TABLE OF CONTRASTS
FOR SPACE AND PROSCENIUM STAGES

Contrasting	Open, Center, or Thrust Stage	Enclosed or Proscenium stage
Acting	Adaptable to realistic or nonrealistic styles.	Realistic.
Audience	Clear view of all action.	There is only one plane from which *all* action can be seen.
Equipment	Less equipment and simpler.	Border, house, and foot lights typical.
Contact	Provides ideal actor-audience relationship.	Audience contact from front only.
Costs	Cheapest.	Most costly of all forms.
Age	Oldest forms.	17th-18th century innovations°
Settings	Need only functional pieces.	Illusionistic; can get very elaborate when aim is to detail real life.
Direction	Greater freedom of movement; experimental; blocking for three sides in thrust or end stages, four in center stages.	Traditional moves; strong and weak stage positions; confined movement; blocking for front only.

°Teatro Farnaze, 1618, in Parma, had a permanent proscenium arch.

Summary

Thrust and end stages, as they exist today, are more modernly equipped and spacious than the older proscenium stages. But central staging seems more confined to modest houses and makeshift equipment. Reasons for the great upsurge of interest in space stages are many, but chief among these would be the following:

1. The costs involved in mounting a proscenium production today have become almost prohibitive except for musicals and instant shock successes. A center stage production seems the most reasonable of all.

2. Playwrights, actors, and directors have been unable to add anything to revive the interest of the public in proscenium productions. Each year there are fewer and fewer of these productions, probably because the distinctive realistic character of the proscenium stage has been acquired by TV and films.

3. There is no place left where beginning playwrights and aspiring actors and directors can learn their professions. By establishing their own theatres in lodge halls, churches, and storerooms, ambitious youngsters eliminate high theatre rental costs, expenses for scenery, and union restrictions. If this could not be done, new talent would be eliminated before it could be developed.

4. Judging by the great variety of drama being presented on thrust and center stages, there appear to be no restrictions on any type of play which can be done. Sophocles, Molière, and Shakespeare are favorites and have an affinity to this type of staging, but O'Neill, Shaw, Wilde, Brecht, Wilder, Ibsen, and Chekhov have also been given noteworthy productions.

There is no one form of theatre which is the only true artistic form. Let good actors today play in a barn or in a theatre, tomorrow at an inn or inside a church, or, in the Devil's name, even on an expressionistic stage; if the place corresponds with the play, something wonderful will be the outcome.

—Max Reinhardt

Further Reading: Different Stages

Baker, Hendrik. *Stage Management and Theatre Craft*. New York: Theatre Arts Books, 1968.

Boyle, Walden. *Central and Flexible Staging*. Los Angeles: University of California Press, 1956.

Corry, Percy. *Planning the Stage*. London: Isaac Pitman & Sons, 1961.

Davis, Jed. *Planning the Stage*. New York: Harper's Magazine Press, 1960. Simple homemade lighting and sound devices, manual dual turntables, dimmers, etc.

Dyer, Ernest F. *Producing School Plays*. London: Nelson, 1959. Clear and practical.

Gassner, John. *Producing the Play*. New York: Dryden Press, 1953. See "Arena Stage," pp. 543–600.

Heffner, Hurbert C.; Selden, Samuel; and Sellman, Hunton D. *Modern Theatre Practice.* New York: Appleton-Century-Crofts, 1959. See "Lighting," chapter 14.

Joseph, Steven. *New Theatre Forms.* New York: Theatre Arts Books, 1959.

Jones, Margo. *Theatre-in-the-Round.* New York: Holt, Rinehart & Winston, 1951.

Mielziner, Jo. *The Shapes of Our Theatres.* New York: Clarkson N. Potter, 1970.

Mitchell, Roy. *Shakespeare for Community Theatres.* London: J. M. Dent & Sons, 1919.

Napier, Frank. *Curtains for Stage Settings.* London: Muller, 1949.

Oenslager, Donald. *Scenery Then and Now.* New York: Russell & Russell Publishers, 1966.

Parker, Oren, and Smith, Harvey. *Scene Design and Stage Lighting.* New York: Holt, Rinehart & Winston, 1963.

Richards, Mary. *Practical Play Production.* London: Evans, 1943. Especially good on curtain fit-ups.

Southern, Richard. *Proscenium and Sight Lines.* London: Faber & Faber, 1939.

Somerscales, Marjorie. *The Improvised Stage.* London: Pitman, 1932. Especially for little theatres.

Wilson, Angus. *The Small Stage and its Equipment.* London: Allen & Unwin, 1930. 130 pages on setting and lighting small stages; illustrated.

Wilson, Angus, and Ridge, Harold. *The Planning of a Stage.* London: 1932. In small halls; in little theatres.

OTHER STUDIES

Abbott, Stanley. "Arena Lighting, Four Methods." *The Theatre Annual.* Vol. 22, 1965–66, p. 76. Cleveland: Press of the Western Reserve University, 2029 Adelbert Road.

Burin, Jarka. "A Case for Arena Theatre." *The Theatre Annual*, Vol. 22, 1965–66, p. 65.

Kook, Edward F. *Images in Light for the Living Theatre.* Ford Foundation Studies in the Creative Arts, 1963. A survey of the use of scenic projection with letters from well-known directors regarding light images.

Lounsbury, Warren. "Dichroic Filters and Quartz Lights." *Educational Theatre Journal*, March 1963, p. 73.

Perry, John. "The Enigma of Flexible Staging." *The Educational Theatre Journal*, December 1965, p. 335.

CATALOGUE

The Edmund *Unique Lighting Handbook* # 9100, $3.00 postpaid and latest catalogue. Edmund Scientific Co., 300 Edscorp, Barrington, N.J. 08007.

Theatre Personnel

The Director's Colleagues

When he leaves his private world in which he has created his image of the production, the director will begin working with people of different temperaments and interests. He will describe to his staff and actors the sights and sounds and emotional content of his concept. It should not be described in one dimension but from many angles: the setting, the sounds, the emotional impact, the characters, and the story. This will be the spirit of the play, its very sum and substance. It is most important that the director be able to inspire all concerned by his own enthusiasm and excitement for the production. If this current of involvement and dedication is successfully passed on from him to his staff, then they in turn will be able to relay their excitement to an audience.

The Director's Staff

Once a director has chosen his play and studied it in relation to the stage on which it will be produced, he is ready for the next logical step, which is the organization of his staff. This should not be delayed until a later date. Scenery may need to be designed, built, and painted. Furniture and props, costumes, scripts, and lights must be procured, and all of this must be done within a few weeks' time.

A knowledgeable director delegates the responsibility for such work to reliable people and does not attempt to put on a one-man show. His energies must be saved for the formidable task of directing and supervising the entire production. The mechanics of directing may be learned, but the sheer physical energy required is considerable and will be needed to combat such problems as temperament, frustrations, and fatigue. Too many directors expend themselves upon details which might be accomplished just as well by others; and the latter way is certainly more democratic.

But the director must use careful and considered judgment in choosing members of his staff. Only those he knows to be willing, capable, and reliable should be appointed. The next step is to inform them of his concept of the production and make sure that some of his enthusiasm is transmitted to them. Unless unavoidable, members of the staff and the stage crew should not be assigned parts in the play. They will be needed at final rehearsals, just when they are needed for technical work. Naturally, each director will have his own preferences as to the organization of his staff, but the following may serve as a guide:

Professional Theatre[3] Chain-of-Command

General Objectives: The management of business, artistic elements, and crafts.

BUSINESS:

In Charge: Director or producer

Financing, capital, investors.

Assisting: Company manager

Accounting, purchasing, box office, tickets, passes, rentals, salaries.

Press representation

---

[3]Some larger universities have staffs as elaborate as this.

Promotion, advertising, photos, publicity, passes, critics, program copy, posters.

ARTISTIC:

In charge: Director

Assisting staff: Production or stage manager

Designer

Responsible for the visual arts, works with crew, heads of crafts, costumes, props, sets, lighting, painting.

CRAFTS:

In Charge: Stage Manager

Head of craftsmen, actors, rehearsals, dressing rooms, backstage, etc.

Assistants: Prompter, call boy

Set up rehearsal, furniture, and props. Give actors their rehearsal calls.

After opening, the stage manager is responsible for performances being "kept up" and is in full charge.

ARTISTS:

Actors

Maintain performance standards. Furnish biography, photos to Promotion Department. Abide by backstage laws.

Outside the professional and university theatres, few directors will need such an elaborate staff. But even in the most modest theatre, one staff position is of vital importance—the director's adjutant:

The Stage Manager

An early appointment of a stage manager will relieve the director of many noncreative details. He will be of inestimable help during casting and rehearsals as well as during the production. He should be chosen because he is reliable, can assume authority without becoming officious, is responsible, and is dedicated to the theatre. It will also help if he is ingenious, as there will be many occasions when the director will depend upon his resourcefulness. Sometimes he is given the title of assistant director, but rarely in the professional theatre.

During staff conferences with the director, one of the stage manager's first duties will be to reserve the conference room, provide chairs, table, paper and pencils, and manuscripts. A more modest staff usually consists of a designer, a property head, chief carpenter, wardrobe mistress, electrician, business manager, and sound engineer. Each of these department heads will appoint, and be responsible for, his own assistants.

At the first staff conference, the director should explain fully his concept of the play and his plan of production. Previously the stage manager will have prepared "plots" for each department head. The designer will be furnished with a ground plot for each setting showing the director's placement of furniture and the boundaries of the acting space. The master of properties will receive a list of both hand and set props needed for each scene or act. A list of costumes required will be given the wardrobe mistress with changes of costumes noted by act or scene.

All of these lists indicate that the stage manager has already begun work on his own prompt book. This entails "breaking down" the script into units of work or "plots." Eventually, this same prompt book will include: all stage direction for actors; cast names, addresses, and phone numbers; sound, music, light, and prop cues; a schedule of rehearsals; and playing time of scenes, acts, and intermissions during the production. In fact, this book will incorporate all necessary information for the successful management of the stage during a performance. It is a "Working Prompt Book" with all *technical* details of production and rehearsals. It will not include any creative aspects of production, such as matters of interpretation. *The director's book and the prompt book serve two different purposes.* If technical and artistic information were combined in one book, that book would become so cluttered that it would be useless for either purpose.

A prompt book must be clear and legible so that it can be easily followed by the prompter, who must be ready at any time to "throw a line" to an actor. The stage manager should make up the book and hold it during rehearsals. Then when all stage directions, cuts, and additions are complete, he will then be able to pass it along to one of his assistants who will then be responsible for the prompt copy and prompting during performances. Need I say that a lost prompt book is a catastrophe?

During performances, the stage manager will have many duties backstage and should never be "on the book." There are no rules regarding prompting. In fact, some directors refuse to provide a prompter during performances, demanding that the actors learn their lines "cold." Others believe that by having a prompter in evidence in the wings, following every line of the play, the actors gain a sense of security. But during rehearsals, when the stage manager is "holding the book," it is sensible for him to prompt only when actors ask for it. The actors should be informed of this as quickly as they put down their parts and are attempting to speak from memory. Otherwise, prompting can grow into a defense mechanism. When an actor declaims, "I know the line, I know the line!" you may be quite sure that he does not. It is best that the actors ask to be prompted, and then they should be given only the key word or phrase, and *without expression.*

When performing any of the classics, and especially Shakespeare, no word substitutions should be tolerated. Many people in an audience will know their Shakespeare word for word. Errors must be corrected early so that the wrong words do not become set in the actor's memory. Rather than interrupt the flow of a scene, a written note regarding his substitutions should be given to the actor at the conclusion of the scene.

A stage manager does not train or direct actors. Even when he is substituting for the director, he should not discuss characterizations or interpretation. When the director is unavoidably detained, valuable rehearsal time might be spent on line rehearsals or walking scenes previously set by the director.

The stage manager is the major-domo of rehearsals. Some of his duties are to post time and place of rehearsals and tryouts, to check rehearsal rooms as to keys, heat, water, toilets, chairs, and scripts. At blocking rehearsals, he should see that tape is placed on the floor to indicate the boundaries of the acting space, doors, windows, and set pieces. Furniture or substitutions for important pieces should be set in place according to his ground plot. In other words, during rehearsals the stage manager is the director's right-hand man, and during performances he will "run the show."

THE
DIRECTOR
AND
THE
ACTORS 8

What a Director Should Be

A director needs to be permissive enough to allow actors to test out their ideas experimentally, and yet he must reserve the right to accept, modify, or abandon their hypotheses. Such experimental ideas originating from an actor may move a director either intellectually or emotionally; he may develop and enrich such ideas, acting, as he does, in the capacity of fellow artist and partial audience. This should be rewarding because an actor is dualistic, developing ideas from mind to matter. The director should encourage the actor to contribute, but this should never degenerate into permissiveness, in which the director loses control. It is the director who decides upon the theme of the play and how it is to be interpreted in stage terms, and it is the director who decides the mood, style, tempo, emotional impact, visual patterns, and characterizations for the entire production. It is his concept which is to be turned into theatrical reality, and therefore, he alone can decide how that idea or vision will be put into concrete form.

The director always has many duties other than working with actors, but that is certainly his most important task. He must serve as other eyes and ears for the actor during rehearsals, when the actor has no audience other than the director. Along with the actors, he searches for the main characteristics in each role, encouraging the actor's own creativity by inspiring and generating ideas. He should not only be a catalyst to the actor, but also a sounding board for all experiments and improvisations. He should also be able to guide the actor back to the main road when the actor gets lost down dark alleys of inconsequentialities.

But, he must never emulate a stern, unyielding parent. He must keep in mind that he is working with sensitive people, and he must not only encourage them to create, but also to blend into the production as a whole. He should not attempt to stamp out characters according to his own steel die, like so many plastic soldiers. The wise director knows the value in keeping a loose rein and realizes that he cannot drive an actor, but that reason, sympathy, and logic can work miracles. Whenever possible, he should offer several solutions to a problem and then allow the actor to choose his own, because the actor must be convinced that whatever is done is right for him and his character. When arbitrarily forced into accepting directions, the actor never makes these his own.

"That's all very well for experienced professionals," a high school director might say, "but I have students who've never set foot on a stage. I have to show them what I want done." I would answer by asking this question: "What is the main purpose of drama in the school? Is it to 'put on a show,' or is it to enrich a pupil's imagination and give him a broader understanding of human values?" I know all too well how frustrating it is to sit by and watch students flounder about. What a temptation it is to jump up on stage and show them what you want and then allow them to copy what you've done. But, they will never learn to create that way, only imitate. Do not solve all problems automatically. Teach your actors how to solve their own. Begin by offering several alternatives and allow them to choose one. The next time they may offer several solutions and allow *you* to choose the best.

A director is not only a teacher; he is also a psychologist, a politician, and a Nana. Directing, on any level, is largely a psychological process of inter-relationships. The fullest performance and involvement from either amateur or professional actor can only be attained by the director's empathetic response to the actors and their problems, and this allows for collaboration and guidance.

What a Director Should Not Be

Your success as a director is going to develop in direct ratio to what you are inside, to your empathetic response toward the play and the actors with whom you will be working.

A director who is either lazy, tired, or uninformed tends to be permissive with actors. The usual results are that the actors, or one particular actor, will fill the breech. When this happens, the production will probably turn into a starring vehicle for the one taking over. Actors are not able to see the play from any perspective. There is a conflict of interests when an actor directs and acts in the same play. For the same reason, a director should not act when directing.

There is another type of director you will not want to become. He is the one who is given to long discussions during rehearsals. His time with actors turns into open forums on many subjects from psychology to philosophy to politics. Usually, these discussions begin by being related to the work at hand, quickly drifting off into tangents until the director suddenly realizes that twenty minutes of precious rehearsal time has passed. That time might have been better used by allowing the actors to rehearse the play. The time for discussion is at the round-table meetings. Once the rehearsals begin, it is time to rehearse—for action, not talk.

Another type of director has been referred to as a drill sergeant, a strict disciplinarian who acts out all the parts and reads all the lines for his actors. Stanislavski has admitted that he was a despot when he began directing. In retrospect, Molière, Reinhardt, Belasco, George M. Cohan, and George Kaufman are generally considered as being on the arbitrary side. In contrast, Arthur Hopkins, Elliot Nugent, Gilmor Brown, and Winthrop Ames were usually receptive to ideas from actors. It is a mistake to believe that it is a director's duty to find fault with his actors. His most challenging task will be to recognize and then develop strengths. Avoid shouting or using sarcasm in your critiques. Criticism must be handled in a constructive, not destructive, manner.

To return to the original thought, the director's motivations, his personal convictions about directing, what he is inside, and his feelings toward a play will always be obvious in his work. His approach, the environment he creates at rehearsals, and the way the play is presented to an audience finally represent his individual style. Mike Nichols' work could never be mistaken for Peter Brook's. In films, Fellini, Bergman, and Hitchcock leave their trademarks on all their work. In fact, the director's name is often featured today rather than the actor's.

Is the Captain on the Bridge?

Most readers will agree that there is much truth in the old bromide that it takes all kinds of people to make a world. Some actors respond quickly to logical suggestions, while others need to be stimulated by involved improvisations. When one technique fails, the director must be resourceful enough to find another. The intellect, the physical, and the emotional work together as one effort in the acting process, and yet the director may need to separate one from the others in order to achieve a satisfying result. One student might be approached intellectually, another emotionally, and another purely through physical exercises. This will mean that from the beginning, the director must gain the respect of his actors by demonstrating that he knows what he is talking about. Tempered by courtesy and patience, his remarks should leave no doubt that he is the final authority and that he expects the work to proceed in an orderly and intelligent manner.

But a director may find himself in a situation where he must deal with temperament or a star complex in an egocentric individual. This is especially true when the velvet glove treatment has been used. Remember that the velvet glove should have an iron fist inside it. Because the director is in command, he must not hesitate to eliminate discordant personalities, and to do so *as early as possible*! This is the iron fist. No cast member must be allowed to believe that he is indispensable. The star system no longer exists in the professional theatre, and it certainly should not be encouraged among amateurs. It is a disservice to tolerate temperament in a trainee. Since the professional theatre will stand for no such nonsense, it is your responsibility as director to teach students the necessity for a community of interests. If not, the profession may not have the tolerance or understanding you might give him.

As director you may do much in setting an example through your own behavior. You must be able to feel emotion and also be able to control it. This implies that you never show fits of rage, and this may prove more difficult for you, who have complete responsibility for the production, than it will be for an actor playing a part. Your field of irritation will be much wider. When you sense that your emotions are beginning to take control, it is then you must remember that you may be jeopardizing the entire production. Raging and shouting is not the way to bring out a performance from a reserved but feeling actor. Your goal should be to become the kind of director who is scholarly enough to make an in-depth study of the play, sensible enough to listen to others, and wise enough to know that art without discipline is impossible.

Once you are in rehearsal you cannot afford doubts about the play, your interpretation of it, your ability to produce it, and above all, in your actors to perform it. Some actors will need more rigid control than others. But those playing smaller parts cannot be given as much of your time as those in the leading roles. And yet each, in proportion, should be made to feel that he is part of the creativity. In fact, each member of the cast should know that he can ask you a question and that if you cannot answer at once, you will give the matter some thought and reply later. They should regard you as a colleague, not a judge. It will be a great asset if you can gain, and maintain, the respect of your cast.

Directing Incentives

Although all of the above applies to most directors, there are individual circumstances which might alter the approach. There are three general fields of occupation for directors and each is specialized. This is born out by the fact that there is little free traffic from one field to another. In America today, we have the professional, the educational, and the avocational theatres. A director might be gainfully employed in any one of the three, so that differences which exist cannot be based upon the amateur or professional standing of the director. Having accepted that most stage directors are professionals, we must consider that some work with professional actors while others are involved with drama students, or amateurs—and this is the vital point of difference.

A Director in the Professional Theatre

Usually the director working with Equity actors has himself started as an amateur, and then distinguished himself by some individual effort. Some have been well known actors, such as Orson Welles, Elia Kazan, or Mike

Nichols. Others may have been trained in television or have been graduates of a college with a respected theatre arts department and then gone on themselves to organize modest but exciting groups.

The point is that all have distinguished themselves and gained a reputation by their own efforts. One seldom finds a request in the want ads for a stage director. And it rarely happens any more that a director is hired because he is the producer's brother-in-law. It is only logical that no one is going to provide a play, a theatre, actors, technicians, scenery, and a salary to an inexperienced director. Broadway, films, and TV are commercial in every sense of the word; that is, success is determined either by the box office or by sales of a sponsor's products.

Ron Rifkin (in wheelchair), Carrie Snodgrass, and Sheree North circle the stage in a nightmarish race as Nehemiah Persoff returns home in Rosenbloom *by Harvey Perr, produced by the Mark Taper Center Theatre Group. (Courtesy of the Center Theatre Group, Mark Taper Forum, Los Angeles, Calif.)*

In the commercial theatre a director works with actors who try to make a living by acting, and he will be expected to respect their professionalism. They may only be Equity apprentices, but they usually pretend they have played a long string of important parts in some remote repertory companies. They are very impressed with their professionalism and expect others to be impressed with their training and experience. These actors may be complete strangers to a director, but that director will be expected to work with each one according to the actor's own method. And there are as many "methods" as there are method teachers. Some actors can be told to enter

151

through door up right, and it will be done; another will ask why, and everything must be made believable to him.

"I don't do tricks, I'm a method actor!"

In working with the novice actor, a director can best identify the actions of a character by relating it to the actor's own reality. For instance, in order to help the amateur plan an emotional scene, it is often related to the actor's own experience. But the professional is supposed to know the tools of his trade. Because the actor believes he is thoroughly trained and experienced, he may expect the director to explain the effect he hopes to achieve rather than suggest the means of accomplishing it.

Whether he is working with amateurs or professionals, the ultimate objectives of the director will be the same, but the *means* of accomplishing these objectives will be different.

Therefore, it becomes a matter of some importance that the director be able to understand enough of the actor's ways and means so that he can work with various techniques.

But like any other specialist, the actor has a limited field to function in, while the director is a general practitioner. The director must be careful not to narrow his larger field of interest or permit the actor to collaborate upon matters which are strictly the director's responsibility. Professional or amateur, the actor cooperates. The director collaborates.

In general, the aims of the regional professional theatres are somewhat loftier than the aims of the New York commercial theatres. Their seasons include a respectable number of classics and they do have a policy of producing new plays. Such standards are possible because of local civic pride and season subscribers. However, in order to survive, they are also dependent upon ticket sales.

The professional or amateur standing of off-off Broadway is fluid. Equity has a minimum salary concession allowed Off-Broadway. Ellen (La Mama) Stewart has said that she employs "amateur-professionals"—whatever that means. Off-off Broadway has no box office; their productions are made possible by gifts, gratuities, and "membership fees." It is interesting that the more worthwhile and experimental theatre productions are found in educational theatre and off-off Broadway, neither of which is shackled to the box office.

A Director in Avocational Theatre

Although to a lesser degree, because expenses are not so high, the community theatre must also keep its eye on the box office if it is to survive. When working in the avocational theatre, a director is apt to find cliques, and these often influence the casting. There is, of course, some justice in it. The people who do the work and support the theatre will want, and deserve to have, some influence on policies.

The community theatre director will be working with actors of various talents and experience. He may deal with the totally inexperienced amateur. In this case he will become a teacher, which should not disturb him, for what is a director, amateur or professional, but a teacher? When working with more experienced people, his concern will be to eliminate poor acting habits and clichés. Finally, a community theatre is a *social* theatre, and the director must be careful that the social part does not become more predominant than the theatre part.

A Director in Educational Theatre

For the director working in educational theatre, or preparing to do so, many questions must be answered before a clear goal can be reached. What purpose should educational theatre serve? To what extent is it education and to what extent is it theatre?

If service to education is its main function, then it should relate to educational areas such as teaching, social studies, literature, languages, and of course, related arts. But if its main function is the preparation of professional theatre personnel, then the program must include not only standards used by professional writers, directors, and actors of yesterday and today, but also new theatre forms and experimentation.

It may be the purpose of educational theatre to fill a culture vacuum which the professional theatre does not. In a complex technological society, we have created machines which reach the moon. An amoeba also creates, and all animals breed, nest, and die; but only man is conscious of self, life, and death. Art examines this consciousness. To do this may be the greatest challenge the director in educational theatre must face. Certainly no other organization is doing it.

Fortunately, educational theatre has the facilities to meet the challenges of the future. A majority of educational theatres are provided the latest theatrical equipment. They are surrounded by culture and are relatively independent of the box office. In no other country has theatre made so large a place for itself in universities and colleges as in America. Just how well this potential will be used and how the challenges will be met will depend

Educational theatre leads the way with the Tufts University Drama Department under the direction of Dr. Marston S. Balch. Above is a scene from their concept of Antigone. (*Courtesy of Tufts Arena Theatre*)

upon how the force will be used. From this training ground great playwrights, actors, and directors should emerge—artists who will equal or surpass O'Neill, Winthrop Ames, and the Barrymores. Colleges and universities should not attempt to compete with the commercial theatre. This would not only cheapen their artistic and cultural aims, but it would also put them to a disadvantage.

The importance of the director's concept in educational theatre is evidenced by the makeup and the use of an artificial hand for the character Claire, played by a student, Evadne Giannini. From the North Carolina School of the Arts production of The Visit, *directed by Ira Zuckerman. (Courtesy of the North Carolina School of the Arts)*

Critics of educational theatre tend to be more tolerant of high school drama. Nevertheless, they insist that the director functioning in grades nine through twelve has an obligation to culture, although to a lesser degree than in higher education. This leniency is granted more on a basis of the student's immaturity than on the expected aims of educational theatre.

POINTS OF DIFFERENCE BETWEEN PROFESSIONAL AND NONPROFESSIONAL ACTORS

Interest and Motivation	
The Nonprofessional	**The Professional**
Pride in group; thrill and excitement in acting before family and friends; director's enthusiasm; local attention.	Advancement of profession-career; salary incentive; pride in job well done; attention of critics and a demanding audience.
May have other activities with priority over rehearsal time.	Complete dedication to the theatre.
Director must teach theatre behavior, makeup, terminology, etc.	Knowledge and experience in theatre ways, which may or may not be an asset.
Pliable as to working methods; social, pleasure motivations.	Working methods are most often set; schedules strictly followed; businesslike.
Youthful energy and enthusiasm; stage fright; element of excitement; of playing a game.	Confidence based on experience.
Actors may be replaced at any time at director's discretion.	After seven days actor must be retained or given two weeks' salary (Equity rule).
Actors need constant reassurance by means of director's approval.	Attitude is that it is a professional's job to be good; some praise advised at selected times.
Must be taught relaxation, muscular control, discipline, characterization, voice projection, etc.	Expected to be trained and have technique in all acting elements.

Actors as Media

> We transport you into a world of intrigue and illusion
> . . . clowns, if you like, murderers—we can do you ghosts
> and battles, on the skirmish level, heroes, villains, tor-
> mented lovers. . . .
>
> —"First Player,"
> *Rosencrantz and Guildenstern are Dead*

All artists must be skilled at using the media through which they make contact with the observer. The painter uses pigments, the author uses words, and the director's chief instrument of communication is the actor. In contrast to other artists, the director's task is made especially difficult in that his media does not consist of inanimate materials, but humans, with minds and wills of their own. He must learn to understand them not only as humans and individuals, but as actors, for actors are a breed apart. Directors with teaching backgrounds usually understand and accept that they must be able to reach an individual on several levels if there is to be any effective communication. Others are impatient to get on with rehearsals, allowing no time to learn how to handle the tools which are so important to their artistic efforts.

Most individuals possess, to some degree, the ability to create genuine works of art. Those unable to do so have never devoted sufficient time in learning how it is done. Some people excel in methodology, others in having the patience and skill necessary to communicate ideas to others. Both attributes are desirable in a director.

Actors, What Are They?

Not only is the personality of each actor different from another, but today each actor varies in his acting approach as well as in his physical and imaginative capabilities. Not all actors can be handled in the same way. Some will need a great deal of encouragement, others a firm authoritative hand. But one of the stimulating rewards of directing is in the way each individual responds to his work with the director. Ideally, the director should receive as much inspiration from the actor as the actor receives from him. "There is something incomparably intimate and productive in the work with the actor entrusted to me," writes Jerzy Grotowski, director of The Polish Theatre Laboratory. "He [the actor] must be attentive and confident and free, for our labor is to explore his possibilities to the utmost. His growth is attended by observation, astonishment, and desire to help; my growth is projected into him, or, rather, is found *in him*, and our common growth becomes a revelation. . . . What is achieved is a total acceptance of one human being by another."[1]

The Acting Temperament

All actors need to grow in a vital and creative way. Characteristic of the actor's constitution is an inner personal and sensitive life. This is the creative power, or rather it is what makes that power function. This creative life has been referred to as "the God element" and is most apparent in children, revealing itself in a love for pretending. A child can easily imagine himself an astronaut setting the first foot on the moon, or some great king shouting orders to his subjects. Early schematic pretendings are usually bound up with the child's wishes, desires, or fantasies. Later, as the child matures,

[1]Jerzy Grotowski, *Towards a Poor Theatre* (Denmark: Odin Teatrets Forlag, 1968), p. 25.

the play instinct becomes more and more difficult to sustain. The demands of the practical world subdue and often truncate the faculty to arouse it.

In the life of a well adjusted adult, this same instinct may compensate for those things which the individual has been unable to achieve in real life. And when such dreams and fantasies are turned into creative channels, the individual gains emotional release and self-confidence.

The adult actor must regenerate this play instinct, whether he be amateur or professional. For the amateur, acting may be only a temporary experience, a social or school activity, but the employment of his inner creative power will be a valuable asset in developing his own character, if nothing else.

So that you, as director, can better understand the people you will be associated with, let us examine other dimensions typical of the actor's personality.

Creativity. In general, actors have a more creative approach to things than other people. An actor's thoughts are apt to be more profound, his problem-solving more imaginative and wide in scope. It is typical of the actor that his life is filled with a series of kaleidoscopic experiences. Such moments in time are, to him, indelible impressions. They may have no basis in fact, and he might even admit this, but somehow these impressions constitute the factual sum and substance of his life. It is these fantasies which the actor has a compulsion to express by his body and acting instincts.

Sensitivity. Most fine actors are known to be more sensitive to people and situations than the average individual. Some people would consider them "an easy touch." Wherever there is a "cause," you will always find actors in the front lines making speeches, protesting, and contributing funds to it.[2] Many star performers appear on benefit shows, performing gratis the same act for which they receive huge sums in Las Vegas.

Emotionality. The typical actor needs love. He must be noticed. Just as the toddler calls attention to himself, the actor seems to be saying, "Look at me, look at me!" When admired and encouraged, he extends himself and blooms with childlike ecstasy. This uncontrolled effort to gain attention causes many less emotional people to suspect that he is not quite as sane as themselves. His easy flights of imagination convince them that he is not well adjusted to everyday living, that he cannot keep household accounts, manage his money or himself in any sensible way. All successful actors pay a sizable amount of their incomes for business management. They readily admit that they are impractical. An actor with any business sense is rare indeed. An exception was the late Al Jolson. Someone once said that he was "too smart to be an actor."

Instead of facing up to unpleasant or difficult problems and devising practical means of changing them, the inner-oriented actor retreats into a fantasy world in which problems either do not exist or are solved with a Cyrano flourish. He knows that these hallucinations are not real but persist in his

[2]It also keeps them in the public eye.

Emotional stress as shown by Michael O'Sullivan as the Emperor in Fernando Arrabal's The Architect and the Emperor of Assyria, *an American Conservatory Theatre production directed by Robert Goldsby. (Photo by Hank Kranzler, courtesy of the American Conservatory Theatre of San Francisco)*

imagination because they fulfill him. Often the dream life of the stage grows into his real life.

This childlike quality in an actor seemed to be indispensable to Stanislavski:

> *The nature of the actor's creative process makes him trustful as a baby . . . his childish belief in the events of the play are an integral part of his creative talent.*[3]

Those actors who are able to move audiences never seem to lose this ability to pretend. They have either retained it since childhood or have been able to recapture it.

Threatening action in Paul Sills's The Metamorphoses. *(Courtesy of the Center Theatre Group, Mark Taper Forum, Los Angeles, Calif.)*

[3]Nikoli Gorchahov, *Stanislavski Directs* (New York: Funk & Wagnalls Co., 1954), pp. 140–141.

Children paint wonderfully. Their drawings are direct and refreshing and their use of paint is intuitive, colorful, and bold. *They do not copy nature, they re-create it.* But they grow up soon and learn to imitate nature. Then, finally, the innocence—that magic spirit of self-expression—disappears. It is that magic spirit the actor needs. The problem is that he must remain a child without ever becoming childish.

Melinda Dillon, Hamilton Camp, and Richard Schaal create "Henny Penny" in Center Theatre's production of Story Theatre, A Night of Fantastical Tales. (Courtesy of the Center Theatre Group, Mark Taper Forum, Los Angeles, Calif.)

Intelligence. There are always exceptions, of course, but most actors are several notches above the ordinary in intelligence. A large percent are actually brilliant, imaginative, articulate, and knowledgeable, with quick recall and a way of assembling words which is entertaining to a listener. Eighty percent of the personalities appearing on TV talk shows are entertainers. Most actors have a nodding acquaintance with a broad panorama of people, places, and things. Because of their vast interests and their ability to concentrate and communicate with others, some have eventually become heads of large corporations, congressmen, delegates to national and international posts, and governors.

Even so, the impression often persists that actors are not very intelligent because if they were, they would not have entered a profession so overcrowded and precarious. *Actors become actors because there is nothing else so worth doing.*

Certainly it is not entirely the search for glamour which still lures thousands of youngsters to Hollywood and New York. They no longer believe that a seat at the counter of Schwab's Drug Store may mean stardom. They know that training will be long and that the career of an actor can be defeating and heart-breaking; and yet, there is something magical and elevating about acting, and so they persist in the gamble—and a few win!

Self-confidence. Those who persist are notable for great faith in their gift and in their potential for development. These are the very dedicated ones who are not easily distracted from their goals.

The need for self-expression. The need for self-expression is not limited to the actor. Prehistoric cave paintings are evidence of man's early deep-seated desire to share his experiences with others. The tribal man demonstrated his prowess as a hunter by dance and rituals. Even today, the lawyer clarifies a point by using hypothesis; the doctor, the salesman, all demonstrate and fantasize. In fact, the general public's revival of interest in all the arts is proof of this basic human need. This is especially true of shy individuals who would not think of walking boldly into a drama class and announcing, "I want to be an actor!" He would be more apt to slip into the class on the pretense of being with a friend.

Personal relationships. It is surprising how many established actors first became involved in acting because of some friend or relative. Most high school directors are aware that many of his acting students first came to class through associates who were already part of the drama effort. Such warm personal relationships demonstrate how the actor needs contact with others. He may be gregarious or shy, but he must, at some time, have the love and interest of others.

Ego-feedback. An actor's need to express himself can only be satisfied when he succeeds in obtaining the approval of others. If he should fail in his first attempt, the true actor will try again. The director must make it possible for him to continue to have that opportunity. There have been many times when an actor has set his heart on a certain part for which I knew, as director, he had little to offer. But special concessions were made to give him every opportunity to convince me that he could play the part. I tried to keep an open mind, gave no word of discouragement, and in a few cases came to agree with the actor. But usually, after many readings, it became obvious even to the actor that he was wrong for the particular part. This kind of effort should never go completely unrewarded. The director should try to find some other part for the actor: perhaps a place on the director's staff or as understudy. The point is that this sort of enterprise and dedication is something the director hopes for but rarely gets, and it should be encouraged. But there is another type of actor who is not so desirable.

The Vanity Actor

Unfortunately, many acting candidates applying for parts are more interested in the exploitation of their own personalities than they are in developing skill as an actor. The true actor is never himself. The day of the "walk-on" is over. Today all parts are character parts. There was a time when good looks and an ingratiating personality could make a career. No longer! The public soon tires of the personality actor and the day always comes when he must learn to create characters.

A director needs to be alert in order to flush out the local "stars" and vanity actors. They can undermine and even destroy all worthy efforts to establish a hard-working and amiable group. The allegation that many applicants are more interested in self-exploitation than in acting can be tested. Announce the production of a play on a given date in a given theatre and actors will tear down your door in an attempt to be cast in that play. But announce the start of an acting workshop where actors may study and develop their art and those same ambitious youngsters will be conspicuous by their absence.

As director you will need a sixth sense to recognize those interested in showcasing their own personalities rather than working to improve themselves. If I were given a choice between a talented actor who wouldn't work and a worker with only a little talent, I would unhesitatingly choose the latter. A vanity actor will frequently unmask his true intentions in statements such as: "I've had lots of training and experience; what I need now is a part to market my wares." My dire warnings regarding those actors interested in personal aggrandizement should not be taken to mean that vanity in an actor is not part of the acting equipment. Vanity is always a part of vision.

The director should also be cautious about accepting anyone into his group who makes a special effort to disguise his feeling of incompetency by rashness and bravado. Later, at rehearsals, he is apt to present an entirely different, and even mousey, personality. Such an actor will require a great deal of the director's time and gentle handling, but if you are so inclined and feel it worth the time and effort, all well and good.

Application Blanks

In most educational theatres, applicants for casting in plays are asked to complete a mimeographed question form stating experience, time available, acting ambitions, and attitude toward theatre, in addition to the usual information, such as name, age, phone, etc. This is an excellent idea and gives the director an opportunity to appraise the applicant's sincerity and ability to work. It can save him much time, and perhaps some sorrow.

Talent

Now and then a director will encounter a person with genuine talent. That word is often used to describe an individual with unusual resources for most problems in acting. Sometimes these resources are intuitive, not easily explained. In others their gift is the result of great effort. Some are specialists, that is, they have a proclivity for one type of acting but lack the facilities for any broader efforts. Even some celebrities are creative in a special field but are not capable of any characterizations beyond the periphery of their specific field, and certainly not with anything approaching the skill used in their particular forte.

Another consideration the director should take into account is that when an actor is identified as being "talented," it means that the actor has been trained and successful under some other director. It does not guarantee that this actor will be as successful working with him. Directing actors is a process of inter-relationships. In the ideal situation, the director and the actors will have been together and worked together for some time. This is impossible when one is a free-lance director in the profession. It is quite possible in educational theatre.

When considering the creative potential in actors and the general attributes of the acting constitution, we can only examine the typical, not the exception. Later we shall deal with the underachiever, the actor who is able to be convincing and reassuring during interviews, and is cast, but then fails to show any growth during rehearsals.

THE
WORKSHOP 9

A Director's Research Center

OBJECTIVES

1. To provide an environment and techniques for relieving tensions in both the inexperienced and experienced actor.
2. To give physical textures to descriptive matter, that is, to put ideas into action.
3. To train actors in concentration, point of focus, flexibility, and working as part of an ensemble.
4. To offer a means for the actor to express something of his true self without the autocracy of the play.

We know that it is almost impossible to create any meaningful artistic work without first removing undue tensions. A student's mind and body must be receptive before he can reveal his true self. This is the foundation upon which characterization is built.

In our society most of us are constantly playing a part. It may be the person we should like to be or the one others would like us to be, or the

Physical training develops the actor's body as an instrument of communication. The Workshop group at right enacts a situation given them by Living Theatre 70 Director Robert Alexander. (Courtesy of the Living Stage, a project of the Arena Stage in Washington, D.C.)

163

part we play may be our sublimation for failure. We may masquerade as a sophisticate with a ready quip or as a reticent dignitary. But before any creative acting can be accomplished, all such pretensions must be removed along with the tensions causing them.

Once primed in physical exercises and muscular control, we may then move into the composition of characters. The body has a way of understanding that physical exercises are not a substitute for speech but an auxiliary to it. An actor must express things he would normally hide behind his defenses. He must not be concerned with what others think of him or how he looks to them. He must stand with all defenses down. How can a director train his actors to remove their masks and reveal *themselves?*

Workshop Environment

A first consideration is that the atmosphere of the workshop be pleasantly informal and noncompetitive.

Secondly, the director must encourage members to recognize that they are part of a select group with each member chosen for special qualities which he can contribute to the ensemble. There are many ways this can be done. One is by imposing regulations and rules. Explain that the Lab work is confidential and should not be discussed with outsiders who have not had the preparation to understand. It is advisable for all members to work as freely as possible. Recommend that they wear jeans or leotards and that they remove shoes.

Essentially, acting involves vibrations with others but is achieved by the actor first acquiring confidence in himself. Then, in a spirit of play and joy he is able to become part of the workshop exercises with others. Conditions must be employed which ensure that an individual will never be afraid of making a fool of himself. Instead he must be made to feel proud that in acting the fool he is part of an exclusive group of fascinating humans usually reserved for idiots, clowns, and geniuses alike. This connotes that visitors are never to be permitted to attend workshop sessions. Each one present must be physically involved in the exercises. *No Auditors!*

Mental and physical conditioning are largely dependent upon the student-actor. This implies the acquisition of much self-discipline on his part.

Tested Workshop Techniques

All sessions should begin with a loosening-up activity: stretching, yawning, grimacing, stooping, squatting, etc. These activities may or may not be assigned within a game structure. Throughout the exercises which follow, a game structure is used as a medium to aid the actor to free himself of stilted, wooden stage deportment and acting clichés. The total organic involvement, which emphasizes the physical, releases tensions and helps the student to become receptive to the more complicated intuitive and intellectual aspects of performing. Warm-up or loosening-up periods at the beginning of the work are no longer considered to be empirical but are now standard procedure—even in professional acting companies.

"The actor is like a physical athlete," Artaud tells us in his *The Theatre and its Double*, "but with this surprising difference; his effective organism is analogous to the organism of the athlete, it is parallel to it, as it were its double, although not acting upon the same plane . . . what the athlete depends upon in running is what the actor depends upon in shouting a passionate curse, but the actor's course is altogether interior."

NOTE: The following exercises should in no way be mistaken for calisthenics or ballet posing. They should be given only a few at a time, in sessions lasting from fifteen minutes to an hour—never more than an hour, as the student will be using muscles, voice sounds, and bodily positions not often used in daily life. All problems need to be presented by the instructor on a physical basis as opposed to any emotional approach.

EXERCISE 1: THE ACTION CIRCLE

Why circle? This is the form used by primitive man for tribal communication, for "getting people together." It is the "all hands around" of folk dancing. The circle has a magic which shifts emphasis from the individual to more communal interests.

We begin by having everyone take a place within a circle and then revolve as the instructor beats time. Physical contact, action, and sounds are thereby combined. Voices begin with the "OHM-m-m" sound. As the circle of students revolve, other sounds are introduced—chants, cries, laughter, monosyllables, grunts, groans, and clapping the hands in rhythm. The instructor guides the players in reaching various harmonies, tempos, and volumes. Taped music may be used. An *imaginary* object (a beach ball?) is thrown from player to player as they continue walking or trotting around the circle.

The imaginary object changes form, weight, texture; sometimes it is hot, then cold—or it may be heavy or balanced on one finger. Spontaneous reactions are encouraged within the action ranging from joy to terror, fear, disgust, etc., all timed to the music or counterpoint to it.

Beginning with total freedom, the students use their *entire bodies and senses as instruments.* Complete relaxation and a spirit of child-play is the essence of these exercises. The more that students become skilled in the physical, the better they are able to get their inner consciousness to respond to the work.

In short, *we are trying to reach characterization and emotions by first relating these to the physical.*

The instructor should help the students in finding their images and then work with them to exploit these preferences. This may be an absolute necessity during the early workshop sessions, but the instructor should allow the actors to continue on their own as quickly as possible.

It may be found that particular members of the group have an almost uncanny ability to star themselves, and often without realizing it. Work within the action circle should be assigned so that the egocentric is required to relate within the group experiments.

During the exercises, the instructor or director is involved as a member, prompter, orchestra, rhythm or mood leader, and as an instigator of nonsense sounds. He should offer neither approval nor criticism of the work, avoiding any kind of domination once the students get into the spirit of the exercises. Results will be greater if he is simply one of a homogeneous group. There will be other times as director that he will need to be firm in asserting his authority, *but not in lab sessions.* Freedom, not discipline, is the purpose of these sessions. Students should also be encouraged to try out their own ideas for exercises and to follow through with them. They might select and develop exercises themselves later and submit these to the director for "polishing." If such a procedure were followed, it would certainly relieve any authoritarian method which might be created by complete dedication to the actor-director discipline.

Lab or workshop is essentially nonverbal. Instructions should be presented in clear, simple language. The parallel to play is both schematic and actual. Watch children at play and you will witness a spontaneous mimetic instinct in action. A cardboard box becomes a space vehicle, a broom handle is a sword, a mongrel pup may become a tyrannosaurus, or Rex the wonder horse. Such creative thinking demands a maximum of concentration and imagination, both essentials of acting as well as playing. Another similarity is that the actors *enjoy* the pretending, just as children delight in play. An infant develops recognizable gestures, babblings, and use of identifiable word sounds often before he begins to walk. The function of communication through play precedes the function of work.

It is possible that some of your students will resent these exercises in the beginning because they seem so childlike, but it has been proven beyond doubt that such exercises make better actors. The "action circle" just described is very deceptive.

Today large, respected industries are using exercises in pretending or "role-playing" as techniques for looking at problems from different angles, for exploration of group differences, and as aids in communication. Black and

white masks are worn in situations involving black and white relationships.
At staff meetings, those agreeing upon a certain point or solution to a problem
do so as the blue group, while those opposing defend their position as the
red group.

Let us look at the objectives of our action circle exercise:

1. To free the body of psychic tensions and muscular tensions.
2. To encourage total relaxation.
3. To heighten concentration.
4. To stimulate spontaneous reactions, as no one will know what is going
to happen next.
5. To relate individual reactions to the group, biologically and psycho-
analytically.
6. To open students to the environment of workshop and to the game
spirit.
7. To accept the body and voice as indispensable tools of acting.
8. To realize that acting is mostly reacting to others.
9. To involve mental, physical, and emotional processes.
10. To discover unstereotyped movements and gestures.
11. To develop the skill to value space and use it, seeing the entire stage
picture while a part of it.
12. To discover and explore untapped resources in the student.
13. To free the student of self-consciousness to the extent that he does
not mind making a fool of himself.
14. To realize that serious work may be accomplished joyfully.
15. To accept that acting demands complete surrender of self.
16. To provide vibrations between members of the group.

All that from one little exercise? The action circle is not merely an exercise.
It is the foundation on which all the exercises to follow will depend.

Exercise 2: Visual Metaphors Through Body Reactions

Rising from a chair is a physical habit. What counts is *what you
do in preparation* for the action. It is the same in movement and
gesture on the stage. Consciousness must be associated with *the feeling of the action before that action is taken.* Muscular coordinations
must be built up with corresponding sensory and emotional data.
The actor's feelings control his body reactions, and these body reactions convey the actor's feelings to the audience.

Word suggestions are given by the instructor, and the students
are to supply mental-physical-emotional reactions. These words may
be given to the individual or to the entire group.

Hate	Love	Fire	Water	Rejection
Joy	Fear	Flight	Cave	Heat
Pain	Cold	Surf	Blind	Threat

Note: If some do not respond to a single-word stimulus, the director should
try relating incidents which might suggest fear, cold, etc.

In everyday living, we express ideas by words, voice inflections, and gestures. Theatre requires that we use our entire bodies for expression and a new vocabulary of hearing, seeing, rhythm, form, silence, texture, and sound.

EXERCISE 3: SPACE DIVISIONS CAN INDICATE MOODS

1. The group is told that they are in a small room and that they are to block out sight. They are not to walk, but only move in place. PROBLEM: By listening, feeling, and receiving impulses, they are to measure the confines of the room.

2. The group is now told that it is standing on a baseball diamond. Same conditions as above. PROBLEM: What are the moods and impulses received in this case?

Objective: To sense moods and atmosphere in a scene. To interpret space by physical means.

Recommended: For actors who depend too much upon facial expressions and small, meaningless gestures.

EXERCISE 4: FILLING SPACE

Each individual is given thirty seconds alone at stage center. He is informed that he has extensions on his arms and must attempt to fill the entire stage space without walking. This exercise is most effective when the student keeps his eyes closed.

Objective: To use the full body in a coordinated physical investigation. To make the actor aware of extending himself to his limits and to make him experience muscle tensions in exertion.

Recommended: For relieving stage fright. By exerting maximum physical effort, then releasing the strain, body tensions relax.

EXERCISE 5: THE LANGUAGE OF MOVEMENT

With their entire bodies, individuals are to shape themselves into hieroglyphics, or short or long lines, circles, triangles, etc. Balance must be shifted as body positions are changed. Note how the dynamics alter the character of the lines. Members of the group perform in teams of three. Others watch and scribble stick figures representing the basic lines of movements. After everyone has completed the exercise, a discussion should follow, concerning what the stick figure drawings symbolize or express in action, mood, or emotion.

Objective: To demonstrate how the body in freely invented attitudes and metaphors can express action, force, or emotion.

Recommended: For awkward, ungraceful actors.

EXERCISE 6: FORMS PROVIDE IDENTITY

A coiled rope is thrown above the acting area. The shape it makes where it falls on stage is used as a pattern for group formation.

Objective: Group involvement.

Discussion: What might such a grouping suggest to an audience?

Recommended: To teach egocentric individuals to fit into an ensemble activity. Especially good to encourage uncooperative students.

Character portrayal by emotional means is dominated by creating a state of mind, or mood. Our next exercise considers the purely physical effects of a mood or an emotion on walking.

EXERCISE 7: WALKING

(a) *The Promenade*. Use rhythm sounds either recorded or live, but not march music.

With the students in stocking feet, start them walking around the action circle to rhythm. Instruct them to step right out to the beat as if they were going somewhere: chest out, leading with the chin, abdomen in, but arms and hands relaxed.

Observe the different ways people walk. You may see the shuffle, the leaning tower, the pigeon-toed, the flat-footed, the droop-walk, or the wet-diaper weave.

In normal walk, the body's center of balance is carried evenly between the two feet. This determines how the feet will be placed. In stocking feet the heel will take the first weight which is quickly transferred to the pads and toes. It is almost impossible to achieve a natural walk while wearing high heels unless unnatural adjustments are made in the movement of the knees and waist.

(b) *Toe Bounce—To Improve the Walk*. Students should stand relaxed, arms at side, feet together, weight evenly distributed. They

should rise on toes, fall back on heels—rise and fall for five counts. Now they are to slow the tempo and movement, still maintaining balance. Instruct them to walk in this rhythm, rising on toes with each step with an energetic bouncing effect. Then they should walk bouncing only with the right foot, then only with the left foot, then only with the right; next, set up various other rhythms.

(c) *Toes In.* If you want to encourage some shy ones to join the group exercises, demonstrate this one yourself. Overdo it and they will think they' cannot look more ridiculous than you. This exercise does wonders for the anterior tibialis, the muscles that correct flat feet.

(d) *Toes Out.* The girls will like this one. It removes flab from the inside of the thighs. It also trains in flexibility.

(e) *Lock Knees.* Students are to pretend knees are tied together. They step forward with lead foot, toes up, heels down, simultaneously snapping the other foot forward to balance the next step but remaining erect. This is a primitive dance step. The exercise must be done to rhythm.

(*f*) *Walk Expressive of Calm and Dignity.* Center of balance is supported by rear leg when stepping forward and is shifted only when the lead foot is placed firmly on the floor. Slow tempo. Insist upon ease of movement.

(*g*) *Walk Expressive of Haste or Impatience.* Heels will touch the ground only momentarily with head leading the forward thrust. Faster tempo. Slight forward angle of body.

(*h*) *Walk Expressive of Opposition or Uncertainty.* Body angles slightly back where center of balance is placed. Toe often reaches the floor first and steps are hesitant.

(*i*) *Walk Expressive of Dread or Fright.* Erratic tempo. Tension shown with entire body.

(*k*) *Walk Expressive of Stealth.* Knees are raised higher than in normal walk, the toes touching the floor first; then weight is slowly transferred to the heel for balance. From the waist up, the body is conventionally erect.

EXERCISE 8: THE CAT WALK

Slow, smooth beat, once around the circle. (Better save this until your group is loosened up.) Place right foot forward, bend knee, then drop entire weight onto right flat palm. Bring left foot forward, knee bent, balancing full weight on left hand. Walk on all fours.

EXERCISE 9: RUNS

Adjust tempo to capabilities of group. This is another toughy, but great for the feet and thighs. This is the straight leg lift often seen in ballet. Start walking the students with legs straight and toes pointed forward. This will positively relax tensions and will improve walk and appearance. Have your students try it slowly at first to

get it right; then have them trot once around the circle. Next, reverse direction.

EXERCISE 10: PEANUT PUSH

Perform in place. Begin on hands and knees, pointing toes out. Bend over, arms in front with palms flat on floor. Lower head to permit chin to push an imaginary peanut. Raise head and shift weight back to knees, then forward again to push the peanut. Have your students perform the exercise only a few times at first. Later it can be done up to fifteen times.

EXERCISE 11: THE ANIMAL STRETCH

From the hands and knees position, strain chest, arms, and shoulder muscles by raising head, allowing pelvis to drop as back arches (catback). Bend up to a back arch, weight on palms and knees while dropping the head and tightening the abdomen. Hold for count of three. This exercise will improve posture and eliminate tension.

EXERCISE 12: THE CALCUTTA

Perform to rhythm. This is one of the main exercises used by the cast of *Oh! Calcutta!* for warmups before every performance. Standing in circle, keep shoulders, hips, and neck still and level. Now face in position to walk, keeping arms extended so there is room between each student. Lower arms, and at the count, twist

lower body by turning toes of leading foot inward with each step while stretching out arms parallel to shoulders. Center of balance should shift with each step from right to left as hips twist.

After students have perfected this movement, it might be made into an exercise in coordination by lowering the arms on every third count, then raising them on the fourth.

NOTE: Insist that students stay with the beat. If music is dull or unsuitable, change it. Music should inspire and make the exercises enjoyable. Let me repeat, these are not gymnastics, but carefully chosen and tested exercises to develop the efficiency of the actor's physical instrument. Exercises should be given which are most applicable to the needs of the particular group and not necessarily in sequence as published here.

Physical training is a vital part of the American Conservatory Theatre's total program. Here Instructor Jewel Walker puts her class through their exercises. (Photo by Clyde Hare, courtesy of the American Conservatory Theatre of San Francisco)

EXERCISE 13: SOUNDS CAN INDICATE EMOTIONS

1. Study texture, pitch, volume, direction, and time of such human sounds as those associated with fear, anger, grief, happiness, suspicion, and "davenning."[1]

2. Make tapes of phrases of different mood sounds and music, waltzes, sirens, merry-go-rounds, etc. Have group react physically to these sounds in any way they feel.

EXERCISE 14: WELL-SPOKEN, WELL-WRITTEN WORDS PROVIDE THE INTELLECTUAL ELEMENT IN THEATRE

1. While all are standing in the circle, the instructor speaks a word; then with *no hesitation* the person on his right adds another

[1]"Davenning" is a rhythmic murmur or humming sound such as old women make when in church or at funerals. It is performed by repeating prayer or lament.

word which continues the thought. This continues around the circle until each person has added a word. When it reaches the instructor, he speaks another word.

2. Repeat the same pattern, but this time instead of words, use nonsense words or gibberish.

3. Students are previously assigned to memorize the same Shakespearian soliloquy. Each student is to speak one word in proper sequence. Attempt to produce a semblance of dramatic flow.

Objectives: To provide individual-group participation. To demonstrate value of ensemble.

Especially recommended: For preparing a comedy or farce. Also good exercise for drilling actors in picking up cues.

Acting is one of the few art forms in which the creative moment is happening in the present, before the eyes of the spectator. This requires that the actor be able to produce an efficacious moment at will.

EXERCISE 15: SENSE REACTIONS

Use only word suggestions such as:

SUGGEST

(*Smell*)	A bakery, a fish market, low tide, a perfume shop.
(*Sight*)	A miracle, maggots, a lake, an auto wreck, a tennis game.
(*Sound*)	Tapping noises, birds, traffic, sirens.
(*Touch*)	Rain, velvet, thumb tacks, marble, corrugated cardboard.
(*Taste*)	Bitter medicine, ice cream, metal, honey, alum.

Some of these words may be given to individuals while other students watch and react. Additional words may be given to the entire group. In lab work, the instructor should begin with suggestions which are common, ordinary, and basic. Word suggestions work best when given without a game structure. Suggested words such as *celebrations, confrontations, tragedy,* and *conflict* are active and lend themselves to less subtle and more easily experienced exercises than those requiring more sophisticated activity.

EXERCISE 16: SPONTANEOUS RESPONSES

Explain to the group that sometime during the session something unexpected will take place and that when it does they should react in any way they are moved. (Arrange privately beforehand for a pistol to be fired, someone to scream, or a person to walk into the room wearing an outlandish costume.) The function of this exercise is to shake students from their frozen, set responses and to demonstrate how different the responses are when spontaneous.

In beginning sessions the instructor will be guiding the students into simple physical problems, the purpose of which is to develop skills in handling their bodies as acting instruments. When they have profited from these exercises, they will be more prepared and competent in dealing with spontaneous dialogue and the subtle situations used in more sophisticated improvisations.

The point has already been made that in workshop, the director learns as much as the students, and especially *about* his students. Quirks, fears, crotchets, habits, temperament, and dedication will all be revealed. You will learn which members of your group are going to need help and in what area. It will also be apparent which students have an ability to express themselves. For others, much of the work will lead into a discovery of skills they hardly knew they possessed.

Here is an exercise I have been using for years, but its results continue to amaze me. It gives free reign to a student's imagination, shows his interests, and tests his ability to convey ideas to an audience. Often a student's ideas are so involved in concept that not even Sir Laurence Olivier could transmit them to an audience without speech. Caution your students beforehand to *keep their concepts simple and to choose only those ideas which they know can be communicated to an audience.*

EXERCISE 17: POINT OF FOCUS

Problem. There is a letter on a table. The table may be anywhere, anytime, any place, *but such details must be communicated* by the student. The character may be any person the student wishes, but this must also be shown because there is to be no speech, only pantomime.

Each student will perform solo, while others serve as his audience.

The only essential is that the letter be read and some reaction shown. Students should be cautioned to concentrate upon the point of focus which, in this case, is the letter, and then the reaction. What is the size of the letter? Is it typed, hand-written, perfumed, or what? Is it from a man or woman? Could you suggest its color to an audience?

In one of my groups doing Exercise 17, a very young man chose to be a very old man. The letter was placed on top of a box containing, of all things, the torso of his mother-in-law. At least that is what he *told* us during discussion after the exercise. His mistake was in choosing a situation without considering how he could communicate it to the audience.

Another rather matronly student found the letter so upsetting that she

175

neglected to wear white gloves to a formal luncheon—evidently a matter of grave importance to her.

I learned a great deal about those two individuals in a very short time. It might have required months of association without that exercise.

It is an advantage to the student-actor if he learns quickly that there is a vast difference between what he *thinks* he is showing an audience and *what that audience actually sees and understands.* This all comes out in the discussions afterwards when the observing students explain what they understood and then the performer tells *what he intended to show.* In this exercise it is impossible to judge the effectiveness of the actor's work unless we know what he thought he was doing. The Zen form of teaching consists of *not* teaching, and valid research has proven that learning is more effective when the instructor assigns problems which allow students to discover knowledge themselves.

The workshop environment provides the student-actor with a high level of experimentation in solving problems, with only limited assistance from the director. Some students must be limited to beginning problems suggested by the director, while others will be inspired to use self-directed experiences. This should be encouraged. Acting cannot be learned by listening to lectures, filling notebooks, or reading books on acting. It must be experienced by the actors themselves. During the learning period, the more self-directed the student can become, the more motivated he will be when given a part in a play. Among the many responsibilities of the director, one of the most important is to bring out the fullest involvement and performance from the inexperienced actor.

In regional acting companies, more and more professional actors are building character by accenting physical action in preference to depending solely on older Stanislavskian theories. Misuse of the psychoanalytical approach has encouraged a stress on feeling to the virtual exclusion of style and physical techniques, so needed and lacking today.

All over the western world, many variations of this physical approach to training and conditioning actors is in evidence. Polish director Jerzy Grotowski was brought to London and New York to conduct classes in his physical-psychic approach to acting.[2]

Other professional companies are using analogous techniques. In *The Theatre and its Double*, Artaud, also a strong influence in the new movement, was most prophetic when he wrote:

> . . . if he truly wants to be a director, that is a man versed in the nature of matter and objects, he must conduct in the physical domain an exploration of intense movement and precise emotional gesture which is equivalent on the psychological level to the most absolute and complete moral discipline.[3]

These fresh approaches to teaching acting are bringing the theatre more parallel to the newer cultures now existing in all the other arts, where the

[2]See *Drama Review* T 24, T 27, T 35, T 41. Also Eugenio Barda, *Allaricera del Teatro Perduta* (Padua, Italy, 1965).

[3]Antonin Artaud, *The Theatre and its Double* (New York: Grove Press, 1958), p. 114.

practicing means have extended away from the realistic and verbal expressions into sensory awareness. Painters and sculptors use unlikely materials such as junk, soup labels, newsprint, and vinyl in their creations. Musicians use auto brake drums, rattles, gongs, and foghorns to produce "sounds." Young people understand at once that these artists are trying to reach them by *physical* means, through the senses, by sight, sound, taste, smell, and touch, rather than in the conventional, intellectual, and realistic representation. They have digested McLuhan, Nietzsche, Levi Strauss, Gyorgy Kepes, and have grown up watching TV. They know about John Cage and Andy Warhol. Is it any wonder they want a theatre of less verbiage and more form and style?

Singing and dancing play an integral part of Paul Sills's Story Theatre transformation of Ovid's classic tales. From left: Judi West, Trina Parks, Avery Schreiber, Lesley Warren, and Paula Kelly in The Metamorphoses, *a Center Theatre production. (Courtesy of the Center Theatre Group, Mark Taper Forum, Los Angeles, Calif.)*

Recordings: For Action Circle Exercises

Antheill, George. *Ballet Mechanique.* Urania: 1924. 134:5134.
Brant, Henry. *Angels and Devils*, Concerto for Flute. Signs and alarms. Galaxy, Columbia ML 4956 II. Lehigh University.
Cage, John. *Amores* for prepared piano and percussion. Time: 580009. Stereo: 8000.
———. *Indeterminancy.* New Aspect in Instrumental and Electronic Music. 2 Folkways 3704.
Cage, John, and Harrison, Lou. *Double Music for Percussion.* Time: 58000. Stereo: 8000.
Schuller, Gunther. *Seven Studies after Paul Klee.* Mercury 50283. Stereo: 90282.

Any recordings will do as long as they are not popular rock, jazz, vocals, or hackneyed "standards." *Pure sounds* are better to stimulate physical expression. Many of the exercises should create their own rhythms.

Methods of Helping the Student-Actor Develop

Fortunate indeed is the director who has had the advantage of spending a training period with actors before he must produce a play. Serious acting faults are not always apparent until the play is cast and well into rehearsal.

While a training period is not a cure-all for all actor ills, it is at least an antibiotic. During lab or workshop sessions, where a *gemütlich* atmosphere prevails and there is not so much pressure on a director, he may be able to discover and treat many of the more common faults of the inexperienced. And training is the answer to the question, "How can a director bring out a performance from a reserved but feeling person?"

Workshops have a way of developing relaxation, a dependency upon others, and a sense of responsibility to all fellow workers. The exercises in themselves are not entirely responsible for this development. They are merely the means of creating a relationship between the body and feelings of one individual and fusing these into the psycho-physical disciplines of the group. Such training makes it possible to react directly to impulse, eliminating blocks which might exist between an inner impulse and the outer expression of it. Within a group, objective questions can be turned into subjectivity. For instance, in workshop we might ask, How does one rage? How does one fight? After such problems are submitted to the group for solutions, the individual is encouraged to open up and to accept certain relationships between himself and other members of the group.

New methods are explored and tested in a continuous training program for company members at the American Conservatory Theatre. (Courtesy of the American Conservatory Theatre of San Francisco)

One exercise might consist of a member looking directly into the eyes of another, then describing what he sees as he touches the other's face with his fingers. After such tactile human contact, with its resultant lowering of barriers, it would be difficult for the individual to think only of himself and not the oneness of the group. An empathy occurs through the senses similar to that felt when a passenger in a car presses his foot on the floor as the driver applies the brakes, or when we yawn because someone near us yawns.

Values of Workshop Sessions

The minimum number of rehearsals usually allowed most directors in educational theatres to produce a play certainly does not provide time to train and develop actors to any extent. Workshop offers a happy solution to the problem. It would be advantageous if workshop were part of a curriculum, but if this is not possible, then sessions might be scheduled at any time suitable to the director and those interested in developing themselves as actors. Any time spent in workshop will balance, or exceed, the time lost in teaching fundamentals during rehearsal periods and will make possible better performances when the play is produced. We might also consider a few other advantages:

In rehearsals, the goal is to get a production together within a scheduled time. Precious hours cannot be spent in teaching acting fundamentals. "The show must go on"—and the result usually is that actors are trained at the expense of a production which is then hastily, even crudely, put together.

Uses of ensemble playing. It supplies the human contact so necessary for group participation; it demonstrates the value of relating to other actors or objects in a meaningful way; it encourages spontaneity and fresh responses to the group or to the individual.

Relaxation. It has long been established that students learn faster and more efficiently in a relaxed atmosphere. In workshop the spirit of play is more apparent than any learning disciplines.

Confidence. Workshop will develop an ease of association in the actor-director relationship, and in the relationships between actor and other actors. It may even create an *esprit de corps*. Because of the mutual understanding and confidence, the student will be spared that feeling of insecurity when walking into a room full of strangers and having to perform for them, as he must at open auditions. The only credential needed in workshop is that the student be willing to make a fool of himself.

Experience. No one can deny the importance of a cast of good actors when producing. Workshop-trained actors will be experienced in playing together, an advantage not possible in most professional productions.

Permanent values. In workshop, actors are not trained for a single production. The basic training in acting will be available for all subsequent productions.

Values to a Director

Students are not the only ones to benefit by workshop sessions. The director will have ample opportunity to study each individual, his dedication to the work or lack of it, his personality, talent or potential talent, and his ability to work with others. The exercises may prove too strenuous or boring for those only interested in exploiting their own personalities. Such people will quickly eliminate themselves from the sessions and this will be beneficial to the director. Potential talent will have every chance of revealing itself, and the inept student will have many opportunities to discover his faults and blocks for himself. He will learn what is right by first determining what is wrong. "Hunch" casting will no longer be necessary, as the director will have full knowledge of his people.

In workshop, all members should be treated with fairness and impartiality. They will be able to observe and therefore understand why the director eventually casts a play as he does. This means that there will be less chance of conflicts and jealousies when a play is cast. In workshop all students begin equally. But it will become obvious during the sessions that those who apply themselves and develop are going to get the parts when the casting is done for a play. And the rewards will be justified, because certain students will improve themselves and demonstrate to all that they possess the sincerity and interest necessary to *deserve* the leading parts in the plays.

Workshop Discussions

I want to return to a point mentioned previously which may not have been given the emphasis it deserves. What is the best way for a director to give criticism to an actor? *The ideal approach is not to criticize, but to lead the actor into discovering his own errors.* This procedure relieves any resentment which might be generated by remarks which are not carefully phrased. Self-discovery fortifies the actor-ego, whereas faultfinding weakens it. One proof of greatness in an actor is in his ability to discover his own faults and then correct them.

Beginning with game-playing in workshop, the director's ultimate goal is to guide the actor in selecting some responses, rejecting others, and then reinforcing those of value. The skill of a director is in strengthening the unseasoned actor's strong points without himself minimizing the student's weaknesses. This is especially true when directing actors in the avocational or educational fields, where they lack the confidence coming from experience. A professional's skin is not quite as tender. He has learned to accept criticism as a means of growth.

Even so, when being critical, the director will be wise to make judgments only after he has given the matter some thought. When giving critiques, never speak emotionally. Once when the celebrated director Granville-Barker was directing Sir John Gielgud in *Lear*, he said, "You did some fine things in that scene. I hope you know what they were."[4] And then the director proceeded to read Gielgud a long list of his mistakes.

Correcting Faults of the Individual

As workshop techniques are designed mostly for the ensemble, it is possible for criticism to be directed toward the group, and there should be very little of that. But later during improvisional work, open discussions may be encouraged.

Some remedial work will of course need to be considered for certain individuals. Exercises given below should be clarified by description only,

[4]Sir John Gielgud, *Stage Directions* (New York: Random House, 1963), p. 43.

without revealing the objectives. A student might wonder about a prescribed treatment for a malady he did not realize he had.

Remedial Exercises and Improvisations

By far the most common malady of actors is—

Stage Fright

Indications: Dry mouth, nervous hand movements, poor eye contact, timidity, quavering voice, restless shifting of feet, general embarrassment, frustration, panicky emotion (even terror) or anxiety at facing strangers.

Causes: Tensions, fear of being unprepared and being judged, of losing status or esteem of others and self.

Treatment: Release body tensions and anxieties by group exercises. Assure student that he is not alone; that he has the full cooperation of yourself and the group.

"You have nothing to fear but fear itself" might be used as the theme for an invented exercise. Fear is lack of knowledge. Walk into a strange, dark room and you are apprehensive; but if it is your own dark room you have no fear. You know the room even though you cannot see it.

Stage fright during rehearsals or performance might be diminished by narrowing the point of focus, by blocking out all but the first words and actions. Deal with just one goal at a time. Use relaxing exercises—head swivel, yawning, stretching, knee bends, etc. Also, see Exercise 18 below.

Stage fright is not confined to amateurs. Professionals experience it also, and with more at stake.

EXERCISE 18: THE COBRA—A TENSION RELIEVER

From a horizontal position, face down, forehead resting on floor, bend elbows in so that flat palms are under the thorax. Slowly lift head only, straining back neck muscles. Turn head slowly to right and left. Gradually push up with arms until they are straight, bending the spine back, stretching it as far as possible. Hold. Return to first position by bending arms at elbow, forehead on floor, palms under thorax. Repeat. (Note: Lower body does not move in this exercise.)

Problems in Speaking

We find many of these problems in amateur acting.

LACK OF PROJECTION—INAUDIBILITY

Causes: Inexperience, poor everyday speech, fear of audience, fatigue, faulty breathing, tensions, anxieties.

Treatment: Student should be made aware that an audience is not an ogre but a friendly, interested group which has invested both time and money to hear what he has to say.

Explain the function of diaphragmatic muscle in assisting to sustain breath and tone. Then use a series of breathing exercises. (See Exercises 34, 35, 36, pp. 199 and 200.)

Workshop of the Arena Stage in Washington, D.C. (Courtesy of the Living Stage, a project of the Arena Stage in Washington D.C.)

DULL MECHANICAL SPEECH—MONOTONE

Causes: Lack of emphasis, recitative quality, caused by hasty memorization or "lazy" everyday speech habits.

Treatment: Explain to student that he is speaking, not reading or reciting. Assign a speech from a play and underline the words which convey the thought. Explain that all the words in a sentence are not of equal importance, even in everyday speech. Verbalize, transpose author's words into student's. Teach coloring of words, sing scales. (See Exercises 13, 14; and Exercises 33, 34, 35, 36, pp. 198, 199, and 200.)

TAKING ANOTHER'S TONE

Indications: Borrowing another's speech patterns, inflections, and tones. Usually done unconsciously.

Causes: Inattention to point of focus: "deaf ear." Needs more work on individual characterization.

Treatment: Rehearse by having the actor transpose the author's speeches into his own language. Use Exercises 13, 14, and 2 on sounds, words, and body actions.

Rushed Speeches

Causes: Anxiety, nervousness, desire to eliminate source of annoyance and "be done with it."

Treatment: Use relaxing exercises, stimulate sense of enjoyment, not irritation. Assign "slow motion" exercises, such as Exercise 19, below; also Exercises 10, 11, 12.

Exercise 19: Slow Motion

Have student pretend he is an astronaut in a no-gravity situation, busy with daily tasks. He then should divide a speech into sections or sentences and give physical movements between each section.

Poor Enunciation—Slurred Speech

Causes: Localized accent, inability to understand and practice the use of lips, tongue, teeth, and soft palate in articulation.

Treatment: Use exercises in vowel and consonant sounds. (Appropriate exercises can be found in *Acting, the Creative Process*.[5])

The training concept as practiced at the American Conservatory Theatre is the belief that it is the responsibility of more experienced artists to pass on their knowledge to younger members. (Photo by Clyde Hare, courtesy of the American Conservatory Theatre of San Francisco)

Lines Misread or Repeated

Causes: Faulty memorization, uncertainty, learning by rote without awareness of "the moment," the lead-on to the line itself, or the event taking place; nervousness, inadequate rehearsal, not enough work in group relationships.

[5]Hardie Albright, *Acting, the Creative Process* (Belmont, Calif.: Dickenson Publishing Co., 1967), pp. 32–38.

Treatment: Give situation for improvisation with others and exercises to demonstrate point of focus; concentration upon the substance, not the words, of a speech.

Falling Inflections—Dropping Ends of Sentences

Causes: Mostly habit and must be corrected for stage work, as it establishes a minor, depressing key.

Treatment: Impress on student that last words in a sentence are often the most important. Give instruction in underlining words which are important and which he neglects. Give exercises singing scales, breathing, and opening voice passages, especially muscle exercises for mouth. (Appropriate exercises can be found in *Acting, the Creative Process*.[6])

Inability to Listen to Other Players

Causes: Not enough work with group, inattention (check with other teachers); lack of concentration upon what is happening on stage; insensitivity to other players (personal reasons?), short attention span.

Treatment: Use an exercise for two, such as Exercise 20, below. Also see Exercises 13, 14, 18, and 19.

Exercise 20:

Have one student begin a narrative, such as where he was and what he was doing when the astronauts landed on the moon, etc. Have him use first person in narrative. At a signal from the instructor, have the other student take over and continue in first person, remembering all the details already given.

Mouthing Other Player's Words—"Lipping"

Causes: Hasty memorization, studying part by rote (or learning words, not sense), poor concentration on P.O.V. of scene.

Treatment: Stop rehearsal. Ask the actor who is lipping what the other player has just said. Assign improvisation for student and partners. Allow student to decide upon theme, and develop it with others by using the "who-what-why" formula (see *Improvisation section*); then improvise for entire group. Also, see Exercise 21, below.

Exercise 21

One student reads a famous speech (Gettysburg Address, Marriage Ceremony, etc.), pausing at ends of sentences to allow time for others

[6]*Ibid.*, pp. 23–38.

in the group to interpret by physical means, some by extending fingers to receive vibrations (finger pantomime), others with entire body. ("Do you, John Smith, take this woman, Mary Jones. . .") It is possible to use any speech which lends itself to graphic interpretation.

Physical Problems

Today's plays, to a large extent, depend more upon presenting their themes visually rather than aurally as before.

Gilmor Brown has said, "The director's great problem is to get the actor to use his body as a metaphorical vehicle for the expression of a dramatic idea." Not that the director should run up on stage and demonstrate a movement, gesture, or rhythm as he sees it; he must reach the actor by more delicate means—giving problems to solve problems. In solving them, the actor makes the movements his own.

In the old days of stock when a new "bill" was presented each week, the director had no time for exercises or improvisations—he *showed* his actors what he wanted. There are times during rehearsals when demonstration might be the only solution, but it should be resorted to only when all else fails. Otherwise, you might have an entire cast of alter egos cavorting about the stage.

AWKWARDNESS

Indications: Dangling arms, poor posture, dragging feet, eccentric walk, and generally odd physical movement.

Causes: Poor everyday habits, self-consciousness, not enough rehearsal or work with group.

Treatment: Improvisations. Isolate offending movement and use corrective exercises. Restage scene more in harmony with actor. (See "Walking" and "The Calcutta," Exercises 7 and 12.)

STILTED WOODEN MOVEMENT

Indications: Hands stuck in pockets, inflexible stiff body, automatism.

Causes: Tensions, resistance, fear of audience.

Treatment: Improvisations, work in action group. See Exercises 2, 3, and 8.

"COVERING" OTHER PLAYERS

Causes: Many amateurs find it difficult to understand "sight lines." It is very important that actors with important scenes to play are not blocked from view by others. The amateur has been given inadequate or ineffective knowledge regarding the importance of "dressing the stage."

Treatment: Instead of *explaining* sight lines to inexperienced actors, here is an exercise which serves to *physicalize* angles of sight.

Exercise 22

1. Arrange four individuals into a team. Line up four teams (as per sketch) in a triangular arrangement, open end facing the audience. Instruct groups to decide upon "who, what, why, when, and where" and to improvise dialogue within their own team. They are to move at will but always within their area. Stop them at intervals and ask them to check lines of sight from all positions in the auditorium.

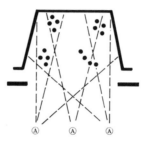

2. Rearrange teams for center staging.

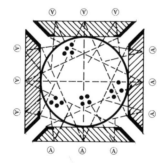

LACK OF POISE

Indications: Wandering about the stage with no motive; shifting body weight; restlessness; repetitive and meaningless gesturing; appearing to be ill-at-ease, uncomfortable, and lost on stage.

Causes: Inability to use entire body as instrument and keep in control; stresses.

Treatment: Use point of focus and space exercises which will help the actor to relax and be in control of his body. Stress the necessity for motivating each move on stage. Encourage visual inventiveness by exercise. (See Exercises 3, 4; and Exercises 23, 24, p. 188.)

Indications: "Ham" or insincere acting for effect; wild unnecessary gesturing and emotion; lack of inventiveness.

Causes: Imitation of idol, fight for status, failure to understand focus of play or scene; egocentric exhibitionism. (So-called Method actors are more susceptible to overacting because of inability to control emotion.)

Treatment: Eliminate mannerisms when not suitable to character. When useful for character delineation, keep them. Use exercises concentrating upon point of focus and those encouraging cohesion with group. (See Exercise 22 and Exercises 23, 24, p. 188.)

Excessive Gesturing

Indications: "Sawing the air," unmotivated use of hands and arms.

Causes: Insufficient study of character, nervousness, fear of competing, anxieties, etc.

Treatment: Young people tend to believe that energy will solve any problem. Instruct student to use hands only to express what he has not expressed by body or voice. Try exercises to develop concentration and relaxation. In severe cases direct the actor to rehearse with hands in pockets.

In reading this list, it seems apparent that most faults can be traced to either nervousness, caused by improper memorization, or inadequate rehearsal time. Another reason might be a lack of attention on the point of focus.

Realizing any of these mistakes, the completely embarrassed amateur might giggle and say, "I wasn't serious about acting anyhow." If this happens several times in rehearsal, take the young man at his word and replace him. You will be justified, as acting is a serious matter.

Lack of Eye Contact

Some faults hurt only the actor making them; others are rude, if not harmful, to fellow actors. It is very distracting for one actor to play a scene with another whose eyes wander, look beyond, to one side or another, at the forehead—anywhere but into the eyes of the person to whom he is speaking. It can destroy concentration and drive every line out of the other actor's head. Some professionals have actually cultivated this habit. Not only do they focus the attention of the audience upon themselves, but they also put the fellow player at a disadvantage by being inattentive to him. When an actor has an important speech and the man to whom he is talking will not pay attention, how can the director expect an audience to do so?

Most amateurs are completely innocent of any such ulterior motives. If they are guilty of this discourtesy, it is only because they are nervous or embarrassed. Usually a polite reminder is all that is needed. But whether done innocently or maliciously, the director must watch for it. It will not be easy to catch an actor at it unless the director moves about the auditorium where he can see the action from different angles.

The actor is to fix his eyes on some focal point, such as the reflection of his own eyes when looking into a full length mirror. He is to hold his concentration on the spot, not allowing his eyes to blink for as long as possible.

The game of Indian wrestling is also effective in teaching eye-to-eye contact and concentration. Watching his adversary's eyes for signs of weakening makes a good Indian wrestler.

Any other exercise in this book which is effective in easing tension or developing control might be used.

Following are some other exercises which have been found effective in workshops. These might be useful if schedules permit more extensive sessions.

Additional Exercises

Exercise 24: Concentration and Relaxation

Objective: To achieve the concentration of the entire ensemble upon a single suggestion. To give awareness to the senses.

Concentration is like listening on the telephone. You must give it *all* your attention. Any small distraction destroys the point of focus. Students must close their minds to any outside interference.

All members of the group are instructed to kneel on the floor in a semicircle within touching distance of each other. An environment is created by dimming the light and playing soothing, quiet, music. The instructor speaks slowly and quietly, almost in a mood of hushed reverence. Students are instructed to slowly sit back on their heels with back straight, eyes closed, hands crossed, palms up, and head bowed. Pause. The next instruction is that the members release all thoughts from their minds, to imagine themselves in a state of grace—at peace with themselves and all that surrounds them.

For the next three minutes nothing is said and no one moves. Then quietly the instructor informs the members that he is going to make certain word suggestions and that from these they are to imagine sensations without moving in any way. Ample time must be allowed for each word to stimulate a sensory experience.

SUGGEST

	A grandfather clock in an adjoining room;
(*Sound*)	A faraway train whistle;
	Barking dogs in the next street.

	The skin of a peach;
(*Touch*)	Rough sandpaper;
	Rain in your face.

	A spicy, hot pumpkin pie;
(*Smell*)	A hospital;
	A pig sty.

	Spoiled meat;
(*Taste*)	A menthol cough drop;
	Mineral oil.

Members are now asked to rise slowly and stand in place. Instructor leads in deep breathing exercises:

Intake deep breath through nose only—hold—exhale with "OHM-m-m" sound.

Intake deep breath through nose and mouth—hold longer than before—exhale with nasal sound.

Continue each time holding breath longer than previously and making different vowel sounds.

End by shaking arms and body in short, palsied movements, and twisting the muscles of the face in grotesque masklike formations.

Either at the beginning of this exercise, or preferably at the end, the instructor orients the students to the importance of concentration, memory recall, physicalizing, and the relationship of these to the skills of creating moods and character. Students are then asked to choose an emotion such as fear, happiness, irritation, anger, anticipation, sympathy, etc. They are then to give evidence of that emotion.

Students are next instructed to sit with legs crossed under them and arms extended to side, palms flat on the floor, looking straight ahead in preparation for the next exercise.

The instructor may choose this time to explain the two methods in use today for creating character and emotion.

Myth and Reality

One hears a great deal today about subjective and objective acting. Those who believe themselves to be practitioners of the Stanislavski System contend that the actor must "get inside" his character, become so identified with it that he becomes interchangeable with that character.

The physical approach (from the outside to the inside) is illustrated by Sir Laurence Olivier, who has said that he begins creating character by first noting someone's walk or tone of voice and builds from that point on.

Before Stanislavski, actors had no difficulty in distinguishing between myth and reality. They realized that they were, after all, acting in a play, before an audience, and that once the curtain fell, the pretending would end. These actors took some pride in their ability to play a comedy at a matinee after attending a morning funeral, or to discuss baseball in the dressing room and then walk out on the stage and convince an audience that they were seeing their father's ghost. They believed that the stage was timeless, transcendental, and universal, beyond the common experience of one man, because it dealt with all men. For these actors, the play, the rehearsals, the makeup, the costumes, and the performance were make-believe—part of a myth. They believed that the theatrical reality of a play could coexist with the thought that it was only a play, and that this was the essence of the aesthetic illusion.

But the subjective actor works from the inside out. He creates character by relating to the mental and emotional states of that character, then recalls some parallel emotional experience or incident which occurred, not necessarily to him, but which affected him personally.[7]

Henri Bergson, the French philosopher, questions the logic of that process. "Analyzing the past is only an example of memory serving the intellect, that memory is not necessarily related to the truth."

I pose a question. Is it possible for a conceptual thinker to work from both inside and outside in order to create a character of many dimensions?

Emotional States

> The only way of expressing emotion in the form of art
> is by finding an objective correlative; in other words a
> set of objects, a situation, a chain of events which shall
> be the formulae for that particular emotion.
>
> —T. S. Eliot

EXERCISE 25: EMOTIONAL RECALL

No claim can be made that this exercise will create emotion. But it should provide the members of your group an opportunity to experience the beginning of the process.

In order to create emotion, one must begin with intense concentration. Student-actors are instructed to close their eyes. Then one word at a time is spoken by the instructor and time allowed for the student to relate that word to some personal experience. The student is to re-create in his mind where he was during the experience, others present, his age at the time, why he felt the particular emotion, what he wore, what was said; in fact, *every detail of the incident*.

For instance, suppose the word "fear" has been suggested. Perhaps one member of your group has been in a car accident and for some-time thereafter will hesitate to get into another car. He will think of that accident. He might begin with an anxiety which will make him tremble, or sweat, or he may become literally paralyzed as he recalls that awful moment when his car careened across the highway into the path of an oncoming car.

Allow some time for reaction after each word suggestion. Students should then be instructed to show the effects of the recalled emotion

---

[7]*Affective memory* is commonly thought to be Stanislavski's term. However, it was borrowed from the writings of French psychologist T. A. Ribot.

by *physical means.* Questions will naturally arise, such as: if we had not the experience to recall, would we be able to summon the emotion now? Or—if the key word had not been heard, would the actor have transmitted the emotion to the audience? The key word is suggested in order to stimulate the actor into a *personal* mental recall of the given circumstance and its specific reaction upon him. When an actor seems unable to do this, then the director might help, but it is more effective, in training, if the actor's own sense of recall and imagination be developed—not the director's. This is the reason for a key word being used.

The Living Stage Company in workshop activity with Director Alexander (in background). This company is one of the programs instituted by Zelda Fichandler's Arena Stage in Washington, D.C. (Courtesy of the Living Stage)

Expressing Character and Emotion by Physical Means

Let us suppose that one of our group has been assigned a part in a play. He has studied the play and his character and has discussed both with the director. From this the actor has decided that the essence of his character is a craftiness and a distrust of others. Ask if anyone in the group has ever seen or known a man who gave them such an impression. If so, ask that student to describe the man's appearance, and then, as he does, have the student who must play the part try to assume the character of the man *physically.* Perhaps someone has seen an animal that left him with such an impression of distrust and hostility.

> NOTE: In demonstrating physical aspects of characters, exercises are more effective if students are limited to the visual. You will have noticed that all simple exercises have certain barriers in order to isolate particular aspects. In this exercise students should be instructed not to speak or walk, but to concentrate upon *posture, stance, attitude, and facial expression.* In other words, they must limit themselves to a display of the visual symbol, the outer image of the character, which will represent and reflect the character.

Suppose the character is old? What happens *physically* in the aging process? **191**

Don't allow students to begin their thinking with clichés for showing age, such as the bent back, the cane, and the piping voice. Guide them into thinking of fading vision, lack of memory, poor balance, lack of self-confidence, arthritis, the way clothes hang, the weariness and despair, all evidenced in the body and facial expression. Instruct them to show the outer image of such a person. As another problem, suggest to the students that our old man or old woman has lived a very active life. Perhaps he is an ex-wrestler or laborer, and she is a pioneer woman who has born many children, driven teams of horses, and chopped firewood. How might they look?

Assignments—"Show Us"

The instructor assigns one character from a well-known play to each student. Out of class each is to read and study the play with particular attention given to the character assigned. In a later session each student presents to the group a *visual* characterization of that role. They may move about or perform short mimes, but they may not speak. Afterwards, they may be able to justify any movements they have made by quoting lines or actions from the play. As an example, Sir Tyrone Guthrie directed *The Taming of the Shrew* with "Petrucio" as a shy, modest character. Are there lines in the play which might justify this concept? (Notes are permissible when quoting lines or author's description of the character.) The purpose of this exercise is to show physical attitudes. This should not be difficult if each player is fortified by study of the play and character.

Additional characters from dramatic literature, novels, and even life might be added by the instructor to the following list of possible characters.

CHARACTER ROLES FOR MEN:

Falstaff: Shakespeare tells us he is fat. What else is he? How will you show it?

A retired economics professor: What is his age? How will his profession be indicated? His subject?

Chris: (In *Anna Christie* by O'Neill)

Marchbanks: (In *Candida* by Shaw)

Firs: (In *The Cherry Orchard* by Chekhov)

Mosca: (In *Volpone* by Ben Jonson)

Rosencrantz: (In *Rosencrantz and Guildenstern Are Dead* by Tom Stoppard)

CHARACTER ROLES FOR WOMEN:

An old librarian: Decide her age. Has she ever been married? Is she head librarian or an assistant? What are her hobbies? How does she dress and wear her hair? Does she enjoy reading, herself? What does she read?

Lady Macbeth: How does Shakespeare describe her? What do other characters in the play say about her? Do her actions in the play tell you what sort of woman she is? How will you show that? Translate Shakespeare's words into visual concepts.

Millamant: (In *The Way of the World* by Congreve) See J. L. Styan, *Dramatic Experience* (London: Cambridge, 1965), pp. 8–9.

The Workshop

Rhythm

Architecture may be judged by its relationship to the space surrounding it. In the same way, rhythm can only be appreciated when it is related to surrounding atmosphere and space, that is, to its silences and immobility. A rest in music is an interruption of sound, and yet it is part of that music. Almost all books on directing make the analogy of a director to an orchestra conductor. A stage director *does* study his score. He does deal in beats, changes of pace, rests (silences), tone, pitch, phrasing, and shadings. The only difference is that he is never in front of his orchestra at the performance. He is in the lobby sweating it out or squirming from a rear seat in the auditorium. His conducting must be done during rehearsals.

Each actor in a play contributes a rhythm for his character which he develops during rehearsals. The constant repetition of lines, movement, and silences serves to blend his rhythm with the rhythms of the other characters in the play. There is a time during final rehearsals when a play takes on a music of its own, a most fulfilling experience for the director. No changes should be made once this point is reached. This imprinted behavior is the security which the actors will depend upon during performances.

What is Rhythm?

Rhythm is the impulse behind words and movement. It is time, pace, and meter all rolled into one—always more physical than mental. Walking is a natural starting point for a child's initiation into rhythm. A regular step is a natural unit of time. Muscles are made for movement, and movement is rhythm which involves time in space. It is impossible to conceive of a rhythm without thinking of a body in motion. It is not enough that the actor possesses natural rhythm. He must develop it into a precision tool by developing the muscles of his body. A feeling for rhythm tells an actor the exact time to pause, when to move or be still and silent. If an actor comes on-stage with a walk which is timed to an uneven rhythm, the audience will be immediately alerted to some disturbance to the natural flow of the play.

Rhythm and *tempo* are terms which are frequently used interchangeably, but a director should have a clear definition of each. *Tempo* most often involves the timing of a scene or an entire play, the rate at which the unit of time is either increased or decreased, and is more properly used as a director's term. *Rhythm* is more personal and generally describes an instrumentality of the actor, just as we speak of the rhythm of the pulse.

Exercise 26: Rhythmic Movement and Coordination

Objective: To develop feeling for time and rhythm. Use for all members of the workshop group. Use metronome or drum. Students should be trained to distinguish between various divisions of time and various accents within the divisions of time. For example, this exercise moves constantly in four-beat divisions (speaking as they walk will help).

1. The group begins by walking around the action circle in response to a regular beat.

step-step-step-step
step-step-step-step

2. At a given signal and without breaking rhythm, *change* the *first step* to a *stomp*.

stomp-step-step-step
stomp-step-step-step

3. When all are accustomed to this rhythm, *change* the *second step* to a *rest*.

stomp-rest-step-step
stomp-rest-step-step

4. Assorted variations of your own can continue the complication and concentration. Try clapping with each step on every group of four beats.

stomp-rest-step-step
clap-clap-clap-clap
stomp-rest-step-step
clap-clap-clap-clap

After constant repetition, muscular actions pass outside the control of the brain into automatism. The instructor may want to combine or substitute speech or song with the already imprinted behavior. Exercise 26 above (second movement) was used in double time for the army in the APA production of *Pantagleize*.

We have all noted the magic of combined and disassociated rhythms in nature, traffic, and in all life around us. When asked if he had any "particular hobby-horse" he rode in his work as actor-director, Sir Laurence Olivier said:

> *I rely greatly on rhythm. I think that is the one thing I understand . . . the exploitation of rhythm, change of expression, change of pace in crossing the stage. Keep the audience surprised, shout when they're not expecting it, keep them on their toes . . . change from minute to minute.*[8]

Some Exercises in Learning to Speak Verse

EXERCISE 27: RECOGNITION OF TONAL VALUES

Assign group members to memorize a certain soliloquy from a Shakespearian play. Later, while they are seated in a circle, have

---

[8]Interview with Sir Laurence Olivier by Kenneth Harris, *Los Angeles Times Calendar*, March 2, 1969. Reprinted by permission of *The London Observer*.

each member speak one word of the speech, in turn. Increase and
decrease speed.

**The
Workshop**

EXERCISE 28: FINDING THE SENSE OF A SCENE

Choose a scene from some verse play, preferably one of dialogue.
Have the actors decide which words carry the *sense* of the scene.
Rehearse: 1. Speak selected words loudly, others softly.
2. Vocalize only the selected words.

EXERCISE 29: IN METER

Have the actors read lines from one of the great Greek tragedies
to the accompaniment of a percussion instrument. Vary the rhythmic
patterns and silences.

EXERCISE 30: MECHANICAL RHYTHM

Here is one Peter Brook uses. Assign all group members to memorize a soliloquy or verse of your choosing. Divide the piece into
three sections. Then have three individuals read the piece as a unit
using no special expressive delivery, but reading it in turn—

1. As quickly as possible.
2. Slowing down gradually.
3. Accenting certain previously selected words, using beats or
silences for other words.

When speaking verse, there are mechanical beats which must be found.
The difference between *intoning* and speaking verse properly is in *adjusting
the emphasis in accordance with the meaning.* The three main faults of the
amateur in speaking verse are: (1) the melodious or "stagey" reading; (2)
an academic sing-song; (3) colloquialism which chops up the verse and is
unforgivable. *Search out the meaning and the verse will appear automatically.
Reality can be achieved only through the verse.*

Gesture

Movement is as much a correlative of gesture as it is of rhythm. Few
gestures can be made without involving the entire body to different degrees.
A person sitting at a desk, handing a letter to another, uses not only his
fingers, hand, and arm, but he has altered his body balance and readjusted
many muscles by this simple action.

The form gestures will take will vary with different play styles. Hands
in pockets, flicks of the wrist, short, jerky, incompleted movements which

we call gestures may be all right for Pinter characters, but unsuitable for Shakespeare. Classical plays require that gestures be free, open, and completed—in keeping with the lyrical intentions.

In *Berkeley Square*, the late Leslie Howard used mundane gestures as the modern young man, but when the same character was transported back into the eighteenth century, Howard used more graceful gestures in keeping with that period.

When properly chosen and executed, a gesture can do a great deal to illustrate character. They give an audience an immediate image of a person. Some actors are inclined to use gestures on the stage which they themselves use in daily life, rather than find those which only the character would use. Where are such gestures to be found? Sir Laurence Olivier said:

> *Sometimes on the top of a bus I see a man. I begin to wonder about him. I see him do something, make a gesture. Why does he do it like that? Because he must be like this. And if he is like this, he would do (gesture) in a certain situation (gesture). Sometimes months later, when I am thinking about a bit of business, I hit on a gesture, or a movement, or a look, which I feel instinctively is right. Perhaps not till later; perhaps weeks after I have been making that gesture I realize that it came from the man on top of the bus.*[9]

It would seem axiomatic to state that gestures should never be used to pump out every word spoken, and yet I have seen actors do it. Evidently Shakespeare did also, for he cautioned players not to "saw the air too much with your hand." Peter Brook defines a gesture as "a statement or wordless language" to be used only when emotion and words will not convey the meaning.

EXERCISE 31

Assignment: The director or instructor gives the following instructions to all members of his group: "Select a phrase from some dramatic work which in your opinion should be accompanied by a gesture." And in a later class—

1. Each member of the group is to come forward, face the others, and using emotion and gestures, attempt to convey the meaning of the phrase, *without the use of speech or mouthing*.

2. He indicates when he is finished by giving some gesture of finality to the group, but he remains in place for evaluation.

NOTE: The test of how well the actor's gesture has conveyed the meaning will be indicated by how quickly others guess that meaning. Frequently they will guess the actual line.

The old game of charades is an excellent exercise in the use of gestures

[9]*Ibid.*

to transmit meaning. But pantomime not only employs gesture, but also requires action of the entire body, utilizing the whole rather than a part.

EXERCISE 32: GESTURE, MOVEMENT

The instructor reads a short scene from a play involving no more than four characters. Actors are assigned roles and as the instructor reads, the actors supply gestures and movements, silently. In short, this will be a silent movie. This exercise is more challenging when the actors are hearing the lines for the first time and reacting spontaneously.

Pauses

In Michael Green's amusing book about English amateur theatricals, he defines an amateur actor as one who "remembers the pauses but not the lines."[10] I do not believe that anyone will deny that it is important for an actor to learn his lines and be able to speak them without hesitation. But the actor must also memorize those intervals of time in which he does not speak, the pauses or silences. These can be as important to a play as rests are to musical composition. Lines of dialogue on a printed page follow an unbroken line of continuity. When to hesitate, to bring out meaning; when to pause for dramatic effect or to elucidate character must be determined by the director. Such decisions cannot be made intellectually, but must be arrived at emotionally.

Silence Can Be Golden

Dialogue is what the characters say, but another form of dialogue exists. Intervals of silences can be pregnant with drama, exploring thoughts the characters cannot, care not, dare not, say. Silence is another means by which the director communicates his ideas to an audience. It has many forms. There is the *pause* of a few seconds between phrases, the silent *break* between one thought and another, the silent *interval* which gives emphasis to a movement or an emotion. And then there is the full *stop*, in which the absence of sound usually indicates that one scene has ended and that another is about to begin. In our context, perhaps a better word to use than *silence* would be *stillness*. Stillness has a creative connotation not implied by the word *silence*.

One of the unique developments in staging by young directors is their rediscovery of the value of stillness. There can be no doubt that immobility and silence create a dramatic effect. It can be used in the same way that modern sculptors use open space, or as they call it, "negative volume," as an integral element of the composition itself. The very first exercise in my

[10]Michael Green, *Downwind of Upstage* (New York: Hawthorn, 1964).

acting book requires that the student stand perfectly still and relaxed in front of the class for a period of time. This is exactly what happens in the beginning of The Living Theatre production of *Mysteries and Smaller Pieces*. A quite ordinary-looking young man in levis enters, takes center stage, and stares at the spectators for ten minutes. When the audience realizes he is not going to *do* anything, they begin to admire his passivity in response to their taunts and catcalls. This in itself is drama and also part of the overall composition.

Many plays have scenes in which a character delivers a long speech while other characters are required to remain silent and immobile. Obviously, the director must see to it that they never stand looking blankly at the speaker. They must be involved by listening attentively and reacting to everything the speaker is saying. The director must teach them the use of the "inner monologue." During early rehearsals he permits them to whisper their thoughts and reactions to what is being said until these become imprinted in their minds. Thereafter, body positions and facial expressions will transmit their thoughts *silently* to an audience.

Exercise 33: Inner Monologue

Select a scene or two from a play and allow members of the workshop to invent lines suitable as reactions to the main speaker.

Suggestions: Marcus Antonious in *Julius Caesar* (Act III, Sc. ii)—"Friends, Romans, Countrymen. . . ."
Hamlet's "Advice to the Players" (Act III, Sc. ii).

Anyone who has seen a production of *Dial M for Murder* will remember those long scenes of silent business with the apartment key which added so much to this suspense mystery.

In *Tovarich* an indigent Russian countess-in-exile applies for the position of maid in the household of a wealthy Parisian businessman. He grants her an interview, but during it appears unimpressed by her attempts to charm him. There is speculation in the audience as to whether or not she will get the much-needed job. After ending the interview, he walks in silence to the French windows at the rear, then closes them slowly behind him; but just as he is about to disappear from view, he frames his face between them, showing a sly, lecherous smile as he looks in her direction. This business is silent but full of action, suspense, character revelation, and comedy. It accounts for the biggest laugh in the show.

Speech, Voice, Dialogue

The voice has always been considered one of the greatest assets of an actor. When Richard Burbage, the original interpreter of many Shakespearian heroes, and the great David Garrick were described by writers of their time, invariably these writers attributed voice as the finest of these actors' superlative skills. Voice and speech dexterity is not acquired easily, but only after long and careful study. This book might well devote an entire chapter to this important subject, but there are excellent texts available on voice and speech which are recommended to the director unfamiliar with the scope of this discipline. Other readers, such as speech teachers, will be very familiar with the discipline. These teachers may be more interested in the more innovative phases of modern direction available in this but not in other texts. However, absence of adequate voice and speech coverage in this book is not meant to disparage those subjects. Correct pronunciation, resonation, diction, articulation, projection, and tonal range, as well as the beautiful melody of the human voice, are assets sadly lacking in a majority of modern American actors.

Often during a performance, an actor may feel he has at last reached a high inner-emotional experience in his work. But what does it mean if the audience could not hear him because he garbled his lines? Many actors have elementary faults of voice and speech which a director will need to correct. Oral patterns are responsible for audibility, intelligibility, impact, and variety. These are also the chief means of expression for the actor. As an illustration, the ability to use a sustained tone is a necessity when playing the classics; and for the truly great roles, an actor must learn how to conserve his voice for those tremendous surges of passion at the end. Voice and speech training should begin with the motor sources.

Training the voice as well as the body is a basis of the American Conservatory Theatre's total program. Voice coach Mark Zeller works with actor Paul Shenar. (Courtesy of the American Conservatory Theatre of San Francisco)

EXERCISE 34: RESPIRATION

(a) *Clavicular Breathing.* Stand and relax. As you raise your shoulders and collarbone, inhale slowly. Exhale. Breathe this way several times; then try speaking a sentence.

(b) *Upper Thoracic Breathing.* Relax in place. As you inhale this time, place your palms against the breastbone and raise the chest. Now speak the same sentence.

(c) *Medial Breathing.* Relax, and as you inhale this time, place your palms against the lower ribs, moving them upward and outward. Repeat. Now read the same sentence.

(d) *Diaphragmatic-Abdominal Breathing.* Stand at ease and inhale as you place your right palm over the soft part of your abdomen just under the ribs. Put your left palm against the ribs and abdominal wall. Repeat. Then try the sentence.

NOTE: Upper chest or clavicular breathing (a) is to be avoided, as it results in fatigue and lack of control. Breathing is a natural and spontaneous process. For acting, (b) and (c) would be best. A test may be made by tightening a belt around the waist, and when breathing is correct, this binding will compress the abdominal muscle.

EXERCISE 35: BREATH CONTROL

Take a full deep breath and count silently: *in*, 1, 2, 3, 4, 5, *hold*, 6, 7, 8, 9, 10, *out*. Now increase the counts each time the exercise is repeated.

EXERCISE 36: PROJECTION

Poor projection is one of the major faults of the inexperienced actor. He simply cannot be heard. Each student should try to reach various distances with his voice. He should use short sentences at first, such as, "Wait where you are; we're coming," or "We're going back to camp," or "Take the luggage out of the car." In doing so, the student should try to visualize the persons with whom he is trying to communicate, even though he is unable to see them. Mentally he should reach out to touch the audience, not with his hand but with his voice. Projection is psychological as well as physical.

QUESTIONS FOR INSTRUCTOR

1. Do the students raise their shoulders and upper chest when breathing deeply? (They shouldn't.)
2. Do they strain to increase loudness? (There should be no straining in proper breathing.)
3. Does the quality of tone become harsh and wavering? (This indicates lack of breath control.)
4. Do they tire after four or five attempts? (They are probably breathing in the upper chest.)

Dialogue

Correcting the faults of the inexperienced in reading dialogue can be done only if the instructor works on an individual basis. The *purpose* of dialogue should never be lost. It is to tell the story, to create atmosphere, to express mood, and to reveal the characters. Thought progressions are indicated by voice inflections, that is, changes in pitch or tone, and by changes in rhythm.

1. Place hand on chest and speak in the lowest possible pitch. Note the vibrations within.

2. Now use the nasal resonators by pronouncing the consonant N-n-n-n.

3. Next try the laryngeal resonators. Inhale. Imitate the "Louis Armstrong" sound (so dubbed by a student).

4. Try the occipital resonators. Inhale. Now speak in your highest possible register. Note how the voice vibrates in the back of the head toward the occiput.

First try making sounds in your natural pitch, then through the various resonance passages. Note how you are producing various tones.

Suggestions: Have students act out stories using a variety of *sounds only*: bells, doors, weather, cars, trains, animals, guns, etc.

Additional exercises and exploration into such subjects as reserve breath supply and control, phrasing and pausing, timing, pitch, range, articulation and pronunciation, dialects, accents, vowels, diphthongs, consonants, and sustained tone may be found in *Acting, The Creative Process.* As in the case of all other lab exercises, the aim of voice and speech work is to move away from theory, philosophy, and psychology into the practice of more physical organic instincts. Work in voice and speech means work with the entire body. Vocal expression begins first with some body action, as when we bang our fist on a table—and *then* shout.

Further Reading

EMOTIONS

Bartlett, F. C. *Remembering: A Study in Experimental and Social Psychology.* New York: Cambridge University Press, 1932.

Blake, Robert R., and Ramsey, Glen V., eds. *Perception: An Approach to Personality.* New York: Ronald Press Co., 1951.

Fromm, Erick. *Man For Himself.* New York: Rinehart & Co., 1947.

Reymert, Martin L., ed. *Feelings And Emotions.* New York: McGraw-Hill, 1950.

Sarte, Jean-Paul. *The Emotions: Outline and Theory.* New York: Philosophical Library, 1948.

Schachtel, Ernest G. *Metamorphosis.* New York: Basic Books, 1959. (Analysis of specific emotions: hope, fear, joy, anxiety, pleasure, etc.)

SPEECH AND VOICE

Brigance, William N., and Henderson, Florence. *A Drill Manual for Improving Speech.* New York: J. P. Lippincott Co., 1939.

Chapter 9

Bronstein, Arthur J., and Jacoby, Beatrice F. *Your Speech and Voice.* New York: Random House, 1967.

Eisenson, Jon. *The Improvement of Voice and Diction.* 2nd ed. New York: Macmillan Co., 1966.

Fairbanks, Grant. *Voice and Articulation Drillbook.* New York: Harper & Row Publishers, 1961. (A standard)

Hahn, Elise, et al. *Basic Voice Training for Speech.* New York: McGraw-Hill, 1957.

Machlin, Evangeline. *Speech for the Stage.* New York: Theatre Arts Books, 1970.

At Stratford, Conn., actors are given physical training to develop their bodies as interpretative tools. (Photo by Alfred Westheimer, courtesy of the American Shakespeare Festival Theatre)

Summary

Group training should never be underestimated. It will:

1. Encourage a sense of pride in the work and in the group.
2. Stimulate a loyalty to and an understanding of the director.
3. Discourage solo performing and foster group interdependency.
4. Provide enthusiasm for the production to come.
5. Provide time for the director to study individuals, to explore their talents, and to train the less talented.
6. Allow the director a solid base of experience with each individual before casting.

Of course, as in any group of individuals, there will be those who are opinionated, argumentative, or uncooperative. The director must win over such students to his viewpoint. But bad temper, hysteria, and star complexes should not be tolerated. If the director feels unable to correct misinterpretations regarding the director-actor relationship, then the offenders should be

202

promptly eliminated. This must be done before they subvert the morale of the entire company.

Harmony must always exist within the group if any creative work is to be done. But in "freeing the actor," direction must not disintegrate into no direction at all. The director should make it clear that he will determine what work is to be done and that the actors are there to accomplish it. One of the directing texts in wide use states that direction consists mainly in telling actors what they should *not* do. This is dangerous advice. It may have been true, in part, some time ago, but directing today is much more complicated than that. In the first place, directing is the exact opposite of criticism. There is no need to criticize and dissect. The director must work constructively, never speaking of something he feels is wrong without being ready with alternatives. More effective results will be accomplished if he remains calm and follows a logical pattern of procedure. This will discourage dissension and create confidence in the director.

Workshop activities are optional. The main objective is to develop acting students within the components of that discipline; to encourage physical relaxation for the individual, replacing that dreadful self-consciousness which students experience when first stepping on a stage. Just as a pianist begins his practice with scales in order to develop physical dexterity and skill, so the actor is trained in the separate parts which eventually integrate into an acting technique. The work includes the use of gestures without words, movement without character, and emotion without situation, until the student is able to locate the precise area of his deficiencies and improve them.

No effort is made to produce anything for observers; nevertheless, in the student's mind is the conviction that one day a play will be produced and by improving his skill he could become part of it. The play may not materialize until next month, or next year, but today it is all fun and games—with a purpose!

One or two of your members may feel self-conscious by the apparent childishness of some of these exercises. *Reactivating a childlike approach in adults may very well be the key to unlocking the acting mystique.* A spontaneous human response to ideas or to a set of circumstances, free use of the imagination, acceptance of an abstract fantasy world—these are elements of acting most lacking in the mature adult. This should be explained to the students. Those who are incapable of accepting these exercises as nothing more than child's play may also lack the imagination to become competent actors. Think of any fine actor and you think of dedication, self-discipline— and imagination.

For the director, in addition to the main purpose of training his students, his interest in workshop is diagnostic. Here he has the leisure to make considered judgments and devise intelligent solutions. The pressures in rehearsals do not provide such an atmosphere or opportunity. Much of that ephemeral spark which ignites and illuminates an inspired production depends upon a vital collaboration between the director and his actors. It can begin in workshop.

CHARACTERIZATION 10

"Who are you?" said the caterpiller. Alice replied shyly,
"I—I hardly know, Sir, just at present. —At least I know
who I was when I got up this morning, but I must have
changed several times since then."

— Lewis Carroll,
Alice's Adventures in Wonderland

To the layman, creating character is thought to be the responsibility of the playwright and the actor. But it would be odd, indeed, if the director, who is responsible for every detail of the production, should permit this vital part to be outside his control.

Characterization can be the lynch-pin of an entire production. An audience is often more interested in what happens to the characters than in any other factor. Unless the director is responsible for the characterizations, how will he be able to decide upon movement, stage business, interpretation of the play, or where to place the emphasis in the production? The function and relative importance of each character will need to be decided before rehearsals begin.

An actor may contribute to, even alter, the director's point of view about a character, but final decisions regarding all characterizations must be the director's prerogative. Only he is able to see the whole as well as the parts.

The Importance of Characters to a Play

All artists deal in symbols. The characters in a play are used by the playwright as symbols by which he conveys his meanings. These symbols are invested with human traits and drives which allow an audience to identify with them. Without characters, a plot would be simply a series of events. The characters are the agents of the plot. Through them the audience becomes involved in the drama because they recognize the human qualities in the characters and imagine themselves in the events of the play. Only events and actions relating to people are theatrically effective. This is what makes an audience care. Artistic fulfillment in any art form is possible only when there is an emotional response on the part of the viewer. An audience needs to feel, not think. This was Brecht's dilemma. His politics seem outmoded today, just as Ibsen's social problems are no longer of interest. But both authors live on because of other values—Ibsen for his characters and Brecht for his theatricalism.

Emotional response in an audience is most often achieved through characters. Events, even action, generate little reaction in an audience *unless these affect characters.* A devastating hurricane sweeps across the Atlantic coast. This is an event, an action. But our interest is in the *effect of the hurricane upon people, their lives and homes.* It is an historical fact that the Continental Army crossed the Delaware river to surprise the British. But to us, it is "Washington crossed the Delaware." History becomes interesting through people. We all remember Falstaff, Sherlock Holmes, Oliver Twist, Scarlett O'Hara, and Holden Caulfield. Most of us can close our eyes and see them, they are so vivid. But how readily can we remember the plots of their stories? Characters keep us interested in the play. We empathize with Romeo or even with a villain like Richard III. Good or bad, we recognize their humanity and associate with them.

Character expressed visually and emotionally in this production of The Lark *by the South Eugene (Oregon) High School, with designs by David Sherman and directed by Edward W. Ragozzino. (Register-Guard photo by Phil Grenon, courtesy of Lane Community College)*

Actor into Character

A playwright can do no more than suggest a character. He has neither the time nor space that is available to the novelist. His playscript serves only as an orientation for the actor and director. The director supplies the substance and form, the actor the flesh and blood. Often the inexperienced actor or a professional lacking imagination will rely heavily upon the playwright, expecting the playwright to carry him. In such circumstances the play presents the actors instead of the actors presenting the play.

The director's task is to stimulate his actors into individual creativity, to suggest possibilities, to find relationships between the actor and his character, to encourage the actor's sense of perception, and to serve as the actor's audience when he has none. Of course, it will always be the actor who makes the final contact with the audience. He is the relay team's anchor man. It is the actor who will finally win or lose the day. This alone should be sufficient reason for him to know his character better than the playwright who created him or the director who collaborated with him. *Understanding is the key to successful characterization.*

Some directors request actors to write biographies of their characters in order to give a more penetrating insight into their roles. Actors rarely seem happy to do this. However, Anthony Quinn is reported to have written some 11,000 words on his part in the film *Flap*. His notes begin with "the character's character (very male), and his weight (193 pounds), and continues for forty-five pages.[1]

In real life we might walk into a room filled with strangers, and after being introduced all around, find that one certain individual interests us more than all the others. We would like to know this person better, to ask him about his background, his means of livelihood, his ambitions; but good manners do not encourage such direct interrogation. We must wait until such information is volunteered, bit by bit. And this may take years. Time alone forges intimacy between people. Older married couples, after years of living together, know each other so well that they actually come to look alike. This is the sort of intimacy the actor must develop between himself and his character. But the actor has not the luxury of time.

Understanding the Character

Not only must an actor know his character, he must also *understand* him. He must know why the character does what he does in the play. When such an understanding is accomplished, and only then, will the actor be able to sense anything false to the character in speech or movement. With the director's guidance he must reason out each problem in characterization. He must adjust to the events in the play and justify all lines and business in harmony with the author's concept.

Rapport by Association

It is an unfortunate truth that most of us understand only that which is within ourselves. An actor will only be able to create in direct proportion to his understanding of his fellow man and through an ability to sympathize with him. Let us suppose that one of your characters is a murderer. How will you get an actor to understand and sympathize with a murderer? If the actor were placed in that character's circumstances, had similar mentality and background, would he not do exactly as the character did? Unless the actor is able to understand, even sympathize, with the character, he will

[1]Joyce Haber, "Anthony Quinn Really Takes Film Work Seriously," Interview in *Los Angeles Times Calender*, October 26, 1969, p. 19.

not be able to bring him alive for an audience and move them emotionally. "The artist need not have experienced in actual life every emotion he can express," states Philosopher Susanne Langer in her provocative *Feeling and Form*. "It may be through manipulation of his created elements that he discovers new possibilities of feeling strange moods, perhaps greater concentrations of passions than his own temperament could ever produce."[2]

When asked by a director to read a line or make a move which seems false, the genuinely creative actor never says, "I don't feel it that way." He relies upon his intimacy with the character to justify the line or move. In so doing, he is also ready with plausible answers should the director ask, "Why do you do that?" or "Why do you read the line that way?" But the hack, the unimaginative actor, never bothers much to create a character. He merely lends his voice, body, personality to a part. He creates nothing, but is simply using what God and the playwright has given him, and does not deserve to be called an artist. An artist creates, using the materials available, to compose by selection, observation, research, experience, inspiration, and discipline something which had no existence before he set his hand and heart to it. Most actors do not study enough. Contrary to general opinion, acting is not a lazy man's pastime. A creative actor is never content to read lines written by an author and to be moved about the stage by a director like a pawn on a chessboard. Any actor worthy of the name does more than read a play once—or twice. It is not enough to be able to follow the story and to decide what he, as an actor, will do with the part he has been assigned. Indeed he does not view the work ahead from an actor's point of view at all, but from the character's. He begins by *absorbing* the play, and this requires much study. He allows it to seep through his pores until it becomes a living part of himself. He knows that his character cannot be pushed and jammed into the confines of an actor's ego. A character only begins to live after the actor knows him, understands him, and is on intimate terms with him. Even then, the character will come in his own time when he feels no longer a stranger and when the actor is at repose. This moment of revelation will be clear to the actor. He may note a different pitch in his voice, become conscious of an unfamiliar gesture or a strange way of thinking, as actor and character fuse into one. When this metamorphosis is complete, the actor will begin to think, act, and even look like the character. Blind confidence will not accomplish this change. Logical steps must be taken. Development comes systematically, piece by piece, requiring intensive concentration, investigation, and self-discipline from the actor and systematic guidance by the director. Here are four steps that the director might use in working with his actors on characterizations.

Character Delineation

1. ORIENTATION:

Study of play, the milieu in which character lives. Character's relationships to others in play. Find the individuality in the character. What makes

[2]Susanne Langer, *Feeling and Form* (New York: Charles Scribner's Sons, 1953), p. 374.

him different from others in the play? Decide his mental and moral traits. Behavior? Dress? What is his importance to the play? To the plot? Who is he? What is he? When? Where? Why?

2. MOTIVATIONAL PERIOD:

What are his biological drives? What makes him do the things he does? What are his dominant characteristics? What does he say—or not say? What does he want? Find a sentence or speech in the part which illuminates the essence of the character.

3. PHYSICAL ASPECTS:

All movements are motivated by thought (we decide to get up out of a chair before we do). Select the inner dynamics of the character which can be shown physically and audibly. Select rate and tension of his moves and what physical aspects can be adapted to the character. How does he fill space? Is he a small man, a fat one? What is the rhythm of his walk? The texture of his voice? Synthesize the character *in action*.

4. EVALUATION:

Remember you are the audience for your actors at this point. Don't *judge* their experimental work, assist them.

EXERCISE 38

Begin with some simple everyday duty, such as washing one's face, reading a newspaper, threading a needle, etc.
1. Instruct the student to pantomime the action as he himself might do it.
2. Next, have the student pantomime the action as several different characters would do it. Select a character from a well-known play, announce the name of the character and play, then have the students improvise a scene which is not in that play, but using the character from it. Pantomime only, then with words (improvised).

The actor can carefully scrutinize a character's background and quickly learn a great deal about him. But to be valid this search must begin with the facts as stated in the play—the author's description of the character, what is said by the character, what others say about him, and how he contributes to the play. In other words, an actor must work backwards—from what happens to the character during the action to the *reasons* for what happens.

The Motivations for Behavior

It does not help much to use adjectives to describe the character. *Everything must be shown and be made clear by action.* To do so, motivations must

be found. These in turn will suggest certain physical behavior. All movement
must come from character impulse.

Developing a Character

Before working with actors on their characterizations, the director himself
will have analyzed the functions of each character in the play and how
they relate to the story. Principal characters will of course motivate the
plot more so than subsidiaries, whose function may be only to contribute
to the protagonists or to lend atmosphere. Therefore, the principals will
demand more of the director's attention than others. Whenever possible,
the facts in the play should be used to reach decisions on the intellectual
or emotional motivations of the characters. If none can be found in the
play, then these must be invented but based upon lines or incidents in the
play. A knowledge of what the characters are inside will help greatly in
reaching decisions which can not be clarified by the script. The director
determines what importance each character will assume in his production
and how it will be coordinated, that is, the relationship between the characters
in each scene, in each act, and in the entire play.

All characters have an identity with a time and place and this must be
considered. The director should work with the actors and decide upon the
social and educational backgrounds of all the characters, mental and moral
attitudes, the drives of each, what action is taken to fulfill these drives, or
the conflicts which might inhibit them. An audience will not be able to
see inside each character, but *the exterior must be shown because it will
mirror inner-dynamic sources.*

Character Progression

Some characters in a play will remain the same, but usually the leading
characters will begin in one way and then, because of what happens during
the play, change for better or worse. This gives the audience the experience
of witnessing an event. Something has happened to someone like themselves,
and they were there to see it. My friend, the late John Gassner, once said
that *Waiting for Godot* should have been a one-act play. For most people,
Godot has not enough character progression to hold an audience's attention
for a full evening.

Other modern plays also disregard progression, which may be one reason
for their limited audience appeal. The function of mounting dramatic scenes
is to reveal the constantly shifting psychic lives of characters. When character
progression is absent in a play, the actor is only permitted to show one
facet of a character. In the great dramatic classics, transitions of the leading
characters can be traced scene by scene. This metamorphosis happens before
the very eyes of the audience, and yet the basic inner-dynamism of the
character is never lost. In any aspect of vital experience there is always
progression—some sequential development. Each living thing reacts to the

world about it by constantly changing its total condition. When it ceases to do so—it is dead.

Exercise 39: In Character Progression

1. Improvise a few lines of everyday dialogue. ("Good morning," "How are you," "Nice day," etc.)
2. Create characters and improvise same.
3. Decide upon some experience these characters have just undergone. Show how they have progressed or regressed because of that experience, using the same dialogue.

Real-Life Prototypes

The director should be cautious about encouraging actors to base character interpretations upon people in real life. It is true that stage characters must seem like real people, but when an actor begins with a living person, his characterization usually ends in imitation. Ordinary living people may seem to have certain aspects similar to a character in a play, but there are points of difference which might nullify their use as models. Stage characters are not ordinary people, they are extraordinary. The great dramatic heroes are wittier, more intelligent, and quicker to act than ordinary men. More happens to a character in a play than to a dozen people in real life. A character is the quintessence of a person, highly concise and richly colored. The magic of theatre is in making devised characters *appear to be real*. Real people would only bore an audience. Chekhov's characters are accepted as being very real, but they are carefully devised intensifications of real people.

In all art, truth is relative. Who can tell how much the Mona Lisa resembles

Characterizations based on animals in the Broadway hit, Story Theatre, *created and directed by Paul Sills. (Courtesy of Center Theatre Group, Mark Taper Forum, Los Angeles, Calif.)*

the model? If an actor bases his character upon someone he knows in real life, it is likely to result in an unreal characterization. A painter or a sculptor will frequently use as models the hands of one person and the posture of another and combine these to create a figure which embodies *the artist's own intent and purpose.* On stage we are not interested in a literal transcription of life but a theatricalization. The most effective means of developing character will be by using observation and experience—then selecting and refining to fit a concept devised by author, actor, and director. Real people are too complex, have too many contradictory and dull traits to be convincing on a stage.

Characterization Must Relate to the Play

So far, we have been considering characters with a high degree of intellectual, emotional, and physical reality. None of what we have said would apply to a character such as Caliban in *The Tempest.* There is a wide range of characters to be found in dramatic writing, some of which are symbolic or *one-dimensional,* such as Good Deeds or The Devil in the morality plays. Others are *two-dimensional,* such as Slander and Waitwell in the Restoration plays. Characters of depth are *three-dimensional.* These are found among Shakespeare's leading characters and in the plays of Ibsen, Chekhov, and O'Neill. It is these three-dimensional characters which we have been considering so far.

In *The Dramatic Experience,*[3] J. L. Styan devotes an entire chapter to this subject and it is well worth reading. Of course, it is obvious that one need not investigate the social mores, family background, or motivations of a one-dimensional character such as The Devil in a morality play. But one should be careful about too much generalizing or pigeon-holing of characters conceived by our best dramatists. On the other hand, we need not hesitate about deciding that Knowledge or Five Wits in *Everyman* are symbols. Nor are G.I., Senator, or Protestor in *Viet-Rock* anything more than labels. Such one-dimensional characters have always existed in the theatre along with more recognizably human characters. Types bear the same relationship to characters as a poster does to a painting. They are sharply outlined, highly colored, and nonrealistic. When the Elizabethan stages were displaying Shakespeare's multi-faceted characters, they were also playing A Good Angel and An Evil Angel in Marlowe's *Faustus.* One year before Ibsen wrote *The League of Youth,* the following cast descriptions appeared in the acting version of Dion Boucicault's *After Dark:*

> OLD TOM (A Board Man—Character Lead)
> CHANDOS BELLINGHAM (Man-about-town—Juvenile Tragedian)
> DICEY MORRIS (Gambling House Keeper—Character Comedy)
> SIR GEORGE MEDHURST (Juvenile Lead)
> GORDON CHUMLEY (Captain of Dragoons—Walking Gent)

[3] J. L. Styan, *The Dramatic Experience, A Guide to the Reading of Plays* (London: Cambridge University Press, 1964), pp. 54–70.

POINTER (Police A Division—Utility)
AREA JACK (A Night Bird—Utility)
JEM AND JOSEY (Negro Minstrel—Bus.)
ELIZA (Sir George's Wife—Lead)

NOTE: During the turn of the century and for some time after, many
theatres had a permanent "company of actors." Each actor was chosen
for his particular "line of business" or range of character. In the more
popular plays an actor was expected to be "up on the lines" for characters
within his range. This custom eliminated most casting problems for the
director. When the acting script arrived he simply matched the role to
the specialist in that line in his company. "Walking Ladies or Gents" were
usually townspeople and not members of the professional company. "Bus"
denoted "general business" or "utility actor," while a "walking gent" meant
an extra, lower in theatrical level than a "bus" actor. Such information
was printed in the acting versions and never appeared on the programs.
("A Board Man" refers to a down-and-outer, who walks the streets carrying
a sandwich sign.)

*Director Ira Zuckerman worked closely with set and costume
designer Christina Giannini for the production of* The Ghost
Sonata *at the North Carolina School of the Arts. (Courtesy of
the North Carolina School of the Arts)*

Guiding the Actor in Character Creation

Objective: To guide and encourage the student in giving imaginative life
to a character as described by the author. This will entail drives and social,   213

psychological, and physical factors, based upon the play and the director's concept of his production.

In general, a character is created by:

1. Playwright's lines and description of characters.
2. What other characters say about him.
3. What the character *does* in the play.
4. His ideas, goals, beliefs, and emotions.
5. His past, heredity, present environment, and appearance.
6. What the actor has to contribute mentally and physically.
7. The emphasis the director cares to give the character.
8. The quality of imagination contributed.

The actor should not begin his characterization until he has a knowledge of the complete play and the period for which it was written. A girl of fifteen in a Shakespearean play will be quite different from one in a farce by Oscar Wilde. Skill at creating character can make the difference between an amateur and a professional. We go to see Sir Laurence Olivier in *Othello*. From his past performances we think we know Olivier the actor, but soon his appearance, voice, walk, and speech convince us that this is another person we are watching. Olivier has become Othello and soon we are transported into Othello's world and we become absorbed in his problems. We have forgotten all about Olivier, the actor. Once an audience accepts the character emotionally and interests itself in his problems, the identity of the actor vanishes. He has become part of the artistic creation. But if a characterization is not fully explored, we see only Sara Jones, whom we have known since childhood, "playing at" being Juliet. An audience must identify with Juliet, not Sara Jones.

EXERCISE 40: CHARACTER CONCEPT BY THOUGHT PROGRESSION (FIRST SESSION)

Objective: To describe a character which an audience would believe capable of a given action.

By the use of logical and orderly thought patterns, the student is to trace back and create a character whose background, age, and

Robert Pastene characterizes Prospero in The Tempest, *as produced by the Minnesota Theatre Company for the Tyrone Guthrie Theatre. (Courtesy of the Tyrone Guthrie Theatre)*

mental, moral, emotional, and physical aspects would cause the character to take the action he does. Put in another way, the student
is to give full justification for the action of the character by understanding the character himself.

This is not a physical exercise, but one demanding orderly thought
progression and imagination. Students are not asked to mime or
improvise, but to *describe* the thoughts, feelings, and behavior of
a character which would be believable to an audience doing what
he or she does.

NOTE: Each member assigned one of the problems below is to *describe*
the situation, filling in the cause and effect from the protagonist's viewpoint
in the first person. At the end of this first session, the director instructs
each student to prepare an improvisation for *the second session.* (Exercise
41)

A. A man who has walked to a parking lot two blocks away finds that
he has left the keys to his car in his office.

B. A girl slaps her mother in the face.

C. A mother slaps her daughter in the face, choosing entirely different
circumstances from above.

D. A young wife hears a noise during the night. She cannot arouse her
sleeping husband and decides to investigate herself. When she enters the
living room, she confronts a burglar.

E. A sensitive fourteen-year-old boy, a music student, is given his first
summer job on a garbage disposal truck. After two days he quits and
attempts to explain to his father.

F. Two office girls from Texas decide to spend their vacations together
in New York. One is offered her plane fare by her employer and she accepts.
She explains why to her friend.

G. A freshman is dared by an upper classman to call the White House
and ask to speak to the President and the President comes to the phone.
Describe the scene.

H. A girl of humble circumstances has saved to buy a fashionable wardrobe in order to be admitted to a garden party of the socially prominent.
At the party she overhears a guest discussing her. What are her reactions?

I. An overprotective mother objects to her daughter dating. A very eligi-
ble young man calls and the mother either changes her attitude, or not.

J. An old rancher, known as a teller of tall tales, tells a whopper—which
comes true. Explain.

K. A young mother forces her eight-year-old son to go to a dancing
class. He returns with a black eye.

L. A young woman is separated from her hiking party and is saved from
a rattlesnake by a man she despises.

M. A protestor sees a wounded policeman lying in the street and helps
him to his feet and to an ambulance.

N. Trapped at a police barricade in an alley, a petty thief believes his
world has come to an end.

EXERCISE 41: CHARACTERIZATION CONCEPT BY THOUGHT
PROGRESSION (Second Session)

Each student who has previously *described* a character and incident now applies it to an *improvisation*. He may use voice to express stream of consciousness or monologue, or play to invisible, related characters, at the director's discretion. He may relate some actual experience he had to the improvisation, or it may be a fantasy. The instructor might judge the results by determining how well the student has

1. Indicated the age of the character.
2. Made the character believable.
3. Shown emotion.
4. Used imagination.

Was there an obvious difference between the actor and the character? Were the thoughts, feelings, and actions explored in such a way that an audience would accept the character as doing what he or she would do in the given situation?

Characterizations in the Newer Plays

There are many playwriting innovations being presented in the experimental theatre. The young director should become familiar with these and judge their efficacy.

An actor already accepted by the audience as one character seems to become another. As a result, an audience is often confused, or as one spectator has put it, "stationless." Also, isolated situations and incidents are reconstruct-

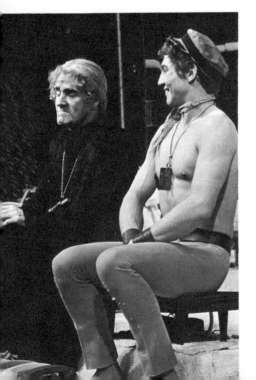

Outward manifestations of inner character is evidenced in this photo of Jay Doyle as Grandma and Scott Hylands (right) in the American Conservatory Theatre's production of The American Dream, *directed by William Ball. (Photo by Hank Kranzler, courtesy of the American Conservatory Theatre of San Francisco)*

ed from different viewpoints. Adding to this distraction is the fragmentation
of the plays themselves. New elements of time and place are introduced,
as well as scenes of ritual, camp, or vaudeville, with little attempt to relate
one scene to another except for polemics.

Transformations

This is the term used to describe the shifting characterizations. As explained
by advocates of experimental theatre, each character has many different facets
of character within, one being dominant and more obvious. This dominant
image or face is the one we present to the world, but underneath are other
people who may burst through the skin of the main identity at any time,
revealing contradictions or complexities. They are careful to point out that
their process is unlike the dual roles found in hundreds of plays from Shakespeare to Brecht to Genet, in which one character pretends to be another.
Their "split personalities" attempt to explore *the many different personalities
within one personality.* The stated objective is for a continuity of progression
to occur, because the same actor plays the various facets of a character.

If this is to be made convincing, it becomes a very difficult acting job.
Not only is the actor required to assume several characters without logic
or without previously preparing the audience, but he must be convincing
in each. By the time an actor has switched from being a condemned prisoner,
to his mother, to General Custer, the audience may be completely baffled.
The acting skill required to make this convincing might even confound Sir
Laurence himself.

The actors are instructed not to attempt any Stanislavskian psychological
motivations, but to make these "transformations" only through physical manifestations. They are to be made abruptly, and the number of characters each
actor must create within a limited time is not exactly conducive to penetration
into any single role.

EXERCISE 42: TRANSFORMATIONS

If a director has time to train his actors beyond a specific production, he might explore a many-faceted character by first having his
students perform a single-character improvisation using established
realities (given circumstances) and then another improvisation in
which several aspects of that character are shown simultaneously.[4]

A majority of the exercises in workshop were those in which the entire
ensemble was to take part. Next we will concentrate upon improvisations
in which some will take part while others observe, and for the first time,
critiques will be offered. Active members will remain on stage after performing for appraisal by the director and observing student-members.

[4]For those interested in further study of this form, there are many examples; for instance,
Van Itallie's *Interview* abounds in transformations.

217

Chapter 10   Critiques: Open Evaluations

The best criticism is always an act of love, written with
enthusiasm and belief—and sometimes sorrow.

—Alan S. Downer

If workshop sessions are to be open to comment by all members, the instructor should caution the students to use tact in giving critiques, as the young can be very cruel to each other. The purpose of general discussions is to be constructive, not destructive.

If a few words of caution are given before these evaluations begin, they will usually prevent possible altercations incited by envy or jealousy. Remarks are to be concentrated upon vital points, and not minor details. Students are to look for and discuss only important values, such as how well the performer solved his particular problem and how well he handled characterization, projection of ideas, and audience interest. If good manners are maintained, analytical discussion can be helpful to both performers and spectators, and most acting studios use this format. But the instructor must remain alert in order to rephrase or amend any harsh remarks which might offend a sensitive performer. Some may resent being criticized by their peers and as a result become self-conscious and inhibited, perhaps even refusing to participate in future work. This would be unfortunate, considering that workshop's great effort is to free the actor of inhibitions and to bolster his confidence, as well as to develop a spirit of camaraderie among the group. But there have been incidents in which open forums have encouraged aggressive students to "take over," usurping the authority of the director. I present the pros and cons, leaving the director to make the choice between opening discussion to all, or keeping critiques exclusively for the director.

Further Reading: Communication

Birdwhistell, R.L. *Expressions of the Emotions in Man: The Kinesic Level.* New York: International Universities Press, 1963.

Carpenter, E., and McLuhan, M. *Explorations in Communication.* Boston: Beacon Press, 1968.

Cherry, C., *On Human Communication.* New York: Science Editions, 1961.

Darwin, C., *The Expressions of the Emotions in Man and Animals.* London: Murray, 1872.

Dittman, A.; Parloff, M.; and Boomer, D. "Facial and Bodily Expression: A Study of Receptivity of Emotional Cues." *Psychiatry,* Vol. 28, 1965.

Frank, L.K. "Tactile Communications." *ETC,* Vol. 16, 1958. A review of general semantics.

Goffman, E. *Encounters.* Indianapolis: Bobbs-Merrill Co., 1961.

———. *Interaction Ritual.* Garden City, N.Y.: Anchor Books, 1967.

———. *Presentation of Self in Everyday Life.* Garden City, N.Y.: Anchor Books, 1959.

Hall, E.T. *The Hidden Dimension.* Garden City, N.Y.: Doubleday & Co., 1966.

———. *The Silent Language.* Garden City, N.Y.: Doubleday & Co., 1959.

Koffka, K. *Principles of Gestalt Psychology*. New York: Harcourt, Brace & World, 1935.

Ortega Y Gasset, J. *Man and People*. New York: W.W. Norton & Co., 1957.

Scheflen, A.E. "Human Communication." *Behavioral Science*, Vol. 13, 1968.

Sommer, R. *Personal Space*. Englewood Cliffs, N.J.: Prentice-Hall, 1969.

Improvisation

Here is a word which is usually misunderstood and generally misused.

> *Improvise*: To compose, recite, sing, play, or sketch without previous study or preparation.
>
> Funk & Wagnalls Dictionary

Applied to theatre, improvisation is a means by which a director and his players locate authentic impulses of a scene or a play by beginning with the given circumstances or established realities, as given by the playwright, or by providing objective points through the use of the "who-what-why" formulae. Improvisation requires the players to supply feelings, actions, and words simultaneously while performing, and *without previous rehearsals*. Pantomime may be improvised, but these are not interchangeable terms. Improvisation is not playwriting, either, but play-understanding. In the professional theatre, actors are disciplined to respect the authority of the play, the playwright, and the director. Improvisations provide release from this authority, allowing the actor to get into direct communication with the essence of a dramatic or comic situation. Improvisation should never be used as an end in itself. Most of the improvisations we see on TV are previously rehearsed and performed "skits." In a strict sense, improvisation is a tool to be used in the training of actors. In fact, public performances of improvisations have been prohibited in England.

The main purpose of improvisation is to familiarize actors with the significant moving parts of a play through an active reference or experience which they can grasp. If the experience is to be meaningful, the player will need to become familiar with the structural qualities of a scene or play. He will need to know why the scene was necessary, for what purpose it was·written, to discover its essence and how that relates to theme, plot, narrative, and characters.

There are many advantages to be acquired by performing improvisations. They teach an actor how to plan his work, respond imaginatively to the given circumstances, and develop a dramatic or comic incident; but most of all they teach him to gain confidence in his acting potential and his work with other actors.

The director may find that the greatest benefit from improvisational work will come during rehearsal periods, where it will become an invaluable aid in clarifying a scene, business, or motivation. If nothing else, improvisation is a means of eliminating imitation and stereotyped reactions, which seem to plague most inexperienced players.

A teenage improvisational workshop, a program of the Arena Theatre in Washington, D.C. (Photo by Fletcher Drake, courtesy of the Living Stage, a project of the Arena Stage in Washington, D.C.)

The Use of Improvisation as a Learning Experience

1. Encourages creation of fresh images.
2. Provides experience in stepping into the world of illusion.
3. Encourages careful preparation through understanding of dramatic presentation.
4. Provides student with means to extend himself from a limited natural environment into wider experiences.
5. Teaches value of flexibility, collaboration, and point of focus.
6. Trains in concentration, observation, and communication.
7. Gives training in creating "the illusion of the first time,"[5] and in following impulses.
8. Provides experience in working from a plan or overall artistic design.

Technique of Improvisation

Although this form is impromptu, there should always be some thought given to it before performing. Improvisation is not entirely ad-lib. It is best when there is a plan or overall artistic design.

"The Given Circumstances"

Improvisation begins with some established realities, a stated problem, or a "given circumstance." In order to develop the given premise, certain cor-

---

[5]"Illusion of the first time": giving the audience the impression that the lines and situation are impromptu.

relative information is usually needed and should be supplied before the improvisation can be considered ready for performing.

The "Who-What-Why"

Who: Are the characters?

What: Happens? (situation)

Why: Did it happen? (motivation, theme)

Where: Does it happen?

When: Does it happen? (today, yesterday, tomorrow)

Rarely are all of these components stated in a given circumstance. Whatever point or points are missing must be supplied by the actors based upon what has been given or implied. When this is not possible, then the actors must create the missing elements imaginatively. When more than one student is involved in an improvisation, all of the involved members should discuss and agree upon the "who-what-why" and from the information they have, invent a plan which will dramatize their answers. Most plans will be improved by the addition of conflict (what happens and why), sequential development, and a conclusion.

As an illustration, let us take the following given circumstance:

A and B have a heated argument in the home of C, who tries to make peace but finds himself attacked by both.

Now let us apply the formula to it:

Who: A and B . . .

What: are having a heated argument . . .

Where: in the home of C . . .

This gives us the characters, situation, conflict, sequential development, climax, and conclusion. The missing elements of *when* and *why* will need to be supplied by us. "Don't stick your nose into other people's business" might at this time function as a kind of theme for us.

Now, in order to perform this as an improvisation, we must create a rough scenario by supplying characterizations, and we must break up the action into "beats," or small developing scenes, beginning with the premise:

A and B are having an argument . . .

Are they friends, relatives, strangers, business partners? How old are they? Suggest backgrounds through body postures, habits, etc. Are they in disagreement about money, wives, gossip, cars, business, ethics, politics, children, religion, or what (decide which will contribute most to your improvisation)? Will you build this scene from a quite innocuous remark to loud insults and threats? Or will you begin with high emotions? Which will be best dramatically? How will you vary tempo and audibility when C enters into the scene?

In the home of C . . .

221

What brings them together? What sort of home has C? Is this meeting social or business? Does C enter from another part of the house or is he present when the argument begins? What is C's relationship to A and/or B? Is he a friend to both? A stranger? What answers will contribute most to the improvisation? Trace down all possibilities.

Who tries to make peace . . .

Obviously this constitutes a fresh development, a new scene, needed for dramatic interest because of what has happened in the first scene. It entails a physical change in positions—an encounter—as C takes central position. If C comes between A and B, this would be understood by the audience as a visual symbol of intervention between opposing forces. The movement alone activates the theme, or point of focus, of this little scene. We must decide the reasons for C's intervention. Will animosity between the men jeopardize some future plan of his? Or perhaps it is simply that he does not want the neighbors to hear, or the baby awakened. What points of argument does he make as he tries to stop the conflict? His statements could lead us into the next scene, in which A and B turn on him.

But finds himself attacked by both.

Why do they object to his peace-making efforts? Do they attack him physically, or only verbally? How is it concluded? Do they knock him out, call the police, call others in, or walk away friends, leaving C their common enemy?

Scenario: Plan of Procedure

Decisive answers to questions such as these will constitute a plan sufficient to begin an improvisation, providing all performers understand it. You will note that no dialogue has been planned, merely sequential development and content for each "beat," or scene. Before improvising, the three actors assigned the problem will have agreed on what is to happen, the order in which it will happen, and the characterizations they are to assume. Narrative, definition of character, and emotional reactions are left to be extemporized. The plan of procedure (or scenario) will be better remembered by all three if written and not left to oral agreement.

Before the improvisation, the director should caution the students to free themselves of all preconceptions and to contact their specific material directly, allowing their sensory equipment and characterizations to create fresh impulses. These impulses are the main reasons for improvisations. The director should also discourage long speeches or soliloquies. Whatever narrative is necessary should be presented physically, in action, rather than verbally. *Don't tell us, show us!*

Director's Evaluation

After presentation of the improvisation, the director usually evaluates not only what has been presented, but the planning done beforehand. This means that he will decide how effective students have been in solving the problem dramatically. Unless one is watchful, improvisations can slip away from the problem as stated, ending as comfortable presentations of what the student is convinced he does best. There is little growth in this.

Improvisation is an instrument for development of understanding. It demonstrates form, a sequence of planning, playing, and evaluating. It is not a show. It will be of value if the director looks for signs of imagination, physical response, and control, and checks how well the players capture the point of focus. Short improvisations are best. Otherwise, students may run low on inspiration.

Although it is important that the director explain carefully the objectives and procedures which are to be followed, improvisations nevertheless provide the highest level of independent study for the individual, being self-initiated and self-directed. They permit students to make their minds work as *they* want them to work. Here they become independent of doing what the director directs them to do. This will help later when rehearsing a play. Proper groundwork in earlier improvisations will encourage individual incentives in the actor. Any director would be happy to have some actors capable of self-help, even if they were inexperienced. During evaluation, in order to discover if the player has been properly motivated, the director should ask such questions as, "Why did you walk away on that speech," "What were you thinking when she showed you the envelope," etc. The student should be able to justify every move, each inflection and attitude. From his answers the director will be able to decide how well the actor has projected his plan to the audience.

Giggling and clowning during an improvisation is usually the result of self-consciousness. Often it can be stopped by pointing out this fact. Of course, there are times when something happens which is genuinely amusing, and laughing will relieve the tension; but *when the work or the players are being ridiculed*, acting the fool should not be tolerated.

In the beginning of improvisational work it is best to have students in roles near their own age and interests. Previous lab exercises should have "loosened up" any reticent members, so that at this point you should not have the problem of forcing anyone into participating against his will.

Everyday conversation and casual movements will not make points so necessary on the stage. *Action and words must be distilled.* Also, there needs to be an intensity in the work as well as tempo, suspense, and complication, and all of these should be built within the overall plan or design.

The "who-what-why" formula used to develop an improvisation is, in reality, a kind of elementary prototype for dramatic composition. There is another method used which is similar, except that different words are used:

Situation:	What happened?
Characters:	To whom?
Locale:	Where did it happen?
Motivation:	Why did it happen?
Atmosphere:	When did it happen?

Enriching an Improvisation by Adding Elements

EXERCISE 43

Let us begin with an everyday nondramatic occurrence and add only one element at a time.

Two people meet.	"Who"	Improvise	Now add the "when"
Two old friends meet.		Improvise	Now add the "what"
Two old friends meet and fail to recognize each other.		Improvise (situation)	Now add the "where"
As both are boarding a plane for Europe.		Improvise	Now add the "why"
One is a CIA agent who does not wish to be recognized and his old friend is a gregarious insurance salesman.		Improvise	

By inventing motivations (the "why") we have also helped in the characterizations and given a conflict-relationship between our two old friends. One is hiding, the other probing.

EXERCISE 44

1. Begin by using only the "why" (motivation element).
2. Each student selects a mood such as anger, suspicion, fear, expectancy, happiness, etc.
3. Each is to improvise a scene consisting of one simple line, "I'll get it," in answer to a telephone or doorbell ringing.
4. All else must be supplied by the player.

EXERCISE 45

1. Use only "where" (locale).
2. Statement of the problem: *A man is standing in line.*
3. Questions to be answered by players: What line? Where is this line? Who is the man? Why is he standing in this line?

NOTE: This is the starting point of one of the off-off Broadway plays. It's title? *Line,* by Israel Horovitz.

EXERCISE 46: The "What" Element

This is a series of exercises in improvisations. The problems state
one or two elements, others to be supplied by the students when
planning what they will do. Mostly these are situations—the
"what"—with other elements, "who-what-why," to be added. Try
to choose elements which relate to each other.

1. A robbery occurs in a busy bank.
2. A suburban home catches fire.
3. A teacher returns to her classroom to find students in an uproar.
4. A job interviewer discovers that one of his childhood idols is applying
to him (or her) for a job.
5. A girl is temporarily blinded by seeing what she believes to be a
UFO. A friend is with her.

EXERCISE 47: The "When" Element

Set up several improvisations of people preparing to take a trip
on a plane. Suggestions:

1. A girl learns her mother is seriously ill in another state and she makes
arrangements to travel to her, including getting permission from her boss.
2. A Cuban exile has reasons to return to Cuba and plans to hijack
the plane.
3. A TV comic who is a "white-knuckle flyer" must fly to fulfill an
engagement.
4. A student who is late for registration.
5. A bankrupt businessman "looking for greener fields."
6. A dignified matron impatient with delays.
7. A strike organizer.
8. An elderly foreign woman on her first flight.
9. A reporter for a national magazine on an assignment.
10.   A couple on a honeymoon.
11.   A rich, former cowboy star.

Perform each improvisation singly and then do another in which
all these people are waiting to board a jet at 4 a.m. Retain the
characters and moods established in previous improvisations. The
boarding gate will not be open for some time, but the passengers
cluster around the entrance hoping to have first choice of seats.
As they wait they strike up conversations. (See *Rimers of Eldrich*,
excerpt, p. 230.)

EXERCISE 48: MISCELLANEOUS PROBLEMS

1. Play an emotional scene without overt emotional display.
2. Create an improvisation which is in direct contrast to a soap-
opera TV program. This will require two separate improvisations

and casts. Play them in counterpoint.

3. Create a printing plant in which the actors improvise noises and actions of machines. (This may require a visit to an actual plant.)

4. Choose a basically narrative description of some character from a famous novel. Reconstruct the narrative into an active or dramatic improvisation. The student should look, sound, and feel like the character. At a signal from the director, another actor takes over the characterization, then another, etc.

NOTE: Several actors should work on this problem so that all are prepared. They need not collaborate as in other improvisations.

5. Character: A tough, wounded Marine is being loaded into a helicopter.

6. Use banal dialogue, such as "Nice day," "What's doing?" "How'ya been?" etc. in

A. A dramatic situation.

B. A comedy situation.

C A situation using characters which are recognizable, functional, predictable, or *one-dimensional*, such as: Smokey the Bear, The Devil, St. Peter, Santa Claus, Pride, Sloth.

D. Now use the same one-dimensional characters and give them some human attributes (*two-dimensional*) in an improvisation which brings out such things as home life, disappointments, success, etc.

E. Present the same characters in *three dimensions*, bringing out individual qualities, such as inner conflicts, background, and psychological drives, all rooted in lifelike situations. Note how the poster-like simplicity of the one-dimensional characters disappears as they are complicated by individual human attributes. As a three-dimensional character, Santa Claus will seem unlike himself. (This should be proof enough that the charm of simple characters is in keeping with their simplicity.)

7. A woman shoplifter being interrogated by a nearsighted desk sergeant.

8. An improvisation between Adam and The Creator, Noah and his sons, a girl and her alter ego.

9. Situation: a freeway accident. Students create characters and improvise action and dialogue. Suggestions: argument, exchanging names and addresses, and finding they know each other.

10. Premise: A series of mishaps caused by attempts to answer phone. May be used for different students portraying different characters. Begins in a bathtub—phone rings—tries to reach towel—it falls in water—phone continues ringing—decides to let it ring—reaches for robe finally—slight slip on floor—phone continues—wipes feet on bath mat which blocks door—struggle to force open door—while trying to dry self with robe, knocks over vase still trying to force door—gets out, answers phone—and says "wrong number"—hangs up—gets back in tub and sighs with relief. Phone rings again.

11. Memorize the lines of a short scene from a play. Use the same inflections and tempo you would in speaking the author's lines, but speak *gibberish* instead as the following characters:

A. As two ghostly spirits. (This is an amusing improvisation when done using two bed sheets.)
B. As two angels. (Use makeshift halos or wings.)
C. As two robots.

12. Adapt *colloquial speech* to a short scene from Shakespeare, using characters' names and situation.

Suggestions: Nurse and Juliet from *Romeo and Juliet*, Act III, Sc. ii; Launce and dog from *Two Gentlemen of Verona*, Act II, Sc. iii (Use people as props and animals); Hamlet and Polonius from *Hamlet*, Act II, Sc. ii; *Taming of the Shrew*, Introduction, Sc. ii.

The most satisfactory method a director can use to create his own improvisations for special requirements is to begin with *characters in a situation.* In this context we may define a *situation* as an incident or event in which characters are involved with each other or with outside forces. Characters which seem to work best in improvisations are those which relate to or confront each other, or some object, or an idea, motivating them into some goal or desire.

Point of Focus

Any object, event, or thought on which all players agree is the focal point of the improvisation. This might be compared to the ball on which all players concentrate in a ballgame. "Keep your eye on the ball" could be paraphrased for improvisations as "Keep your eye on the point of focus." The established realities, as stated in the problem, scene, or play, will be given circumstances, in other words, information supplied to the actor by the instructor or the author. What is *not* stated must be supplied by the actor.

NOTE: The action of an improvisation should consist of a conflict and have development. It should never be planned so that it ends as it began.

Note point of focus in this production photo from We Bombed In New Haven *by Joseph Heller, as staged by George Lauris for Lane Community College, Eugene, Oregon. (Courtesy of Lane Community College)*

Some Suggestions of Characters

1. A person with a gambling problem
2. A person influenced by East Indian philosophy
3. An ambitious young music student
4. A brilliant but arrogant young student
5. A plain but wealthy young woman
6. A young married man or woman
7. A young mother
8. A bill collector
9. A person of ideals
10. A ranch hand
11. A black police officer
12. A perfume saleslady
13. A detective
14. An apartment house superintendent
15. A man hater
16. A teacher
17. A real estate agent
18. A sign painter

Some Suggestions for Situations

Select two of the above characters and involve them in one of the following situations:

a. Undergoing an experience that results in a change of viewpoint.

b. Forsaking cherished goals to carry out a moral duty.

c. Seeking a crafty way to avoid misfortune.

d. Annoyed by unwelcome attention from opposite sex, a person pretends to have a spouse.

e. Becoming involved, through curiosity, in an unusual enterprise.

f. Implicated in an accident which has its bright side.

g. Finding an obligation at variance with pleasure or ambition.

h. A threatening complication because of misjudgment.

i. Seeking revenge for a fancied wrong which proves baseless.

j. Secretly hiding another from a danger.

k. Happening upon an important secret which might endanger personal ambitions; a decision must be made.

l. Becoming involved in a situation in which there seems no solution, but one is found accidentally.

m. By involving himself in a risky situation, a timid man proves heroic.

n. Assuming the personality of a criminal in a legitimate enterprise.

Improvisation and Playwriting

Improvisations are now being used extensively in the creation of new plays for off-off Broadway productions. In workshop the director gives "notions" to the actors as a starting point for the development of improvisations. Later, these are put together by the director, using paste-pot and scissors, and are jig-sawed into plays. These are not so much playtexts as a pretext for a production. Despite claims of originality, this is not exactly a fresh technique for creating drama. Down through theatrical history a great deal of drama has been created by actors using no playscript. Who were the playwrights of the Commedia dell'Arte, or, for that matter, the authors of the morality plays?

EXERCISE 49: "WHEN"

Assign situations, characters, and season of the year; then improvise in the following periods:

1. Modern
2. Elizabethan
3. Eighteenth century
4. Victorian

Several years before off-off Broadway, *A Hatful of Rain* was developed by the improvisational method. Joan Littlefield has been using improvisational techniques in her productions for some time, notably in *A Taste of Honey* and *Oh! What a Lovely War*.

Comings and Goings, according to the playwright, was created by actors as "an enjoyment of technique, pure virtuosity on the part of the actors." The repertory of The Living Theatre is now almost exclusively improvisational. The Open Theatre, led by Joseph Chaikin, conducted improvisations on the Book of Genesis, and later performed it under the title of *The Serpent*. Richard Schechner's Performance Group attempted, through improvisations, to refashion Euripides' *The Bacchae*, retitled *Dionysus in '69*. In the performance of that play, the actors adjusted their actions to the reactions of the audience, eventually "storming into the audience in a frenzy of orgiastic violence and total nakedness," as one critic reported. Peter Brook's productions of *US* and *Marat/Sade* owe much to the improvisations of his actors.

There can be no doubt that today improvisations are the "in-thing." However, when improvisations are presented as plays there are some hazards. Notably, the language is never much better than the actor's intelligence can make it while speaking extempore. What actor could improvise language such as this:

> *Dying is not romantic, and Death is not a game which will soon be over . . . Death is not anything . . . Death is not . . . It's the absence of presence, nothing more . . . the endless time of never coming back . . . a gap you can't see, and when the wind blows through it, it makes no sound . . .*[6]

Also, when improvisations are offered as plays, there is an ever-present danger that actors will become involved with their own involvement, exposing a slipshod amateurism and self-indulgence.

[6]Tom Stoppard, *Rosencrantz and Guildenstern are Dead* (New York: Grove Press, Inc., 1967), p. 124. Copyright © 1967 by Tom Stoppard. Reprinted by permission of Grove Press, New York, and Faber & Faber Ltd., London.

To hire a hall and pay for tickets, lights, and scenery requires playing to more than a single audience, and this means repeating something rehearsed, set, and complete—which is the exact opposite of improvisation.

Improvisational Collage

Once a director has become facile at training his actors in improvisations, and a certain skill has been acquired by his students, he may care to experiment further with the technique. Selected improvisational scenes may be combined into a collage, giving a total result which is somewhat different from the effect created by the parts. As an example, let us look at a scene from Lanford Wilson's *The Rimers of Eldrich*, considered by some to be one of the best of the new plays. Various self-contained plots are presented in *The Rimers*. During the following scene, lines from these subplots are used to build tempo and excitement and to remind the audience of the contributions each has made to the main development.

THE RIMERS OF ELDRICH[7]

EVELYN is walking out onto her porch calling EVA, who is approaching the porch. An area may be EVELYN's porch and part of the courtroom at the same time—the effect should be of the entire cast moving in a deliberate direction with lines coming in sequence from all over the stage. CORA enters the café area from upstairs, sleepily, calling softly, exactly as she will when the scene is repeated at the end of the first act.

JUDGE	A travesty of justice.
PECK	We, the jury—
CORA	Walter?
PECK	—find Nelly Windrod—
CORA	Walter?
PECK	—not guilty.
MARTHA	Not guilty.
CORA	Walter?
EVA	Robert
NELLY	Oh, God; Mama?
EVELYN	Eva?
TRUCKER	Not guilty.
WILMA	Papa?
MAVIS	Peck?
JOSH	Not guilty. (He begins whistling softly, calling a dog.) Here Blackie, here, boy.
WALTER	Cora!

[7]From *The Rimers of Eldrich and Other Plays*, by Lanford Wilson. Copyright © 1967 by Lanford Wilson. Reprinted by permission of Hill and Wang, Inc.

CORA	Walter?
JUDGE	Not guilty.
PATSY	I know.
EVELYN	Eva? You come on, now.
CORA	Oh, God, oh, God, oh, God, oh, God, oh, God.
JOSH	Blackie? Here, Blackie?
EVELYN	You better get on in here now.
EVA	I'm coming.
JOSH	Come on, boy.
LENA	The poor thing.
PATSY	Really, I get so damn tired of all that nonsense.
LENA	I know, but they insist I wear it. (The movement subsides)
EVELYN	(continuing). You better put a sweater on if you're going to sit out there.
EVA	(approaching the house). I'm coming in directly.
EVELYN	Not directly, you come on in now.
EVA	All right.
EVELYN	Where were you all day?
EVA	I was wandering around the woods.
EVELYN	Now, you know I don't want you running around alone. What if you fell and hurt yourself and who'd ever know it?
EVA	I wasn't alone; Robert and I went walking.
EVELYN	Well, don't you go off alone.
EVA	I won't.
EVELYN	Not all afternoon. Wandering around; God knows what could happen to you.
EVA	I know, I don't.
EVELYN	You look so fatigued.
EVA	I'm not at all.
EVELYN	I don't want you spending so much time with that boy.
EVA	What boy?
EVELYN	That Driver Junior. Wandering around with that boy. Spending all afternoon and evening with him.
EVA	Well, who else would I spend it with?
EVELYN	Well, why do you have to go off every day of the week? Doing God knows what? You could visit the Stutses, you shouldn't be running around. It isn't good for you; you have to be careful. You're not like other kids; you know how easily you get fatigued; you run yourself out every day; perspiring like you do; wandering off with that boy. If something happened, who'd know? And don't think he's responsible; his brother might have been different; devil and his angels wouldn't know if something happened. I don't know why you can't stay at home like everyone else. Traipsing around the woods half-naked, what do you do out there in the woods alone, the two of you, anyhow?

231

EVA   Nothing.

EVELYN   I said you answer me.

EVA   (rapidly). Nothing!

EVELYN   I said you answer me the truth, young miss.

EVA   We don't do anything. Whatever you think.

EVELYN   Don't you talk back to me, what do you do, little miss smarty pants? All day gone from the house, smarty? (Hits her.)

EVA   We talk.

EVELYN   We talk, you talk. I'll just bet you talk; now you get in that house this minute do you hear me!

EVA   (running to the witness stand). I don't know what you think.

EVELYN   You get on in to the supper table! You're going to be the death of me. I swear, I swear, I swear. (everyone is assembled in court)

JUDGE   —to tell the whole truth and nothing but the truth, so help you God?

ROBERT   She didn't see anything.

JUDGE   Eva, as a witness to this terrible—

EVA   I don't know! I didn't see! I didn't see! I told you I didn't see anything! (A long run into her MOTHER's open arms.)

EVA	Mama.	EVELYN	Leave my daughter alone! Can't you see she's upset? My God, what are you trying to do to her?
CORA	She told me.		
CORA	I talked to her; she told me.		
ROBERT	(his lines overlapping CORA's). She didn't see.	EVELYN	(to EVA). Poor baby—(to CORA). You know what I think of you? Before God!
EVA	I don't know!		
NELLY	It's not true, none of it, it's like I said. You're trying to make a murderer of me; it was God's will be done.	JUDGE	(his voice rising above theirs, simultaneously, trying to quiet them). We have all long known Skelly Mannor; we have known of his past—that latent evil in him, that unnatural desire, and we have long been aware that at any time the bitterness in his soul might overflow.

NOTE: For groups contemplating the use of a center or thrust stage for the first time, it might be well to move now into the room which is to be used for performances. If at all possible, avoid rehearsing a space production on a proscenium stage.

    1. Fill the acting area in geometrical patterns such as star, checkerboard, circle, etc. Move everyone into a tight circle at dead center, then spiral out in N.E.S.W. columns. Move out to periphery and back.

    2. Try groups of three people just off center.

3. Walk everyone around the periphery clockwise; turn and reverse.

4. Play a scene which has previously been done on proscenium stage using exact movements.

Does it play as well in the new acting area?

What adjustments must be made for central or thrust staging?

Further Reading

IMPROVISATION

Hodgson, John, and Richards, Ernest. *Improvisation, Discovery and Creativity in Drama.* London: Methuen & Co., 1967. New York: Barnes & Noble, 1968.

Spolin, Viola. *Improvisation for the Theatre.* Evanston, Ill.: Northwestern University Press, 1963.

MIME

Barlanghy, Istvan. *Mime Training and Exercises.* New Rochelle, N.Y.: Sportshelf, 1967.

Bruford, Rose. *Teaching Mime.* New York: Barnes & Noble, 1958.

Hunt, D. and K. *Pantomime.* New York: Atheneum Publishers, 1964.

Laban, Rudolf. *The Mastery of Movement.* London: Macdonald & Evans, 1961.

Lawson, Joan. *Mime.* London: Pitman, 1957.

Lucian. *"On Pantomime," Works.* 4 Vols. New York: Oxford University Press, 1904.

Marash, Jessie Grace. *Mime in Class and Theatre.* London: Harrap, 1950.

Mawer, Irene. *The Art of Mime.* London: Methuen & Co., 1932.

Sayre, Gweanda. *Creative Miming.* London: Herbert Jenkins, 1959.

Shawn, Ted. *Every Little Movement.* Published by the author, 1954. (A very interesting volume from many angles.)

Walker, Kathrine Sorley. *Eyes on Mime.* New York: John Day Co., 1969.

11 CASTING

Auditions

A notice is posted on the bulletin board in the main hall:

AUDITIONS FOR THE NEW PLAY

will be held in Room 214

7 p.m. Tonight

and

every night thereafter
until play is cast.

The Director

And the crush begins!—people pushing into a room expecting to win a part in the play. Forty hopefuls—and only three leading parts! When his name is called, each aspiring, anxious actor walks to the front and faces his competitors. Perhaps he has never before seen the book from which he is now asked to read. He stumbles, hesitates, and finally stammers out some sounds that make little or no sense to him. Finally, the ordeal is over, and in relief, he returns to his seat.

This is the sort of frantic and ineffectual scene which has happened many times in preparation for the production of a school play. What is wrong with holding such an audition? It is certainly democratic. The play can be explained to everyone at one time, and students may learn something by hearing each other read. Indeed they will, and consciously or unconsciously, each will be affected by the others' readings. But the truth is that at such a mob meeting, a director has little chance for an appraisal of any individual's latent talent or imagination.

Good sight readers are generally thought to be poor performers, whereas poor readers, after study and rehearsal, are often able to turn out a fine performance. If a director is aware of this and casts a poor reader believing he will improve, how secure will he feel as he begins rehearsals? His decision has been made by basing it upon what he feels is the student's *potential*—and this is "hunch casting."

Auditions can never gauge the hidden talent in a candidate or uncover personality quirks which may later appear at rehearsals. It is even more difficult for the new director attempting to evaluate students he does not know.

Some directors conduct auditions in which students are asked to perform prepared speeches or scenes which they have done previously or learned for tryouts. How satisfactory is this method? In the first place, the director can never have any indication of how the actor will perform under *his* direction. Often the material the student chooses will be something learned from a recording which he reproduces down to the last tone and inflection. (How many times I have heard, "My brother Essau is an hairy man. . . ." from that *Beyond the Fringe* recording, or a Bill Cosby monologue!) But the chief objection to tryouts, open readings, or auditions is that they have a built-in capacity for creating competition, gossip, and resentment—at a time when the director is making every effort to create a friendly, civil atmosphere. After tryouts are over and the play has been cast, there is always some disgruntled individual ready to broadcast, "Everyone there said I read better than she did except *him*."

Even when circumstances force the director to conduct tryouts, many of those having to do so would admit that auditions are the least enjoyable part of their work. Not only are they tedious and frustrating, but the director often feels he is being deprived of time which might be better used in rehearsing. This time is being sacrificed in the name of the "democratic process." He must read every Tom, Dick, and Mary who fancies himself a star, even though he knows they are physically and temperamentally unfitted to act his leading parts. But if you must cast by this method, be wise enough to inform your cast that you will expect them to keep working and that you expect to test their willingness to cooperate. Some actors relax into inactivity when cast.

Casting by the Interview Method

An alternative to the tryout method of casting is to set up personal interviews with those expressing interest. You will learn more about a candidate from a face-to-face talk than you ever will from readings. The talk need not be concentrated upon the play. Get to know your potential actor: find out all you can about his home life and his ambitions, and try to determine his intelligence. I have said before that directing is largely a matter of interrelationships, and this is a good example. "That's going to be a pretty long, involved method of casting," someone is sure to say. But by moving slowly at the beginning, you will save time, and possibly a lot of grief, in the end.

A director should learn all he can about someone he will work closely with during the weeks ahead. These will be tiring weeks. Nerves will be on edge, and polite social manners will rub off to expose raw personalities.

It is best if a director understands at the beginning what kinds of people he will be dependent upon. Once that curtain goes up on opening night, his efforts and possibly his future are in the hands of his actors. That is why we rarely see a director sitting in the audience on opening night. Not until the show is over and the verdict in can the director be sure that the choices he made at the beginning were good or bad. That is precisely why all early decisions must be unhurried and carefully considered. A director must be reasonably sure he has cast the right actors in the right roles. It cannot be claimed that casting by interview is infallible, but you will certainly have more information with which to reach a decision than by holding "a cattle call."

Interviews should be scheduled by posting a notice on which those interested in being cast in the play may sign for a definite appointment. After each student has been privately interviewed, those making a favorable impression are given a call back. Even during the second interview it is best not to ask a candidate to read the part you have in mind for him. Then what does happen during these interviews? For one thing, you should ask about the candidate's health. After classes or a day of work, energy might be low for rehearsals. It would be unwise to cast any but the most healthy individual. A listless, tired actor will not derive any benefit from rehearsing. Another aspect which should interest a director is in learning how the candidate's parents (or family) feel about his appearing in a play. It has happened that after several weeks of rehearsal the director is suddenly informed that the student's parents have other plans for his time. Learn before casting if he has any duties or obligations which might interfere with rehearsals.

Also, try to determine the student's intelligence, imagination, voice quality, and physical appearance in relation to the part you have in mind for him. Has he satisfactory grade-point averages? Has he a full academic schedule? Has he any special talents, such as singing, playing an instrument, juggling, tumbling? But most important, what are his reasons for wanting to be part of this production?

Are you able to "see" him up on your stage playing the part you have in mind for him? How receptive will he be to direction and to you as a director? Human relationships can never be disregarded in casting. When in doubt as to a candidate's sincerity and commitment, you might ask, "Would you play a small part?"

Even if students have never been part of a workshop group, improvisations may be used to advantage during interviews. Describe a scene similar to one in your play, explain the given circumstances of the scene, and ask the student to improvise. If workshop sessions have been held previously, many scenes from the play, or related ones, might have been worked out so that actors might have literally cast themselves. In addition, the time would have been spent in performing exhilarating exercises while anticipating the production to come.

There are those who might nettle at the interview or workshop method

of casting, feeling that either might void pet theories. Let me offer justification. If workshop or careful interviews can eliminate the tensions, the fierce
competition of tryouts, and the bitterness when final choices are made, then
these are reasons enough to experiment with them. But no matter what has
been said here, I know that not all directors will be able to, or care to,
avoid tryouts.

Casting in the Professional Theatre

There are always exceptions, of course, but in the professional theatre,
casting usually proceeds in the following manner. A producer submits a play
to a director, who, if he agrees to stage the play, receives a retainer, and
with the author and producer, considers the casting. The author may have
preferences for actors he had in mind when writing the play, and the producer's interests will normally be in obtaining "name" actors who he hopes
will stimulate interest in the production and provide "box office draw." In
either case, these actors may or may not be suitable to the director. The
director must then decide if he will resist casting of which he does not
approve, or if he will work with actors chosen by the producer or playwright.

Casting is often a matter of compromise. How much influence does a
director have on the casting? According to the Dramatist Guild contract,
the playwright is the final authority. In cases of conflict he may withdraw
his play from the producer or the director. Therefore, the director is low
man on the totem pole, or third in command.

When the leading parts have been cast, the director has more freedom
in selecting actors for supporting roles. But always in the professional theatre
the director will be working with a scratch cast, actors who have been trained
in different acting methods or techniques. Unless the director is familiar
with each actor's background and training, he must learn quickly, but judi-
ciously, how the actor works and speak to him "in his own language." While
he would not dare talk "method" to Sir Laurence Olivier, this would be
expected when directing Marlon Brando. In short, he must know how to
draw from each actor the most that that particular actor can contribute
to his part.

Casting in the Educational Theatre

A director in the educational theatre often has the advantage of training
his own actors and is therefore aware of the capabilities of each. There
is also an invaluable teacher-student relationship which exists because of
previous work together. This is an ideal climate for creativity.

A disadvantage of directing in educational theatre is that desired actors
cannot be depended upon for the continuous and concentrated hours needed
to produce a polished performance. There is always the possibility that academic, family, social, and other activities may call them from rehearsals at
crucial times.

To Type Or Not To Type

Typecasting consists of giving a role to an actor who, in real life, most resembles the character in the play. The teacher-director is unable to use typecasting as frequently as it is done in the professional theatre. His actors are mostly within a certain age group and possibly within a certain ethnic group. He will need all of his skill to make students convincing in parts for which they are not really suited. Although firmly rooted in the profession, typecasting is possible in educational theatre only in a modified way.

There is nothing wrong with young actors playing character parts. In fact, this was formerly the way young actors were trained. As a boy in the Yiddish Art Theatre, Paul Muni played nothing but old men. Later, when he was cast in straight parts nearer his own age, he greatly benefited by that earlier training. Old age is more easily portrayed by young people than is middle age. Since it is shown more obviously, old age may be simulated more impressionistically. But a more subtle inner approach must be made when interpreting characters in the forty- to sixty-year-old group.

The director can do much toward solving this problem by casting in older roles only those actors who have settled mannerisms and mature voices. But he should not depend too much on makeup, beards, and other hackneyed expressions of old age. When used by any but specialists, makeup does not create an illusion of age, but merely calls attention to itself. A student with a dignified carriage and mature gestures, with vocal resonance and authoritative manner, will be more convincing as a judge or an army colonel than will an eager youth with a makeup box.

Other less obvious examples of typecasting used in educational theatre, and mentioned before, are those occasions when an actor is cast in a part similar to one he has done previously. If a boy has been amusing playing Grumio in *The Taming of the Shrew* and the next play to be cast is *The Merchant of Venice*, he is very likely to be cast as Launcelot Gobbo. Not only does this encourage a young actor to develop tricks, but there is no opportunity for any growth in his acting training. Cheryl Crawford, a Broadway producer and former casting director for The Theatre Guild, had some definite opinions regarding typecasting.

> When in casting a play I run across a dull businessman part, for instance, I immediately put out of my mind all the actors who quickly leaped to the fore as perfect examples. I rack my brains for someone with some eccentricity in color, voice, appearance or general style of acting who will give an extra touch to the part and keep it from being dull.[1]

Casting Leads

On the stage, as well as in real life, the first impression we make on others is through our physical characteristics. Posture, voice, and facial ex-

[1]John Gassner, *Producing the Play* (New York: Dryden Press, 1953), p. 204.

pressions are all indicative of our personalities. These outward manifestations of the inner person are tools to be used by a director. They afford planned responses in a potential audience. Voices—tired, excited, high- or low-pitched—are also audience symbols. Immature voices have limited range, while the mature voice suggests flexibility and an ability to adapt. A colorless, monotonous voice will, of course, detract when trying to convince an audience that an actor is a bold, dashing hero. But physical aspects as they appear in real life may not appear the same on stage. A girl who seems chubby and very ordinary on campus may exude a charisma when on stage that is irresistible. When working in her garden, Marilyn Monroe seemed quite plain. The most popular boy in school life might, on stage, have a sinister manner which could be just what you are looking for in your Richard III. Richard Brook has said that "the fascination of actors is in their capacity for revealing unsuspected traits during rehearsals." This is true, but a director should never count on it. It is usually a happy accident. Your leading players should not be chosen to benefit actors, but should be chosen for an audience. Technical skill in acting is not as important in school productions as the actor's suitability to the part. You may wonder if this isn't just a gentle way of saying "typecasting." But go back a few paragraphs and carefully reread what Cheryl Crawford has said. Probably the most effective test a director can use in making a final decision about his leads is to put himself mentally "out front" and imagine he is part of an audience. You have come to see a play. Imagine you do not know these actors in the play. Will you believe they are the people they represent? Will you empathize with them and their problems?

Let us suppose you are planning a production of Shakespeare's *Romeo and Juliet* and you are searching for two outstanding young people around whom you can build your production. Let us also imagine you are new to this school and have not had the opportunity to establish workshop sessions. Therefore, you are unfamiliar with the students and any previous work they may have had in theatricals. Please don't begin with those destructive tryouts, at least not until you have accomplished some preparatory exercises in basic stage deportment.

In the beginning, you will want to feel confident that you can train these students to speak the English language without localized accents. You will want to create pantomimes and improvisations on the theme of young love, to note carefully how they react to your direction. You must learn if they have any proclivity toward self-help or if they have a complete dependency upon others, yourself included. Will they keep looking to you for approval? In other words, you should search for a good measure of self-acceptance and self-confidence. Assign them scenes to learn from *other* Shakespearian plays in the hope of teaching them an appreciation for the great poetry. Finally, with these things accomplished and with the assurance that your choices have been carefully considered and are the best you can make, *then* begin talking to them about *Romeo and Juliet*.

Supporting Parts

These roles are so called because of their relationship to the play's story structure, but not necessarily because the parts are inferior. *Othello* is not a story about Iago. He is in this play because he is a vital force in the downfall of the protagonist. But it is far from an inferior role for an actor. Many great stars of yesterday have toured together alternating the two roles.

Often, supporting or secondary parts are so meaty that they "steal" the audience's interest from the lead. John Barrymore once said that Shakespeare had to kill off Mercutio early in the play in order to save Romeo. George Arliss inscribed a book to Romney Brent, "To the only Launcelot Gobbo who stole the show from Shylock." There are other supporting roles which are not so glamorous, but are long and exacting. In the profession such parts are known as "work horses." A well-known example is Rosse in *Macbeth*. He carries the burden of a great deal of narrative for Shakespeare and yet he is rarely remembered by an audience. Such parts, while less attractive and conspicuous, are nevertheless pillars of strength in supporting the structure of the story.

Character Relationships

When two people are mutually attracted, we call what happens between them chemistry. Chemistry should also exist between actors who work together. An actor playing Romeo need not be in love with the young lady playing Juliet, but there certainly should not be any animosity between them. In very mysterious ways, relationships between actors have a way of traveling over the footlights.

Also, it would not be convincing to an audience if a lanky Mediterranean actor were to be cast as the son of a short Nordic father. When actors are supposed to represent members of the same family, one character should not speak in cockney English and his brother in Texas drawl; and yet that is precisely what happened in a recent college production of Pinter's *The Caretaker.*

Double-Casting, Understudying

The chief reason for having two casts for the same production is usually to give a larger number of students a chance to play good parts before an audience. Double-casting means double work for the director, robbing him of concentration and energy which might otherwise be spent on perfecting a smooth workmanlike production.

An alternative to double-casting is to appoint understudies for the major roles. This may be difficult, as few students are willing to take time from other activities just to understudy. But when a regular member of the cast is prevented from attending a rehearsal, it is handy to have someone around who knows the lines and the business of a part. Just how useful this is to the other members of the cast might be debated. A strange personality in the part is liable to so upset other cast members that they soon give up any attempt to gain anything from the rehearsal. Also, absenteeism usually begins to happen just when a cast is beginning to mesh together as an ensemble. This is tragic. In fact, I have known productions to be ruined, even abandoned, because of too many absences from rehearsals.

To cancel a rehearsal because the leading lady had made a date previous to being cast in the play means that all rehearsal progress comes to a dead halt. For these reasons I have repeatedly warned those reading this book *not to give important parts to any potential absentees. Before casting, investigate completely into any previous commitments which might conflict with rehearsals.*

Rather than depending upon understudies, a much better plan is to cast those in supporting parts who will also memorize and study the leads; then, in case of unforeseen legitimate sicknesses or accidents, they can take over with much less confusion. In such circumstances, the stage manager can read the smaller part and, if there is a shift in the female characters, a prop girl could cover the small part.

Always list three potential candidates for each important part and do so in preferential order. Compare finalists both physically and stylistically.

When you have finally completed casting, by whatever means, see that the stage manager receives a copy of the cast to enter into his prompt book along with addresses, phone numbers, and alternate numbers where they can be reached.

Summary

In casting, consider the following:

1. Intelligence of candidates.
2. Ability to work with others—
   Is the actor cooperative?
   Will he take direction?
   Is he capable of working in a team?
3. Physical characteristics—
   Is the actor in good health?
   Does he move well while walking, gesturing?
4. Personality—
   Is he shy, gregarious, morose, happy, inhibited?
   Does he have charisma?
5. Voice and Speech—

Harsh?	Nasal?
Mellow?	Affected?
Resonant?	Obvious localized accent?

6. Imagination.
7. Dedication—

To the play?	To the part?
To himself?	To the theatre?

8. Availability—

THE
DIRECTOR
AND
REHEARSALS 12

*The power of the creative artist is infinite, but only when
he masters the technique in which he creates. Yet all
these production aids, these minute details, must be made
practical and must be carefully timed and rehearsed. All
the environmental background, born in excitement and
high imagination, must be transposed into controlled and
disciplined technique.*

—Jo Mielziner,
The Shapes of Our Theatre, p. 97

Importance of Scheduling

In a large sense, directing evolves from a director's own inner motivations
and the harmony he is able to create between an analytical approach, intuitive
insight, and manual skill. His enthusiasm will help to overcome obstructions,
frustrations, and the depletion of energy during the rehearsal and production
phases.

Also, many of the difficulties he might face may be relieved or eliminated
by careful preplanning on his part. To leave the many details of a production
to chance and to adopt a laissez-faire attitude is to invite failure. Never
allow yourself to become convinced that "The show will get on—somehow."
It may, but you might be sorry it did. Take time to plan each and every
step beforehand. Even unforeseen contingencies must be considered, along
with solutions.

With a bare minimum of two hundred hours to be spent in producing **243** a play, it seems obvious that careful scheduling of that time must be made *before rehearsals begin.* Next, make a point of keeping strictly to that schedule. This is a requirement when working with nonprofessionals who must carry on with regular studies or occupations as well as rehearsing with you.

The problem becomes one of balancing time and energy spent—with accomplishment. A step taken before it is practical to do so could be most harmful to the progress of the actors and to the entire production.

In most high schools and colleges, schedules of events are set up by administrators. It is up to the director to work within this master calendar. It will be his responsibility to make his own schedule detailing the work to be accomplished on the play during every hour of rehearsal. This allocation of time can only be made by the director himself. Each play, each production will need individual attention, and different directors might have different schedules for the identical play.

The director might consider the time allotted to him for a production as being divided into four basic units of work:

1. Orientation
2. Blocking and Movement
3. Synthesis of Actors into Play; "Polishing"
4. Technical Aspects of Production

In this chapter, and in the chapters to follow, we will detail the work to be done in each of the above units. Let us begin with Orientation, or table sessions.

Table sessions are a theatrical tradition. At left, André Antoine and members of his Théâtre Libre in a table session. At right, Chekhov reads The Sea Gull *to Stanislavski and members of the Moscow Art theatre. (Reprinted from Cole and Chinoy,* Directing the Play, *courtesy of the Bobbs-Merrill Company, Inc.)*

Value of Table Sessions

There are many historical photographs and paintings titled "The Reading of the Play," depicting a cast of actors sitting around a table listening to a director. With the great rise of American stock companies all over the country, this custom of conducting early rehearsals seated around a table was, of necessity, abandoned. Stock actors began rehearsals "on their feet," working out business, movement, and characterizations simultaneously. Because of the haste in preparing a new play each week there was usually no alternative but to fall back on conventional stock characterizations. The juvenile part was generally played with awkward, youthful energy in a fluctuating and unmanageable tenor voice. The unctious heavy wore a permanent sneer and a black moustache. The ingenue often was so innocent and flighty that she seemed constantly on the verge of going into orbit. But the hero was a man of the earth, handsome and full-chested, kind to all living creatures—but to wrong-doers he was a lion of vengeance.

Some directors even today begin rehearsals in the old stock way. However, most rehearsals do begin with table sessions. Even some TV series have one or two such meetings for the principals. Clifford Odets has described beginning rehearsals of a new play for The Group.

> After the play was chosen, [Harold] Clurman would call the company together and would talk with extraordinary brilliance for anywhere from two to five hours, analyzing the meaning, talking from every point of view, covering the ground backwards and forwards. And if the actor's imagination was touched somewhere, which was his intention, then the actor would catch something and begin to work in a certain way, with a certain image or vision of how the part should go.[1]

There is a period when the only way a play can become a smooth and exacting production is by constant, repetitive rehearsing. Of course it is futile to run on and on when the actors are not properly prepared. There are wrong times for doing right things and right times for all things, and a director learns to recognize both. He will come to know the expression on an actor's face who is not following what the director is explaining to him. But when the right time occurs, a nod or a gesture from the director will be instantly understood by that same actor.

At least some part of rehearsal time should be spent in reading and discussing the play while the cast is relaxed and receptive to ideas. An actor cannot be expected to grasp and retain an idea about the play or his characterization while he is moving about the stage rehearsing. From the very beginning, the cast should be given a general idea of the play and the director's visual and emotional concept of the production. They should also be told what sort of experience the director hopes to transmit to the audience, and each actor should be allowed to hear the director's suggestions regarding his character and its relationship to the play and the other characters in that play.

The director should also try to convey to the actors some of his own enthusiasm for the play and production. Drawings or models of the settings, photos of other productions, concordances, bibliographies, magazine articles, indeed any and all material relative to the play's background, characters, or author, should be placed at the disposal of the cast.

Remember that at these early meetings you will know much more about

[1]Clifford Odets, "How a Playwright Triumphs," *Harper's*, September, 1966.

the play than the actors. Later, they will probably catch up with you as you encourage and receive their cooperation. Rehearsals constitute a learning experience in which all must take part as the play develops from an idea to an actual living production. You will learn along with your cast, for even a director will not know everything about a play without the living material he must work with—the actors. A mutual understanding, an exchange of ideas, and reciprocative stimulation should begin in an atmosphere of relaxation.

It should be admitted that some directors consider table sessions a waste of time. Margo Jones, of Houston's Alley Theatre, preferred to start blocking the play early, her cast memorizing their lines—and working out characterizations and movement "on their feet." But then, she had a resident professional company who had scripts to study at the beginning of each season. Her conviction was that blocking would provide a knowledge of the play and the characters. This is very like "Which comes first, the chicken or the egg?" Most directors will not have Miss Jones's obvious advantages, and for them, table sessions are a happy alternative.

There are many benefits to be realized by establishing table sessions. Among the most significant is that they begin a logical step-by-step development for the work and practically eliminate those dreary discussions and intellectualizing later when people stand about instead of rehearsing. Nothing is more demoralizing than a walking rehearsal interrupted by a discussion of characters and situations. Naturally, this is an important part of the work, but it is misplaced once actors are on their feet. When actors do approach movement, knowledge gained during table sessions creates an identity of aim between the actors and the director and encourages a mutual trust.

> NOTE: The sample rehearsal schedule which follows is not to be interpreted as a procedure for every circumstance. It is only a guide or matrix which will give a director some basis from which to make his own schedule. Experienced directors have their own tested methods of rehearsals and may approve or disapprove of the procedure as presented here. Others may find the work plan sufficiently stimulating to experiment with it—in part or in whole. It represents just one method which has been practical in producing both classics and modern plays.

Meetings Prior to Table Sessions

STAFF CONFERENCE

In charge: Director and/or stage manager.

Present: Designer, head of craftsmen, costumer, business head, etc.

Orientation: The director presents his plan for the production, including his floor plans for sets, sketches, and all relative material. Books or sides for cast are now available.

AUDITIONS OR TRYOUTS (See detailed discussion)

In charge: Director and stage manager.

Present: All candidates.

Cards are to be filled out listing available time for rehearsals, addresses, comments by director, etc.

Orientation

In charge: Director and stage manager

Present: Cast (No absentees, no visitors)

At this meeting, the director tries to pass along his enthusiasm for the play and production. He explains the atmosphere, theme, characters, plot, style, period, and historical significance, along with his concept for producing the play. He discusses what the audience is meant to enjoy. Any material relating to the play or era is displayed along with the setting schema. If films are available, they are shown.

Reading by director: The director reads the entire play aloud privately, and then reads it to the entire cast. Read smoothly and intelligently, making sure you do not stumble over words, maintaining flow and story line. Establish names of characters supposed to be speaking, but do not make as important as the lines. Do not attempt to characterize or "act," and have a glass of water handy if you are not accustomed to reading an entire play without stopping.

The stage manager next assigns to each cast member his playbook or sides along with rehearsal schedule showing dates, time, etc., for each meeting. Each player is made responsible for his script by signing a receipt. The director asks if there are any questions. If not, he asks if there are any reasons why each member cannot attend the rehearsals as they are scheduled. He makes clear that these table sessions are for the purpose of discussions and readings and that once the walking rehearsals begin, there will be little time for further discussion or intellectualizing. "Once we are on our feet, our drive will be to get a production on the stage."

Unlike workshop sessions, it should be made clear that the atmosphere of all meetings from this point on will be businesslike, that a play is to be staged and that there is a definite time in which to do it. The cast has a duty to be on time for each rehearsal, ready and eager to work. Tardy members will be required to apologize each time they are late to the entire company, whose time they have wasted. After each rehearsal, the stage manager will announce the time and place of next rehearsal in case there is any deviation in schedule. A no-exception rule will be that no visitors are to be admitted to rehearsals.

The above may seem to suggest that there will be an unnecessarily severe or authoritarian attitude on the part of the director. This is exactly what is needed at this time, and especially for those who have enoyed the relaxed play atmosphere of workshop sessions. To state the rules clearly and concisely now is to discourage requests for special concessions later. It is better to deprive yourself now of the fainthearted than to have them break your heart later.

SECOND TABLE SESSION

Reading by the Cast:
The director should instruct actors not to try for characterizations at this point, as they are not ready for performances. Rather, they should read for sense and meaning. Remember, a director works now by persuasion and suggestion. He instructs the cast to read through the entire play without interruption or comment.

Discussion:
After reading, the director should interrogate the actors: "Why do you think the character said that?" "Why did the author need that scene?" There should be an exchange of ideas regarding motivations and character relationships. What did the playwright do to give certain impressions? Form collective and general impressions of each character *by lines and actions.* What would be each character's visual statement? How would he look, sound, and feel? Remind each actor of the *actions* of their character and relate this action and emotion to some similar experience of the actor. The director should explain the point of view he has taken, the rise and fall of action, the importance of certain key scenes to the texture and atmosphere of the play, and what he expects in tempo, movement, etc. It might be well to explain the rise and fall of the play by means of charts drawn on a blackboard. Actors should be told to prepare to perform improvisations of their characters in scenes not written by the playwright.

Once agreement is reached on the form, content, and characterizations, the work of synthesizing begins with the director treating his actors as intelligent, sensitive, individuals. Actors are questioned for the reasons behind each opinion. By his answers, the actor becomes confident that the interpretation is sound. When the director senses that a characterization is not developing or is veering off on a tangent, or that the actor's interest is lagging, then he must, by improvisation or discussion in private sessions, restore progression. The director should never be ashamed to admit that he does not know the answers to all questions put to him, but should promise to have the answer at the next session. If none are forthcoming, the director should invite questions regarding content, theme, etc., and appraise opinions offered by the cast. There should be a meeting of the minds on fundamentals.

The stage manager makes a cast "plot" which includes the names, addresses, and telephone numbers (and alternatives) for insertion into his prompt book.

Limitations of Table Sessions

It is not necessary during table sessions to spend much time on such matters as tempo or mood until the actors have become involved with situation and characters. Analysis of the play by all members of the cast is as important

to an effective production as it is to creating character. Each play has an
emotional and visual mood and background which must be realized now
and evidenced in the rehearsals to come. For example, in the New York
success, *Plaza Suite*, the background dominates the thoughts of the audience
as they contemplate the different stories of many people being enacted in
the same hotel room.

How Many Table Sessions?

The objectives listed here are only suggestions for the work which might
be accomplished during table sessions. If it is true that a production is developed best by taking one step at a time, then it seems valuable to spend
as much time as possible learning the foundations of the play.

The time for moving on from table sessions and into walking rehearsals
will be when the director feels there is a complete understanding by all
as to his concept of the production. The characters and the flow of the
play will develop during subsequent rehearsals, but this is where they begin.
Before leaving the table sessions, the director should feel confident that each
actor has made a personal friend of the character assigned him.

Check List for Table Sessions

1. What did the cast experience when first hearing the play read?
2. Did they empathize with the characters?
3. What is the play's theme as they see it?
4. Did they agree with your statement of the theme? The story? Atmosphere?
5. What relationships do they believe exist between the characters?
6. How does this relate to the story? The theme? The play?
7. Are they excited by your ideas of the production, its color, line, and
form, its stresses and climaxes?

Assignments: Collateral readings of other plays by same or contemporary
authors. Any study of period, modes, and manners sources.

Rehearsal Discipline

*Freedom is not what you like, it is what you want; but
you cannot have freedom to express yourself until you
have discipline.*
                                              —Dame Ninette de Valois

There is a child-state in all of us, and in many ways it is one of our
most valuable human assets. Normality consists of attaining a delicate balance
between immaturity and maturity. But to a great extent, an actor must depend
upon his childlike qualities: imagination, intuition, creativity, and spontaneity.
The acting spirit is fulfilled only while the actor is pretending. A director
should not only accept this, but encourage it to some extent. There is also
a great deal of insecurity in an actor's composition. This is one of the reasons

he likes being someone else. There is a kind of humiliation in that, for the actor exposes himself cruelly before an audience. Because of this exposure, it is very easy to destroy his confidence. He is vulnerable to a glance of the director's eye, a disapproving movement. The better the actor, the more sensitive he will be—"it comes with the territory."

While the workshop atmosphere is free and loose, and one which fosters participation in game-playing among a group of friends, rehearsals have a climate of dedication about them. Businesslike, nonsocial, they reflect a respect for professional ethics and a realization that an important set of tasks must be accomplished during each meeting.

Social amenities are left for the refreshment breaks to relieve fatigue. Only by relaxing a grip now and then are we able to take a better hold when work is resumed.

Directors come in several different varieties. There is the permissive sort who may be timid, uninformed, or just plain dilatory. His rehearsals are fun times, and production of a play is simply a good excuse for getting a party together. Another type is the humorless, pedantic martinet, who insists that every gesture and inflection be done *his* way.

An ideal director must be capable of imposing his will, of being at times stern and arbitrary, but at other times genial and receptive. Together with the actors, he will explore the form and content of the play. He will set dates for all lines to be learned and will insist upon that being done. He will conduct no-nonsense rehearsals, insisting that there is an opening date to be met and that that date *will* be met. But he also will be receptive to ideas of others, although they may change his own ideas of movement or characterization. He will recognize and encourage imaginative thinking and appreciate anything that will improve the production. But he must always guard his position of final authority. A group without a leader could mean the deterioration of all efforts to stage the play. This implies that he will be more often right than wrong in his judgment. He will show confidence in his actors and in himself, displaying logic, calm, and enthusiasm. Always thoughtful of his cast, he will call only those immediately needed in a scene and not keep actors sitting around as others rehearse. Actors will accept authority if it is handled in a fair and intelligent manner. Authority implies responsibility and service to be rendered to others. Actors enjoy the relaxation authority brings. But actors can also detect insecurity in a director. Once they become convinced that the director is unsure of his job or himself, rehearsals can become unruly and may eventually end in chaos. Grumbling and insubordination must be dealt with quickly and finally. Group spirit is more important than technical efficiency.

There is no certainty that individual freedom is a vital factor in the release of creative energy. Indeed there are many outstanding examples of artistic achievements being made under highly disciplined circumstances. The chronic insecurity of the actor needs a solid reliable milieu in which to nourish his confidence. Therefore, discipline which also allows him deference and appreciation of his sincere efforts might be more effective in releasing the actor's creative expression than would an atmosphere of absolute permissiveness.

—Do have an attitude of resilience, but also firmness.
—Do maintain a pleasant disposition; be patient and absorbed in your work.
—Do be calm, businesslike, professional.
—Do be pliable, but also faithful to your own judgments.
—Do be friendly but reserved.
—Do all you can to stimulate the actor's contributions.
—Do encourage an actor in finding himself and his character.
—Do behave in such a way that demands respect.
—Do remember that all moves or interpretations must be right for the actors.
—Do begin and end rehearsals on time.

—Don't insist upon preconceived ideas if those presented are better.
—Don't conduct rehearsals in confusion or permit late starts.
—Don't order—explain.
—Don't permit undisciplined behavior at rehearsals.
—Don't have favorites or discuss personal problems.
—Don't indulge in temper, shouting, intimidations, or exaggerations.
—Don't use sarcasm or show impatience, frustrations, or anxieties to the cast.
—Don't allow distractions, interruptions, or late arrivals.
—Don't socialize too much.
—Don't pretend to be an oracle or think you must answer all questions.
—Don't be ashamed to admit that you don't know—but promise to find out.
—Don't settle arguments on the spur of the moment. Talk about it after rehearsal.

> *No one but the staff, the actors and the author can be admitted to a rehearsal. This is an ironclad rule in our theatre, and I think an important one. The presence of one outsider frequently forces the actor to attempt a performance (for which he is not yet ready) and ruins the rehearsal. Fear of criticism and desire for commendation inevitably appear if a stranger is in the house. We have a serious job to get done in the theatre and must not be disturbed by visitors during working hours.*[2]
>
> —Margo Jones,
> Founder and late Director of
> The Alley Theatre, Houston, Texas

The Director Inspires

Next to the satisfaction of watching an audience enjoy a production you have directed is the pleasure of seeing actors develop under your guidance.

[2]Margo Jones, *Theatre-In-The-Round* (New York: Holt, Rinehart & Winston, 1951), p. 122. Reprinted by permission of the publisher.

The setting, lighting, music, and makeup are only window dressing for the actors. Creativity, according to Aristotle, is "bringing something into existence," and in order to develop creativity, the mind needs to be stimulated.

Many students are not able to use the creative power of the mind at home, and all individuals should have a time and place to reflect, to open their minds to imagination. Not that all imaginative thinking is constructive; it can also result in futile hallucinating, daydreaming, and even delirium. It can be destructive, as in self-pity, martyrdom, or delusions of grandeur. Imagination is creative only when controlled and directed toward some goal, and this can happen only in the proper environment. It is the director's responsibility to see to that environment and to guide the actor into setting effective goals for his thinking.

Finding Goals

At the very first meeting with his cast, the director should be prepared by his earlier study to lead his actors into understanding the physical and emotional components of each character. He must avoid clichés and stock responses and concentrate upon subtle and explicit reasons given in the play for the behavior of the characters in each scene. Beginning with a feeling of the play and its milieu, the actors can reflect upon the actions and motivations of the characters in a plausible and meaningful way. The problem for the director and actor then becomes one of utilizing this knowledge in the actor's creation of his character. Different directors use various methods of procedure.

THE PHYSICAL APPROACH

Instinctive
Positive
Arriving at emotion by first reproducing physical responses

THE EMOTIONAL APPROACH

Memory recall
Comparison of similar experiences

DEMONSTRATION

This method is no longer popular. Great directors of the past used it— Molière, Reinhart, George M. Cohan—but they were also fine actors. Few directors are competent enough as actors to demonstrate how to play a scene.

Guiding Intuitive Research

A director should plan learning activities for a definite period, organizing the time, spacing, and sequence of these activities. An introductory period of discovery is needed to create a provocative, problematic climate in which actors are prompted to develop concepts and relationships of characters for themselves. Rarely can nonprofessional actors do this unaided simply by drawing from their own experience. Most often it is the director who must develop, reinforce, and challenge the actor to operate so that perception will invite comprehension. Frequently the director must create his own exercises which will serve as a springboard for inquiry and discussion.

During this period, the director's attitude should be that of a fellow worker who has no pat and final answers but who searches for them with his actors. He rewards imaginative and creative thinking and incites his actors to prove the defensibility of their points of view. He suggests, encourages, even praises, in order to correct faults, but he never commands or discourages.

The intuitive search into characterization begins with a discovery—some action of the mind which produces a fresh insight or image. Often the impetus is a line, an action, or some sympathetic recall which can set off the creative mechanism. But it is the director who must constantly be the stimulus. He must strive to stir the actor's imagination for creative responses for a revealment of the character, before any attempt is made to act it.

Exactly how does this collaboration between director and actors work in practice? There must never be any confusion about final authority. The director is the motivating force. He comes to the first rehearsal after long and careful study of the play. He presents a broad general outline of his plans for the production and the characters as he wishes the actors to portray them. I certainly do not mean that he describes one character as having a lisp or another as walking with a cane; such physicalizations are within the province of the actor. But the justification for a character's behavior is the responsibility of both the director and the actor. A production would never reach opening night if actors were encouraged to challenge every facet of the director's concept. Even characterizations must be related to the general plan. If a director has not done his homework, an experienced or bright actor may discover its flaws. The director must then be able to defend his idea of characterization or become convinced of the accuracy of the actor's insight. This is one more reason for the director to do a thorough and well-considered job of preparation.

Further Reading: The Director's Ability to Inspire

Arnheim, Rudolph. *Visual Thinking.* Berkeley and Los Angeles: University of California Press, 1969.

Mearns, Hughes. *Creative Youth.* Garden City, N.Y.: Doubleday & Co., 1930.

Osborn, Alex P. *Applied Imagination.* New York: Charles Schribner's Sons, 1963.

Parnes, Sydney, and Harding, Harold F. *A Source Book for Creative Thinking.* New York: Charles Scribner's Sons, 1962.

Torrance, E. P. *Guiding Creative Talent.* Englewood Cliffs, N.J.: Prentice-Hall, 1962.

Blocking and Movement

In charge: Director and stage manager.

Present: Cast as required.

First Walking Rehearsal

The stage manager has marked a ground plan of the acting space on the floor before rehearsal begins. There are to be no props while scripts are being held. When working with inexperienced players, the director should make clear that his blocking is tentative and may be improved as rehearsals develop, but that at this time actors are to move as directed. The director should block the first act only, then repeat it in order to imprint the moves with the lines in the minds of the actors. This second run-through should not be interrupted, even if wrong moves are made. These can be corrected later by the director. This rehearsal should be a short meeting, approximately two to three hours.

As previously indicated, pre-blocking is a highly controversial matter. When there is time, it is preferable to allow the movement of the actors to grow organically out of "the moments," that is, the events taking place in the play. This is the *modus operandi* of some professional directors, and it is a method often followed in college and university theatre.[3] But it is not always possible to do so. In films and TV, the actor is expected to come on the set with his lines memorized, and he is given the blocking of a scene at once by the director. If there is no elaborate business with props, animals, etc., and it is a simple scene of dialogue, there may be no more than one walk-through before shooting. However, in high-budget films, more time is allowed for participation by leading actors in the interpretation of moods, motivation, and movement.

Importance of Movement

"Action!"

> Drama begins with action and spectacle; the deed comes before the word, the dance before the dialogue, the play of the body before the play of the mind.[4]

It has long been accepted that movement is the first, most basic, and universal means of communication between human beings. Human figures drawn in movement were some of the earliest symbols used in writing.

As a play evolves on stage, we watch action, for that is the essence of theatre. Action is composed of two elements—what we see and what we hear. Both can affect us emotionally. Because visual impressions are more

[3]The late Sir Tyrone Guthrie, for one, preferred to skip even the first readings and have his actors on their feet from the very beginning. This is possible with experienced actors.

[4]Frederick S. Boas, in *Encyclopaedia Britannica*, Vol. 7, p. 576.

important to an audience's understanding of a play than what they hear, movement must be carefully planned and rehearsed.

We can be thrilled by the physical feats of the Grotowski performers, a sword fight, a ritual procession, or a silent suspenseful moment as the detective in a mystery play walks toward the telltale evidence.

Stage compositions are similar to, and use the same elements as, the other arts: proportion, balance, line, variety, and mass. The great difference is that a director's pictures are *alive*. They move about in space constantly, and this makes his compositions different from other arts. On a stage, movement is feeling in action and action is movement within a given space. But what is this given space?

Rehearsal Movement

In a proscenium theatre, this space may represent outdoors or it may be a series of flats lashed together to represent an interior. Either will be the acting space to be used by the director and the actors in the proscenium theatre which we inherited from the Italian Renaissance. Today that barrier between actor and audience is challenged. Thrust and circle staging bring the actors into the audience section. Grotowski even brings the spectators into the acting area.

A director must know what space he will use before he can plan any action or movement for his players. The actor in space, his relation to other actors, to the furniture, doors, windows, etc., will not only determine positions, but can either underline or mute everything said. The actor-audience relationship is always to be considered, but the old rules for proscenium staging, such as weak and strong positions, upstage, downstage, right and left, must all be reconsidered in open or circle staging.

In the latter, it is as if an artist who has always painted on a small one-dimensional canvas were assigned to paint on a wall of many planes. So it is with the proscenium director when he contemplates staging in a circle theatre. Suppose we have an actor with a long, important speech to deliver; should he be placed center stage by the director? Inside a box set with no platforms, perhaps yes. In this position he would dominate and have the audience's focus of interest. But this may not be the most advantageous position to be found on a thrust or open stage.

Action in Movement

Both the director and his actors must be constantly aware that on any stage, they are dealing with an ever-changing, ever-moving series of pictures. They are working with time in movement. The stage must flow from one action into another. If the audience has time to consider and admire your "groupings," you have failed to convey the overall impression of grace in motion. During the rehearsals, you may have reasons to stop the action in order to correct errors in composition or interpretation. All well and good.

But be careful not to lose that look of action when you resume, such as the forward thrust of the actors in movement or the sequential build of the scene. Movement is physical; "build" is emotional. Both the physical and emotional aspects should be repeated when you resume the rehearsal.

Using Your Space

Composition or design is created by using mass to organize stage space. Mass, used in this sense, might be thought of as the degree of bulk, density, or visual weight. When Orson Welles directed the Mercury Theatre in New York, he found the stage too small and confining for his concept of *Danton's Death*. He raised the curtain several stories high and created a spatial effect which was breath-taking in its sense of mass. Mass need not be heavy to give the impression of weight.

(Photo by Steven Keull)

Your design might trace geometric lines, curves, or areas related in values, these values achieved by the use of actors, scenery, and light. A moving line in space might be identified by scenery, and travel to weight and mass supplied by a group of actors, then continue along to open forms of light, allowing space to penetrate. Light is equally as important as matter. By its luminosity or its sensuous texture it can balance mass. The outline of your composition is an invisible silhouette by which you have divided space. It organizes all the various parts into a moving symmetry or design. It may form a square, or a rectangle, a triangle, circle, ellipse, or other geometric structure. It should form a pleasing arrangement and never be a jumble of unbalanced, undesigned shapes and sizes unrelated in value or hue.

Influences Upon Movement

Movement can be used to create atmosphere or characterization, or can
be used for strictly technical reasons, such as balancing the stage or adding

variety to a long static scene. As you reach the rehearsal period and you have actors with which to work, you will be able to direct movement more organically than when you sat alone moving cardboard figures about your floor plan. It is never enough that your stage compositions look good. They must also add to the interpretation and communication of the play to the audience. By means of your former study, you should have mental images of scenes. You should know where you want the focus of interest to be placed. The key to this is in the lines, but a more reliable guide will be a knowledge of what characters are feeling at particular moments. Movements may be gauged by your empathy with them.

When we speak of action in staging, we must be careful not to exaggerate it into restless activity. This will only convince an audience that the director wanted to be novel at all costs. The present mode of having everyone running up and down stairs, shouting and clamping about, only distracts and confuses an audience, rather than gaining their interest.

Quality of Movement

All movement should be stimulated by motive and the nature of characters. The young will move more impulsively, faster, than older characters, while a quiet, reserved person will move in a way that is well-balanced and poised. But movement can never be described solely by externals, and now we are back to the point made before: that actors will now make it possible for you to check all movements *organically*. You should also remember that movements will hold an audience's attention only when they are advancing the plot or revealing character. In the execution, movement should be direct, definite, and complete. So often the mark of the amateur is evidenced in a blurred, indecisive movement, an unsureness in handling of details, whether these be connected with the voice, characterization, or gesture. The director must help such an actor to move with authority and precision, to make every action clear and concise. There should be no easing into a position, and no garbled delivery of lines, for this could ruin an otherwise well played scene.

Everything on stage should direct attention toward the immediate point of focus. Movement and speech should correspond. If an actor says, "I'll see him at once," and then sits, this seems inconsistent. In general, an actor moves on his own line, providing the line or speech does not hold some information which is vital to the story. He may also move effectively under the following circumstances:

1. To express character, situation, or emotion.
2. To emphasize speech or a line, such as "It must be somewhere in this room."
3. To shift the focus of the audience.
4. To build an entrance, an exit, or a climax.
5. To break up a static scene, or comply with a move requested by the playwright.

257

These moves apply to an actor moving on his own lines. An actor may move on another's line—

1. If it does not distract.
2. If it is not weak or unsure.
3. If he maintains the point of focus.

But he should not move when another speaker is moving unless it is indicated in the script, or unless it is for comedy purposes, and never on an emotional line or scene.

Covering

In Chapter 6, we discussed the lines of sight and their importance. If one of your actors seems to be blocking another from the audience's view, these rules should be explained to him and the angles of sight drawn upon a blackboard. A director has every right to expect his student-actors to "dress the stage," that is, to make a compensatory movement or to counter when another moves. This should be done unobtrusively, by a slight adjustment of position upstage or downstage, to the right or left. This will prevent the actor from covering or being covered.

EXERCISE 50

Group five people in a half-circle, facing front.

Student at center is given an interesting speech to read, while others are instructed to concentrate upon the reader—except that one of the four has previously been instructed to hedge back on a certain word in the speech.

From this demonstration you can point out how an audience's attention can be lost by this apparently innocuous move.

Differences Between Movement and Business

These terms are closely related and frequently confused. Most stage movement indicates distance, but this is not so with stage business. Directions for crosses, walking, running, and sitting will sometimes be given by the director at blocking rehearsals. Movement may be found in an author's directions: "She crosses to the fireplace." "He runs to his mother." Stage business generally comes when the director is working out the details at later rehearsals. Business usually conveys an idea, such as "George lights a cigar," "They toss her knitting back and forth," or "There is a look of distrust between them." A sword fight such as those in a Shakespearian play would be termed business and rehearsed separately, but the preparation for the fight, that is, the lines spoken immediately preceding the fight, and the lines following it would be rehearsed in the regular way as movement. Business often involves a prop, or object, or it may be strictly a pantomimic move, gesture, or action.

An audience will only be interested in business which relates to the characters or plot, and even then, not for long. Nevertheless, a great deal of nuance in characterization or in the relationships between characters can be added by the director's invention of business during later rehearsals.

Objects Affecting Movement

Doors. Request your set builders to hinge doors so that they open down- and off-stage. An otherwise well coordinated actor will often find difficulty opening a door at dress rehearsal. It should be opened with the up-stage hand; the actor then steps through, makes a quarter turn towards front, and closes it with his downstage hand.

Furniture. Most plays, whether produced on a proscenium, thrust, or center stage, require furniture of some sort. Even on Shakespeare's thrust stage, a throne was required now and then. Marks for furniture are usually placed on the ground cloth, and lights are adjusted to this placement. A matter of a few inches off these marks can alter the lighting on an actor or an important scene. The stage manager should check these marks before rehearsals and during each scene change.

A good rule to follow is to have walking room around each piece. An actor must be prevented from the natural habit of looking back to see where he intends to sit. He should accustom himself to a chair during rehearsals and feel it with the calf of his leg as he faces front. Other natural actions such as pulling up trousers before sitting, sitting with legs crossed, or slumping in a chair are poor stage behavior, especially in period plays.

When placing two actors on a sofa, be sure that the upstage actor sits forward and the one downstage sits well back. This applies particularly when the one upstage controls most of the dialogue in the scene. This will prevent him from being covered. The actors might also be seated or standing with their backs to the audience. I leave this up to the experienced director, but dare not recommend it generally to amateurs who might overdo it because they believe it "chic." Another solution to covering is to rake the set at a slight angle or use higher chairs upstage, or cushions, if the chairs must match.

Hand props. Some plays require that tea or cocktails be served, or (it shouldn't happen to you!) a full meal. All props to be used in such scenes should be provided for rehearsals just as soon as the actors have the scripts out of their hands. Time all movements carefully in rehearsals so that the clatter of dishes, or the movements themselves, do not distract from important dialogue.

Other small pieces of "business," such as arranging pillows, lighting cigarettes, or leafing through magazines, are apt to interfere with the audience point of focus if not expertly done. During later rehearsals when the play is moving along, watch for spontaneous little pieces of business invented by actors who are beginning to get inside their parts. If these seem effective to you, develop them. Such happenstances do occur frequently and they can be delightful in a performance.

Business for Love Scenes

Inexperienced actors are usually self-conscious when required to play love scenes. A director can help relieve the embarrassment. It might be well to rehearse these scenes privately at first until the students feel more sure of themselves. Begin by simply walking the movements slowly. Eliminate books or parts and keep strictly to the technicalities. Positions of the feet are as important as the use of hands. Don't allow the boy to give any impression of "pawing." If a kiss is required, it should be done slowly. When the couple face each other, keep positions close and perpendicular so that there is no bending at the waist. If dialogue is to be delivered while two actors are parallel, they can face a little toward front so that their faces will not be in profile. The director can help alleviate the couple's difficulty by choosing a weak playing area and by careful use of furniture in the staging. If there is to be an embrace, it is not advisable to seat them on a sofa, as it will make them appear awkward and invite giggles from the audience. Platforms or staircases may be used to advantage, and slow movements around furniture are often helpful. Don't begin a romantic scene with a face-to-face encounter. Bring your lovers together gradually as the scene progresses until they meet for a standing embrace, preferably with a unit of furniture masking all but the tops of their bodies.

Invented Business

This term indicates some elucidation of character not in the author's playscript. They are usually happy accidents found during rehearsals, either performed spontaneously by the actors or the result of the director's momentary inspiration. Other business may be invented for purely technical reasons, such as to motivate a cross for an actor or to break up a long, talky scene. Contrary to general opinion, silent moves can hold an audience if the moves are well motivated. The audience wants to see as well as hear. But invented business should never detract from dialogue vital to the audience's understanding. If, in your judgment, the author is holding interest by his dialogue, do not resort to "busy business." In building to a climax, it is often effective to reduce the tempo and pitch the voices lower in order to start building again. This prevents a scene from seeming like a shouting match. Remember, invented business must always be in character.

A production is actually a composition made of many elements. These might be likened to the pieces of a mosaic, some of which are best set in place tentatively to be adjusted later to other pieces as the work on the master design proceeds. Rehearsals constitute a developing process, and like the play itself, will have sequential growth. Certain aspects of staging are carried to a point only to be interrupted by other factors or considerations which clarify and illuminate those earlier points.

Improvising Non-textual Scenes

Improvisations of off-stage scenes not written by the playwright but employing the subliminal or unconscious involvement of the characters may be found valuable at this point. They can add much to characterizations. The audience is told what happens to Hamlet when he is sent to England. If this action were dramatized in an improvisation, it would certainly deepen the actor's characterization when Hamlet returns to Elsinore. The events of the voyage to England are going to make him a different person than when he left.

By these off-stage improvisations, an actor is afforded an opportunity to bring something on stage with him rather than simply making an entrance.

Ensemble Playing

> *An interplay between two actors, by the exchange of looks and subtleties of vocal color and of rhythm, can only occur when two imaginative actors can react to suggestions of the other's performance, when they create and feel their scenes together.*[5]
>
> Sir Tyrone Guthrie

Many years ago I saw the Moscow Art Company perform when Stanislavski was one of the actors, and I was most impressed by their superb ensemble playing. If there is any single factor which is outstanding in the efforts of the new groups, it is not in their acting or playwriting, but in their ensemble playing. Much can be accomplished by a warm relationship between actors. A movement, a look, a gesture, or a turn of the head can add a richness to a production which goes beyond the spoken word. A dedicated group of actors training constantly in physical and mental exercises will bring to any play they produce an expertise in ensemble playing and an enthusiasm which would be impossible in a cast that had never before worked together. What, then, exactly *is* ensemble playing? Perhaps the nearest definition might be found in creating a company relationship in which the individual is inseparable from the ensemble.

Acting is a sensitive discipline. Those who find it irresistible often have a certain amount of emotional instability. An actor needs to have faith in what he is doing and in the people with whom he is working. Barriers which might block creativity must be removed. It is essential that the individual become involved in the common experience of the play, and this is best accomplished by establishing an *esprit de corps.* An empathy among cast members consists of an emotional response being created which circulates throughout the group.

Empathy occurs when one individual identifies with another through group

[5]Sir Tyrone Guthrie, *In Various Directions* (New York: Macmillan, 1965), p. 106.

activity. No imagination or emotional association is required when we join a club, and yet in the sharing of a common goal we acquire a stronger self-identity, and this is a source of personal reassurance. In sports this is known as "team spirit."

A new group coming together because of a common goal but without previous association must be stimulated into mutual psychological and physical involvement. The common goal of getting a production of a play on a stage will encourage a sense of ensemble. An added advantage will be the training each member receives in role playing. The common dependency upon each other can and must be stimulated by the director. If effective workshop training has previously been operative, the director might be assured of a cast which is relatively free of such hang-ups as selfishness, anxiety, competition, jealousy, and resentment. Workshops have a way of developing a dependency upon others and a sense of responsibility to all fellow workers. The exercises in themselves are not entirely responsible for this development. They are but a means of bringing a relationship between the body and feeling of one individual and fusing these into the psychophysical discipline of the group. Such training makes it possible to react impulsively, eliminating the blocks which often exist between an inner impulse and the outer expression of it. Within a group, objective questions are turned into subjective ones. For instance, in workshop we might ask: How does one rage? How does one fight? Such problems are submitted to the group and solutions are sought. The individual is encouraged to open up, to accept certain relationships between one human and another. One exercise might consist of a member looking directly into the eyes of another and describing what he sees as he touches the other's face with his fingers. After such human contact, with its resultant lowering of barriers, it would be difficult for an individual to think only of himself and not the oneness of the group.

Balance

Center stage seems to have a magnetic attraction for most actors, whether amateur or professional. In order to balance a stage, characters who are not the center of interest at the moment must be placed in positions to the right or left or in the background. A large group of characters up left of center must be balanced by giving others a stronger position or a lighted area down right. Geometric balance should always be considered along with the emphasis which is possible by the use of light. This means that during rehearsals a stage may appear in poor balance but during performance, when the final lighting is seen, it might then appear in perfect balance.

As no grouping should remain static, compensatory movement will help a director to constantly balance his stage. The type of play you are producing will also affect your stage picture. More formal arrangements are possible when presenting one of the classics, but in modern plays you will have much more freedom.

Clustering

When it is necessary that a great many people be on stage at one time, as in *Cyrano De Bergerac*, they must be prevented from huddling or clustering into a single mass. The director should design groups which can be placed at various points so that they balance the stage. Even members of a mob with similar emotions or convictions must be somewhat divided for purely artistic reasons.

Emphasis

During each scene, the audience's attention should be directed to the main actor of the moment or the main actions. On the stage, action should never seem a three-ring circus. A play is too concentrated in form to permit diffusion. If certain words or actions are not emphasized in each scene, the audience will become lost in the spectacle. Spectacle is useful and impressive at times when creating atmosphere, but not when vital points need to be understood.

Relationships between characters and their individual reactions are made clearer to the audience when actors are properly positioned. It might help the director if he watches the blocking from a pantomimic point of view. Could a deaf man follow your story?

In a scene with two characters of equal importance, *they share*; that is, they are positioned on a level with each other, and their faces will be either in profile or with three-quarters face to the audience. This level should not be used for more than two characters. It is very likely that during the scene one character will become dominant. He will have a long speech or some important business. In this case, the other actor will "give" by turning three-

Audience focus provided by an active character, to an inactive one, for comedy effect is seen in this scene from Goldoni's The Venetian Twins, *as adapted by director Macdonald for the Tyrone Guthrie Theatre. (Courtesy of the Tyrone Guthrie Theatre)*

quarters back to the audience and the dominant actor will "take stage" by moving from the level to upstage facing three-quarters to the audience.

There are many variations of this stage deportment, or courtesy, which are used to achieve emphasis, but the above example contains the essence of such techniques.

Variety

As you watch the play's movement, it may become obvious that you have repeated certain groupings or positions too often. There may be a monotony of scenes played between two characters just off center stage. It may be that a single piece of furniture seems constantly occupied by one of your characters. Remedy such faults as soon as possible. In order to do so, listen carefully to the dialogue of the scene, and this may give the key to other positions which might be available to you.

Symbols

By the positions you give to the actors, it is possible graphically, or symbolically, to indicate emotions, which will help to express the mood of a scene. A warm relationship between characters can be transmitted to an audience by their closeness in a confined area. Hostility or conflict might be suggested subconsciously by the use of some barrier between the opposing forces, such as a table or chair. Fear or indifference separates people, while strength can be suggested by placing your hero in front of a group of sympathizers or by placing him on a platform above other characters. Even an area can become a symbol of a character or of a condition, such as the acting space around Lear's throne, Crichton's hut, or Snoopy's dog house.

Symbols of wooden royalty, these handladies of the Court are seen in the repertory of the Award-winning Company Theatre. (Courtesy of Company Theatre, Los Angeles, Calif.)

Memorizing Lines

Not much that is artistically significant can be accomplished until actors have the scripts out of their hands. While they are struggling to get their lines memorized, they are going to be preoccupied and somewhat irritable. This is a time for you, as director, to exercise patience. Once the words are learned, the actors will be much more receptive to direction. Point out that it will be of great value to them, and to the production, if they free themselves of books as soon as possible. Some will learn their lines quickly, but others may procrastinate. Therefore, *a deadline must be set for learning all parts.* It is very frustrating to a director who wants to get on with the dynamic and significant aspects of rehearsals to be prevented from doing so by a few who have not memorized their lines even after the deadline has passed. This is a grave breach of discipline and harsh remedies must be used. Seat your cast in a half-circle on stage. Speak seriously, pointing out that you do not intend to waste your time listening to them stumble and "fish" for lines when there is so much important work to be done; that you are ready and anxious to proceed but cannot until they cooperate. Instruct them to sit here as they are for the remainder of this rehearsal and speak the lines by rote. *Then leave, putting the stage manager in charge.* At the next rehearsal, you will probably find that all lines are memorized and that you have a very conscientious group of actors. I mention this problem because it does happen, and it may happen to you.

Significant Action

Suppose you and I are sitting comfortably in your living room conversing. Also, suppose that without speaking I make a small move. Instantly, that mental computer of yours feeds information into your brain and several answers come out. "Oh, he's going for a cigarette." "He wants to leave." "He's offended by my last remark." "It's about time he's leaving." In real life such reasoning is automatic, but on stage the process is reversed. For purely technical reasons, a director might decide that an actor has been sitting too long in that chair. Remember, we are considering an incident in which no such move is indicated in the playscript. The director and the actors must consider many reasons which will justify the move, such as the ones mentioned above, or others, and then select one that seems most significant and believable. The actor then mentally stamps in the reason for moving. He is not moving out of the chair because the director thinks the scene has been static for too long. He is moving because he is urged to do so by a motivated impulse. If he is "offended by some remark," he may develop that idea by a subtle, instant irritation at the remark, a glance, a tightening of the mouth—and a regaining of control—then a silence, and then the decision to leave transmitted by slapping his palms on the arms of the chair and rising. Or, suppose we have chosen "he wants to leave" as our justification. The actor might show some preoccupation during the dialogue—a wandering of the eyes, a furtive look at his wrist watch, and then the move. Such

Workshop training in significant action is demonstrated by actors of the Shakespeare Festival and Academy of Stratford, Conn. (Photo by Alfred Westheimer, courtesy of the American Shakespeare Festival Theatre)

thought processes could enrich a moment which began from pure mechanics. Such constructions rarely occur when reading a manuscript; but when working with actors, they become apparent, and the solutions are possible by collaboration with the actors.

You will recognize that the above is an example of how an action which began out of practical necessity can be so motivated that an audience will not recognize it as mechanics. In addition, by justifying the move, we add to the characterizations and to the relationships between the characters. Moving, speaking, and reacting are the results of a living response to continuous thought processes.

Rehearsing Isolated Scenes

All really good plays have a cyclic movement, like a wheel turning on its axis while advancing in a straight line. Like the spokes on a wheel, each scene follows another, each contributing to the acceleration of the forward thrust. A play is a series of accumulative actions, or fragments which create collectively a dramatic unity. It would seem, therefore, that if scenes are rehearsed out of context for any period of time, the sequential acceleration, or build, of a play would be jeopardized.

Rehearsing isolated scenes is not the best procedure for other reasons: actors are not afforded the opportunity to experience the flow of the entire play, nor are they able to test their ability to sustain the effort necessary when playing a long part in a complete play. Instead, they become accustomed to concentrating and expending physical energies for only short periods.

Nevertheless, it is hardly possible for every rehearsal to be a complete run-through. Certain scenes will need more time and attention than others. A rehearsal may include working on various scenes throughout the play, *but you must always keep in mind the location of these scenes and how they fit into the development of the complete play*, for that is the way the audience will experience them and not as isolated scenes. An opening scene of narration or character exploration will not have the speed or the intensity of a scene near the climax. The playwright has made an effort to keep interest rising by disclosing situations in careful steps, one scene growing progressively out of the preceding one and in relation to it.

What is a Scene?

When characters are brought together for a particular objective and that purpose has been reached, the fragmented action is known as a *scene*. The objectives may be to narrate, to explore characters, or to put the characters into a situation or conflict. A scene may also increase tension or relieve it from a preceding scene. The overall objective, however, is to contribute to the play as a whole.

If it is absolutely necessary to rehearse isolated scenes, the objectives should be kept in mind and also how the scene strengthens the entire play. This will help both the director and the actors to understand the scene's particular character. Study each scene by employing the "who-what-why" formula to it.

Summary

At this point, let us recapitulate briefly. Hopefully, we have had table sessions with the cast and have spent some time analyzing the play's theme, plot, period, action, and characters in open forum with everyone contributing questions and answers. Then the actors have been given their movement and instructed to learn their lines. What is the next step?

13 THE MIDDLE REHEARSAL PERIOD

A Checkpoint

Now we enter a phase of the work which is flexible and exploratory. Decisions reached at the table sessions and all the movement devised for the actors will now be subject to appraisal.

In order to do this, we must have an audit of the work done so far. We begin by calling for a run-through of the entire play. Inform the cast that no props, no books are to be used and that you will now, for the first time, take a place in the auditorium. Instructions are that there will be no interruptions and that notes will be prepared by you for a later critique. The stage manager is to keep the rehearsal moving with no stops. If any difficulties arise, the actors are left to their own resources. This will be your opportunity to evaluate not only the work done thus far, but the work yet to be done. The cast will have the opportunity to experience and accustom themselves to the long period of concentration necessary to sustain an entire play.

Try not to be too critical and don't expect to see a finished performance. And whatever happens, don't reveal discouragement. This run-through will seem rough, but you have many rehearsals ahead to smooth out the production. So far, most of your time has been spent upon construction and not on the fine points. The time for polishing is ahead. As you watch the run-through, try to arrive at a general, not a particular, impression.

Does the dialogue and movement correctly express the characters and the meaning of the play?

Are there wrong inflections or readings which give an opposite or confusing impression?

Are the actors projecting their voices and communicating?

Where can the movement and business be improved?

Are the rise and fall of the action adequate?

NOTE: If extras or minor character parts are to be used in the production, you might give them permission to see this first run-through. Up to this time there has really been no necessity for them to attend rehearsals, but it might be well to allow them to see this one so that they can see how they will fit into the play. After this, call them only when you intend to use them.

There is an important reason for the director to have seated himself in the audience section during this first run-through. Up to now he has been working closely with the actors, and his view has been completely subjective. Their problems have been his problems. But sitting in the audience, his viewpoint should change, become more detached, objective. He will now see the play as the audience will see it.

Moving From the General to the Specific

After this run-through, move back on stage with the cast. This rehearsal should provide you with enough notes for work to be done in many rehearsals ahead. Do not go into much detail in your critique to the cast. Keep all remarks general and encouraging. You may wish to give them some idea of what they will be working on during the next rehearsals. This work should be broken up into improving various individual scenes. Perhaps one was poorly motivated. Try alternatives. Not all motivation or business depends upon character. Human will, emotion, or drives can also be the stimulus for action. Experiment with new ideas, retrace the character's pattern of conduct, modify what you have, or correct, adjust, refine, and improvise to find alternatives for scenes you found dull or misleading. Inquire as to the actors' feelings of a scene. Listen to their suggestions, and if they seem valid to you, try them. Actors will not be disturbed by changes at this time, especially if they participate in suggesting the reasons for the changes. The actors should now know almost as much about the play as you do. If a movement suggested by one of the cast looks better to you than your own blocking, substitute the actor's idea for your own. Remember:

—Don't find fault.
—Don't shout.
—Don't deal in personalities.
—Don't indulge in snide remarks at the expense of others.

—Do stimulate the actor's imagination.
—Do give praise whenever possible.
—Do retain high morale in your company.

At least one or two rehearsals during this period should be devoted exclusively to motivations. Each actor should have a reason for everything he does. Every action is the result of a previous action. Above all, be receptive to those "happy accidents" or inspirational moments some actors have when they do something that is outlandish but exactly right for the character.

During this time you are concentrating upon improving details of characterization and motivation, but care should be taken that you do not do so at the expense of vital scenes, such as the opening of the play, or the climax. After this middle rehearsal period, it would be unwise to upset the cast with further changes. Smoothness and polish in a performance depends to some extent upon uninterrupted repetitions of the entire play. In order to meet your opening-night deadline, you must conscientiously follow the schedule you have made.

Judging Emotional Scenes

What the spectators experience during an emotional scene is a carefully fabricated stimulus devised to set off their own latent emotions. Some actors devise this by relating the situation in the play to some similar experience in their own lives. Other actors believe that emotion can be realized by first "doing the act." As an example, when danger threatens us in real life, we first run instinctively, the adrenalin flows, and we *then* feel the emotions of fear.

The director must gauge the impact of emotional scenes such as this one from Saint Joan *by Shaw, featuring Kitty Winn and Philip Kerr, as presented by the American Conservatory Theatre and directed by Edward Gilbert. (Photo by William Ganslen, courtesy of the American Conservatory Theatre of San Francisco)*

Whether the actor acquires emotion physically or mentally, the only valid judgment to be made must depend, not on what *he* feels, but on how the stimulus he has created is projected and how it affects *the audience.* An audience is not interested in the process, only in the result.

Encouraging Actors

A sensitive director will appreciate the enormous effort his cast has made in sustaining a long run-through at this time. Only partially prepared, fighting to remember lines, and not yet sure of their characterizations or movements, their only security is a blind confidence that eventually all the pieces will fit perfectly into a smooth production. This is a time when the actors need a director to give them courage, for creativity cannot grow in an indifferent atmosphere. The director himself may not feel like keeping up the spirits of others, but he must never show, or even imply, that he has been disappointed in their efforts. Certainly, something good can be said about a run-through. The actor's enthusiasm must be retained. His further growth will not depend entirely upon more rehearsals but upon his mental and physical readiness to continue. Disappointment and despair are the enemies of growth. Expectancy, encouragement, and curiosity will motivate the actor to continue his efforts.

We must always remember that the function of a director is not only to blend many elements into a performance, but also to guide and inspire everyone connected with the production. *Inspiration* is a term not easily defined. When a production seems dull and reminiscent of other productions, it is usually because the director himself was not inspired. Inspiration is the result of looking more deeply into one's self, of giving more energy, more concentration to the task at hand. You should never appear bored, preoccupied, or tired. You must, as Grotowski has advised, "exceed your limitations."

Show or Tell?

Should a director correct actors by means of explanation or by demonstration? This question has been debated for some time. With such directors as Reinhardt, Stanislavski, and George M. Cohan, who were also superb actors, it is reasonable to accept that they could reach an actor faster and more completely by demonstration than by verbalization. These men spoke the actor's language with their bodies, voices, and instincts. Most directors today explain what they want to the actor by stimulating the actor's imagination and channeling his thinking. Actors can then respond with creative results which will be entirely their own. But even a nonacting director should not feel timid about demonstrating a gesture, walking a movement, or giving an inflection. He should simply admit that he is not an actor, then add, "but perhaps I can give you some idea of what I want here, and then *you* can do it properly." Often demonstration takes less time for small points than verbosity.

Private Sessions

There are many good reasons for holding rehearsals in which the entire cast is not called. Private sessions are closed rehearsals during which the director is able to concentrate upon the problems of only a few actors. If a director has had no previous opportunity to study individuals in workshop or table sessions, then such private meetings are almost required. The demanding and collective problems of play production are so all-encompassing that it is impossible to concentrate to any great extent upon the individual during regularly scheduled rehearsals. Also, it would seem unfair to keep others sitting around waiting and listening to instruction which should be privileged and private. Much can be said privately which might be embarrassing if said within the hearing of the entire cast.

Special coaching is not exclusively for those who have failed to improve with the rest of the cast. Actors who carry the heaviest work loads of principal parts will need guidance even if they are well on their way to achieving a characterization. The director will be able to help them in formulating the right plan of attack and in finding the means to sustain a long emotional scene. Long speeches or soliloquies will need variety, tempo, and a plan which will help conserve energy for a time when needed.

If for some reason there have been no workshop or table sessions, then during private coaching the director might begin by offering his ideas regarding the actor's role, and in so doing, encourage the actor to contribute his thoughts. The next task will be to find some relationship between the role and the actor's experience, to stimulate the actor's imagination into a creative response and encourage his collaboration. Once a director feels that he has done this and that the creative potential is properly directed, he should then "give him his head," serving from then on as a sounding board for the actor's ideas. Such ideas are more likely to be offered during private sessions where there is the proper climate for experimentation and improvisations. In lieu of workshop training, these private meetings may also be used for releasing inhibitions and tensions. Ease and simplicity are cherished qualities in an actor and worth every effort to attain. In subsequent meetings, the director and actor might examine the character's needs and goals, pre-play history, physical traits, intellectual and emotional characteristics, present mode of living, in fact, everything the author has not stated or made clear. After agreement on such points has been reached, selected lines and scenes should be read from the play which demonstrate and fortify the decisions reached. An actor can then approach a general rehearsal with the assurance and confidence that he understands the director's point of view. As rehearsals proceed, the director should be watchful that the actor is progressing along the lines discussed, and if the actor should get off on a tangent or is showing no development, further private meetings may be scheduled.

In summary, then, the actors playing leading parts, those who most conspicuously motivate the play, are going to require more of your time in private sessions than others. However, those playing supporting parts should not be overlooked. The leading characters and the quality of the production can depend upon them. Each supporting actor should also be encouraged to give his character something of himself—something uniquely his own.

Private sessions are also useful in working on scenes requiring special handling. Neophyte actors are often embarrassed when asked to rehearse love scenes for the first time in front of a group of their peers. One effective solution is to block and rehearse such scenes in private sessions. Fight scenes and weapon play must first be carefully planned and walked slowly. Patterns can be blocked carefully in a confined area, which is preferable to using the full stage, where it is difficult to control the spirits of young players.

Just as in other rehearsals, the stage manager will be present to insist that private sessions are short and that they begin and end promptly. However, these rehearsals may be scheduled at the convenience of the director and actors. They will require an extra expenditure of the director's time but will be well worth it. In ancient Greek and medieval times, the producer of a play was also a priest. You must not permit actors in these private sessions to burden you with personal problems. Private sessions are not confessionals. The stage manager can help you to prevent this from happening.

Correcting Individual Faults

An actor may have a complete understanding of his character, and yet if he is unable to convey that character to an audience, his theories and psychological probings are worthless. The means by which a character is projected presents a problem to the inexperienced student-actor who has no technique and is also burdened with the slovenly speech and awkward body movements which are accepted as normal behavior among his peer group. When he realizes that there is something more to acting than shuffling on stage and mumbling words, and that he is completely inadequate as an actor, he is besieged by fear. Tensions may cause him to lose control of his hands and he can find no place to put them. His legs do not behave properly; they stiffen his walk. And his voice waivers. An audience immediately senses such tension and from that time on, any effort to convey character is difficult because the illusion has been shattered.

In order to correct such faults as inadequate projection, meaningless gesturing, and all the other maladies which beset the neophyte actor, the director must *remove the cause—tension.* This can be done if the individual is willing to improve. But this means change, and some people resent change, especially in their personal habits. The exercises found in Chapter 9 will be of value to the director who is forced to produce a play with a completely untrained cast. Some of these exercises have proven to be most effective in easing tension. Others are used to correct common faults. When no workshop classes are planned, it is advisable that particular exercises for particular faults be given during private sessions.

Actors enjoy being singled out for special attention, and even the more competent members of a cast will benefit from individual sessions with the director. Let us suppose that the director has decided that one of his actors sounds as if he were reading the lines instead of speaking them. He should work privately with this actor to help him find the *meaning* behind each of his lines and point out that they are to be regarded as *thoughts* which are being spoken for the first time. In another instance, a director might find that during certain scenes one of his actors does not seem to be listening to what is happening. Anticipation is deadly to a play and is usually the result of an actor being out of character. The director should work with such an actor by using the reacting and listening exercises.

Most of the time spent in private coaching should be devoted to developing subtleties of character and to correcting personal idiosyncrasies in speech or movement. Now and then one will find an actor who sincerely believes that acting on stage should be "real." To such an individual, the word *technique* is synonymous with *hammy*. This "tell it like it is" ideology is in direct opposition to all that theatre stands for. The stage is both a magnified and simplified view of life. An actor can be true to life and a liar to the play. Truth on stage is *theatrical truth*. The launching pad is life, of course, but from this a character ascends into another atmosphere, into sights, colors, sounds, and behavior of another world—the world of the play. Considered by some to be an arch realist, Mordecai Gorelik has said:

> In spite of steaming family dinners, glowing fireplaces, the swearing, the truck driver's sweaty shirt, our realism is as much a convention as the theatre of the Greeks.[1]

A director should always encourage the actor who achieves results by relating the situations and characters in a play to himself and his own everyday life. In this way an audience will recognize and identify with the authenticity. Technique is the means by which this is conveyed to them.

Replacing an Actor

We have considered the use of private sessions to help actors who are not progressing on a level with other members of the company. A small-part player who does not listen to the main players but allows his eyes and thoughts to wander into the audience can ruin the most important scene in a play. But a director cannot spend a limitless amount of time with such an actor. Some favorable results must be quickly evidenced. There are actors who cannot or do not choose to improve. In such a case, the director is forced to consider a replacement. But even replacing small parts means extra effort for the already intensely occupied director.

The replacement of leading parts at this time could endanger the entire production. But there are times when even this is necessary. At this time the actors have had an ample opportunity to improve. Perhaps the actor is not entirely at fault. Even careful directors make mistakes in casting. The first run-through should show the director which actors need help; then one or two private sessions should give him an indication if they are ever going to improve. A decision can then be reached by considering the actor's general attitude toward the work ahead. There are those who enter into rehearsal with a sincere desire to work, only to change their minds later. The work is so demanding and concentrated that each participant must derive an inner satisfaction from it. If this does not exist, then it is obvious that the actor is not going to derive anything from the training and can seriously jeopardize the sincere efforts of those with the proper attitude. When the director decides to eliminate an actor, the best time and place to do so is in a private session

[1]Mordecai Gorelik, *New Theatres for Old* (New York: Samuel French, 1957), p. 65.

when the director can explain his feelings to the actor and soften the blow. It is surprising how many times it is not a blow, but a relief.

The Duality of the Director

When reading various plays in search of one to produce, a director has an objective approach. When one particular play is chosen, his attitude becomes more personal. Then, as he studies his play, selects his cast, discusses it with them during table sessions, works with them performing improvisations, helps develop their characterizations, works out movement with them, and supervises the scenery, props, costumes, and lighting, he does in fact become the subjective center in a hive of activity. Then, just at the time when it seems he would be most intensely involved, he must shift this position of personal involvement, walk across the footlights, and observe the work objectively, as one of the audience. He must pretend that he does not know the play or the people in it, and forget his physical exhaustion or the mental anxieties of rehearsals. He must convince himself that he is devoid of prejudice and that he is, in fact, a complete stranger coming into the theatre expecting to be entertained, thrilled, or educated. If he can detach himself in this way for a few rehearsals, he will not only be able to appraise his work honestly, but will be able to visualize the work still to be done. He might begin an analysis by asking himself—

1. Is what I am seeing interesting?
2. Do I like these characters?
3. Does this story concern, amuse, or enlighten me?
4. Does this play relate to my life, my thoughts, my wishes?
5. Could I recommend seeing this production to others?

He should then move into another section of the house and ask himself—

1. Have I transmitted those qualities which first made me want to do this play?
2. Is my production going to tell the author's story? Have I treated it imaginatively or only conventionally?
3. Have I successfully withdrawn from a participating position to a critical one?
4. Do the actors understand this play and their characters?
5. Do they work well together?
6. Is the action visible from all parts of the audience?
7. Is the main focus of interest clear in each scene?
8. Is there variety in tone and pace? Does the interest build to a climax?
9. Are the emotional scenes moving?
10. Have I anticipated events, or am I pulling rabbits out of a hat?
11. Do I sense trouble in any scene? Is this trouble physical or psychological?
12. Are the actors working with or against me?
13. Have I been too permissive with them? Have I driven them too hard?

14. Are they showing boredom in rehearsals? How can I stimulate their
interest again?
15. Do I have a show?
16. If not, why not; or, more to the point, how will I fix it?

Before you rehearse again with your actors, get out that Director's Book
you made during your study of the play. Carefully read all the notes you
made when you were planning this production, and especially those relating
to your *concept*. Are you satisfied that your original concept has been
achieved?

At this point, which is just before beginning the polishing rehearsals, some
directors arrange for a tape to be made during a run-through. It is then
played back for the actors so that they may judge their own work. It is
supposed to stimulate actors into correcting their own faults. I have never
used tape for that very reason. Who wants an actor to be objective?

Creating Audience Response

From the first rehearsal to the last, the director should continually keep
in mind that there are two essentials of theatre: (1) that which is seen and
heard, and (2) an audience. Leave the audience out of your thoughts at your
peril. One false move, a line spoken out of character, can so jar an audience
that it will be difficult for them to regain the illusion that what they are
seeing are real events happening to real people. Not only Juliet, but even
Peter Pan, must seem real—that is, *theatrically real*. It is especially difficult
for a high school student, known personally to many in the audience, to
be accepted as a character without first subjugating his or her identifiable
personality. The final and most effective test of all production effort will
depend upon the reaction of the audience.

Audience Focus

It should not seem odd to you that a director not only directs actors but
also directs the audience. They must see and hear what the director thinks
is necessary for their full understanding of the play. Focal points must be
highlighted if the director is to get their interest and maintain it. Audiences
are more aware of what they see than what they hear. Should you have
a scene played by a group at stage left and it is important that the focus
of the audience be shifted immediately to stage right, the simplest means
is to have those in the group look to the right. The practical joker who
stands looking up in the sky never fails to attract a crowd trying to see
what he sees. Should you have an important prop that needs to be established,
such as a jewel box, a letter, or a passageway, arrange that important scenes
be played around it; make it the central element of a grouping, stamping
it in the spectators' minds *visually*.

Make sure that plot lines are not swallowed, spoken hastily, or confused
with activity. Check that other actors are not distracting attention from the

ıe grouping of your characters on stage can mean
e focus of the audience to necessary business, props,
r locations on stage. If a stage is unbalanced, the
expects it to be balanced soon and their eyes will
empty space in the design. Contrasts in lighting are
ˌhlighting certain areas of a stage. Usually an audience's
d to the top of a flight of stairs, and this is a very strong
ıng up or down stairs, the actor is placed in a very weak
either with or without movement, is another effective tech-
ˌng the focus of attention from one character or place to
ˌding it can be motivated. A direct cross by a character draws
ı from the audience than a curved one. The groupings of your
every scene should strengthen that scene's values. Groupings
beautiful but should always help the audience to focus on what
to their understanding of the scene.

ˌon

ıle or late rehearsals, and even performances, are all part of the training
ım. Begin each rehearsal with some simple group exercises found in
ˌter 9. They will stir up the blood, clear the head, and revitalize weary
ˌcles. When a scene seems lifeless, decide what happens in the scene
ˌd have the actors improvise. A "dead" entrance is most often the result
ˌ actors who are not in character. Improvise some scenes which are not
ˌn the play, using the characters in a time immediately preceding their entrance.

*"Loosening up" exercise before begin-
ning rehearsal. (Reprinted courtesy of
Theatre Crafts, May/June 1969.)*

14

SCENES REQUIRING SPECIAL HANDLING

Crowd handling by Oskar Schlemmer in his Maskenchor *at Bauhausaus-*
bümde, Dessau, Germany. (Courtesy of Frau Schlemmer)

Directing Crowds

Years ago in America there was a very lucrative phase of theatre known
as "the road." After a New York run, a star would pack up his production
and travel to towns all over the United States. Many of these tours would
last over a year and frequently meant the difference between profit and
loss for the production. Because these road companies traveled light, extras
or supernumeraries were recruited from among the local citizenry—usually
from schools and colleges. As an undergraduate, I received the princely sum
of one dollar a performance (one dollar and fifty cents on matinee days)
as a "super" for such stars as Otis Skinner, David Warfield, Walter Hampden,

Robert B. Mantell, John Barrymore, and others. My late father-in-law never missed an opportunity to boast that he had once "acted with Sarah Bernhardt."

As supers we were required to report to the stage door on the morning of the opening day. The stage manager would then take us on stage and "walk us through our business." He would next send us to the wardrobe lady to be fitted with some sort of costume from the company trunks. At performances, a group of three or four of us would be elbowed about the stage by one of the regular members of the company. I remember particularly that Walter Hampden's wife, who was playing the Queen in *Hamlet*, never took her eyes off us. She did not intend that we would move an inch or detract in any way from the main players. Later we learned that in another town, during the scene in which Gertrude pleads with her son, "I pray thee stay with us, go not to Wittenberg," an overly ambitious extra had blurted out, *"That's right, Hamlet, stay here!"*

Before working with extras, a director should be quite sure that they are absolutely necessary to the production. He will need to devote much time and effort transforming totally inexperienced actors into an aroused Roman mob. Even when supers are reliable and show up for each performance, they add to the confusion and backstage traffic. In the professional theatre, the salaries of extras must be considered. This may not apply to the avocational theatre, but there will be the cost of furnishing costumes, which can be quite an item when they are rented. These are a few reasons why some directors try to avoid supernumeraries in their productions. Some are successful in substituting even more imaginative effects. Mark Antony might be placed upon a high platform, using only a few partly hidden extras to represent the mob. A more stylized effect might be to place him directly before the audience as if they were the citizenry of Rome. Even more imaginative handling might be possible by throwing shadows against the cyc or by using rear projection. If at all possible, try to avoid the many problems that come with the use of extras. Unfortunately, this is not always feasible and the director must then resign himself to the necessity. He will first need to decide just how many people he will require, and how he will move them about the stage in order to give the best effect. As has been suggested earlier, all extras and small-part players should see a continuity rehearsal, but extras must be rehearsed separately by the director until he feels that they are ready to be combined with the rehearsals of the principals.

Crowds are usually used by a playwright to indicate the emotional impact of the protagonist's ideas upon his contemporaries or to create an atmosphere. Often the crowd is hostile to the protagonist's ideas at first and then later swayed into a more favorable view by his fervor. Even if supers are required to react as a group, it is advisable to think of each member as an individual— not as townspeople, courtiers, soldiers, etc. The director should create characters and provide improvisations for them. For instance, instead of thinking of Roman citizens, you might decide that one is a forty-year-old armorer who is married to a nagging wife and suffers with arthritis. Improvise a breakfast scene in which this man, his domineering wife, and whining ten-year-old daughter are joined by a neighbor who brings the awful news that Caesar has been assassinated. The neighbor is now on his way to the forum to hear the speeches which are to be made. By such improvisations, these characters will not only react with the group, but will also have individual reactions. As an example, the armorer's wife may continue her nagging, while his only interest is in finishing breakfast. Forced into attending the speech-making by his wife, he may bring a roll of bread to munch on as he listens. Many such individual traits will result from improvisations and a little imagination. And in turn, these will provide motivation, life, and color to what might otherwise be an impersonal and uninteresting mob.

Break up your crowd into small units. Appoint the most experienced and intelligent member as leader and put him in charge of the group. Determine a basic on-stage position for each of these social or family groups, and call it "position one." Move them about to position two, position three, etc., but always return them to position one. It is probably unnecessary to remind you that an individual business (such as munching the bread, the nagging, etc.) must never be allowed to intrude or interfere with the main focus of interest, as an audience is easily distracted by anything visual. Any business must be carefully adjusted to the dialogue by means of direct cues. Costumes and makeup for extras must also be carefully supervised. Nothing can break the illusion of King Lear's court so easily as seeing one of the courtiers with his wig slightly askew, or old-age makeup plastered upon a baby face.

In addition to motivating interplay between the various units within the group, the director might choose to have some dissent in the main group which would finally end in agreement. Improvisations should begin by deciding upon the "who-what-why" factors, but once they are developed the director should be careful that his invented characters do not detract during a scene, but that they listen to the dialogue and stay in character. The main value in working out individualities for members of a crowd is to eliminate that usual "blah, blah, blah" or "rhubarb, rhubarb, rhubarb" conversation and to give some status to the demeaning title of "one of the mob."

Once the results of the improvisations have been developed, they must be blended with the action of the play and the principals. Carefully thought out positions must be settled and ad-libs must be rehearsed until the supers understand where they are to be on stage during each speech of the principals. Never leave the action of the crowd to be improvised during performances. Take special care to establish entrances and exits so that these do not resemble a stampede of buffalo. Move your people on and off gradually, in small groups, using different openings.

Extras always seem to need handling with a tight rein and need more strict discipline than principals. It is possible though, that you will have little trouble directing crowds if you contribute some insight and imagination to the task.

Fight Scenes

One of the first things to remember about staging a fight on stage is that none of the basic fundamentals of a street fight apply. The latter deals with

Exciting fight scene as staged by director George Lauris for Lane Community College, Eugene, Oregon. (Courtesy of Lane Community College)

emotions and violence. The prime objective is to hurt the opponent. Short hidden punches are used to surprise him. The fighting area is confined and the opponents continue to stand on their feet until one of them is finally knocked out. But a stage fight has two main requirements: it must *look* like a fight, and yet *no one must get hurt*. Emotion and violence are simulated. Each blow is telegraphed and then pulled. The movement in a stage fight utilizes as much space as possible and the orthdox boxing stance is not used. Each move is meticulously planned and executed. The truth is that the most effective fights from an audience's viewpoint are those which have been as carefully developed as a dance routine. If given a choice between two evils, it would be much better to stage a fight that is not so convincing rather than one that is a wild, uncontrolled melee in which someone gets hurt. Should this happen, the aesthetic distance is destroyed for the audience. They will be more concerned about the injured actor than the play, and you might just as well lower the curtain. A stage fight is a *prima facie* example of how theatre must *seem* real without *being* real.

Charting a routine. In order to stage a fight, the director should prepare a ground plan of the setting with symbols indicating platforms, furniture, stairs, etc., and the positions of all actors on stage at the time when the fight is to begin. He must decide upon the overall movement of the fight, how it is to begin and end, what blows are to be used and by whom, and what furniture, props, and people will be involved.

Fight technique. The opponents must be trained in pulling punches. An audience must see each blow coming, if only for a split second, but long enough for it to register. This is mostly a matter of putting the move into their line of sight. No surprise blows or short jabs are as effective to the audience as one in which they participate. In a street fight a right to the opponent's jaw might begin parallel to the body, but in a stage fight it would first be initiated by cocking the fist back to the side of the body before being delivered. The more force simulated at this point the better. The force is then diminished as the blow is delivered. The most important

281

point, however, is how the opponent reacts to the simulated blow. He must ride with the punch by doubling over for a body blow or jerking back his head and moving with the direction of the force if the blow is meant to simulate a punch to the head.

Pulling punches. During training for a stage battle, all concerned should wear rehearsal clothes, or a clean drop cloth should be provided. The first exercise should consist of placing your fighters so that they face a blank wall and deliver punches toward it, stopping the force of the blow just as their fists are about to make contact with it. In a stage fight all punches are "pulled." Continue this exercise until each actor actually seems to be hitting the wall with some force.

Stance. A crouching position with knees bent, feet apart, and fists to the side of the body indicates to the audience that an opponent is threatening his adversary and ready to fight. This prepares the audience and actually focuses their attention upon the action. Should they be distracted, they will miss the action of the fight and its effect will be lost.

Dramatizing the fight. An impressive stage fight will depend greatly upon how the director maneuvers the fighters about the stage space so that the audience is able to see the start of the blows, lose sight of the blow contact, but see the effect upon the victim. Instruct the actors not to hurry when showing the effect of a blow upon a recipient. The actor might stagger, shake his head to clear it, or use other means of dramatizing the fight, including receiving encouragement from other characters. Fight action should be sporadic. Rolls, falls, and the use of furniture or props are all effective, as are Judo cuts, kicks, and, indeed, any means that *looks* exciting to an audience but is perfectly safe for the actors.

Falls. The body must be completely relaxed for a fall of any kind. Body weight in motion generates a force. When planning a fall, it should first be decided how this force is to be met. Bent knees will diminish some of the force, and complete relaxation will distribute the fall over several areas of the body. It is dangerous to take an unplanned fall, as the full force of the falling body could break on one point. Many elbows and knees have been shattered in this way. A full back fall is executed by bending the knees, which partly breaks the force of the fall and then letting the fleshy part of the end zone cushion the rest of the fall. A good general rule to follow in planning all falls is to make sure that fleshy parts of the body and not the bones take most of the force.

Use of space in fights. A stage fight would not be very convincing if the opponents were confined to one area. Use of space and props is as important to a good stage fight as are simulated blows. The movement must be kinetic, the excitement generated by the bobbing and weaving of the players and by the utmost use of the playing area.

Begin by rehearsing simulated body and head blows, covers, parries, and counter blows *in slow motion.* Then get out your ground plan and decide where each exchange is to be used, and in what order. Now work on the progression of movement and do it slowly. Variety and proper timing will come later. Don't allow the opponents to become excited or emotional. *Walk* the set routine over and over until it becomes smooth and automatic. You will notice that after many repetitions, a rhythmic pattern begins to develop.

Just a few nicely timed and precisely executed blows are all that are needed, providing there is plenty of other action. Noncombatants can be helpful in breaking falls, changing focus, or altering the timing. Breakaway plates, vases (thinly cast plaster of Paris), and balsa wood clubs can be used with discretion. Scuffling and pushing movements will help the combatants to cover ground. Movement and use of tables, chairs, and props will give more excitement to a fight scene than a dozen blows. Be sure to use your space to advantage by moving your fighters into various locations on the stage. Suspense is increased when it seems in the beginning that the protagonist is getting the worst of it.

Keep in mind:

1. Safety of your players
2. Movement and action
3. Fullest use of space
4. Precision of blows
5. Effective reaction to blows
6. Use of furniture, props, etc.
7. Necessity of rehearsing slowly
8. Necessity of avoiding emotional excitement during rehearsals, unavoidable during performances.

Further Reading

Hobbs, William. *Stage Fight.* New York: Theatre Arts Books, 1967.

Sword Duels

All of the above procedures for stage fights are also applicable to staging duels, either with broadswords or foils. First, learn the thrusts and parries. Make a plan for the routine you will follow and walk the movements and action slowly. Points and edges of swords should be tipped or dulled. Consult books listed in Further Reading for detailed information on basic positions, thrusts, etc. Mask the fatal thrust by movement of the players rather than by using the hackneyed thrust between the arm and chest. Never permit the victim to collapse immediately. There should be a moment of suspense

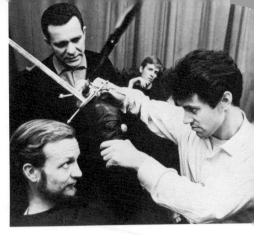

At left, sword duel from Henry IV, Part I, *as produced at the American Shakespeare Festival, Stratford, Conn., Douglas Seale, director, starring Hal Holbrook as Hotspur and Eric Berry as Falstaff; Motley created the costumes. Philip Bosco at left, with Jared Reed at right. (Photo by Sam Siegel, courtesy of the American Shakespeare Festival Theatre) At right, students get daily lessons in swordplay from fencing master Christopher Tanner in preparation for* Romeo and Juliet *at the American Shakespeare Festival Theatre, Stratford, Conn. 160,000 college and high school students from New York State, New Jersey, and the New England area witness such productions. (Courtesy of the American Shakespeare Festival Theatre)*

before he staggers and falls to one knee first. From this position he can be carried away by his supporters or fall slowly to the floor—if a "dead" body will not interfere with further action. Most directors prefer to have victims die behind furniture or set pieces where they are partly hidden from the audience. This is important, as an audience will watch to see if a "dead" actor is breathing, and therefore may miss some important action of the moment.

Further Reading

Crosnier, Roger. *Fencing With The Foil.* London: Faber & Faber, 1951.
————. *Fencing with the Sabre.* London: Faber & Faber, 1954.
Editors of Sports Illustrated. *Book of Fencing.* New York: J.B. Lippincott Co., 1962.
Wise, Arthur. *Weapons in the Theatre.* New York: Barnes & Noble, 1968. Sword fights related to history: rapier, broadswords, etc.

Gun Fights

Much of the above also applies to shoot-outs. Guns must be respected and handled carefully. One prop man should be exclusively responsible for guns and their working order. Firing should not be done in close quarters, as even the paper discharged from blanks can burn those near. Most directors arrange to have the guns discharged from the wings. At any rate, a cover gun should always be there at the ready and as near the stage action as possible.

Drunk Scenes

Everyone knows that alcohol interferes with the drinker's muscular coordination and that he loses some control of balance. Also, we know that his eyes never quite focus upon an object and that he has difficulty with articulation and enunciation. An actor who thinks only in surface aspects will base a drunken characterization upon these obvious facts with the result that his characterization will be just about as obvious as the facts.

In order to avoid "indicating"[1] and to be more than stereotyped, the actor must delve deeper into his character. A tipsy gentleman will not behave the way a drunken sailor will. Some drunk parts are written for comedy, while others may be pathetic or even tragic. As in all interpretation, the director and actor must be in direct contact with the character and the environment. Not all inebriated characters stagger and garble their words. Some might behave stiffly, speak precisely, and overemphasize in an effort to prove they are *not* drunk.

Actors usually like to play such characters, feeling that they are easy to play and that audiences always enjoy them. And for this reason they are often overacted and unoriginal. "Cliché is like a weed," Sir Michael Redgrave once said. "No garden is free of it all the time. The greatest performances are those in which every detail has been freshly conceived."[2]

Death Scenes

From the time they play "Cowboy and Indian" to the day they play *Hamlet*, most actors hope that one day they will have an opportunity to play a death scene on stage. In the Tony Award-winning play *Rosencrantz and Guildenstern are Dead*, the Player King explains to Guildenstern that dying ". . . is what actors do best. They have to exploit whatever talent is given them, and their talent is dying. They can die heroically, comically, ironically, slowly, suddenly, disgustingly, charmingly, or from a great height."[3]

But the old Player King and the ambitious young actor fail to recognize that a convincing death on stage is perhaps the most difficult task an actor is ever called upon to perform. To begin with, an audience must always be wrenched from the fact that the man dying is an actor, and therefore cannot be dying. They must be made to disbelieve what they believe—to become so involved in the play that they have no other thought but that Mercutio's body has been pierced by a rapier and that he lies dying. They must be under a kind of spell, and nothing done by the director or actor must break that spell. A death scene is the final and most convincing argument in the case favoring aesthetic distance. There must be no gruesome or harrowing details in the dying, for those would break the spell, bring the audience back to reality, and ruin the aesthetic distance.

Authenticity and accuracy should be used in planning all death scenes. Here again, the character and environment will be a foundation on which

[1]*Indicating* is a derisive term meaning obvious work done for effect only.
[2]Sir Michael Redgrave, *Mask and Face* (New York: Theatre Arts Books, 1958), p. 177.
[3]Tom Stoppard, *Rosencrantz and Guildenstern Are Dead* (New York: Grove Press, Inc., 1967), p. 82. Copyright © 1967 by Tom Stoppard. Reprinted by permission of Grove Press, New York, and Faber & Faber Ltd., London.

to build. Hotspur, the philosopher, will die differently from a violent man such as Richard III. Some characters might be shocked by the coming of death and may reject it, curse it. Others may give up life out of loyalty or love, with a quip on the lips, as does Mercutio. Authenticity begins by learning exactly what causes a particular death. You need a kind of Coroner's Report. Some of the greatest lines in dramatic literature have been written for death scenes. Mercutio does not die immediately. Where was he hit by Tybalt's blade which allowed him consciousness for a time? Consult a physician, give him all the facts you have from the play, and ask for an analysis of what caused the death. In this way, the director and actor will then have accurate and authentic information on which to base an attitude toward a scene, the staging of it, and the use of the actor's voice and gesture. Details, when authentic, have often resulted in an extraordinary moment on stage.

THE
DIRECTOR'S
FINAL
REHEARSALS 15

It is now time to review what has been accomplished in rehearsals thus far and decide which scenes need extra work. An updated schedule for that purpose should be devised with the help of the cast and stage manager for intensive work on particular scenes or acts. For instance, if you are producing a classic, it is important that the actors get back to the exact lines as written by the author, even if it is necessary that certain actors be directed to hold scripts once again. It would be even better to insist that procrastinating actors ask that lines be "thrown" to them. Much repetition of this will embarrass the actor into memorizing his lines correctly.

As director, some of your duties at this time will be as follows:

Build to important scenes or climaxes, and in order that scenes do not sound like a shouting match, retard, then accelerate a build again in intensity.

Check a run-through of the complete play for tonal patterns. (A play has a sound track just like a film.) Keep variety in pace and tone.

If actual costumes are not as yet available, players must simulate difficult-to-handle period costumes, such as capes, swords, farthingales, or bustle skirts, with make-shift articles.

Avoid making any major changes at this time which will require that actors not only learn new lines, business, or cuts, but also unlearn the old.

Do anything that is going to familiarize the actors with their surroundings. Try to have something of the setting, if only some platforms or a set-piece.

(This will not be possible on a professional stage unless the management is willing to pay a stage crew.)

Actual sound effects, such as bells and telephone rings, should now be used. Up to this time, the stage manager has probably been serving as telephone, barking dog, or earthquake. The stage manager should now be timing all scenes and acts and keeping schedules for the director to compare.

During earlier rehearsals, you have set a time limit on the holding of scripts and have insisted upon it. The serious work to be accomplished from now on cannot be done while actors are holding scripts. There should be no fumbling for lines at this date. If so, the stage manager should cue those unsure of their lines privately.

Certain scenes should now begin to look, sound, and "feel" good. If not, decide quickly what is wrong and experiment with totally different concepts.

The play should now be "living" and looking much better than it will during the period to come when everyone will be concerned with sets, costumes, lights, and props.

Continuity Runs

Any competent performer knows that excellence is achieved in large part by constant repetition. The musician and the athlete drive themselves into a discipline which is the boring drudgery of practice, practice. If an actor ever tells you he fears growing stale by many rehearsals, inform him that nothing grows stale when used. Many unseasoned actors are under the impression that there is no connection between routine procedure and the art of acting. This is not true. Going over and over the play without interruptions gives the actor confidence, stamps in the movements, and leaves the mind free for inspiration.

Now frequently seated in the audience, the director will be unable to make comments to the cast during continuity runs. He has no alternative but to devise some system of making notes for later discussion with the cast and crew. One of the great values of a careful director at this time is that his detached view of the acting is invariably better than the subjective eye of the actor.

Techniques of Criticism

Every director has his own personal method of conveying criticism to actors. During a continuity rehearsal, some directors make mental notes, and when it is over, come on stage and speak to the actors. Individual scenes, entrances, exits, speeches, etc., are then repeated until the director is satisfied. Such oral criticism leaves much to be desired. In the first place, the director is completely dependent upon his memory; also, the actor singled out for criticism often feels on the defensive, and discussions at this point waste precious time.

Another director might take written notes during the run-throughs. By the time he has written a sentence, he has missed the next scene, and to read scrawls which were made in a darkened theatre is often impossible.

Paul Sills gives critique to Metamorphoses *cast.*
(Photo by Steven Keull)

The most efficient method of giving critiques is to have someone sitting with the director who can take down his comments in shorthand on a lighted clipboard. At the end of the run-through rehearsal the weary cast may then be dismissed immediately without long, tiring discussions. Notes pertinent to each individual are distributed after they are typed. This will prevent any unfavorable remarks by the director from being made in front of the entire cast, which could be embarrassing to a very sensitive individual. Then, before the next rehearsal begins, the director asks if there are any questions regarding his notes. Certain scenes may then be given attention when the actors are rested and have had time to study the comments and to use their own initiative in correcting faults.

Bridging

When an actor persists in reading a line stressed incorrectly, some directors resort to a device known as "bridging," that is, having the actor speak the line in response to various questions proposed by the director.

EXAMPLE

The Director	*The Actor*
I know his name, do you?	*I* don't remember his name.
Why do you persist that you don't remember his name?	I *don't* remember his name.
They introduced you, what's his name?	I don't *remember* his name.
You met the family, what's his name?	I don't remember *his* name.
You identified his picture?	I don't remember his *name.*

289

Before memorizing lines, the late Walter Huston often accented various words in a sentence in order to find the reading which would best express the meaning he sought.

Self-Criticism

The director should not confine all of his critical judgments to the actors. He should analyze his own work, too. Has he corrected the technical weaknesses in his actors? For instance, he might ask his actors if they have any problems in interpretation or technique which he might help solve. Is he asking more of his cast than they are capable of giving? Has he used his space effectively? Is the focus of the audience correctly directed in each scene? Does the production have atmosphere, variety, style, and progression?

It is also important for a director to consider the well-being of his actors. He must not drive them to the point of exhaustion. An actor drained of physical energy cannot improve. When your players seem lethargic and unresponsive, stop the rehearsal and allow them to relax for a few minutes. And do not hesitate to tell them that you are pleased with the improvement in rehearsals.

Especially sensitive actors often grow apprehensive as opening night approaches. The director can help a great deal simply by assuring the cast of his confidence in them. The dress and technical rehearsals yet to come will be disturbing, and at this point the cast should be assured that the production, at long last, is coming to life. Try to imbue your cast with a genuine excitement about the opening.

Supporting Parts

In a sincere effort to fully interpret his character, an actor might give his part more importance than it deserves. This could interfere with the intention of the author and put an emphasis where it does not belong. Exactly where the emphasis is to be placed in each scene is determined by the director. No actor has his point of view. Often a one-scene actor determined to "steal the show" keeps his intentions hidden *until this time*. Continuity rehearsals usually bring him out into the open. He may try to make certain business, movement, lines, or pauses seem vital to the play when they are not. All lines and actions must relate to the play as a whole. Some parts may be flat, one-dimensional. They are types—and should remain so. The factor of time alone makes their use a necessity for the playwright. He must devote the time he has to his leading characters, those who deal directly with the progression of his plot and development of his theme. He has no time to devote to long biographies on the life of a maid with two lines in Act II. She must become a symbol, and drama is full of symbols. If a part seems shallow and one-dimensional, don't allow an actor to make a Hamlet out of it. Stereotypes are found in Greek drama, Shakespeare, Molière, and Shaw, and in some of the newer plays, even the principal parts are no more than stereotypes. Watch out for the actor who would project his own personality at the expense of the play. Supporting parts are only as important as they relate to the protagonist and the story. During important scenes or speeches by leading characters, Tyrone Guthrie creates the proper emphasis for the audience by keeping supporting actors immobile, and then, almost imperceptibly, dimming the light on the inactive area while highlighting the important players. This is a common device used in films.

Cuts

All substantial cutting should have been made during the director's study, or at least during table sessions. If cutting is left to this late date, it might seriously interfere with the progression of rehearsals. Should several favorite speeches of an actor be eliminated now, it might create a psychological problem for a very sensitive individual. He might suspect that the lines were cut because he had failed to make them interesting. A notable exception might be when rehearsing a new play professionally. Cuts and changes are often made until the opening, and sometimes even after that.

Rehearsal Control

By this time, the director should have established indisputable command of rehearsals; but there are always those who cannot help testing authority, if only to see just how much they can get away with. If, after several warnings, an actor should continue to be late for rehearsals, or chatter off stage while others are trying to rehearse, or consistently disregard any other rule of theatre discipline, then he should be given a severe and sharp reprimand—in the presence of the entire company.

Polishing Rehearsals

This is a favorite phrase with those who enjoy seasoning their conversation with showbiz terminology. I once worked with a producer who used "polishing" to describe almost every rehearsal after the first week when there was really nothing to polish. Unfortunately, few school productions have any polishing rehearsals. "There is only one way to overcome the difficulty," John Dolman advises, "and that is to announce certain rehearsals as polishing rehearsals, and to carry them out as such no matter how many details of study and experiment have to be left unfinished."[1] Unfortunately, this seems to be a general attitude in many productions. Rarely is there time for polishing. If a rehearsal schedule is improperly planned or casually followed, the poorly organized director has only himself to blame when he reaches this

[1]John Dolman, Jr., *The Art of Play Production* (New York: Harper & Row Publishers, rev. ed., 1946), p. 194.

point and finds his production so crude and amateurish that he must spend the remaining time doing basic work which should have been accomplished weeks ago. An effective schedule for rehearsing is one which provides an unbroken line of progression not only for the actors but also for the director. The production of a play is a process of construction. Like building a house, it begins with blueprints. A foundation is laid and the work proceeds within a structural framework. No one in his right mind would paint a house before the building was completed.

The blueprint of a production is the director's concept as recorded in his book. The foundation work is done during table sessions. Movement and characterization begin the structure. Improvisations, private sessions, continuity rehearsals, and detailed rehearsals add the necessities, and the sets and costumes provide the utilities. When these are all developed in sequence, you will have a construction and a production ready for those final touches which mean so much.

After several run-throughs or continuity rehearsals, inadequacies should be obvious. It may be that there is a monotony, a lack of variety in the playing which makes the play seem boring. A typical fault is an absence of adhesion, where nothing seems to relate to anything else. It is all bits and pieces, the probable result of rehearsing isolated scenes. Although rehearsing individual scenes is practical, convenient, and frequently necessary, if too much time is devoted to working with fragments (or units), then the actors never have an opportunity to experience the *accumulative drive and overall design of the play.*

A Graph for Dramatic Intensity

Provide yourself with a sheet of graph paper. Draw a horizontal line across the middle of the sheet; at the left, put the label "Opening," and at right, "Final Curtain." If your play is divided into acts, divide the graph horizontally and label. Now mark where the "Climax" of the play will occur and label it. Do the same where the "Exposition" will be as well as the "Complications," "Denouement," etc.

The "Climax" will be at the top of the chart and everything will rise to that position or fall after it has been reached. But the rising line will have a zig-zag progression, indicating minor climaxes.

No two plays will have identical graphs. In some the "Climax" will be reached at the end of Act II; in others, in Act III. But all plays will have a series of rising and falling dramatic or comic incidents leading up to the high point of interest—the main "Climax." On a graph, this zig-zag line of interest or sequential build should make clear to you those scenes which need tempo and excitement, those which are suspenseful, and those which merely narrate. The relationship between each of these will also be seen in the rising and falling line. Up until the "Climax," each scene must have a higher point of interest than the one preceding it. The juxtaposition of these scenes, the variety of interest until the "Climax" is reached, will add suspense and keep your production from being monotonous to an audience.

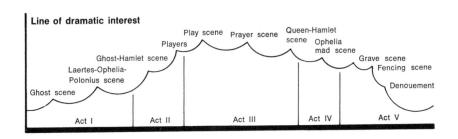

Line of dramatic interest

Ghost scene

Laertes-Ophelia-
Polonius scene

Ghost-Hamlet scene

Players

Play scene   Prayer scene   Queen-Hamlet
scene   Ophelia
mad scene

Grave scene
Fencing scene

Denouement

Act I   Act II   Act III   Act IV   Act V

Building a Climax

The major climax of a play is much more than a playwright's term or the high point on a director's graph. True enough, the author prepares the way for an effective climax when he writes his characters, clarifies their drives and ambitions, and describes the obstacles in the path of fulfillment. But these values must be more than words on paper.

Progressive tensions can only be conveyed to an audience by the director and his actors. A play may have only one or two scenes of minor complications, consisting of mere intellectual suspicion or threat, or it may have strong physical confrontations. In any case, the important value of every scene is in how it involves the spectator in a growing expectancy toward the win or lose climax. The director must therefore guide his actors in achieving a mounting tension toward the climax.

However, any play dealing with human needs does not move in a straight line. Such plays consist of action scenes in which tensions are temporarily eased only to prepare for another emotional drive forward. Each scene containing a minor crisis should be started in low key, then built toward the main climax. No scene should begin and end on the same level of intensity and no minor climax should ever reach the intensity of the main climax.

One of the most discouraging remarks heard in the theatre is "A good first act." To help actors visualize this build to the climax, the director might ask them to think that they are climbing a mountain. It is impossible to reach the summit in a vertical straight line. Sometimes they must veer to the right or left horizontally or even drop back a distance in order to reach the top. This zig-zag way to the main goal is typical only in traditional plays. Some of these have such strong minor climaxes that the major climax is overshadowed, resulting in disappointment for an audience. If you suspect that this is true of the play you are producing, you have little choice but to play down those minor climaxes and build steadily to the main climax.

Plays of the absurd do not have such structure, and the typical experimental plays are not conceived of as a group of small scenes contributing progressively to a central unifying idea. At their most typical they are a collage of impressions, usually the result of being created through improvisational methods. Whatever they convey dramatically is by the juxtaposition of scenes, moods, or the convictions presented. Such scenes may be rearranged in other

293

orders with little notable difference, because the scenes do not build to any central climax. Such plays may be rehearsed out of sequence, as units, such as in revue theatre.

But structured plays build the tensions toward a climax, and a climax may be helped in several ways by the director. He may proceed by purely physical means, beginning with actors in relaxed, static positions. Then the movement of the characters, the tempo, the atmosphere created, and the involvement of the audience builds gradually to more excitement and greater traffic about the stage. In some plays, crowds of extras may be used to encourage a sense of mass participation.

Another means, less physical, is by increasing the volume, pitch, and intensity of the voices and by stimulating emotion. In less subtle builds, such as in melodrama, the director might overlap the dialogue or instruct each actor to top the previous speaker. Off-stage sounds or a different effect in lighting may be used if such means are in harmony with the play. Old melodrama actors were masters at building a scene slowly to a climax, and it is still a technique practiced—although it is done much more subtly now through emotion.

A Danger in Complacency

I have known directors who were so pleased with what they had accomplished at this point that they could do little more than sit watching rehearsals, enthralled by their creation. This type is so astigmatic that it is unaware of faults which would be obvious to any outsider. These final rehearsals which come just before dealing with technical problems are so important that they could mean the difference between an exciting or a boring evening for an audience. This is the period when a really artistic director adds his masterly touches. Such a director might add a pause or a piece of business which will illuminate an entire scene. This is the time for detail, now that the run-throughs have shown you just where refinements are needed. Inspirational touches emerge out of responses to the actors as they are finally "living" the scene.

That Conversational Quality

In our everyday conversations, we somewhat anticipate the end of another's thought, and therefore the interval between speaking is negligible. Directors should discourage the "you speak; I speak" habit. It is both unnatural and stilted. Another fault may be that the actors are not picking up their cues. Perhaps they have not been told that the lines they have learned from the printed page are to be spoken as conversation. They wait for another actor to finish his line completely before speaking, instead of somewhat anticipating the end. Pauses in dialogue, which may seem short when considered individually, can add minutes to the playing time of an act.

This does not mean that all lines in all plays are to be delivered without pauses of any kind. Any production will benefit by variety, and we have previously recommended the values of silences and pauses. But one of the genuine necessities in playing comedy or farce is that cues be picked up. Ask your stage manager to show you his records on playing time during all your rehearsals, and compare them.

Dropping the Ends of Sentences

Not too much attention should be given to a playwright's punctuation marks. It is up to the actor to gauge pauses by his breathing and the sense of the line. Having recommended ordinary conversation as a guide in picking up cues, it should now be admitted that when speaking ordinarily to others, we tend to drop the end of a sentence by decreasing breath pressure and tone. We use this as an indication that we have finished our comment and that it is time for another to speak. However, one of the most important requirements for speaking on stage is that the last words in a sentence be sustained by breath control and emphasis. This prevents the dialogue from having a monotonous cadence, which always results in a loss of audience interest unless done for a specific purpose.

Another poor habit which the director should correct as soon as the lines are memorized begins during early rehearsals when actors are still reading from scripts. They develop a method of glancing at their parts to register four or five words and then looking up to speak these words. If this pattern of speaking continues after memorization, the actor should be reminded that he is not speaking words—but sense. Actors must forget that their lines were ever written or memorized.

Broken Lines

    A. Weren't you here a minute ago when I . . .
    B. Not a chance, since I only arrived . . .
    C. I'm sure you came into this office while I was . . .
    B. (Laughs) No, I couldn't have, you see . . .
    A. Oh stop! You sat over there on that chair and . . .
    B. Tell me something, do you always see things that don't happen?

A line of dots after an incomplete sentence indicates that the speaker is to be interrupted. In this case, the sense is *the sense conveyed by the complete scene* and not by the individual sentences. Each actor concerned memorizes not only his own lines but those of his colleague as well. He learns the entire scene as one speech. Also, if his partner does not respond quickly, he must be prepared to carry his thought further. Once this happens in rehearsal, the slow-responding actor will learn to pick up his cue quickly. Broken lines need not be spoken quickly—but cues must be anticipated and responded to at once.

Telephone Conversations

The telephone is a boon to playwrights. Unseen characters may be developed and affect the story without the director having to cast a flesh and blood actor. In *The Collection*, Harold Pinter begins the play with a man in a telephone booth. Lights come up on another part of the stage as a telephone rings. A man appears and answers the telephone, and as they converse, we see them both. This is a technique more common to films. Generally, on stage, telephone conversations are one-sided. It is up to the actor, by his reactions during pauses, *to show* the audience what the person on the other end of the line is saying. This usually can be accomplished by having the actor himself write suitable lines for the unseen conversant and memorize them. In this way, not only is he able to get the correct timing of his pauses, but knowing what is being said will key him into the proper reactions.

G. Wood phones his client in The Latent Heterosexual, *Paddy Chayefsky's comedy directed by Allen Fletcher for the American Conservatory Theatre. (Photo by Hank Kranzler, courtesy of the American Conservatory Theatre of San Francisco)*

Listening

Telephone conversations should not be very difficult for any actor who listens well on stage. Someone once said that "acting is reacting." The truth of this remark is apparent in film technique. During a scene between two people, the camera first focuses on the character who is speaking, then cuts to the listener for his reaction to what has been said. In most cases we hear what the first character is saying and we are more interested in the second character's reaction.

A good listener responds, not always audibly, but with his thoughts, and these stimulate emotional and physical reactions which can convey thoughts to the audience.

Dialogue should be accepted as a method by which one person attempts to influence another. Silent reactions to another's speech may be accomplished by creating a subtext, or as Stanislavski called it, an "inner monologue." In another instance, a character may be saying one thing and thinking something quite different. Such reactions may be difficult for a novice to project to an audience. But the main point is that an actor should not stand expressionless as others speak, waiting for his cue, and then suddenly spring to life when it comes.

Maintaining the Play's Distinctive Qualities

This may seem a bit late to be concerned about your concept of the play and your production of it. Casting, table discussions, improvisations, blocking—indeed every working hour has been guided by that plan. But during those weeks of concentrated involvement, a director can lose sight of his initial goals by becoming confused in a mass of detail.

Suppose you had started out to produce a fast and funny farce; but now as you watch a run-through, your production seems more like Chekhov than Feydeau. Now, when the basic form of your production has already evolved, recall your first intuitive responses to the play and your first ideas about it. Have another look, now, at your Director's Book and judge for yourself whether or not you have fulfilled your goals.

Moods

We have previously discussed the importance of the atmosphere of a production, along with some suggestions for creating it. Atmosphere is such an all-encompassing influence that it must be in the director's consciousness from the beginning and remain there during all the work to follow. It represents not only the climactic condition and period of the play, but also its parochial milieu, the characters, action—indeed, the total environment. A director has many tools he can use in creating atmosphere—sounds, scenery, lighting, dance, music, language, color, costumes, and of late there have even been experiments in using scents.

Most people have difficulty in differentiating between atmosphere and mood. The creation of a mood is more dependent upon characters than upon other directing devices. We say, "Good morning," to a friend. His smile, shrug, silence, gesture, or even slight body movement might convey a different mood to us. A director is able to impart moods to an audience without help from the playwright, whose only tools are words. Beyond the author's effort is another zone of expression dealing with the present, what is happening now—those electric currents which ensue when characters contact each other in a situation. Also, the moods of these characters will be in constant flux. A character's state of mind, his convictions, and his feelings will be influenced by his contact with other characters in a scene. He may begin a scene in one mood and finish it in another. This is character development as well as play progression. These changes keep an audience interested and involved.

Tempo

The most common epithets used to evaluate direction emphasize tempo;—the direction is "fast," "slow," "lethargic," "well-paced," "rapid-fire," etc.[2]

—Harold Clurman

[2]Harold Clurman, in *Contest and Craft of Drama*, Robert Corrigan, ed. (San Francisco: Chandler Publishing Co., 1964).

Just as critics are frequently unable to recognize any line of demarcation between the work of the playwright, the director, or the actors, they often confuse tempo with pace, timing, or rhythm. Tempo cannot be judged by comparing it to the measured ticks of a metronome, or whether or not a scene is played with loud voices or a rapid pace. Some scenes in *The Great White Hope*, when seen in production, seem short, but when compared to others in script form, are really no shorter than others. When what is happening on stage is exciting and we are enthralled, tempo appears to be quick. This is especially true in melodramas such as *The Front Page* or *Child's Play*.

Tempo depends a great deal upon the actor learning to change emotions quickly, going from one mood to another by means of deep involvement in his role. Of course, it goes without saying that cues must be picked up, that there should be a variety of sounds, and that the director should use his acting space to its full extent. Such factors are much more important in achieving tempo than a fast pace and loud voices.

When a scene lacks tempo, it is probably boring. Stop the actors and rehearse the scene slowly. Analyze again for meaning. Find an attitude for each character during the scene, pointing up their relationships to each other. Variety in characterizations can produce variety in sounds, which may be interesting in themselves and add clarity to the meaning of a scene. Strip the scene down to its essentials and decide which are the guiding and vital moments without which the scene would have no meaning. Next, use your ingenuity and imagination to identify these for the audience.

Sometimes certain scenic elements can be beneficial in specifying tempo and elaborating rhythmic moments. Examples of how sound and lighting effects can achieve artistic results are evident in the chopping of the cherry trees at the end of *The Cherry Orchard*, or the flash storm, with its thunder, lightning, and light changes, which underscore the text of *Cat on a Hot Tin Roof*.

Although the establishment of proper tempo is the responsibility of the director, others also contribute. The playwright may suggest tempo in the way he has written a scene. Chekhov's lines frequently indicate the tempo. Shakespeare wrote breathy words and phrases indicating excitement, and his romantic scenes are filled with soft, liquid word sounds. Actors also inspire a director to find the correct tempo for a scene after they begin playing it and have a full understanding of their characters. To sum up, tempo will depend more upon characters and language than upon speed and noise.

Rhythm

This subject has been discussed previously as an acting device, so that it need not be treated in depth at this point. Rhythm deals more with an actor's emotional response to his part than with almost anything else. It is *organic*, independent of mechanics, whereas meter deals in feet and stress. Preparatory work in rhythm can be considered during table sessions when emotional drives are considered. Later, when the actors begin feeling their characters in late rehearsals, the director is able to refine the work by coordinating tempo with each player's rhythm.

Timing

When a ball is thrown toward you, there is an instant when you must gauge distance and coordinate muscles to catch it. This is learned by practice and instinct. It is the same with speaking a line on stage. There is an instant when a line must be spoken if you are to achieve the most telling theatrical effect. Monologists, or as they are called today, "stand-up comics," depend heavily upon timing for their effects. A good joke can be greeted by an ominous silence if the timing is wrong. Those schooled in vaudeville or night club entertaining are expert at it. Timing should be as precise, accurate, and inevitable as a dripping faucet. In the army I learned that not everyone is born with the ability to keep time. Evidently, it is an instinct which some do not possess. But it can be learned, if only mechanically, and it can mean the difference between getting an effect on a stage or losing it. One method of doing this is by counting beats. As an example, here are a few lines from *The Importance of Being Earnest*, by Oscar Wilde:

LADY BRACKNELL: . . . are your parents still living?

JACK: I have lost both my parents.

LADY BRACKNELL: Both? (one-two-three) That seems like carelessness.

This method is not infallible, because no two audiences are exactly alike. But it is an effective beginning effort, and is adequate as a training aid. Timing can only be mastered by experience before various audiences. An experienced performer can walk out on a stage, deliver one or two remarks, and "feel" an audience so accurately that from then on, his timing becomes automatically adjusted to that particular group.

An instinctive sense of timing happens now and then in a completely inexperienced player. But in most cases the director will serve the actor as his audience during the rehearsal period and whatever seems most theatrically effective to the director in final rehearsals must be the gauge for the actor's timing.

Rate

This is generally accepted as the differential from the regular beat at which an individual speaks words. A long speech or soliloquy may be delivered at a fast or slow rate, but it should always be diversified by changes in rates. The same holds true for the rate of speaking during a scene. There should be variety in the speaking rate of the different characters. This along with each individual's tone can provide a kind of pleasant and varied musicality for the audience.

Volume and Pitch

These are also valuable tools for the director, especially when he senses the need to create a dramatic interest and variety in the production. If a careful schedule has been followed, the gradual development during adequate rehearsals should have provided proper pitch and volume. These are needed when building a scene through the use of force and intensity. Volume and pitch can also be used in developing characters or creating atmosphere. High-pitched, tense voices transmit a sense of fear or suspense, just as volume indicates force or dominance. Rhythm, tempo, timing, volume, and pitch are not as important during early rehearsals as they are later when the time for polishing has been reached. But the director should know from the start whether a scene is to be played *allegro, forte,* or *diminuendo,* and it must be the director who has the final decision. He alone is responsible for the emotional or comic aspects of the production, the points of tension, the playing of major or minor climaxes, as well as the pace of the entire play.

Pace

As rehearsals proceed, it may develop, almost imperceptibly, that the pace becomes slower and slower. This often happens after actors have mastered the lines and movements and are now adding "improvements"—without the director's approval. Slow pace may also be the result of improper memorization, and it is typical that performances by nonprofessionals frequently drag. Check on former timing of scenes with the stage manager.

Before combining the work of the actors with the settings, lighting, props, and music during the technical rehearsals, the director should reserve some time for polishing rehearsals in which he can build to emotional tensions and make sure that the entire play accelerates from the opening to the final curtain. Begin these rehearsals with an uninterrupted run-through of the entire play, and tell your cast that you would now like to see a performance. Make notes, and keep your mind free of other details except the sweep, or thrust, of the play. Note the scenes which seem uninteresting, and check the variety and drive of the action toward the climax. At the end, come up on stage and rehearse scenes you wish to correct, and if possible (or even if impossible), say something nice to your actors.

Director's Check List for Polishing Rehearsals

1. If, up to this time, you have been unsuccessful in motivating actors to pick up cues, you must now force them to do so mechanically.

2. Be on guard that actors are not taking on the intonations and rhythms of others.

3. Vary tones and pace throughout in order to indicate different moods and characters.

4. Take out nonessential ad-libs and ineffective movements which may have been added during late rehearsals.

5. Before each rehearsal, relax the cast with one or two exercises as a warm-up (see Chapter 9).

6. Check visibility and projection from all parts of the house.

7. If certain scenes have become dull and lifeless by repetition, remind actors of original motivations.

8. Guard against any fidgeting by small-part players during important scenes. See to it that nothing interferes with the audience's main point of focus in every scene.

9. It is probably not necessary to say that this is no time for discussions. Your main interest now is to get on with rehearsals and preserve your concept of the play as a whole.

10. Do not waste time now over slips in business or words unless they seriously interfere with the story.

11. Actors may now show signs of fatigue because of intense concentration and depletion of physical energy. When this happens, they must be stimulated by sincere praise for a worthy effort.

12. Make sure that any apprehensions you may have are not shown to the cast.

13. If necessary, introduce the stage crew to the cast and inform all of procedures you intend to follow at "Tech" rehearsals.

Tech Rehearsals

The most efficient, as well as the most practical, means of conducting tech rehearsals is to divide the work into separate phases, as suggested in Chapter 12. (See also pp. 302–303, Technical Rehearsals, items 1–10.) If this plan is followed, some of the technical work required during late rehearsals may be accomplished without using the actors. This is an advantage, as the cast is more apt to show fatigue at this time than at any other.

But eventually there comes a time when the acting must be blended with the technical aspects of the production. Let us hope that up to this time rehearsals have progressed steadily so that the play is now coming to life. But no matter how the director has tried to familiarize the players with the acting space, describing the lighting and the sets, he may find during tech rehearsals that an important prop is not in place, that doors are out of position, and that the big scene is almost in total darkness. Such errors can so upset actors that their timing is off, concentration ruined, and characterizations impossible. If it is all so chaotic, what *can* be accomplished during tech rehearsals? It is imperative that actors become familiar with the setting, props, furniture, lighting, and costume changes. They will also need to adapt to the architectural confinements. The setting cannot be adapted to them at this late date. In realistic productions, food and cocktail scenes must be rehearsed early with the actual food, knives, dishes, glasses, and liquids which are intended for actual performances. All difficulties should be solved by the director in such a way as to be least upsetting to formerly established and rehearsed business.

During technical rehearsals, the director will probably need to abandon any idea of getting continuity in the play, or performances from the actors, but only for the time being. He should resign himself to the important technical business at hand. If he begins with the lighting, he should "walk" the actors through the important scenes. Then, with the wardrobe staff at hand, he must give full attention to the costumes, making notes of changes to be made before the dress rehearsals. If there are scene changes to be made, he should have the actors read curtain or light cues and time the set changes. The director should remain in the front of the house and relay messages to the crew through the stage manager, who should be on stage and in full charge. Tech rehearsals should be managed in a no-nonsense, no-discussion manner in which the director's word is law. All work must proceed with practicality and efficiency, as there is no time left for fun, subtlety, or tact. Property people must organize themselves so that they know exactly what is expected of them during performances. Actors should be trained to return props to the property tables after they use them, and to keep clear of the stage during scene changes unless assigned certain duties. If off-stage sounds and music have not been rehearsed previously, these must now be set and marked. Tech rehearsals can be a time of utter confusion for the cast and a frustrating experience for a director. Backstage traffic will be congested due to the addition of the various staffs and technicians. The director will find himself jumping from the play's climax to someone's entrance in Act I—but that is the normal *modus operandi* of technical rehearsals. You may even feel like walking away from it all. Approach each problem separately and calmly, solve it, then go to another. Just as you might have been shocked by all the difficulties appearing suddenly, you will also be surprised at how quickly they can be solved—with patience and industry.

Technical Rehearsals: A Sample Schedule

In Charge: Director, stage manager, and designers.

Present: All technical personnel and cast as called.

1. *Tech rehearsal.* For technicians only. Scene changes rehearsed and timed by stage manager. Crew and prop technicians set up and prepare for cast rehearsal. Lights in place and set by director.

2. *Costume parade.* For cast and technicians. Work with costumer. Cast dresses and comes on stage to demonstrate how costumes look under lights and if any changes in costumes are advisable.

3. *Prop rehearsal.* For cast and technicians. Run-through of scenes in which complicated props, such as traps, mechanical effects, guns, etc., are used.

4. *Set rehearsal.* May be combined with prop rehearsal. Curtain timing given. Complete run-through with lighting. No costumes unless actors prefer to get accustomed to them. Do not be discouraged by this rehearsal. Everything will come apart at the seams. The play will seem awful, the props will not work, and the sets will look terrible. *Whatever your frustrations are, do not allow the cast to see them.* Dismiss the cast early on this one as they have dress rehearsals coming up and need all the rest they can get.

5. For any last minute corrections or coaching, have private rehearsals off the stage somewhere. The technicians will need the stage now every minute.

6. *First full dress.* Critique at end. Complete run-through with entire cast, props, lights, sets, music, off-stage sounds—everything. Time all acts and curtains. Rehearse final curtain calls. (See p. 306.) Some companies take photographs at this time.

7–10. *Subsequent dress rehearsals.* Critique at end. Try to schedule at least two more rehearsals as first one will probably be a shambles. Invite a few special guests whose opinion you respect. Do not allow cast to invite anyone. Ask your guests to avoid cast and *speak only to you.* Choose strangers to the cast if possible. Full dress rehearsal means just that; everything exactly like a performance before an audience.

11. *Opening.* If desired, a short sit-down line rehearsal may be held during the early afternoon. Visit all members of the cast and wish them luck.

Addenda

12. Keep off the stage during the opening night performance. If the set falls down and the cast forgets everything you have taught them, there is nothing you can do now. The play is in the hands of the actors, the stage manager, and the technicians. Your job is finished. Keep out of the workers' way!

Dress Rehearsals

It is often necessary to combine dress and technical rehearsals. If at all possible, schedule your time so that this can be avoided. The members of the cast will need time to collect themselves after solving the technical problems and approach dress rehearsals with a somewhat different attitude. In dress rehearsals, the actors will be trying to get back their characterizations, to experience once again the continuity of the play, and to begin to give a performance. The difference between a rough or smooth opening night often depends upon the number of uninterrupted rehearsals the cast and crew have had previously. A cardinal rule is that there be no changes in lines or business once dress rehearsals begin. Curtain calls should be rehearsed at this time.

During long evening rehearsals, it is advisable for the director to arrange rest periods, and if possible, to serve some light food and coffee.

Most directors permit a few invited guests to attend the final dress rehearsals. Preview audiences stimulate the cast and permit the director to study reactions other than his own. This is especially valuable when producing a comedy or farce. *But an audience made up of close friends and relatives of the cast will not provide the cast or the director with a fair appraisal of the production.* Beginning directors can be deeply hurt by a "raw" audience the night after a "loving" house. It is also poor business to give seats away to those who might otherwise pay. Senior citizens and underprivileged groups who would not regularly be able to afford the cost of tickets might be invited, and they will give the director a more unbiased reaction.

After each dress rehearsal, the cast should assemble on stage, and when the spectators have departed, the curtain should be raised in order that the cast be given the director's critique. If this plan is followed, the stage manager should be so informed, so that he can arrange for all members of the cast to be present without delay, and also arrange for the set to be left intact.

Another plan is to dismiss the weary actors after rehearsal and see that notes are given to them as soon as possible, so that they may study them before the next dress rehearsal.

Photos are usually taken after one of the early dress rehearsals with the cast in costume and in the settings. This should also be arranged beforehand with the stage manager. He has the additional responsibility now to see to it that after each dress rehearsal costumes are placed on hangers by the actors and that their dressing rooms are left in order.

A Few Words on Makeup

Many amateurs forget, or do not understand, that the purpose of makeup is to compensate for the washing out effect of stage lighting on natural skin colors. Makeup should never *look* like makeup, except in nonrealistic, stylized productions in which it serves some carefully planned purpose. In most amateur and professional stage productions, it is the actor's responsibility to design and apply his own makeup. In films and TV, this is a job for professional makeup artists. When the actor is left to his own devices, he should study the subject of makeup carefully. Usual errors in applying makeup are wrong color base, inexpert lining, and failure to apply crepe hair properly. I once saw a college production of *The Beggar's Opera* in which Macheath wore an orange makeup base, a vivid blue coat, and a snow-white wig, worn slightly askew, and made of some glistening cellophane. I was disappointed that they did not play the national anthem on his entrance.

David Holmes as Ariel in John Ingle's production of The Tempest *at Beverly Hills (Calif.) High School. Makeup by Bill Corrigan.*

Remarkable makeup from the North Carolina School of the Arts enhanced a production of Duerrenmatt's The Visit, *directed by Ira Zuckerman. (Courtesy of the North Carolina School of the Arts)*

A Word or Two on Costumes

Few actors in avocational theatricals have the proper regard for the costumes they wear. These should be respected as *clothes, and not costumes.* Ask your cast to study the customs and manners of the period about which the play was written. Characters should appear to live in these clothes and have pride in the way they look. Wrinkled or drooping tights are not exactly conducive to an appreciation of Shakespeare's "mighty iambs." Instruct your male actors to wear suspenders and to make buttons for the tights by inserting dimes through the cloth and into the suspender loops. If yours is a costume play, you will certainly want to examine an inspiring book by England's chief costumers, Sophie Devine, Margaret Harris, and Elizabeth Montgomery (known collectively as "Motley"). The book is *Designing and Making Stage Costumes* (Studio Vista Ltd., London, 1964). Also recommended are Irene

Effective lighting on masks and sculptured costumes heightens the classicism of Antigone, *as directed by Marston Balch for the Tufts University Arena Theatre. (Courtesy of Tufts Arena Theatre)*

Corey's handsome *The Mask of Reality* (Anchorage Press, Anchorage, Kentucky, 1968), *Costume Design and Making, A Practical Handbook*, by Mary Fernald and E. Shenton (Theatre Arts Books, New York, 1967), and for American costumes, there is *Early American Dress*, by Wyckoff, Warwill, and Pitts (Benjamin Blom, New York, 1965).

Curtain Calls

Devote a few minutes of your final rehearsals to instructing your cast in proper curtain calls. The most typical order of calls usually runs something like this:

> 1. Entire cast "discovered" as curtain rises, arranged in a straight line across the stage, principals in center. Cast takes two steps forward and bows.
> 2. Principals only, in place. Bow to audience, then to each other.
> 3. Leads only. Same as before.
> 4. Lead.
> 5. (If applause continues) Leads.
> 6. Leads bring on other members of cast as selected by director.

Some English companies have adopted the charming custom of having the actors applaud the audience on the final curtain call.

Advice to the stage manager. In giving signals for the curtain, the stage manager should compensate for the time it takes to get the curtain closed (or down). Do not leave the curtain open after the applause has reached its zenith.

Thrust or Center Calls

Action calls are frequently used on these stages. The cast join hands and run out in serpentine to form a half-circle, bow, and run off. They may also be given their calls in groups entering and exiting via different openings. In absence of curtains, lights are used from black-out to full-up. Design a routine, and then rehearse the actors in it several times so there is no confusion at the end of performances.

Limited Runs

After the opening of a production which has only been scheduled for one or two performances, there is little for a director to do unless an actor becomes ill or the scenery falls down in the middle of the climax. So, rather than annoy your cast with nit-picking, it is wise to join the audience, smile, and graciously accept any plaudits which may be forthcoming. If your job has been done properly, that is, the actors sufficiently rehearsed, the stage manager given full responsibility for running the show, and your staff drilled in its responsibilities, you should now be able to enjoy the fruits of your labors.

Runs

But it is an entirely different matter if your production has been planned for a longer run. If this is the case, you must constantly work to perfect the production and the performances.

Any and all alterations which you feel will improve the production must be made. Actors must not be allowed to let down their characterizations or performances. After the initial excitement of the opening, the cast may begin to slip into habits of uninspired performances and clichés. They must be constantly revitalized by your attentions. They must feel that you are out front demanding the best they can give—even if an audience is unresponsive. The tempo you have established must be retained. If a scene is playing too slow or too small, have the actors mime the situation to music. In some circumstances, you may think it necessary to call additional rehearsals. Read notes to the cast which you have made during performances. Discuss the reactions of audiences. They will tell you a great deal about your production, for they are the Supreme Court of the theatre. If a particular scene is giving you trouble, give an analogous situation to the actors for improvising. Improvisations will also help actors you suspect of losing characterizations or falling into comfortable patterns in their playing.

In staging a new play with the author and producer present, there are many additional problems. A playwright can never consider his work finished until he sees it performed before an audience. There are many things which he could not possibly see when working alone on the manuscript. But on stage with the actors, and before an audience, faults in a play become immediately apparent. Therefore, the director will often be handed entirely new scenes to stage. This means that the actors must unlearn old lines as well as memorize new ones. Whole acts may be cut, transposed, or rewritten—but "that's showbiz." (When working with the actors during rehearsals, the director might discover obvious faults in the text, recognizing these failings before the author himself. Often he will himself instigate late changes, if he is sincere.)

Out-of-town tryouts of a new play can be a traumatic experience for a director, but these often mean the difference between success or failure when the production reaches New York. Among many notable examples was the Boston tryout of *Any Wednesday*, during which everything that could go wrong, did—including the need for replacing the leading man.

16 AN EVENING OF THEATRE

More and more these days, the school or community theatre director is called upon to produce something other than a straight play. The Chamber of Commerce or the Rotary Club may ask him to provide a fifteen-minute diversion for one of their meetings. Or, funds may be needed to buy uniforms for the school band or Christmas dinners for the underprivileged.

Rather than consider this an imposition, a sagacious director could turn it to his advantage. The effort could prove to be a showcase for the work of the director and actors and become a means of obtaining community support for their efforts.

Usually, there are no funds available for scenery, lighting, or royalty payments. Also, most drama instructors have a full work load, and any extracurricular activity must come out of their private time. Under these circumstances, it is foolish for a director to consider producing a regulation full-length play. He should, instead, regard the project wholly as producing an entertainment. Very serious and dedicated directors are apt to think of entertainment as being commercially crass and shallow. However, it is a fact that true entertainment could make it possible for an audience to absorb some wisdom and a better understanding of human nature while being amused.

A director fortunate enough to have instituted workshop sessions may find that some of the improvisations worked out during these meetings are good enough to be developed into material which might be performed before an audience. Three or four of these, some monologues, and one or two excerpts from plays, if all tied together by an overall theme, could make an enjoyable "Evening of Theatre," with no pretensions other than entertainment. The possibilities are boundless. Verse readings, music, or dances might be added, providing they can be incorporated into the main spirit of the program. No scenery, costumes, props, or special lighting are necessary. The cast could be seated on an empty platform or curtained stage and come forward only to perform. Royalties for one or two excerpts or one-acts may be kept to a minimum.

The choice of some overall theme will be important, and it is best to choose one which has universal appeal, such as love, taxes, children, business, suburban living, in-laws, or adolescence. It is also possible to use actual quotes from the writings of such famous American personalities as Mark Twain, Lincoln, Jefferson, and Franklin. Foods, diets, and eating habits are also amusing themes and interesting to everyone. And since most people are fascinated by theatre, it might make an entertaining evening to present short scenes from the various styles in acting popular in different eras. This would also be of great benefit in training your actors. Another rewarding theme might be found in demonstrating man's changing thoughts through the use of historical and contemporary play excerpts.

Of course, each director will have his own ideas for "An Evening of Theatre," which he can tailor to his individual actors and audiences. But the general plan as indicated above has the advantage of pliability. It can be scheduled for a full evening, or one or two segments may be given at meetings or assemblies. A full evening presentation should be divided into two parts and separated by an intermission, with the strongest material placed at the end of each half.

The narrator becomes a most important figure in an entertainment of this kind. He serves as the integrating force between the various forms, setting the premise in his beginning remarks. He narrates that which is not acted and explains to the audience what they need to know before each scene is performed. In other words, he is the liaison between the players and the spectators, while establishing the theme and mood for the entire evening of entertainment. If at all possible, the director himself should assume the duties of narrator, as this will provide added importance to the evening.

Please do not imply from what has been said that the sole raison d'être of "An Evening of Theatre" is to buy uniforms for a band. It will serve you and your group as excellent training in that most important aspect of theatre—*facing an audience*. It will also provide more cultural and more lasting results than a production of *Curley McDimple* or *Guys and Dolls*—and with less effort.

Following is a list of plays and scenes which are offered as examples of the kinds of material which might be used in planning such a program. They may also be used as rehearsal scenes in workshop. Individual scenes may suggest overall themes not previously suggested which might be extended by finding other scenes or by inventing improvisations which can be related under a common theme.

Monologues: Male

Henry IV, Part I, by Shakespeare. Falstaff, Act V, Sc. i.
Ceremonies in Dark Old Men, by Lonne Elder. Mr. Parker's final speech in the play. (Farrar, Straus, and Giroux, pp. 178–180).

1776, by Peter Stone and Sherman Edwards. Thomson, Sc. 7 (Random House, p. 139).

Phormio, by Terence. Act I, Sc. i. Davos as Prologue. (In *Chief European Dramatists*, Houghton Mifflin.)

Tartuffe, by Molière. Cleante's "False and True" speech, end of Act I.

From Morn to Midnight, by George Kaiser. Sc. iii, The Cashier.

As You Like It, by Shakespeare. Act III, Sc. vii, Jacque's speech, "All the world's a stage . . ."

Blood Wedding, by Garcia Lorca. Act III, Sc. i. Leonard's speech, "What glass splinters . . ."

The Zoo Story, by Edward Albee. The story of Jerry and his dog.

Rosencrantz and Guildenstern Are Dead, by Tom Stoppard. Long speeches by Player, pp. 64, 70–71, 110 (Grove Press, 1967).

Little Murders, by Jules Feiffer. Pp. 78–80 (Random House).

The Lower Depths, by Maxim Gorki. Act IV, Satine's speech.

Richelieu, Arthur Goodrich version. "The curse of Rome" speech, pp. 243–245 (Appleton-Century-Crofts).

Dutchman, by Imamu Amiri Baraka (née LeRoi Jones). New Theatre in America. Pp. 212–213 (Dell).

The Devils, by John Whiting. Pp. 94–96, pp. 102–105 (Hill & Wang).

Hadrian VII, by Peter Luke. Talacryn and Rolfe, Act I, Sc. ii (Knopf).

Henry V, by Shakespeare. "Chorus."

Our Town, by Thorton Wilder. Prologue by Stage Manager. (Coward-McCann).

Night, by Leonard Melfi. Man, pp. 132–133 (Random House, 1968).

The Mundy Scheme, by Brian Friel. Ryan, Act III; pp. 270–273 (Doubleday).

Indians, by Arthur Kopit. John Grass, pp. 9–10; Buffalo Bill, pp. 68–70; Sitting Bull, pp. 70–72 (Hill & Wang).

The Only Game in Town, by Frank Gilroy. Joe, Act II, pp. 103–104 (Random House).

No Place to Be Somebody, by Charles Gordone. Act II, Sc. i; pp. 45–48 (Bobbs-Merrill).

The Tempest, by Shakespeare. Epilogue: Prospero.

Many Stand-up comic routines may be found in:

Son of Encyclopedia of Humor, by Joey Adams (Bobbs-Merrill, 1970).

In a Fit of Laughter, An Anthology of Modern Humor, Veronica Geng, ed. New York: Platt & Munk, 1969. Humorous pieces by Ring Lardner, James Thurber, Mike Nichols and Elaine May, and others.

Monologues: Female

"*Eh?*" by Henry Livings. Mrs. Murray, pp. 76–77 (Hill & Wang, 1967).

"*America Hurrah!*" by Jean-Claude van Itallie. See "Interview" and "The Girl at the Party" (Coward-McCann).

Life Is a Dream, by Calderon. Rosaura, Act I, Sc. ii.

Antigone, by Jean Anouilh. Antigone's speech, "Tomb, bridal-chamber, eternal prison . . ."

King John, by Shakespeare. Constance, Act III, Sc. iv.

The Taming of the Shrew, by Shakespeare. Katherine, Act IV, Sc. ii.

The Devils, by John Whiting. Pp. 63–67–68 (Hill & Wang).

The Rivals, by Sheridan. Mrs. Malaprop, Act I, Sc. ii.

Death of Bessie Smith, by Edward Albee. Sc. iii.

The Physicists, by Friedrich Dürrenmatt. Frl. Dokter, Act II, pp. 90–92 (Grove Press version).

Medea, by Euripides. (Robinson Jeffers adaptation) Her farewell to her children.

The Jewish Wife, from *The Private Life of the Master Race*, by Bertolt Brecht.

Mourning Becomes Electra, by Eugene O'Neill. "The Hunted," end of Act I, Christine.

Strange Interlude, by O'Neill. Nina Leeds, Part 1, beginning of Act V.

The Cherry Orchard, by Chekhov. Lynbov, Act II, beginning with "Oh, my sins . . ."

The Merchant of Venice, by Shakespeare. Portia, Act IV, Sc. i.

The Effect of Gamma Rays on Man-In-The-Moon Marigolds, by Paul Zindel. Pulitzer Prize and Drama Critics Award 1970–71. Beatrice's telephone conversation, pp. 3–6; also, Janice and the cat monologue, pp. 91–93 (Harper & Row).

Noon, by Terrence McNally. Allegra, pp. 83–86 (Random House).

Two Females

The Rimers of Eldrich, by Lanford Wilson. Act II, p. 34–35 (Hill & Wang).

The Way of the World, by Congreve. Act II, Sc. ii.

√*Hedda Gabler*, by Henrik Ibsen. Hedda and Mrs. Elvsted, Act I.

√ *The Physicists*, by Dürrenmatt. Frl Dokter and Frau Rose, Act I, pp. 31–37 (Grove Press).

Lysistrata, by Aristophanes, Lysistrata and Kolonika, Act I.

The Screens, by Jean Genet.

√*The Prime of Miss Jean Brodie*, by Jay Presson Allen and Muriel Spark. Act I, Sc. ix; Act II, Sc v (Samuel French).

√ *The Night of the Iguana*, by Tennessee Williams. Maxine, Hannah, beginning of Act II.

The Cradle Song, by Gregorio Martinez Sierra. Teresa and Sister Joanna of the Cross, middle of Act II.

√ *A Flea in Her Ear*, by Georges Feydeau. Lucienne and Raymonde, Act I, pp. 5–10; 11–13 (Samuel French).

Lemon Sky, by Lanford Wilson. Ronnie and Carol, pp. 25–27 (Dramatists).

Promises, Promises, by Neil Simon. Fran and Miss Olson, Sc. viii (Random House).

Three Females

The Women at the Tomb, by Michel de Ghelderode.

The Killing of Sister George, by Frank Marcus. Act II, Sc. ii, p. 51, "Alice: Do sit down Mrs. Mercy" to p. 55, "Mrs. Mercy: She'll be dead, that's all" (Random House).

Blood Wedding, by Frederico Garcia Lorca. Neighbor, Mother, Bride, Act III, Sc. ii.

Two Males

Child's Play, by Robert Marasco. Dobbs and Malley, Sc. i, pp. 15–16 (Random House). A "Best Play," 1969–70.

Galileo, by Bertolt Brecht. Little Monk and Galileo, Sc. vii (Grove).

✓ *The Subject Was Roses*, by Frank Gilroy. John and Timmy, beginning of Act II.

– *Othello*, by Shakespeare. Act III, Sc. iii–Act IV, Sc. ii.

✓ *Volpone*, by Ben Jonson. Volpone and Mosca, Act I.

The Price, by Arthur Miller. Victor and Solomon, Act I.

I Never Sang for My Father, by Robert Anderson. Any scene between Gene and Tom (Random House).

✓ *Tartuffe*, by Molière. Cleante and Orgon, Act V.

Beckett, or The Honor of God, by Jean Anouilh. Act IV, pp. 110–114 (Coward-Mc-Cann).

Santa Claus, by E.E. Cummings (in *Theatre Experiment*). P. 81 (Doubleday).

Home, by David Storey.

The Two Orphans (Kate Claxton Version). Pp. 98–99.

Phaedra, by Racine. Act V, Theramenes describing death of Hippolytus.

Miles Gloriosus, by Plautus. Act I, Pyrgopolynices, Artotrogus (see *Introduction to Drama*, Roby-Ulanov, p. 61) (McGraw–Hill).

Barabass, by Ghelderode. Herod and Barabass, Act III.

The Dumb Waiter, by Harold Pinter.

Julius Caesar, by Shakespeare. Brutus and Cassius, Act IV, Sc. iii.

Henry IV, by Luigi Pirandello. Act I. Henry, Landolph, Henry's speech beginning "It's like this . . ."

Sodom and Gomorrah, by Jean Giraudoux. The Angel and John. Beginning with Angel's speech, "I'm not joking . . . ," Act I.

Camino Real, by Tennessee Williams. Block Eight. Gutman and Byron.

The Man with a Load of Mischief, by Ashley Dukes. Nobleman and Man, pp. 21–28 (Doran, 1924).

Muzeeka, by John Guare. Argue and #2, Sc. vi, pp. 16–20 (Dramatists).

Hunger and Thirst, by Eugene Ionesco. Jean and First Keeper, pp. 37–45 (Grove).

The Picture, by Ionesco. Painter and Large Gentleman, pp. 109–125, (Grove).

Three Males

Rosencrantz and Guildenstern Are Dead, by Tom Stoppard. Beginning of Act II (Random House).

The Physicists, by Dürrenmatt. Newton, Einstein and Möbius, final scene of play. (Evergreen).

The Alchemist, by Jonson. Subtle, Face, and Drugger, Act I.

Man and Superman, by Bernard Shaw. Tanner, Mendoza, and Straker, Act III.

The Caretaker, by Harold Pinter. Aston, Davis, and Mick (Evergreen).

The Knack, by Ann Jellicoe. Tom, Colin, Tolen, pp. 31–33 (Delta, 1964).

The Indian Wants the Bronx, by Israel Horovitz (Random House).

Press Cuttings, by George Bernard Shaw. Orderly, Mitchener and Balsquith, pp. 1–15 (Constable).

One Male, One Female

"Eh?" by Henry Livings. Act II. Val and Betty ("Betty: Val, are you there?" to "I've got no money!" pp. 41–55 (Hill & Wang).

Pantagleize, by Ghelderode. Act II, Sc. iv.

It's Called the Sugar Plum, by Israel Horovitz.

Amédée, by Eugene Ionesco. Medeleine and Amédée, Act I (Evergreen).

✓ *As You Like It*, by Shakespeare. Rosalind and Orlando, Act III, Sc. ii; also, Act IV, Sc. i.

✓ *Twelfth Night*, by Shakespeare. Scenes between Viola and Orsino.

✓ *School for Scandal*, by Sheridan. Sir Peter and Lady Teazle, Act II, Sc. i; Act III, Sc. i.

The Lion in Winter, by James Goldman. Act I, Sc. iii (Random House).

✓ *The Physicists*, by Dürrenmatt. Frl. Dokter and Inspector, Act I (Evergreen).

There's a Girl in My Soup, by Terence Frisby.

The Way of the World, by William Congreve. Act IV, Sc. i.

I'm Herbert, from Robert Anderson's *You Know I Can't Hear You When the Water's Running*. Pp. 83–85 (Random House).

Luv, by Murray Schisgal. Milt and Elen, Act II.

A Delicate Balance, by Edward Albee. Tobias and Ellen at breakfast, beginning of Act III (Random House).

"The Diary of Adam and Eve" from *The Apple Tree*, by Harnick and Block from Mark Twain. (Another dramatization of Twain's "The Diary of Adam and Eve" may be found in Irene Coger's *Readers Theatre Handbook*, p. 175) (Random House).

You're a Good Man, Charlie Brown, by Gessner and Schulz. Snoopy and Patty, beginning of Act II (Random House).

Hey You Light Man! by Oliver Hailey. Lulu and Knight, Act I. (In *Three Plays from the Yale Drama School*, edited by John Gassner. New York: E.P. Dutton, 1964.)

The Applicant, by Harold Pinter, in *The Dwarfs and 8 Review Sketches* (Dramatists Play Service).

George Dandin, by Molière. Dandin and Angélique.

The Merchant of Venice, by Shakespeare. Lorenzo and Jessica, Act V, Sc. i.

✓ *Desire Under the Elms*, by O'Neill. Abbie and Eben, Part III, Sc. iii.

The Great White Hope, by Howard Sackler. Ellie, Jack (Dial).

Village Wooing, by George Bernard Shaw. "A" and "Z" in three conversations.

✓ *Forty Carats*, by Jay Allen. Billy and Ann, Act I, Sc. vi (Random House).

No Place to Be Somebody, by Charles Gordone. Johnny and Mary Lou, pp. 30–32 (Bobbs-Merrill).

The Only Game in Town, by Frank Gilroy. Fran and Joe, Scs. i–v (Random House).

Crystal and Fox, by Brian Friel. Episode 6 (Farrar, Straus & Giroux).

✓ *Cactus Flower*, by Abe Burrows. Igor, Toni, Act I, Sc. i; also Julian, Stephanie, Act I, Sc. iv, pp. 31–36 (French).

✓ *A Delicate Balance*, by Edward Albee. Act III, pp. 68–73 (French).

Two Males, One Female

✓ *A Slight Ache*, by Harold Pinter. Edward, Flora, and The Matchseller.

"*Eh?*" by Henry Livings. Act I, pp. 15–30 and pp. 51–55 (Hill & Wang).

Scuba Duba, by Bruce Jay Friedman. Harold, Miss James, and Dr. Schoenfeld, beginning of Act I (Simon & Schuster, 1968).

The Alchemist, by Jonson. Subtle, Face, and Doll, Act I, Sc. i.

The Dance of Death, by Strindberg. Kurt, Alice, and Captain, end of Part I.

Lovers, by Brian Friel. Winners/Losers (Farrar, Straus & Giroux).

✓ *Hadrian VII*, by Peter Luke. Act II, Sc. vii.

After Dark, by Dion Boucicault. Act II, Sc. i.

John Brown's Body, by Stephen Vincent Benet (Dramatist Play Service).

The Picture, by Ionesco. Painter, Large Gentleman, Alice, and Neighbor, Act I (Grove).

Cactus Flower, by Abe Burrows. Julian, Toni, and Igor. Act I, Sc. iii. A "Best Play" 1965–66 (French).

Acte, by Lawrence Durrell. Petronius, Nero, and Flavia, Act II, Sc. iv (E.P. Dutton).

Philadelphia, Here I Come! by Brian Friel. Kate, Public, and Private, pp. 22–31 (Faber & Faber, London). (A "Best Play" 1965–66)

One Male, Two Females

You Know I Can't Hear You . . . by Robert Anderson. The "I'll be home for Christmas" act, final scene.

J *The Cherry Orchard,* by Chekhov. Act IV. Lopakin tells of cherry orchard sale to Varya, Trofimov, and Anya.

Motel, in *America Hurrah!* by Jean Claude van Itallie.

J *A Day in the Death of Joe Egg,* by Peter Nichols. Brian, Sheila, and Grace, pp. 70–76 (Grove Press).

Three Males, One Female

The Mistress of the Inn, by Carlo Goldini. Marquis, Count, Cavalier, and Mirandolina, Act I.

Man and Superman, by Shaw. Don Juan in Hell—Ana, Don Juan, Statue, and Devil.

The Knack, by Ann Jellicoe. Colin, Tom, Tolen, and Nancy, pp. 34–40 (Dell).

Hunger and Thirst, by Eugene Ionesco. Jean, Adelaide, and Marie, pp. 17–24 (Grove Press).

A Delicate Balance, by Edward Albee. Julia, Agnes, and Tobias, Act II, Sc. ii (French).

Ensemble

Miles Gloriosus (The Braggart), by Plautus. Act IV.

Tiger at the Gates, by Giraudoux. Act I.

The Devils, by John Whiting. Trial of priest, pp. 110–114 (Hill and Wang).

In the Swamp, by Bertolt Brecht. Scene i. Skinney, Garga, Shlink, Maynes, The Worm, Baboon, and Jane.

The Devil and Daniel Webster, by Stephen Vincent Benet. A one-act play. (Dramatists Play Service)

Solitare and Double Solitare, by Robert Anderson.

The Great White Hope, by Howard Sackler (Dial).

Child's Play, by Robert Marasco.

After Dark, by Dion Boucicault.

Saved, by Edward Bond.

Conduct Unbecoming, by Barry England.

Happy Birthday, Wanda June, by Kurt Vonnegut, Jr.

Sleuth, by Anthony Shaffer. (Dodd-Mead, 1970)

All the Living, by Hardie Albright. Pp. 141–148 (French).

What the Butler Saw, by Joe Orton.

Subject to Fits, by Robert Montgomery.
The Bald Soprano, by Eugene Ionesco.
The Long Voyage Home, by Eugene O'Neill. One Act.
Interview, from *America Hurrah!* by Jean-Claude van Itallie.
In the Matter of J. Robert Oppenheimer, by Heinar Kipphardt (Hill & Wang).
Forty Carats, by Jay Allen (Random House).
Slag, by David Hare.
Blood, by Douglas Dyer.
House of Blue Leaves, by John Guare (Grove) (Best American Play 1970–71.)
The Effect of Gamma Rays on Man-In-The-Moon Marigolds, by Paul Zindel (Harper
   & Row) Pulitzer Prize Play, 1970–71.
No Place to Be Somebody, by Charles Gordone (Bobbs-Merrill).
And Miss Reardon Drinks a Little, by Paul Zindel.
Adaptation, by Elaine May. (Dramatist Play Service) One act.
Next, by Terrence McNally (Random House) One Act.
Scuba Duba, by Bruce Jay Friedman (Simon & Schuster).
Hotel Paradiso, by Georges Feydeau. Act III, beginning with Bouchard's entrance
   (French).
The Man in the Glass Booth, by Robert Shaw. Act II, the trial (Grove Press).
After the Rain, by John Bowen (Random House).
I Knock at the Door, adaptation from Sean O'Casey by Paul Shyre (Dramatists).
Hunger and Thirst and Other Plays, by Eugene Ionesco. See *Salutations* (Grove).

> NOTE: The above list of suggestions is meant to be used in the director's
> study and as illustrations of the kind of material which might be used
> for "An Evening of Theatre." A majority of these are copyrighted and
> should not be considered or used without written permission or payment
> of royalty. The copyright owner of each play is listed on or near the title
> page of the published play.

Additional Scenes

Wells, Orson, and Hill, Roger, eds. *Everybody's Shakespeare*. Woodstock, Ill.: Todd
   Press, 1935. Three plays edited for reading and staging (J.C., M.V., T.N.). Delightful
   sketches and extremely helpful in suggesting characterizations and stage business.
Feiffer, Jules. *Feiffer's People*. New York: Dramatists Play Service. Sketches for
   various number of male and female actors.

Verse Reading

The Golden Treasury. Best songs and poems in the English language collected by
   Francis T. Palgrave. New York: Macmillan Co., 1929.
The Oxford Book of English Verse (1250–1918). Oxford at the Clarendon Press, New
   York, 1957.
The Hollow Crown, Devised by John Barton. New York: Samuel French; and London:
   George G. Harrap & Co. An entertainment by and about the Kings and Queens
   of England.
Mark Twain Tonight, An Actor's Portrait. Clements' writings arranged for theatre
   by Hal Holbrook. New York: Washburn Co., 1959.
Mr. Clements and Mark Twain, by Austin Kaplan. New York: Simon & Shuster,
   1966.

Stanyan Street and Other Sorrows, by Rod McKuen. Cheval-Stanyon, Box 278, Holly-wood, California. Also by Rod McKuen, *Elephants in the Rice Paddy, The Rod McKuen Song Book, Christmas Times Ten*, and *Lonesome Cities*, the last a musical play.

Further Reading

Aggertt, Otis J., and Brown, Elbert R. *Communicative Reading.* New York: Macmillan Co., 1963.

Armstrong, Chloe, and Brandes, Paul D. *The Staged Reading.* New York: McGraw-Hill, 1963.

Bacon, Wallace. *The Art of Interpretation.* New York: Rinehart & Winston, 1960.

Coger, Leslie, and White, Irene and Melvin R. *Readers Theatre Handbook.* Glenville, Ill.: Scott, Foresman Co., 1967.

Geeting, Baxter M. *Group Performance.* Dubuque, Iowa: William C. Brown Co., 1966.

Grimes, Edgar. *Reader's Theatre.* Belmont, Calif.: Wadsworth Publishing Co., 1961.

NEW
THEATRE
FORMS 17

The Happening

Art is anything you can get away with.
            —Marshall McLuhan

The word *happening* is a misnomer in that it implies that no one concerned knows what is going to happen. Certainly the actors are not supposed to respond spontaneously to unexpected events, because there is a scenario, or list of preconceived elements, which the participants are to follow.

What is *not* happening in a happening is a plot, sequential development, continuity, characters, theme, climax, logic, and suspense. It depends solely upon its collage of pictorial activity, sounds, recordings, wordless words, props, shock, flashing lights, and odors.

Happenings have no permanence, since they cannot be performed twice. In order to repeat a happening, it would need to be fixed, and when it is fixed, it is no longer a happening. Rather, the attempt is to create a nonverbal theatre, although in this the happening is far less successful than pantomime.

Typical of the happening is that it does not require or encourage an audience unless that audience is willing to become physically involved in the action. From this description, it is logical to assume that the form was not the idea of theatre people but of painters and sculptors. Actors in a happening are no more than a medium to be used in space by the artist exactly as he would use paint or clay. Participants are not permitted to characterize or emotionalize, but are simply to carry out assigned tasks. In fact, one of the happening entrepreneurs tried actors but found them "useless." Also, plays as we know them are simply nonexistent in the happening. Content or message is of no importance. What is important is the *means of communication*. To paraphrase McLuhan, the medium is the message.

Ardent devotees of the form believe that happenings are closely related to ancient tribal rituals or ceremonies. Detractors consider them merely another op-pop put-on which burst into our consciousness early in the '60's and have been publicized less and less each year since that time. A purely objective view might be to consider the happening as a possible future influence on dramatic technique, eventually to become absorbed by the theatre.

An Example of a Happening

During the Edinburgh Drama Festival in 1963, the following happening took place:

A platform speaker (Charles Marowitz) making a pseudo-serious proposal that the conference formally, accept as the definitive interpretation, his explanation of *Waiting for Godot.*

An audience member (Charles Lewsen) attacking the speaker for being unclear and not heroic enough.

From outside a tape of cable-pullers at work.

Low and barely audible organ sounds.

The silhouette of a large head at the top of the dome of the hall.

A second tape made from fragments of speeches at the conference.

A man walking the tiny ledge high up at the base of the dome.

Figures appearing at other windows high above the hall and occasionally staring down at the people.

An actress on the platform (Carrol Baker) beginning to stare at someone at the back of the hall (Allan Kaprow), eventually taking off a large fur coat and moving toward him across the tops of the audience seats.

A nude model (Anne Kesselaar) being whisked across the organ loft on a spotlight stand.

The men at the high windows (Rik Kendell and Patrick De Salvo) shouting, "Me! Can you hear me? Me!"

Carrol Baker reaching Allan Kaprow, and both running out of the hall together.

Tape, organ and debate continue.

A bagpiper (Hamish MacLeod) crossing the top balcony.

A sheep skeleton hung on the giant flat with Cocteau's symbol of the conference.

The piper reaching the other end of the hall as all other sounds stopped, and a blue curtain behind the platform being dropped to reveal shelves containing about fifty white plaster death masks (or, to be more precise, phrenological head studies).

A woman with a baby, and a boy with a radio entering the hall, mounting the platform, looking at everything as if in a museum, and leaving. The piper tapering off in the distance.

(Running time of the piece was calculated as seven minutes.)[1]

Further Reading: Happenings

(Also known as Ray Gun, Action, Environmental, and Kinetic theatre.)

Armstrong, William, ed. *Experimental Drama.* London: G. Bell & Sons, 1963.
Becher, Jurgen, and Vostell, Wolf. *Happenings.* Germany: Rowohlt, 1965.
Benedikt, Michael. *Theatre Experiment.* Garden City, N.Y.: Doubleday & Co., 1967.

[1]John Hodgson and Ernest Richards, *Improvisation, Discovery and Creativity in Drama* (London: Methuen & Co., Ltd., 1966), pp. 62–63. Reprinted by permission of the publisher.

Fowlie, Wallace. *Age of Surrealism*. Bloomington, Ind.: Indiana University Press, 1960.

Kaprow, Allan. *Assemblage, Environments, and Happenings*. New York: Harry N. Abrams, 1966.

Kirby, Michael. *Happenings, An Illustrated Anthology*. New York: E. P. Dutton & Co., 1965.

Kostelantz, Richard. *The Theatre of Mixed Means*. New York: Dial Press, 1965.

Weales, Gerald. *The Jumping-Off Place*. New York: Macmillan Co., 1969. American drama in the '60's.

Multimedia

Most people associate multimedia with projected images as a background for performers. While the use of visuals is an important element, there are other components of equal value. To begin with, there is a total objective which is often overlooked. This is an effort to create a controlled electronic environment in which the spectator forgets he is in a theatre.

Media refers to means of communication. Light would be one medium; live and electric sound are others. *Multi* implies that there are many—and there are: actors or performers, movement, scenery, music, dance, film and slides, shadows, kinetic images, poetry, recordings, and words, both spoken and projected. A few or all of these may be combined in a single production. But the primary goal is to provide the audience the sensory experience of *becoming a part of the total created environment.*

Visual light images are not new to man. As the Neanderthal man sat around his fire in his cave, he probably spent some time forming his hands and fingers into shapes of animals which were reflected as shadows on the walls. Perhaps he also learned that he could make the shadows move.

Light images are not new to the theatre, either. History records many instances of the use of projected light from the spatial visions of Craig, Appia, and Brecht. But as technical resources multiplied, artistic experiments were few. Then the light shows at Canada's Expo 67 flashed upon us, inspiring a revived interest in the use of projected light.[2]

The ballet, the opera, discotheques, the advertising media, and industrial shows were quick to experiment and develop multimedia equipment which is now accessible and suitable to all sorts of budgets. Most colleges and high schools have at least some sort of primitive projectors on which experiments may be begun with front, overhead, and rear projections. Almost anything can be used as a throwing screen: translucent Mylar, canvas, shelf or wax paper, cheese cloth, brick walls—and people, especially people. But don't try projecting on a 4-by-4-foot home movie screen and expect to get anything unusual.

The use of these new tools and techniques are so much in infancy that their application is mostly a matter of individual experimentation. The discov-

---

[2]The Czech Pavilion at Expo 67 featured Emil Radok's "Creation of the World," a unique variation of the motion picture with its immense wall of 112 separate box screens. Each screen operated individually by rear projection. The images were sometimes one huge mosaic and at other times a collage of many different images.

Director Leslie Hinderyckx's concept of All the King's Men *at Northwestern University Theatre included use of rear projections to heighten the drama. Setting by Samuel Ball. (Courtesy of Northwestern University Theatre)*

ery of new applications resulting from personal experiments will rely chiefly upon a director's imagination.

Following are a few simple little experiments in visuals to whet your appetite for further and more complicated investigations.

PROJECTED SHADOWS

1. If an actor moves toward the light source in rear projection, his reflected shadow will assume giant and distorted proportions on the screen, but if he moves toward the screen, the image will grow smaller and sharper in outline. Try reflected shadows on various surfaces and planes.[3]

Possible applications: Ghosts, witches, ghouls, apparitions, symbolic fate, gods, etc., such as in Dunsany's *Night at an Inn* and in *Prometheus Bound, Peer Gynt,* and many Shakespearian plays.

SILHOUETTES

2. Experiment with various cut-outs, found materials, etc., in front of a floodlight. Reflect shadows on various textured surfaces. Experiment with degrees of light in different positions and intensities away from the flood.

Possible application: Background scenic patterns.

COLOR

3. Use red, green, and blue gels on three different lights, then adjust intensity until all three are focused together and look white. Note how shadows look purple, yellow, and blue-green.

---

[3]Illusions of flashing lights, moving trains, flickering light of old movies, etc., may be produced by a device known as a Lobsterscope, which is mounted in front of an ellipsoidal spot.

4. Use the same three lights, but focus on three mirrors. Adjust mirrors at different angles to reflect on various surfaces. Note colors.

SYMBOLS, WORDS, SIGNS

5. Use transfer tape letters to form words, and apply to glass slides or gels; then frame and project onto various surfaces with different lenses.

Possible application: Plays of the absurd, Brecht, etc.

FILM

6. Paint various patterns on clear, undeveloped (raw) motion picture film with colored felt pens so that images animate when projected.

Possible application: Project this film using actors or dancers as screen.

SLIDES

7. Cut frames of raw film, decorate, and mount inside two filaments of glass; hold together at edges, using transparent tape. Try strings, seeds, thread, crushed moss, and oiled tissue paper between glass slides. Use slide projector with various lenses and projected surfaces.

Possible application: Clouds, waves, patterns, etc.

CLOUDS

8. Using an overhead projector, place a large (15-inch-diameter) glass dish on top, fill with water, and put a few drops of different colored mineral oil on surface. Blow the oil into streams across the water.

Consideration has been given to the use of scoops or floods in providing patterns for back walls and cycloramas. These lights are manufactured with grooves so that frames may be inserted. By mixing colors and cut-outs in the gels, various effects can be created, such as tonal variations and cloud-like formations.

Rear Projection (For Thrust, Open, or Proscenium Stages)

Another interesting effect is possible by using translucent panels set as a background to the acting area. To the rear of this panel or panels, a projection lamp known as a *lamphouse* is placed anywhere from six to twelve feet behind the panel-screen. The beam from the lamphouse transcends a small stenciled panel, and this pattern is then projected onto the large screen. Color washes may be accomplished by gels inserted into the grooves of floods or scoops, which are placed on the floor near the screen or panels. The stencil is placed fairly close to the lamphouse. Plants or objects may also be used in conjunction with the cut-outs or used individually.

Obviously, rear projection cannot be used unless there is something to project upon. This creates a problem in central staging. Also, the units of projection would need to be stationed above, for in center staging there is no rear. This distorted light from above, however, could suggest certain psychedelic effects, which might reach the subconscious. If handled well, this could provide movement, intense color, time distortions, and graphic variation. The mechanics might include perforated discs which are turned before a follow spot. Strobe lights and the older lobsterscopes are now available for such effects.

Adaptation of Artaud's Jet of Blood *Scenario; multimedia as used by director Richard E. Mennen and designer Kenneth Bendell.* (*Courtesy of Richard E. Mennen*)

Possible Applications

Once the mechanics of rear projection have been perfected, the imaginative director will be able to conceive many uses for the device, such as using shadowed ghosts of Richard III's victims projected inside his tent. (Act V, Sc. iii). The furniture engulfing Ionesco's *New Tenant* might be effectively staged by using distorted silhouettes on screens. Or a panorama of a district or town so much a part of a play might be projected on a screen or back wall of a set, such as the dominating Welsh mining town in *The Corn is Green.* Many truly aesthetic concepts have been inspired by such mechanical equipment.

Further Reading: Multimedia

At this writing, there is no definitive book on the many innovations in modern lighting. The best lighting books were a product of the thirties and fifties when more modern, sophisticated equipment was not available.

Recent manuals and catalogues from lighting equipment firms are worth requesting. Here are only a few such addresses:

> Castle Lighting, 2858 South Robertson Blvd., Los Angeles, Calif. 90034.
> Hub Electric Co., Inc., 2255 West Grand Ave., Chicago, Ill. 60612.
> Olesen Company, 1535 Ivar Ave., Hollywood, Calif. 90028.
> Kleigl Bros., Inc., 32–34 48th Ave., Long Island City, N.Y. 11101.
> Capitol Stage Lighting Co., Inc., 509 West 56th St., New York 10019.

Write also:

> National Audio-Visual Association, 3150 Spring St., Fairfax, Va., requesting their Audio-Visual Equipment Directory, for information on various projectors and accessories.

THE
NOT-SO-DEAD
THEATRE 18

That perennial bromide about the theatre being dead is still with us. But the eager pall bearers, while putting on their white cotton gloves, fail to note that Broadway has recently experienced the best financial years it has ever had—annually approaching sixty million dollars. True enough, this may be mostly the result of higher ticket costs, but for those with know-how, such as Neil Simon, there is more money to be made on Broadway today than ever before.

Ticket costs are certainly not responsible for the success of the current London theatres where prices are modest indeed when compared to ours. The Royal Shakespearian Theatre recently had a £390,601 season, and The National Theatre collected £150,000 while playing to 92 percent capacity at every performance.[1]

The real hope for a healthy English-speaking theatre does not rest solely upon Broadway or the West End, but upon the resident companies both in England and America. Walk among the crowds at the Ahmanson or the Guthrie Theatres and you realize that people must have theatre because they *need* theatre. Films and TV do not reach spectators in the same way that theatre does. People go to the theatre today for the very same reasons that audiences sat on Athenian hillsides or stood in the pit at the Globe. It is an institution which will not die—*if* it remains receptive to fresh ideas and change. But the general ticket-buying public cannot be expected to pay to see unskilled experimental work in a commercially oriented theatre. Theorize all you will, the critical question regarding all innovation remains, "Is there a market for it?" Sir Tyrone Guthrie wrote, "The dominant purpose of theatre management is success and the objective way to measure success is in terms of the box office. Artistic success is a matter, not of fact, but of entirely subjective opinion."[2]

[1] *The Theatre Today*, a report by a Committee of the Arts Council.
[2] Sir Tyrone Guthrie, *In Various Directions* (New York: Macmillan Co., 1965), p. 35.

Off-off Broadway is constantly experimenting. And yet the groups performing there seem to be each other's best audiences. Hermetically sealed inside
their own little ideological theatre world, their contact with the outside comes
only when the check arrives from an occasional grant from the very institutions they condemn. Evidently there is no compunction against biting the
hand that feeds.

A director or a management who thinks only in terms of selling tickets
is no more than a pitchman, but those who completely ignore the box office
must be forever content to beg for handouts.

Problems in the Commercial Theatre

Broadway's very existence depends upon profit and loss statements. It
cannot afford to gamble exclusively on new plays by untried authors or to
experiment in new forms. At the same time, Off-Broadway and off-off Broadway have produced more new plays than ever before in American theatrical
history. Broadway's costs are monumental.[3] Real-estate values and union
demands mount steadily, so that if a production is to survive beyond a few
days, most seats in a theatre must be sold. And there are too many seats
to fill in these big houses.

One great advantage theatre has over films and TV is the human contact
possible between actor and spectator; but in these big houses, that is impossible except in the front rows. Also, in most of these houses the backstage
area is so antiquated that it is impossible to accommodate modern audio-visual
equipment. The old-fashioned proscenium limits the view of the audience
to looking through a peep-hole into the box settings. In the audience section
there are poor acoustics, and in the lobby orange juice stands and a box
office staffed by the most imperious personnel since the Medicis. Compared
to the easy accessibility of tickets to see films, the prospective theatre cus-
tomer often loses heart before he begins.

These objections must be considered if Broadway is to survive. Such problems stifle any significant experimentation and growth in the commercial
theatre. It must be free to advance, to welcome untried playwrights with
new plays and to provide young directors with modern facilities which will
inspire and support fresh concepts of our classical literature.

Problems Off-Off Broadway

So far, most of the experimental work in New York has been done without
proper funds, equipment, or technical skill by off-off Broadway amateurs.
The professional theatre cannot forever retreat into those dank and musty
interiors of nineteenth-century playhouses, quoting from Stanislavski. Already
eager young theatre lovers are walking in from the outside with contemporary
ideas. Never mind if some of these ideas are impractical, immature, or even

[3]To produce a non-musical show on Broadway today costs between $75,000 and $100,000,
and musicals cost upwards of $250,000, plus operating costs in each instance.

naïve. They may well be what is needed to breathe new life into our theatre and make it the exciting place it has been. At any rate, the future theatre is going to belong to the young, and the profession might just as well welcome them and offer them the benefit of their experience and expertise. If not, the theatre must remain fragmented. One theatre will aim at giving audiences what they want, while the other continues producing nihilistic plays in lofts and churches for its own coterie.

Propaganda is hardly new in theatre, as indicated by *Uncle Tom's Cabin*, *The Drunkard*, and *Ten Nights in a Barroom*. However, there is one significant difference between these plays and our present doctrinaire dramas. Theatregoers supported the older plays.

More often than not, proselytizing in the theatre succeeds only in converting the already converted. After ten years of struggle, most of those in the politically motivated theatre are still working gratis. Perhaps they are content, as long as they are part of showbiz, to go from relief rolls to old-age pensions.

A New Spirit in the Arts

The element of accident seems prevalent today in all the arts. Young people "dig" Jackson Pollock's splashes and splats, Kandinsky's cold, intricate, disoriented work intended to woo the beholder's emotions, Van Gogh's impasto, Picasso's distortions, plus other artists who shred the fabric of realistic painting to bits.

Does this mean that all theories of art, all conventions, structures, and traditions are worthless—that all art and drama instructors (and books such as this) are sinking into a functional obsolescence? And are those impulsive onslaughts and crude accidents better than intellectually and emotionally organized designs?

Teacher-training program in workshop techniques by the Arena Stage to increase sensitivity, awareness, and effectiveness of the public school teacher. (Photo by Fletcher Drake, courtesy of the Living Stage, a project of the Arena Stage in Washington, D.C.)

Opposing such thoughts is the longing in most humans for order, under-standing, and arrangement—and in theatre art, some energizing and elation of the spirit. Teachers now learn from students. All the arts are returning to the workshops where accidents and practice finally make for skill. But after all the impulsive protean accidents have happened, there always remains a time when decisions must be made. *The truly artistic must be selected from the abortive, and it is at this time of choice that a knowledge of theory, structure, tradition, and design is required.*

Form and Content

A young director just entering the field must look to the future, but he must also remember the past, for theatre is a very ancient and honorable art. It cannot be wholly an orgiastic dance of death. He must accept its disciplines and the necessity for craftsmanship. Form and content, content and form, can they ever be separated? The thing to admire in the "New Theatre" is the search. The product has too often been embarrassing in execution (form) and deadly in its pseudo-intellectual didacticism (content), but now and then, and in spite of its form and content, something emerges out of the screaming, the nudity, and the ugliness, that is delightfully theatri-cal. Picasso is an innovator, a slap-dash surrealist, but underneath his work is a solid discipline of traditional painting.

Now, more than ever, when religion, morality, law, government—even the earth itself—is insecure, we look to the theatre to show us some logic, some reason, some stability, and some value in self-discipline. We need faith to assure ourselves that no matter how dark it looks for the hero in Act II, before the final curtain falls he will be safe with his ideals.

Should Theatre Entertain?

In an introduction to his collected plays, Arthur Miller writes, "I do not believe that any work of art can help but be diminished by its adherence at any cost to a political program, including the author's." Even Brecht himself, in his "Short Organum," states, "From the first it has been theatre's business to entertain people as it also has of all the other arts. It is this business which gives it its particular dignity; it needs no other passport than fun."

In a theatregoer's study initiated privately for William Goldman's book, *The Season*, The Center for Research in Marketing Inc. asked a number of people what they wanted Broadway to be. Here are the results of that survey in order of preferences:

1. Entertaining
2. Good theatre
3. Funny and witty
4. Socially aware

5. Enlightening
6. Provocative[4]

These results seem to substantiate Mr. Goldman's comment, "If a critic calls a show 'A genuinely thought-provoking evening of literate theatre,' he is dooming it to a quick death. If, on the other hand, he says, 'I had a hell of a time at this musical, in spite of its flaws,' he is writing what is called in the trade, 'A money review.' "[5]

If there is one fault which stands out above all others in the emerging theatre, it is the replacement of entertainment with instruction. Entertainment can be instructive, but instruction is seldom entertaining. In a *Newsweek* interview (February 2, 1970, p. 53), Neil Simon said, "I used to get these horrible letters from people saying, 'You don't know how nice it is to go to the theatre and be able to laugh without thinking.' But humor isn't anything if it can't make you think and feel." Unfortunately, many young theatre enthusiasts consider entertainment as something left over from vaudeville, a word and a theatrical technique no longer relative today. It is their loss.

The Realistic and the Theatrical Theatre

There are many phenomena which make it difficult to sort out and identify just what are the new directions in contemporary theatre. As we have seen, the new directions are not new. The open stage, inprovisations, audience participation, the propaganda play, and nonrealism in acting and setting are older than the realistic theatre which the innovators are in revolt against. This rejection of the realistic theatre by the young seems a corollary of their denial of parental standards. Re-examination of accepted standards is typical of each new generation, and with maturity, usually results in retaining some former standards, while rejecting others. It does not follow that all traditions are wrong because they are old. Nor is it true that all changes are for the best. At its finest, the realistic theatre does not aim at authentic reality, but only enough to orient an audience to the play. Also, at its best, the traditional play is literate, technically impeccable in craft, and inspirational in concept. It presents us with ideals, hope, and much understanding of the human predicament. In its characters and philosophy it is larger than life, inviting admiration for any number of timeless virtues, devotion, honor, morality, and a belief in the transforming power of love. It shows us other not-so-admirable characters as a reminder that humans can also be cowardly, mercenary, and disloyal. Plots have a beginning, a middle, and (sometimes even a happy) ending which gratifies a spectator's sense of order and justice.

[4]William Goldman, *The Season, A Candid Look at Broadway* (New York: Harcourt, Brace & World, 1969), p. 398. (Mr. Goldman is also author of the 1970 Academy Award screenplay, *Butch Cassidy and the Sun Dance Kid.*)
    [5]*Ibid.*

Summary: The New Directions

It seems to be a necessity that a summary deal in generalities. The difficulty in generalizing or cataloguing the new directions in theatre is that they are so emergent and tentative. The task is somewhat like trying to describe what color a chicken will be while it is still in the egg.

One fairly safe generality is that the modern theatre is in revolt. How this will be evidenced depends upon the aims or goals of the individual group. One group will concentrate upon new techniques in training actors, another will use the theatre to further special interests, while another, such as a professional resident company, may seek to please audiences while searching for a new methodology of theatrical expression. Such groups as the latter seem to portend more permanency than others. Acting styles change; so do politics. But groups aimed at the inspirational and financial support of subscribers are in a better position to search out and perfect new forms. They are not using the theatre to sell an unpopular product, but theatre itself—to those who want it. The security they enjoy provides them with the resources to experiment, to find new directions in which to express the personality and the tempo of today.

The following is an attempt to abstract the innovations *of all groups*, to condense many different aims and goals under specific identifications. And yet there are even exceptions in this. *The Rimers of Eldrich* deals with a milieu as realistic as any play by James Herne or George Kelly, but the presentation is stylistic. We might note as a generalization that all new plays lack fully developed characters; and yet, *The Madness of Lady Bright* has a deep and touching portrait of its leading character. We cannot say that all new plays are lacking in sequential development, but this is more typical than in older plays. Distinguished language is not common in the play of today; and yet, most of Tony Richardson's plays excel in language.

And so, the experimental theatre cannot be fitted into neat pigeon holes and labeled, probably because it *is* an experimental theatre. Therefore, the following should be accepted only as being *generally* typical of the new directions in theatre.

DIRECTION

Use of new symbols, masks, puppets, film, slides, dance, pantomime, audio-visual effects, metaphors, sound patterns, and fantasy.

Time often alternates with intent to see two time elements at once.

Discontinuous situations or events fragmented. Transformation of form and content. Nonliterate language. Use of voice sounds.

Improvisations: Development with actors and later editing these into a play. Diversity of tempo, mood, and pace. Complete reliance upon intuition, not intellect, in directing.

Objective: To create a form so pure in sensory involvement that it is divested of all formal content.

ACTOR TRAINING

Accent on the physical, not psychological depths. "Transformations"—characters dissolve or converge without logical transitions, making exceptional demands upon the audience's imagination.

Elaborate use of improvisation in training and in rehearsals. Use of fantasy and childlike insights. Abandonment of the "let's pretend" syndrome—not "living" on stage, but *acting* on stage. Disavowal of "aesthetic distance" for direct contact with audience. Lines studied for sound, not meaning. Denial of words for beauty. Language substandard—obscene, profane, may even be inarticulate. Emotion described as a sense bath. Great reliance upon *ensemble playing*.

Objectives: To use the actor as a performing medium, not as an artist creating character. It is the activity, "the thing done," which is of prime importance.

AUDIENCE

Exposure to physical, emotional, and intellectual contact with performers. Instead of stimulating emotions, the goal is to call the spectator to action. No attempt to entertain audience or have them escape from reality, but to become involved.

Objective: To force, even abuse, an audience into an involvement with its own existence—to have the "soul's unhealthy elements extracted!"

PLAYWRITING

A great many of the printed plays of the experimental theatre are, in reality, edited improvisations. All rules of play construction are broken; exposition, unifying plot, sequential development, crisis, climax, and protagonist, some or all are discarded.

Elimination of the playwright as a controlling figure in the theatre. Plays not inspired by overall design, but an actor's improvisations finally edited into a theme. Use of intuition, nonsense, irrationality, inspiration, nudity, ambiguity, immorality, nonacademic forms, and substandard language. Anti-traditional, anti-establishment, anti-entertainment, and undisciplined.

Objective: To be free of, and transcend, traditional realism and psychology and to develop sensory levels, physical attacks—which means that theatre as a branch of literature must be reappraised.

Another change in playwriting today is the tendency to eliminate the third act, or the material the third act might contain. In other words, after the part built up in the first act, the stresses of the second, and just after the point of decision or climax has been reached, the whole matter is dropped.

This may be done for several reasons:

1. To allow the audience to draw its own conclusions.
2. Because the author believes that the results are predictable.
3. Because the author believes that the results are less important than the causes.

BACKGROUNDS

Scenery as a function of the play not merely representative or decorative. New projected images or other imaginative devices to replace old fashioned box sets. Furniture and props also functional. Elimination of the actor-audience separation by proscenium. Actors to move into audience, or spectators placed into acting area, as has been done by Grotowski. Rejection of architectural areas such as lobby, house, stage, backstage, etc. Now all one—theatre. Space as a medium.

Objectives: To more fully involve the audience into the action, not merely to observe, but to encounter a complete actor-spectator confrontation.

Directors for Tomorrow

If Maureen Stapleton is correct when she says that actors are "the deformed children of the world," then stage directors must surely be the neglected children of the world. One of our most constructive theatre critics, John Simon, points out that there are grants, subsidies, and foundations for actors, playwrights, and critics, but only marginally, or none at all, for the training and creation of directors.[6] What we need is a national program exclusively for the study and training of young directors, with grants for internship under the finest American and European directors. Until such a program is activated, we shall have to content ourselves with specialists, such as Mike Nichols, who directs comedy brilliantly, but fails with a melodrama such as *The Little Foxes*; or Elia Kazan, a master at the brooding naturalism-plus-Freud style, but who drives himself out of the theatre with a noncontemporary, poetic, and unrealistic production of *The Changeling*.

Perhaps we will have no great American theatre until we have great American directors. All exciting theatre movements have been spear-headed by outstanding director-actor-managers.

In this book we have attempted to consider how a director might work in a variety of theatrical styles, how he selects a play for production, his concept and preparation for that production, how he develops his actors, manages technicalities, and attracts audiences. All the great directors have understood these requirements.

But the finest textbook is experience. Our manic search for new playwrights, new ways of saying things, whether the play be staged in a circle or a square, will avail us little unless we have a knowledgeable and experienced director guiding it all.

The relationship between time and change is intriguing in that there can be no limitations in our thinking. But one prediction is simple: the theatre of today is no more what it was yesterday than it will be tomorrow. And tomorrow belongs to the young director with imagination and experience.

[6]See *New York* magazine, Aug. 17, 1970, p. 48.

INDEX